Ecological Printmaking

a maker's guide

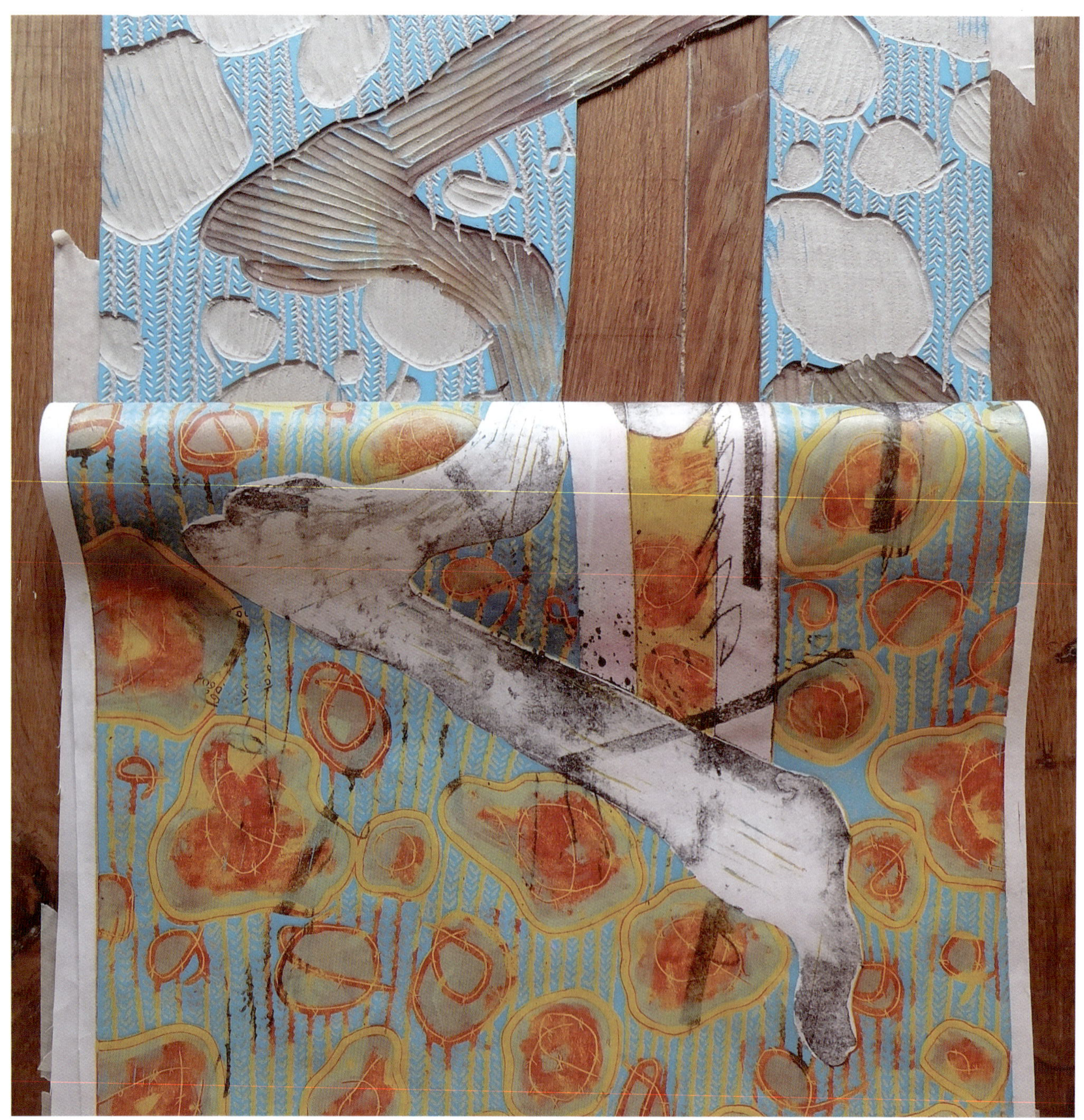

Mary Dalton

Ecological Printmaking

a maker's guide

THE CROWOOD PRESS

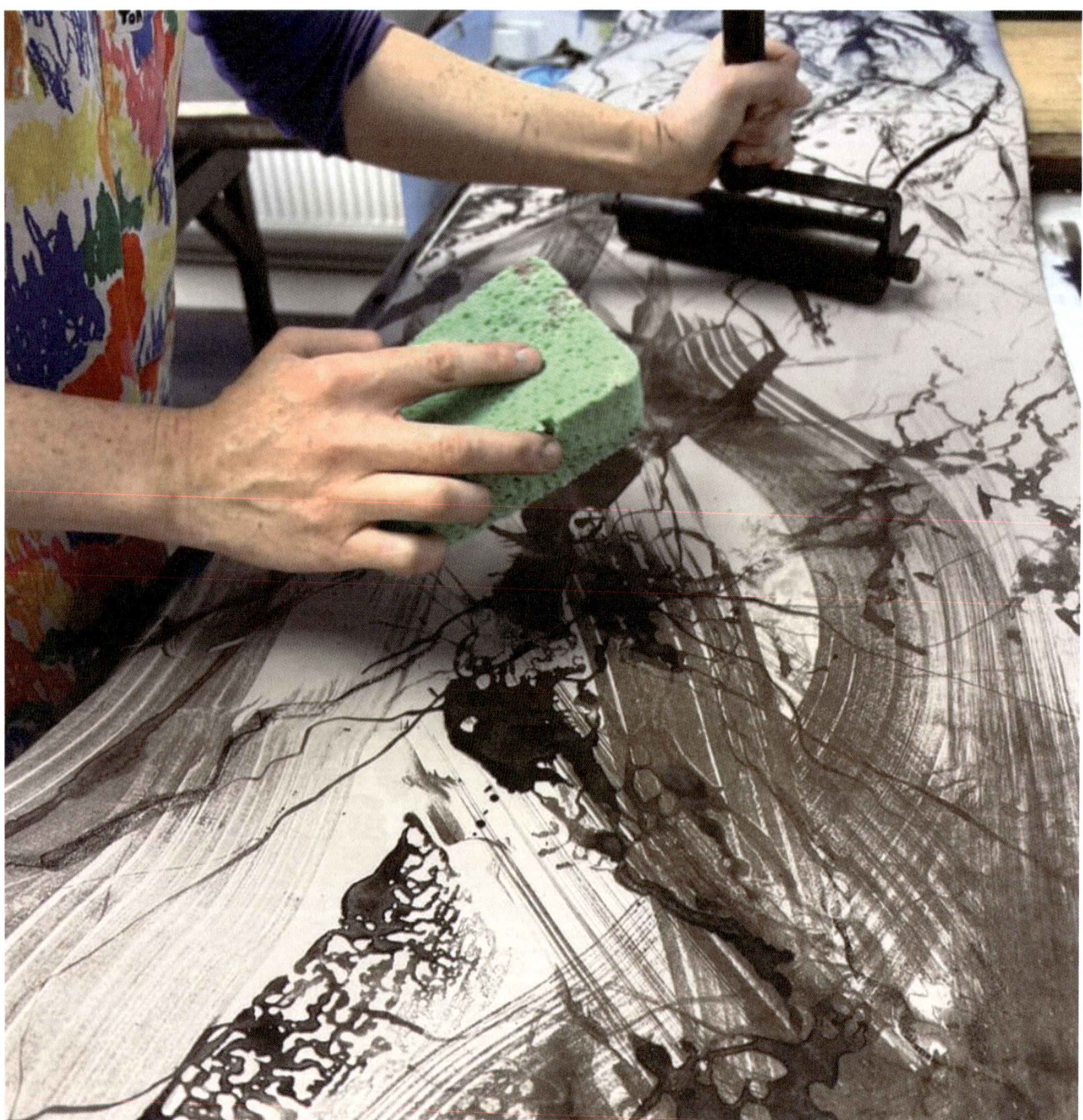

CONTENTS

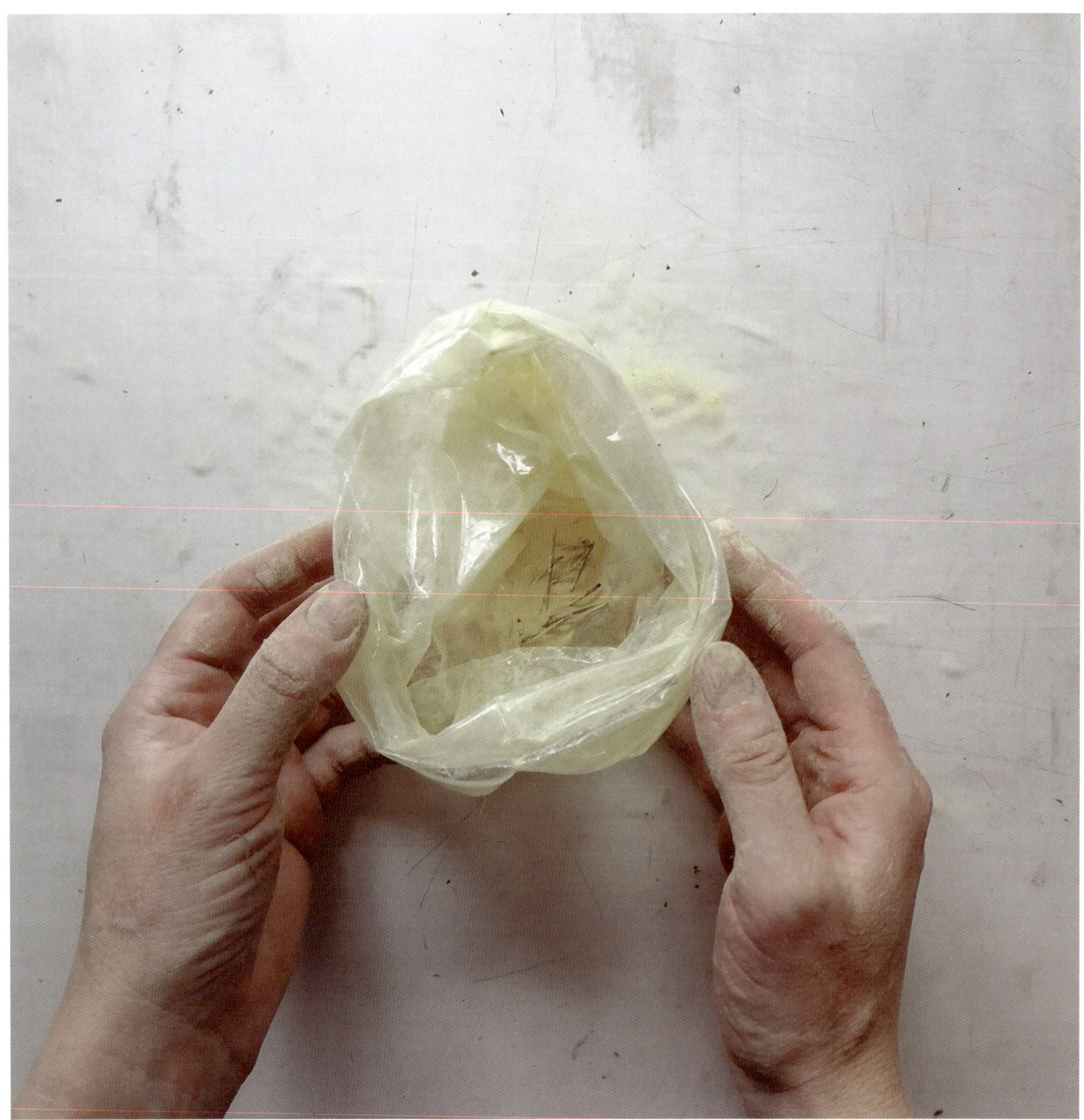

INK

nk starts off all printmaking journeys. It is the backbone of how a printmaker translates the image they have created into an impression. Nowadays, we have an array of inks available on the market, from water-based to oil-based and even water washable oil-based inks. Depending on the medium used, the ink chosen by the printmaker will vary in viscosity, tackiness and binder. Building up our backbone of printing, the focus of this chapter is looking at traditional oil-based printing inks as their uses are diverse and they can be used across all the methods of relief, planographic and intaglio that we will look into in this book. We will understand what oil-based ink is, how to make a considered decision when buying pre-bought inks and how you can make your own artist-quality printing ink.

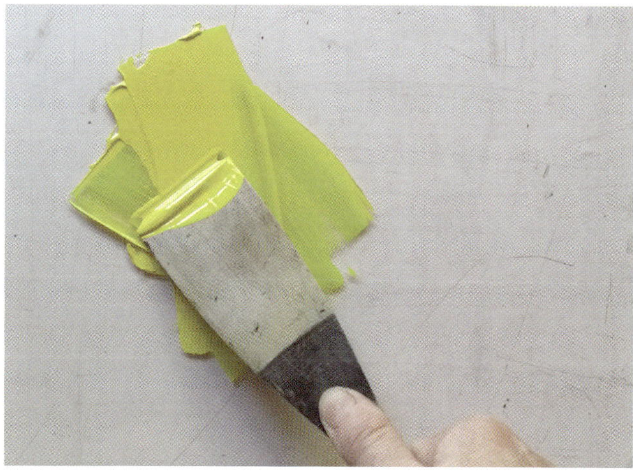

Oil-based ink is luscious in colour and texture, and highly versatile.

OIL-BASED INK

Printing ink is very unlike other oil-based artist's mediums, such as oil paint or oil sticks. They share similarities, particularly in reference to the linseed oil binding agent, but the texture and viscosity are quite different. The ink has to be able to work for intaglio, where a stiffer ink is required for ease of wipe down, and relief, where a tackier ink is required for smooth and even rolling. Then we have inks required for lithography, which have to be loose and able to be rolled out thinly and evenly. The ink consistency can really affect the end result of the print, both aesthetically and technically in how well it prints.

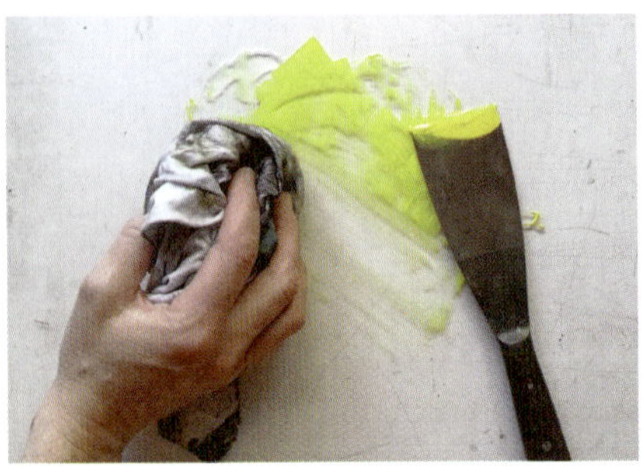

Cleaning oil-based inks is easy and sustainable with oil and rags (*see* Chapter 8).

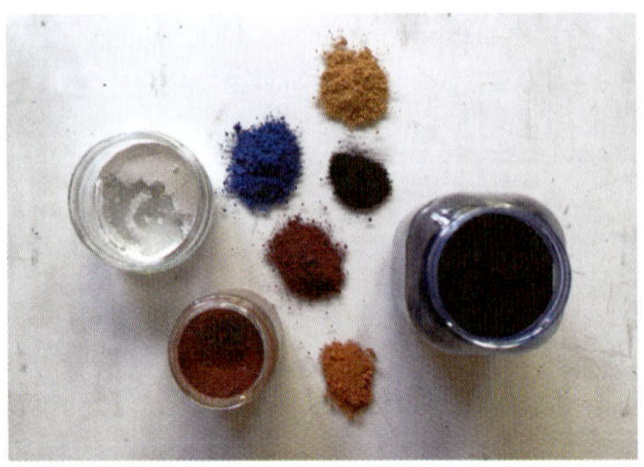

Pigments of different types contribute to the colour in printing ink.

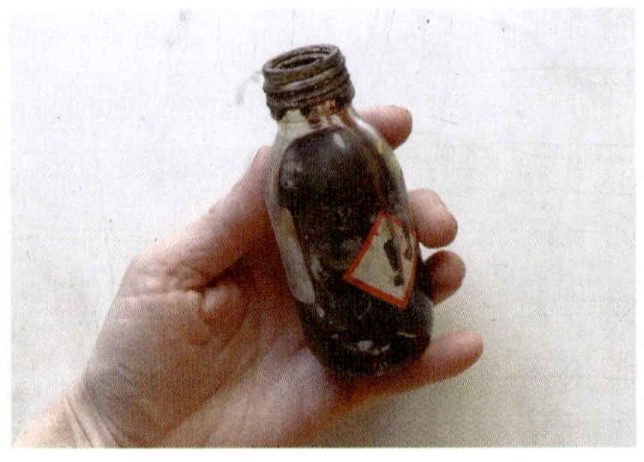

Cobalt or magnesium driers are not ecological and not always necessary.

Oil-based inks have a sheen, a colour strength and a diversity that I find is unlike their water-based modern counterparts. Traditionally, oil-based inks would have been used for relief, lithography and many other printing methods. However, in the modern age, harsh solvents were being used to clean up the inks, which were hugely damaging for both human and planetary health. This is completely unnecessary, because all oil-based inks can be cleaned up using simple oil and a mild soap solution. Easy, effective and non-toxic, it saves washing lots of pigments and modifiers into our watercourse.

Oil-based inks are made by grinding a pigment with thickened linseed oil. The linseed oil is heated to various degrees to achieve different thicknesses, and this is referred to as copperplate oil or plate oil. When making studio-quality inks from your own pigments, a base plate oil is used for the main grind and the viscosity is altered using a very heavy, tacky plate oil. Making your own ink allows for you to change the consistency according to your individual needs. It also guarantees complete transparency of all ingredients used, creating a very ecological approach.

Oil-based inks have a longer drying time than their water-based counterparts. However, this is a distinct advantage when it comes to working time. Oil-based inks will stay 'open' (or wet) for lengthy periods on your work station, and in some cases can even be covered and left overnight to continue working the next day. If you are working on a print but need to pop out or make lunch or have a break, no need to clean up, just leave it all and the ink will stay open. A huge advantage for both flexible working and editioning. They will take longer to dry on the paper, but I always see this as a game of patience and planning, and I often have multiple works on the go at once to allow for layers to be built as other layers dry. Some artists will add cobalt or magnesium driers to their inks. Cobalt driers are surface driers, meaning they allow for the top surface of the ink to dry more quickly, so that the next layer can be added. Magnesium driers are body driers, speeding up the drying time of all the ink layer evenly. Both these driers are extremely hazardous to human and planet health. I avoid them unless absolutely necessary. When buying oil-based inks, check the ingredients. Some modern inks have these driers added to speed drying time, and so you may think you are buying an ecologically safe oil-based ink, but double check.

Pigments

Every ink is made from a pigment. Usually just one pigment ground with plate oil. The traceability of each pigment used for modern pre-made inks is very easy. Every pigment has a unique pigment number, which usually can be found on the side information of the ink container.

This unique pigment number can be searched for on the internet and you can pull up details of what the pigment is made from, how it is made and its ecological data. Much of this information is contained in what is referred to as a Material Safety Data Sheet (MSDS). These sheets are invaluable when researching and finding out about materials you bring into the workshop. Many of the modern inks use pigments that are manufactured in laboratories, and the ecological effects of the pigments used varies hugely. It also

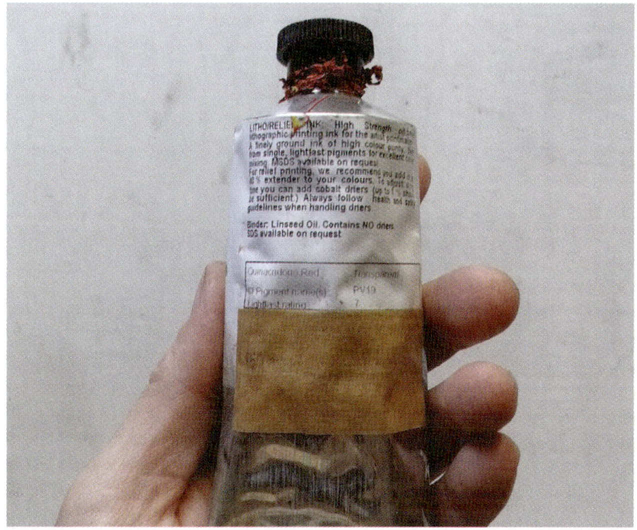

Individual pigments can be traced according to their pigment number.

depends on how much you want to delve into the subject. If you choose to buy pre-made inks, but wish to have as sustainable a model as possible, then a little bit of research goes a long way. Firstly, look at the MSDS for the ink you are buying and importantly avoid the use of driers, either in the ink as bought or added by yourself. If you fancy a bit more in-depth research, have a look at the pigments used in each ink and you can make a very informed decision that suits personal practice with all the new-found information presented to you. The only sure way to ensure that the ink you use is ecologically traceable is to make it yourself, which is what we will be looking at next. This is very dedicated but is also great fun and allows for complete traceability of the ink.

MAKING PRINTING INK

This step-by-step guide is a very basic introduction into the wonders and variance of making printing ink. The ink produced here will be an all-round, oil-based tacky printing ink. Further on in the chapter we will look in more detail at collecting and grinding pigments, changing the texture of inks and how to store them. We are starting by using a pre-ground

natural English red ochre pigment. The principles of this procedure can be followed with other pre-ground pigments. Note that each pigment requires different amounts of grinding and oil, and this is something that you will learn the more you feel the materials. You will also need an ink muller and grinding slab. These are essential for ink making. You can purchase a whole range of mullers, from glass through to granite ones. You can also make your own using a lovely smooth, large stone.

All ink materials are cleaned up with vegetable oil and a rag.

Materials
Copperplate oil weak
Copperplate oil strong
English red ochre pre-ground pigment
Ink muller
Ink grinding slab
Palette knife

Using your ink
The ink we will make is a good all-round basic ink. Let us take a look at how it performs over relief, intaglio and planographic methods.

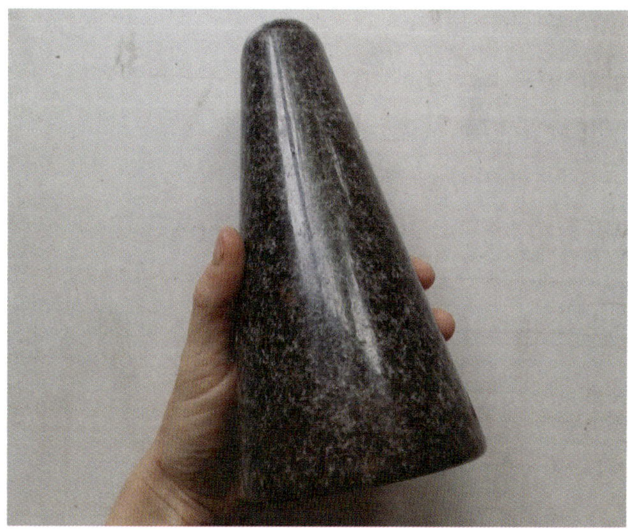

Using a muller helps grind pigment into the oil. This one is made from granite.

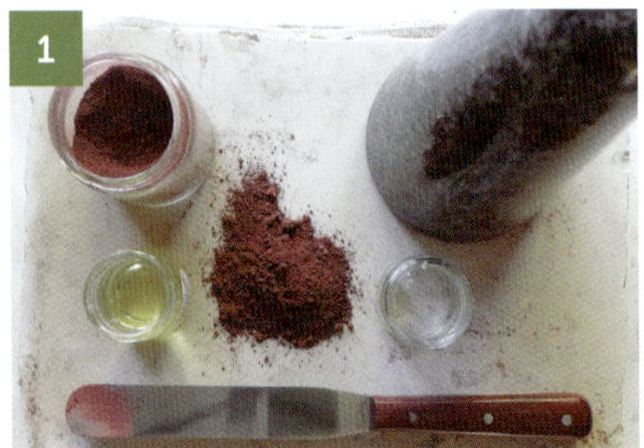

Materials needed for making a basic ink.

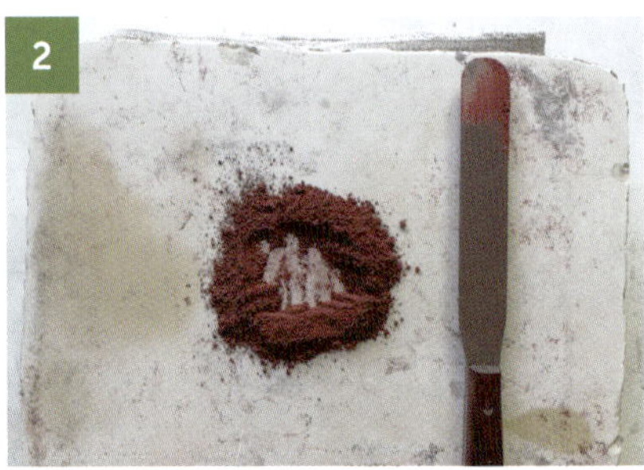

Place your pigment in the middle of the grinding slab. Make a well.

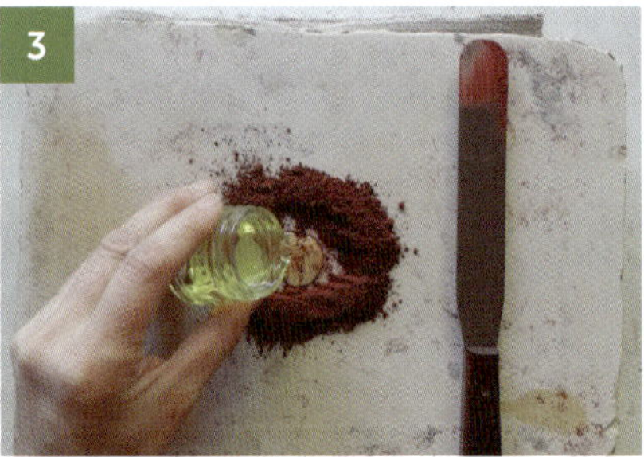

Add weak copperplate oil to the well. You can always add more later.

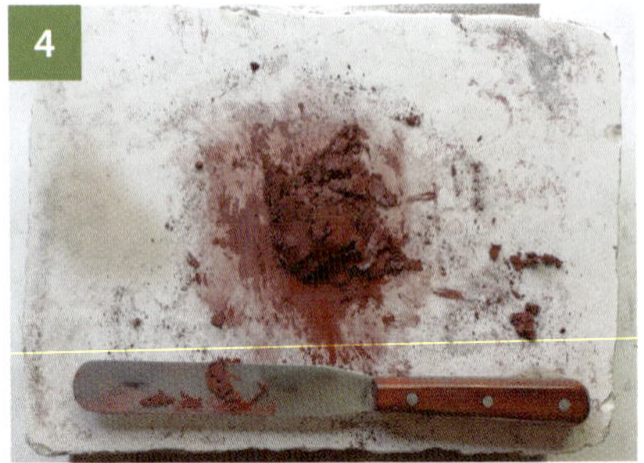

Use a palette knife to slowly work the oil into a dry paste.

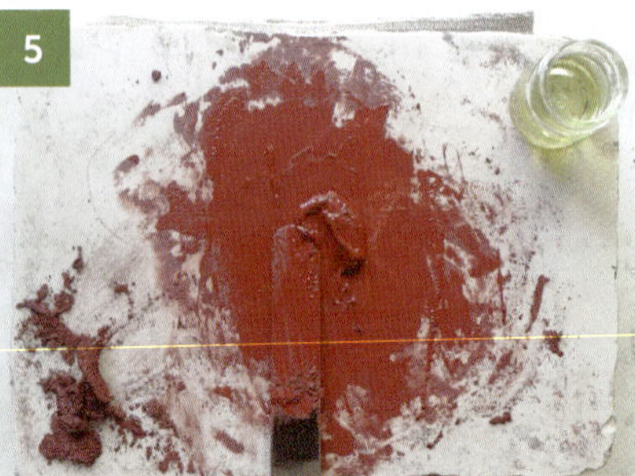

Add more weak oil in small amounts, work with a palette knife until smooth.

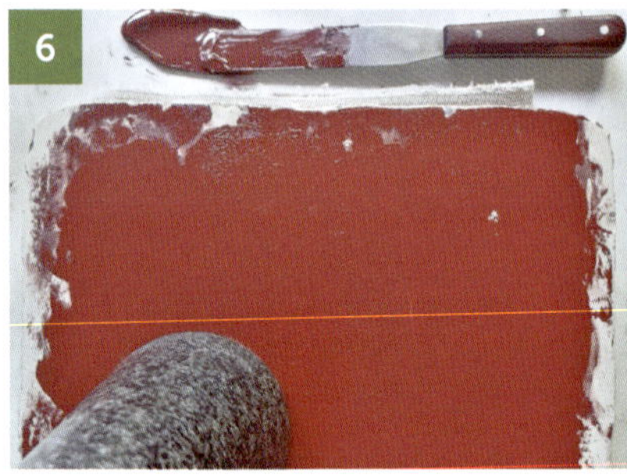

Use the muller to grind ink across the slab, small amounts at a time.

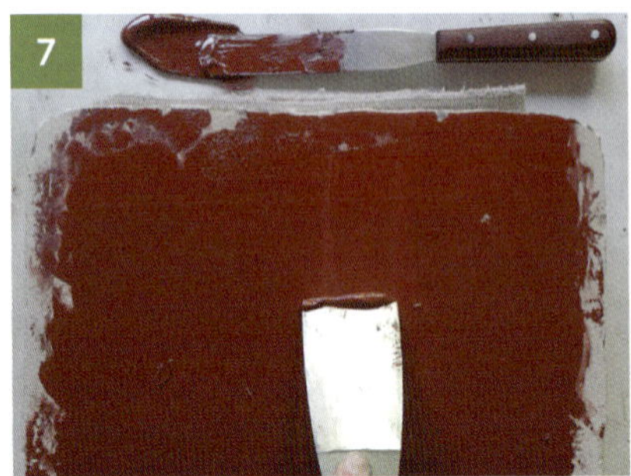

Use a push knife to scrape up ground ink and put to one side.

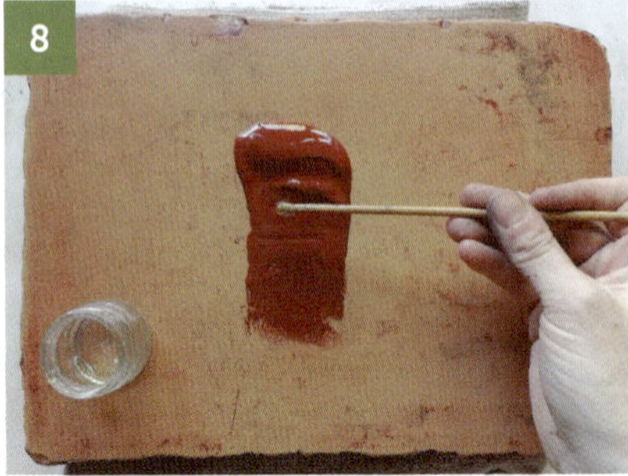

Add a couple of drops of strong plate oil to the ground ink.

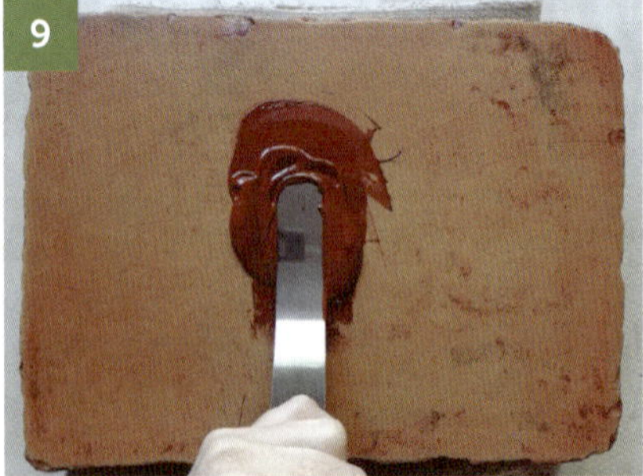

Mix oil in with a palette knife until tack is desired consistency.

To test the relief qualities, I am inking up a basic lino cut carved on traditional artist's lino. The ink rolls out well and has a good gloss and tackiness. I will roll up and print under a press on Fabriano Rosaspina 220gsm paper and by hand on 39gsm Japanese washi.

To test intaglio, I am inking up a paper dry point plate using reclaimed Tetra Pak from an old long-life plant-milk carton. Details on how to utilise paper dry point can be found in Chapter 5. Because we have not stiffened the ink a little to adjust for the intaglio process, it was quite oily and

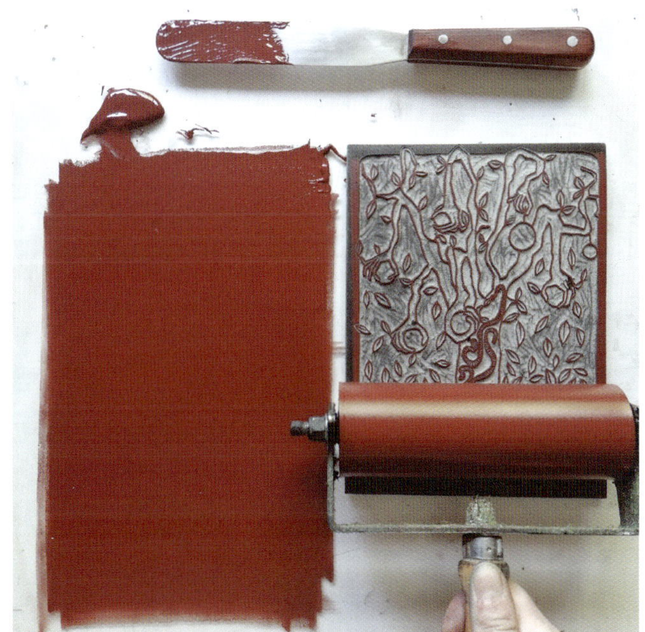

Testing the roll-out strength of homemade oil-based ink.

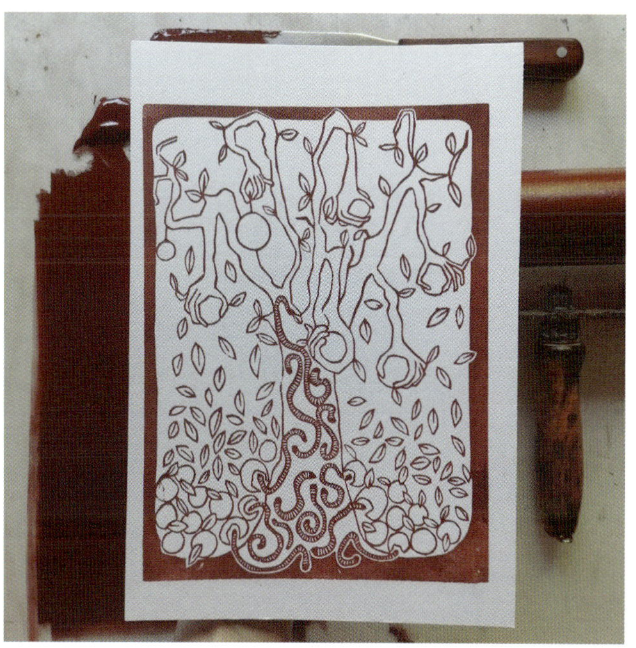

Results from printing a lino cut under a press on 220gsm paper.

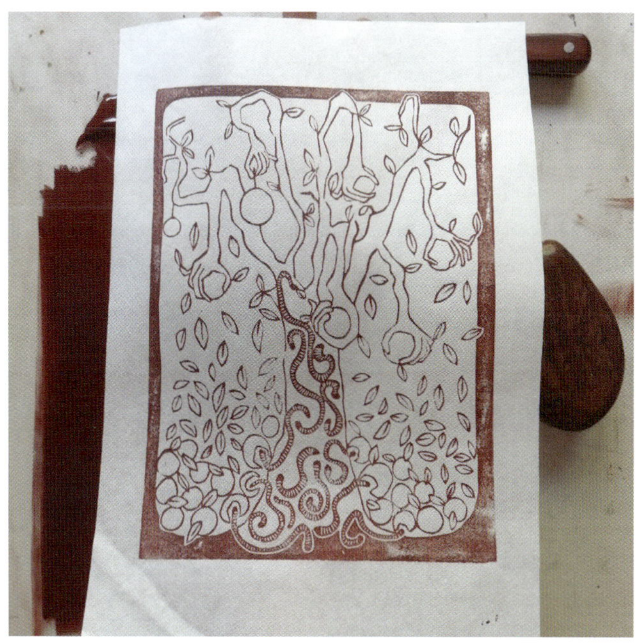

Results from hand printing a lino cut on 39gsm paper.

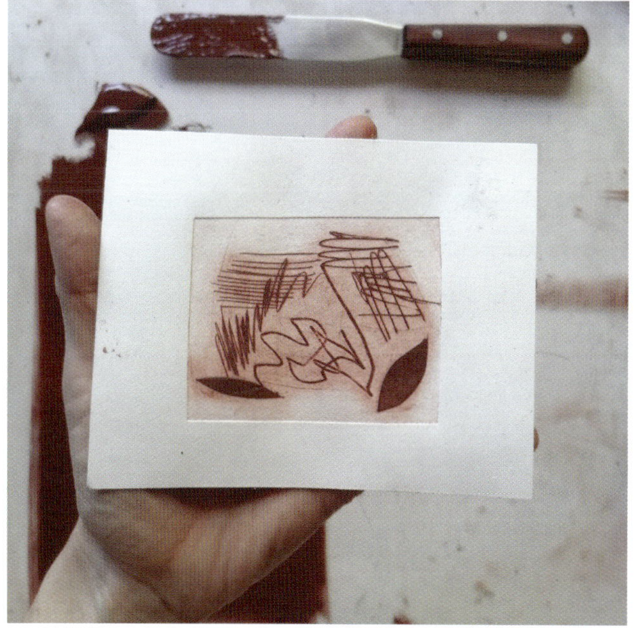

Results from using homemade ink with an intaglio process.

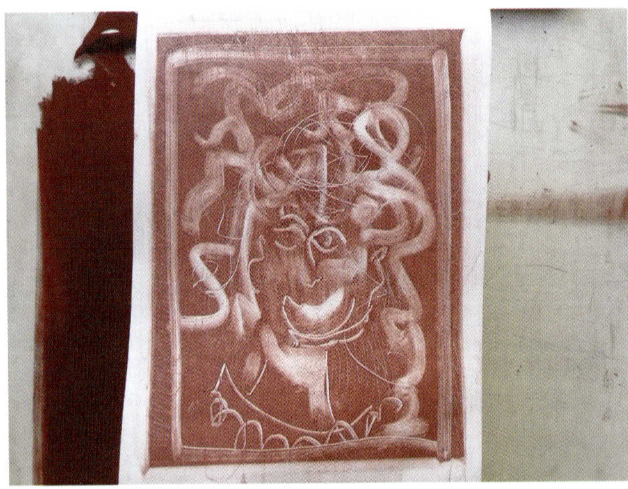

Results from using homemade ink with a monoprint process.

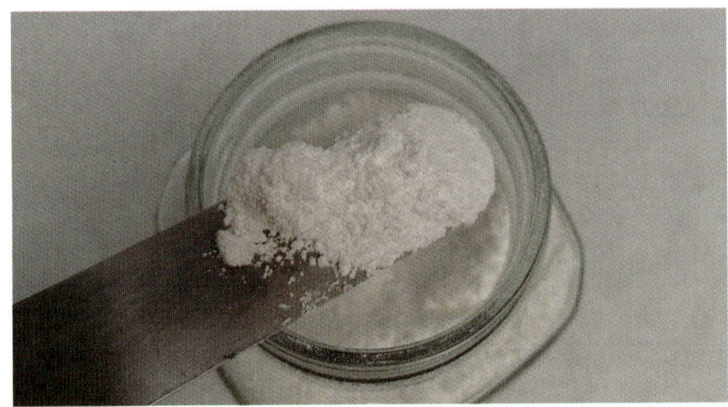

Magnesium carbonate is a non-toxic additive to stiffen inks.

created a strong plate tone, but it held well in the marks and softer elements such as the areas of sanding.

Finally, we are testing the ink through a planographic process – this could either be lithography or monoprint. To cover a good base that would be suited for both these processes, particularly checking the use for the thin layers of a lithographic roll up, we are going to apply a very thin, even, solid area on a sheet of Perspex. We will then remove this solid area using rags, fingers, knitting needles and any other tool that in essence creates a negative drawing upon the surface. This allows us to test the quality of the ink over a thin area, as well as whether it can hold textural effects from rag wiping.

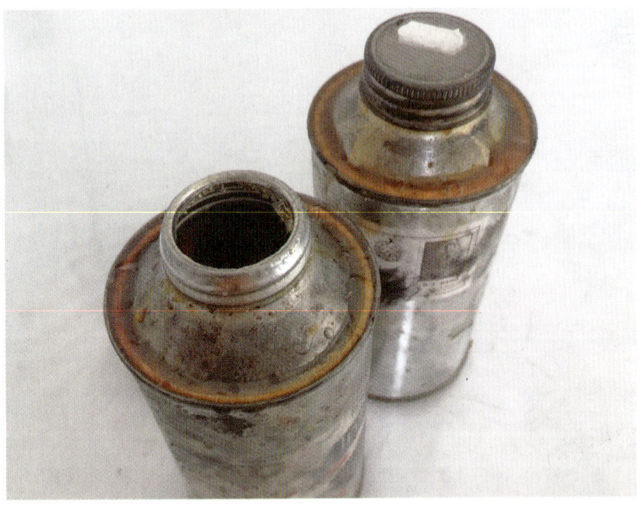

Different strengths of copperplate oil change the ink viscosity.

Developing ink

The studio basic oil-based ink works really well across the board. However, the more you delve into printmaking and ink use, the more you wish to be able to influence the viscosity of the ink so that you can play with texture, gloss, layering and numerous other effects in your final impression. Commercially ground oil-based inks undergo minute oil changes, different grinds and tweaks in recipes to achieve the reliable consistency we all love and that is so accessible. But these nuances can be achieved on a smaller scale in the workshop, and indeed this allows you to be able to have individual inputs into the qualities of each and every ink made. If you gather or sustainably source your own pigment, then the ink becomes fully traceable and ecological.

To change to texture of the ink, to make a stiffer ink for etching, then you can add some magnesium carbonate. It will reduce the gloss but make for easier wiping if needed.

If you wish to increase the tack of an ink to help with a roll-out for relief work or for monoprint purposes, then a strong plate oil can be added drop by drop. If you wish to loosen the ink for perhaps some viscosity work as we will explore in Chapter 4, then a weak plate oil will do the trick. Changing the consistency of oil-based inks is a useful skill to get to grips with, so do have a play.

WHERE TO FIND PIGMENT

Sources of pigments are all around us. Earth, stones and clays are common sources of richly coloured pigments that can be made into inks. For many years we have also developed pigments using laboratory techniques that generate pigments based upon synthetic chemicals or metals. The collection and sourcing of the pigments can be a fun adventure, and if you are wishing to know what makes up the inks you use in your studio practice, then tracing the pigments back to the original source is really the only way.

Pigments can be bought pre-ground, or you can source your own rock or earth. In order to have a sustainable approach to it all, an element of common sense and balance needs to be exerted. Gathering a small lump of chalk washed up on a beach to use to make your extender for a year, in balance, is far better than going along to the cliff face with chisel and bag and hammering away to take kilograms to then sell on as a wild pigment. Stampeding off designated pathways in protected lands to raid a patch of ochre-shaded earth in a woodland will invariably destroy much-needed protected habitats. Whereas asking a group of building workers if you could take home a section of the ochre-coloured clay they are digging up as part of the site works is a far more sustainable approach. Collecting sources of pigments means being fully attentive and aware of the land and the situation in it. If you are wishing to gather from land that is not your own, do seek permission or open a dialogue with those who manage the land. People who protect the lands for future generations are often very friendly and amicable if you are honest and open in the first instance. And I always make sure I never, ever, collect in greed. Over-consumption and waste is a huge sustainability issue.

Pigments that are collected from around the globe and shipped to us are part of a long history of trading resources, dating back to the ancient world. Again, use common sense if you wish to partake in the sharing of rich-coloured pigments from around the globe. There is a reason lapis lazuli was so rarely used, or that certain ochres from Roussillon, France are used in abundance to colour the village limewash. Some pigments are more plentiful than others and if we respond and listen and reflect this in our own practice, then I think making one's own inks can be fully sustainable. Vitally, I always remember to give back. If my practice involves using some pigments shipped from the South of France, or a piece of sea-washed chalk, then I will endeavour to make sure that areas in my lifestyle are also contributing positively to the earth, such as choosing to walk or cycle over driving, reducing plastic use or growing food. Ecological awareness is a big picture made up of many smaller moments, which include our art practice and lifestyle choices.

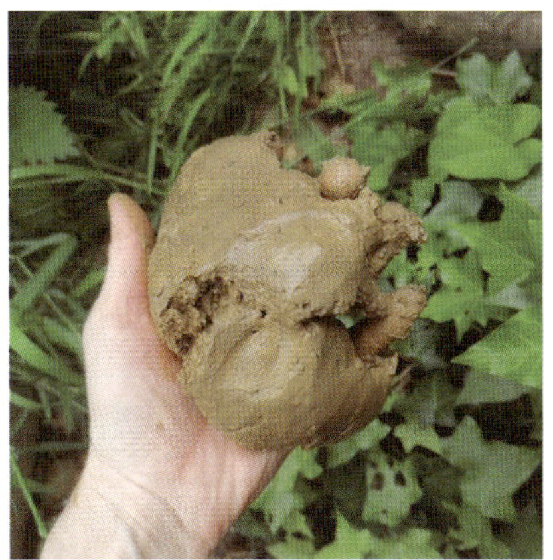

Clay rich in earth ochres can be found readily in back gardens.

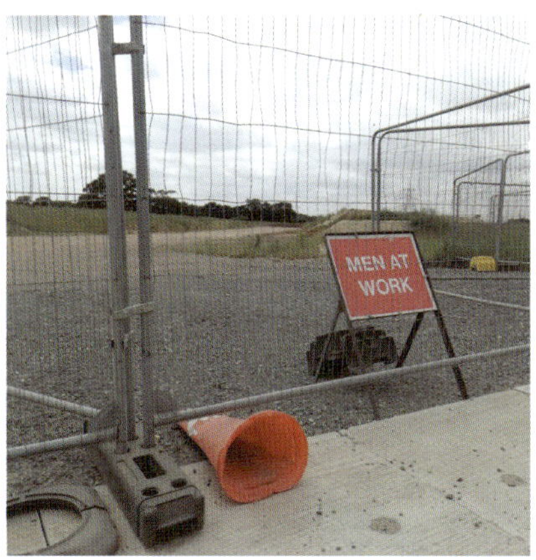

Building sites often dig up coloured earths and are usually happy to spare some.

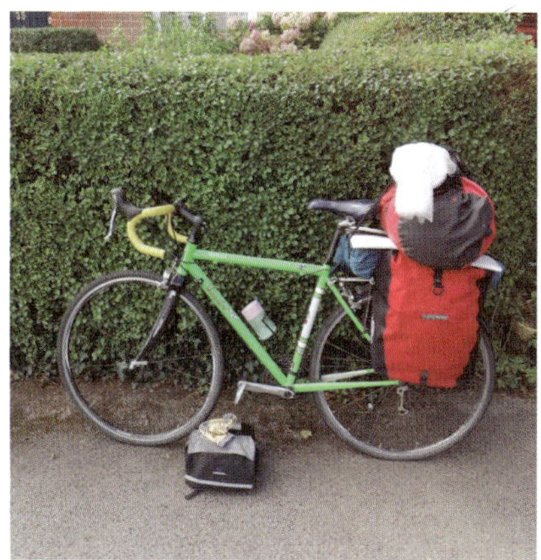

If we do take, can we give back? Is that car journey necessary?

HOW TO PREPARE PIGMENT: EARTH

In this project we will be looking at how to extract earth pigments from an ochre-rich earth. I will be using a rich orange/red ochre-coloured clay-heavy earth that was gathered from my back garden. Basic coloured earths are usually a good sign of ochre existing. Ochres are iron-based pigments that are heavy in iron minerality and it is the oxidisation of this iron that produces the rich yellows to reds we know. Ochre can be found in soils and earths as well as in ochre-rich stones, or even bricks, due to the ochre-rich clays that were used. We will look at processing minerals in the next section.

Materials

Approximately a small handful of ochre-rich clay/soil
Three standard jam jars, cleaned out, with lids
A small bucket
Source of water (I use rainwater)
Clean fine muslin

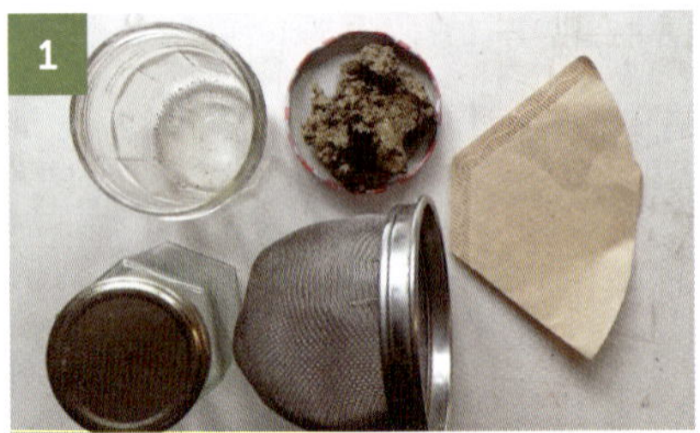

Materials needed to extract the ochres from a clay sample.

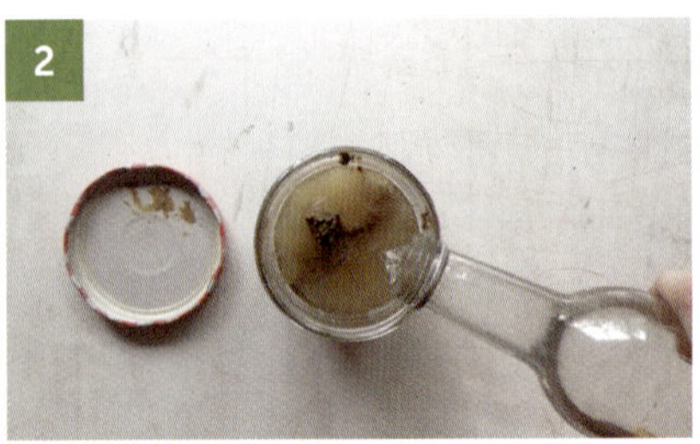

Place clay sample in jam jar and cover with water.

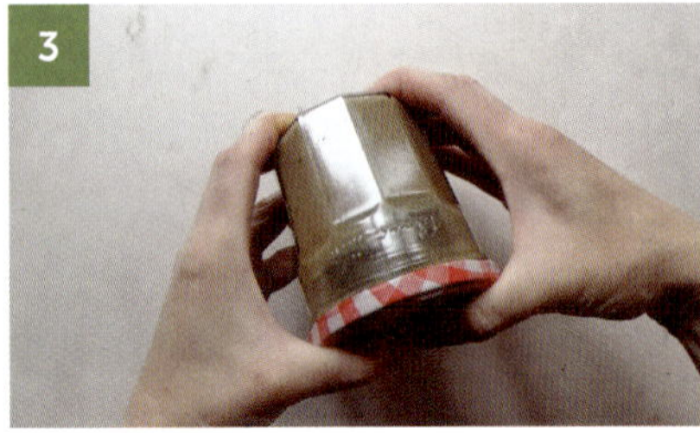

Put the lid on and shake the jam jar vigorously until the clay is dispersed.

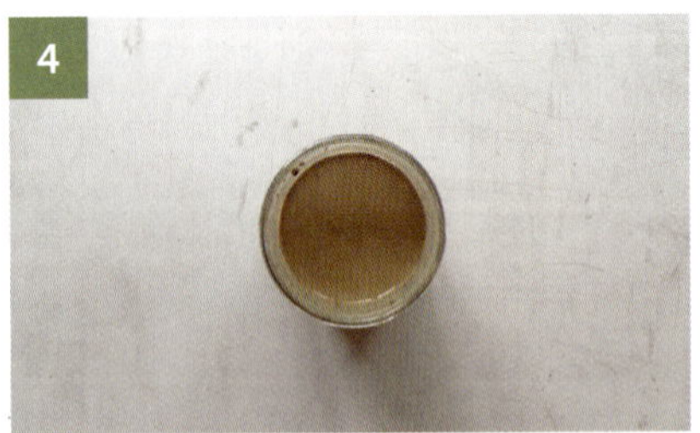

Let the mixture sit for a few minutes to let sediment gather at the bottom.

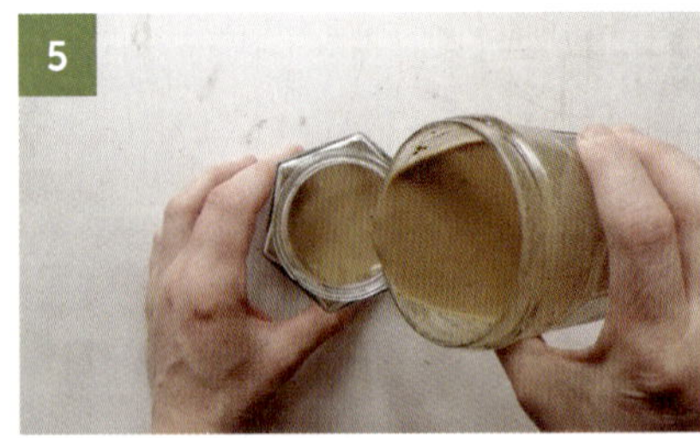

Carefully strain off the top ochre water into a clean jar.

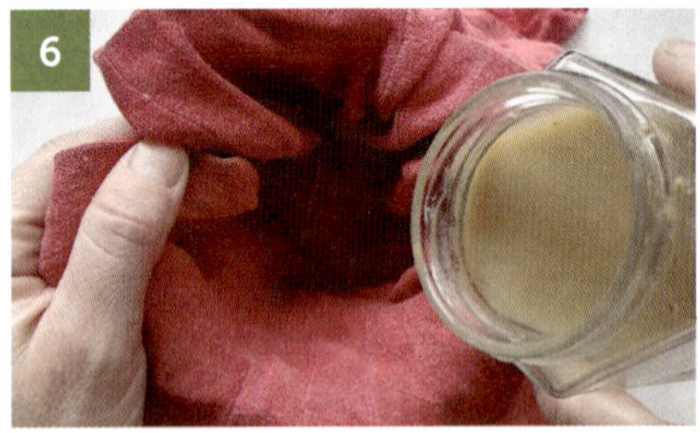

Strain ochre water through a fine muslin into another jar. Discard sediment.

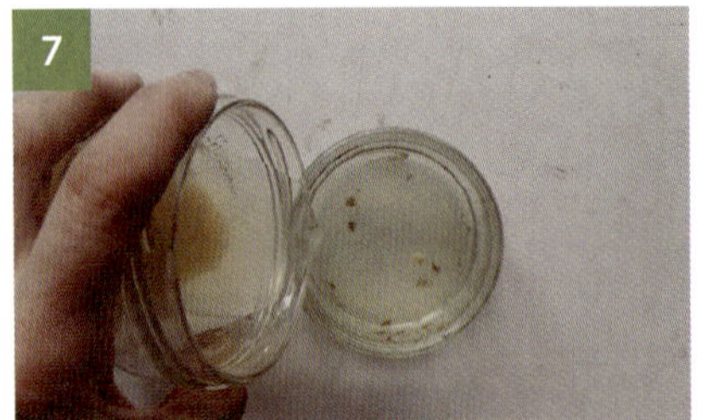

Let pigment settle to the bottom and carefully strain off clear water.

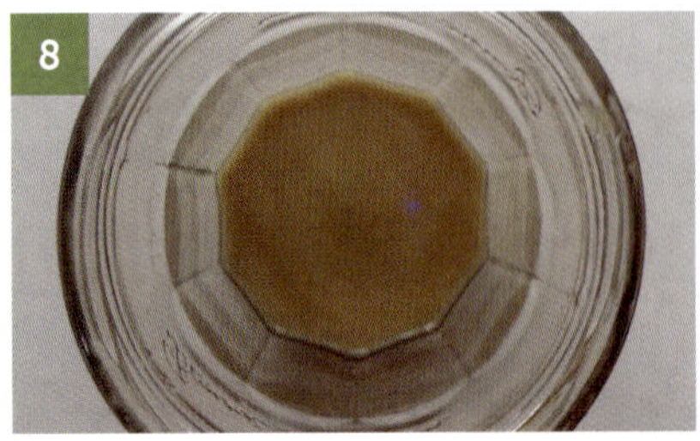

Let the remaining pigment settle, and the water evaporate over time.

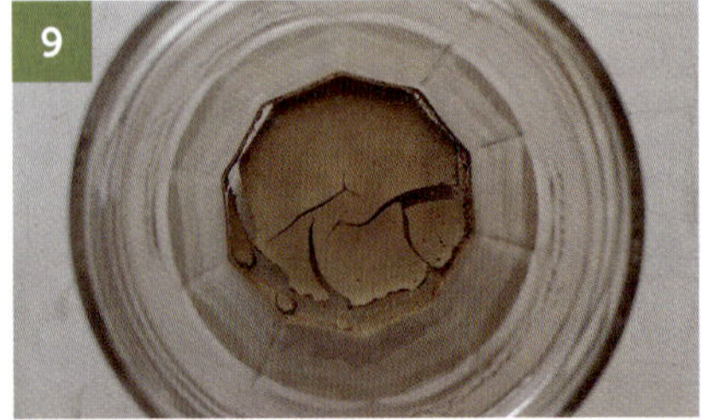

When the water has evaporated, you have a fine ochre pigment ready to grind.

HOW TO PREPARE PIGMENTS: MINERAL

Stones are a rich source of many pigments. Their processing from stone to pigment can vary in method and ones such as lapis lazuli require a lot of time invested to gather the rich blue pigment. Stones such as chalk, or iron-rich ochre stone, slate, even bricks, are great sources of colour that are more accessible to make into pigments. In this project we will be using a small lump of brick gathered from my garden. This is where you will need a pestle and mortar for grinding. I use a stone one to withstand the heavy bashing that comes from stone smashing. Please also wear a face mask as you make the pigment and/or work in a ventilated area. I tend to work outside. Although we are not grinding up heavy metals, insoluble particular matter is still airborne during the grinding process and precaution is sensible.

The grinding of the red ochre into an ink can take time, as with many of the earth pigments. However, the colour is wonderful and all from a resource otherwise left to go to waste.

Materials

Small lump of brick. The older bricks are better – you can find some great old brick samples on pebbly shorelines
Stone pestle and mortar
Two jam jars and lids
Fine muslin
Water source

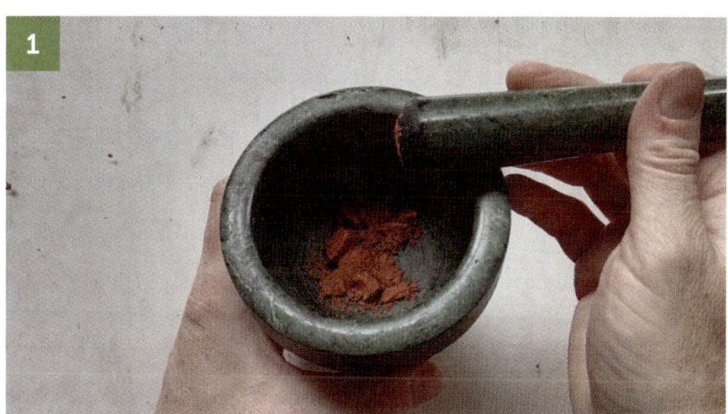

Using a pestle and mortar, grind up a brick sample to a fine powder.

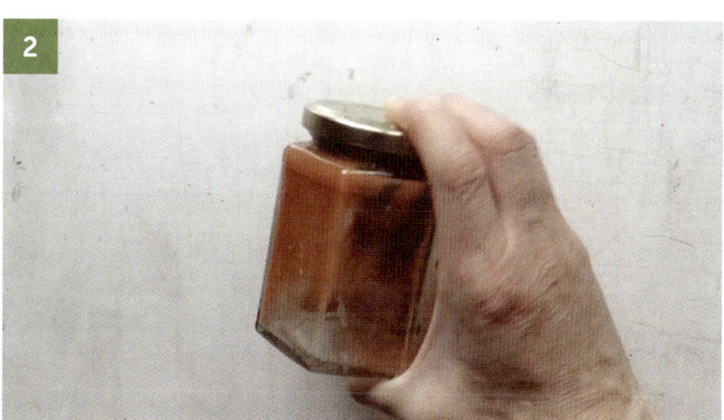

Place powder in a jam jar, cover with water and shake vigorously.

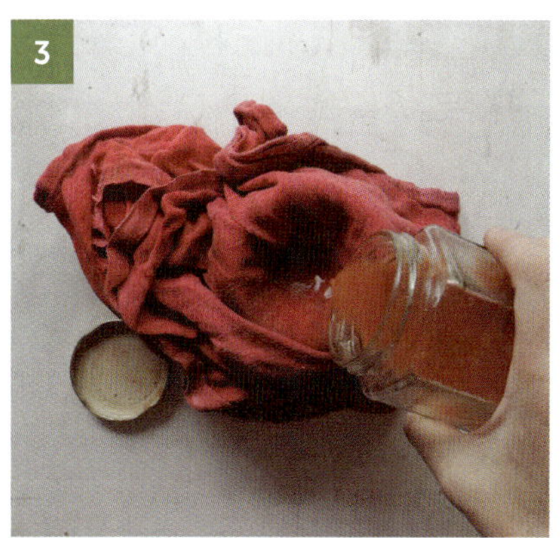

Strain the brick solution through a fine muslin into a clean jar.

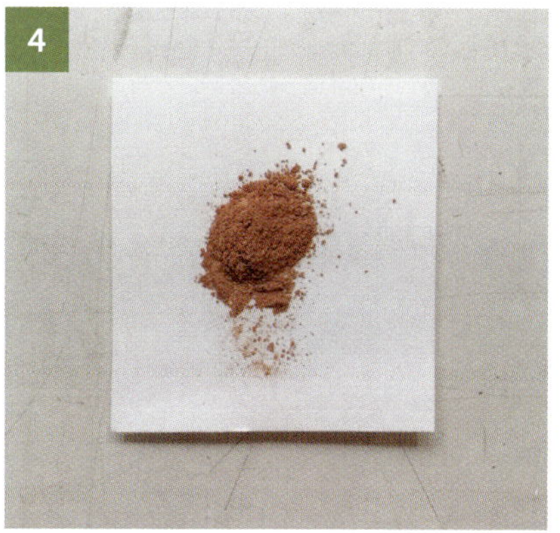

Let pigment settle and water evaporate leaving red ochre pigment.

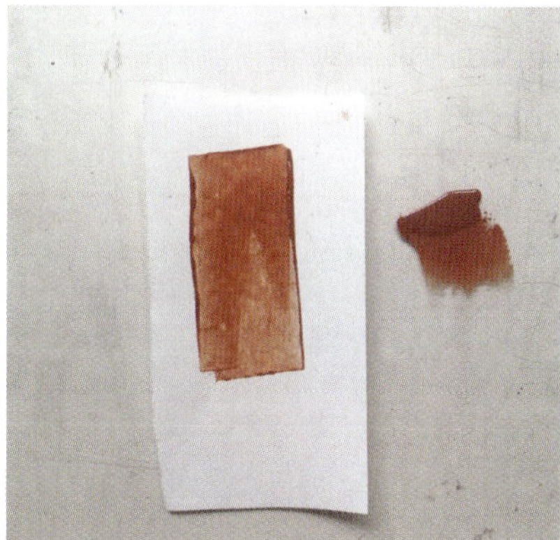

Resultant red ochre ink extracted from a brick in our back garden.

HOW TO PREPARE PIGMENTS: DYE AND LAKES

A lake pigment is describing a pigment that has been extracted from a dye. A dye contains a pigment that is soluble in water and thus methods were invented to extract this colour to acquire a solid pigment that can then be ground in suspension with a binder. Lake pigments are often fugitive, that is, they fade in UV light, because they are based upon dyes that are also sensitive to light. The extraction of the dye colour to a solid form involves the use of a metallic salt for the dye molecules to adhere to, so you end up with a solid coloured powder. Most commonly used is alum, or aluminium sulphate. Alum is also used widely as a mordant for textile dying. Alum has mixed reviews on toxicity, and like many substances if used in huge amounts – if kilos were emptied into a watercourse – then it would cause high levels of damage to the aquatic life. On a smaller scale it is significantly less harmful but in principle, should not be entering the watercourse when making lake pigments. It is technically classed as a hazardous waste, and thus its disposal should be treated in accordance with your local authority disposal regulations, and it should be handled with care to avoid skin irritation. I am still pondering the use of lake pigments with regards to ecological printmaking, so for now, the focus of ink making in this book is upon solid pigment from earth and minerals.

Pigments around the home

Pigment making and thus ink making is hugely rewarding and even if you do not make all your inks, a small contribution of homemade ink from well-sourced pigments is a huge step to more ecological printing. It also adds a direct connection to the landscape around you, which tells a story in the artwork itself. There are some pigments that can be made and sourced readily from around the home that offer the artist some fun experimentation. When we cleaned out our wood-fired ranges, beautiful ultra-fine soot came down the flue and promptly was gathered up for future soot black making. Old bones from the ground can be used to make bone black, and if you know of anyone with a grape vine, then gather their pruned branches and try making vine black. This is a beautiful deep black pigment that developed from charring the yearly pruned stems from grape vines. If you have access to a wood-fired stove, then you can make your own. It is a fun introduction into the various deep blacks that can be acquired from the carbons created through charring substances.

MAKING VINE BLACK

Materials
A handful of dry vine clippings
A metal tin with lid that fits all clippings
Access to a wood-fired stove or small fire box
Ink-making equipment as per previous demonstrations

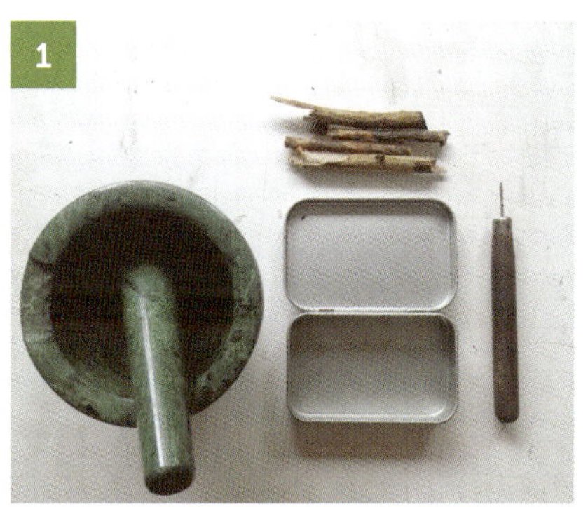

Materials needed to make a basic vine black pigment.

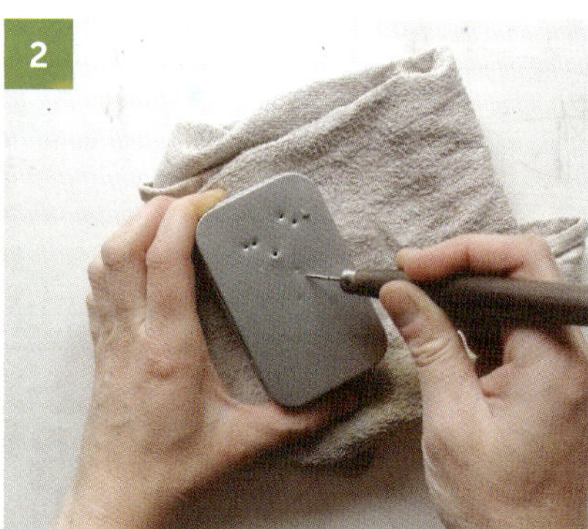

Carefully stab holes into the lid of your metal tin.

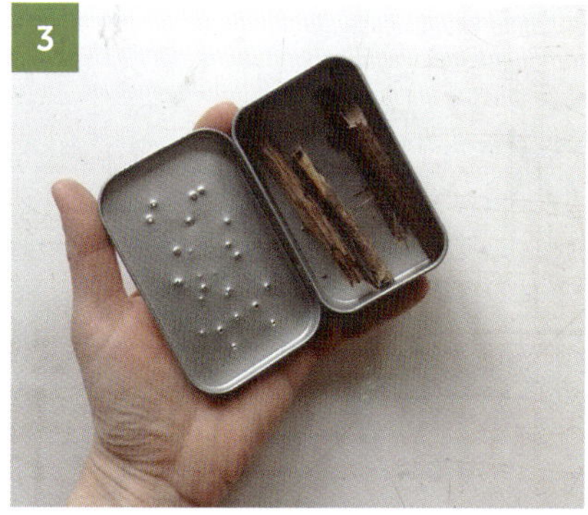

Fill the tin with the dried-out vine cuttings, close lid.

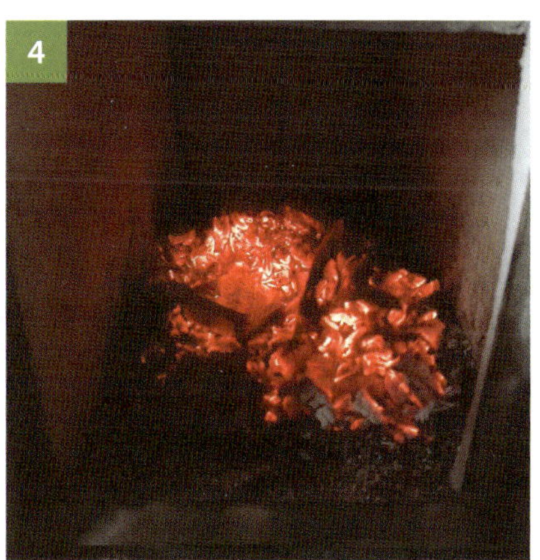

Carefully place tin in hot embers of a fire and leave overnight.

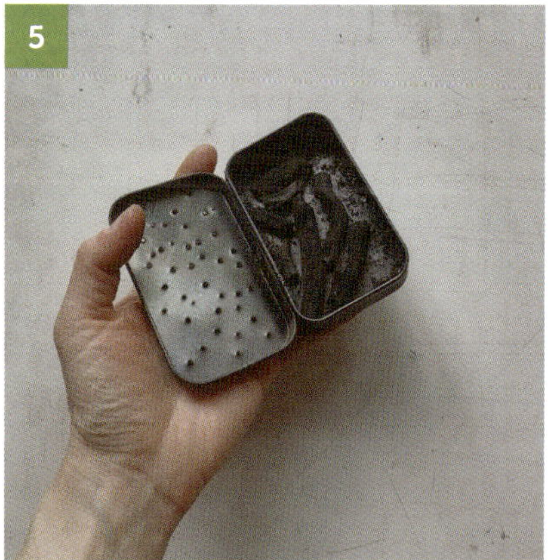

After the tin has cooled, you can check the vine charcoal.

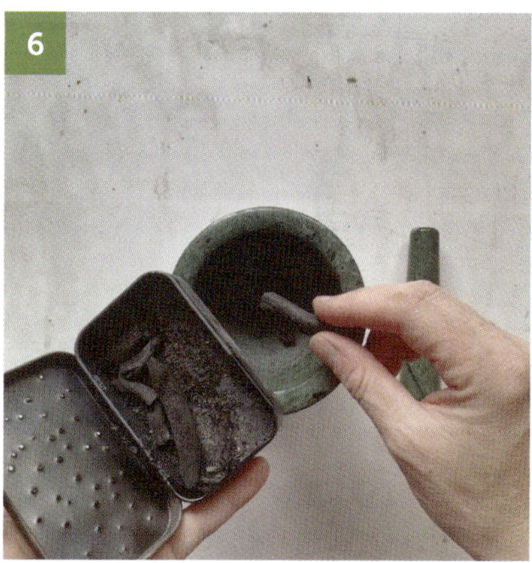

The vine charcoal can now be ground into a fine pigment ready for ink.

CHECK YOUR PIGMENTS
FOR THE FUTURE

After exploring pigment making, you may notice that individual pigments grind differently, they sit differently in oil and they also change colour once bound with the linseed oil. It is a huge journey with much fun along the way. A note to bear in mind for the future; some pigments change colour rapidly when bound with linseed oil and are not suitable for an oil binder. One such is green verdigris made from the reaction of acetic acid upon the surface of copper. Binding with linseed oil causes it to go brown rather than the luscious neon blue-green. There is a wealth of supportive information on pigments online and in books, so if you are taking the joyous powdery plunge, then it is worth checking out the background of the pigment you wish to make to check its stability in oil. If not for oil, then why not try it as a watercolour for paste printing or mokuhanga, but that is a whole new book…

Pigment collection and ink making can be highly addictive and beautiful. It can, however, make you feel daunted about trying to be sustainable and overwhelmed with the amount of work required to fully overhaul an ink system. My advice is, as with all things, to find a balance that is manageable within your own set-up and lifestyle. Even changing one commercially bought ink to an inert handmade one is a huge step. Massive, in fact. It is important to make change but also make sure that change is sustainable and manageable so that it stickily sticks into the future. One of my first investigations, and a true learning curve it turned out to be, was extender or transparent medium. Transparent medium is used to make highly pigmented inks more transparent. I use it a fair amount in my work, so the following investigation turned out to be interesting. One day (and this is a true story), my five-year-old daughter started collecting the chalk found naturally in our garden and smashing it up with a rock, filtering it and sifting it with a sieve and making beautiful white water, which she and her sister played with as magic milk. I collected some of the milk (in exchange for biscuits) and followed the standard filtering procedure to produce a very fine chalk pigment.

And it made me realise how simple it is to make a very fine chalk pigment and how on earth had I not been already doing this when it had been staring right at me. Immediately, I thought I could replace the titanium dioxide white inks with a chalk white. But, no, this did not work because when calcium carbonate is ground with linseed oil it does not retain the white depth; it actually goes transparent. Of course it does, I use calcium carbonate occasionally as a filler to stiffen printing inks knowing it does not affect their pigmentation. And so my homemade extender ink started. One change at a time, we can all make a shift.

Where does this leave us?
We have seen that making ink is completely possible and allows for traceability in materials, thus making it a very ecological approach. There is also a balance to be had. It may not be feasible to entirely shift overnight the practice embedded for years. So take it step by step. Is there one particular ink colour made from home-sourced pigment that you really like? Could this be made in smaller batches to allow it to be used as a spot colour for a specific print run? Even that simple change and using homemade inks here and there is a huge positive step.

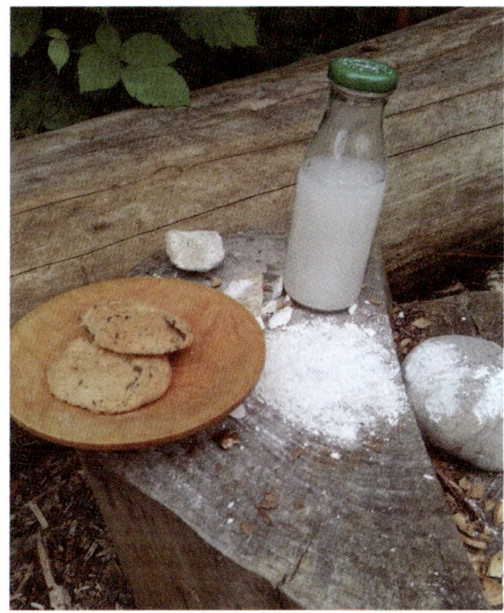

The process of making 'magic milk' in exchange for biscuits inspired making oil-based extender.

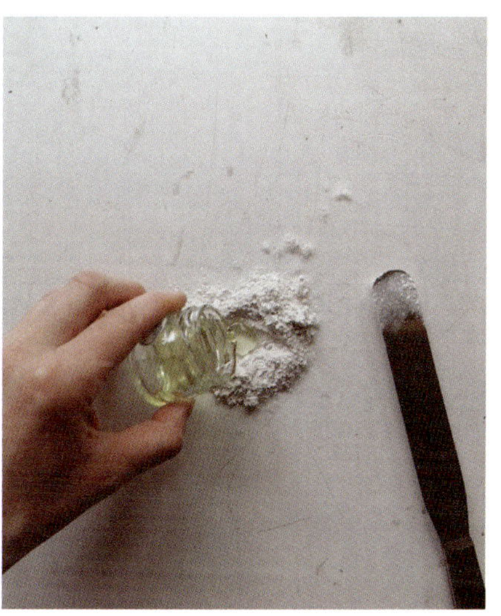

Adding weak copperplate oil to finely ground chalk from our garden.

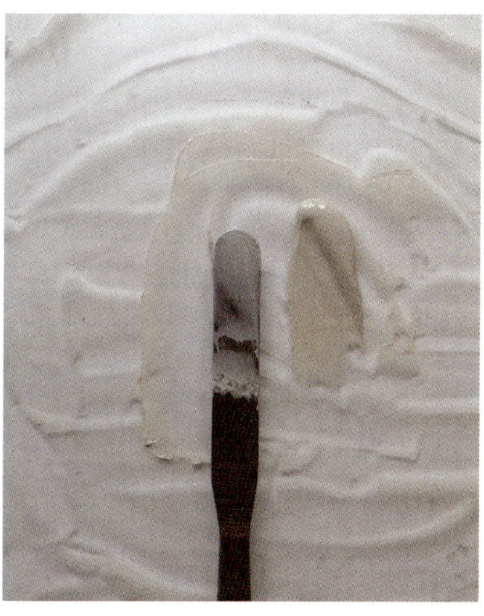

The extender after being ground with muller and strong plate oil added.

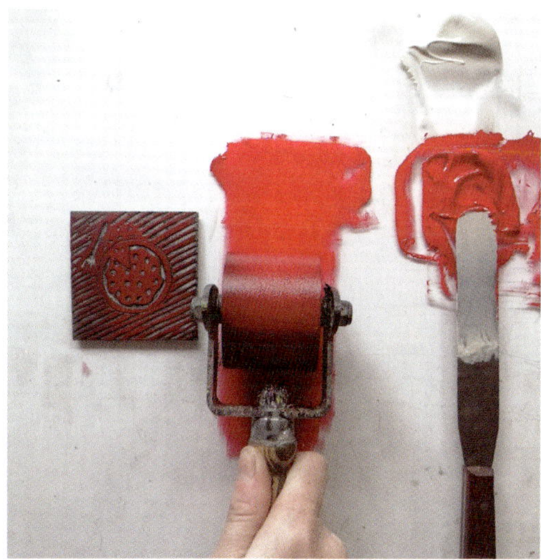

Rolling out a mix of three parts extender to one part neat carmine red.

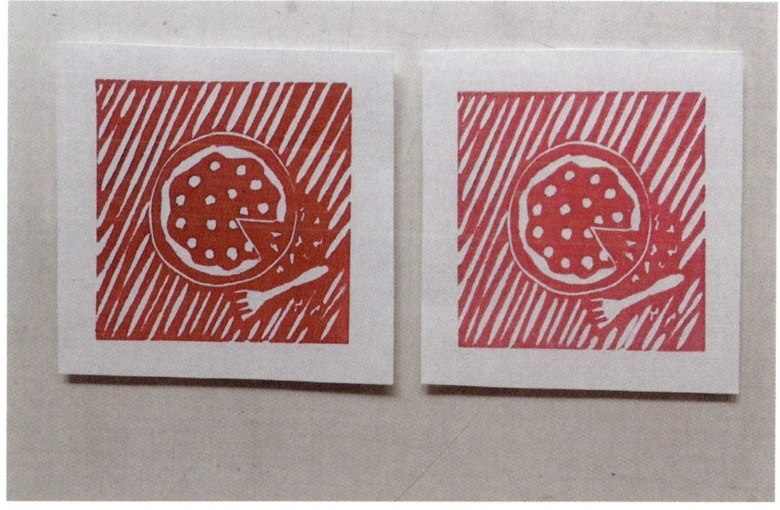

The resultant prints from neat carmine red (left) and extended.

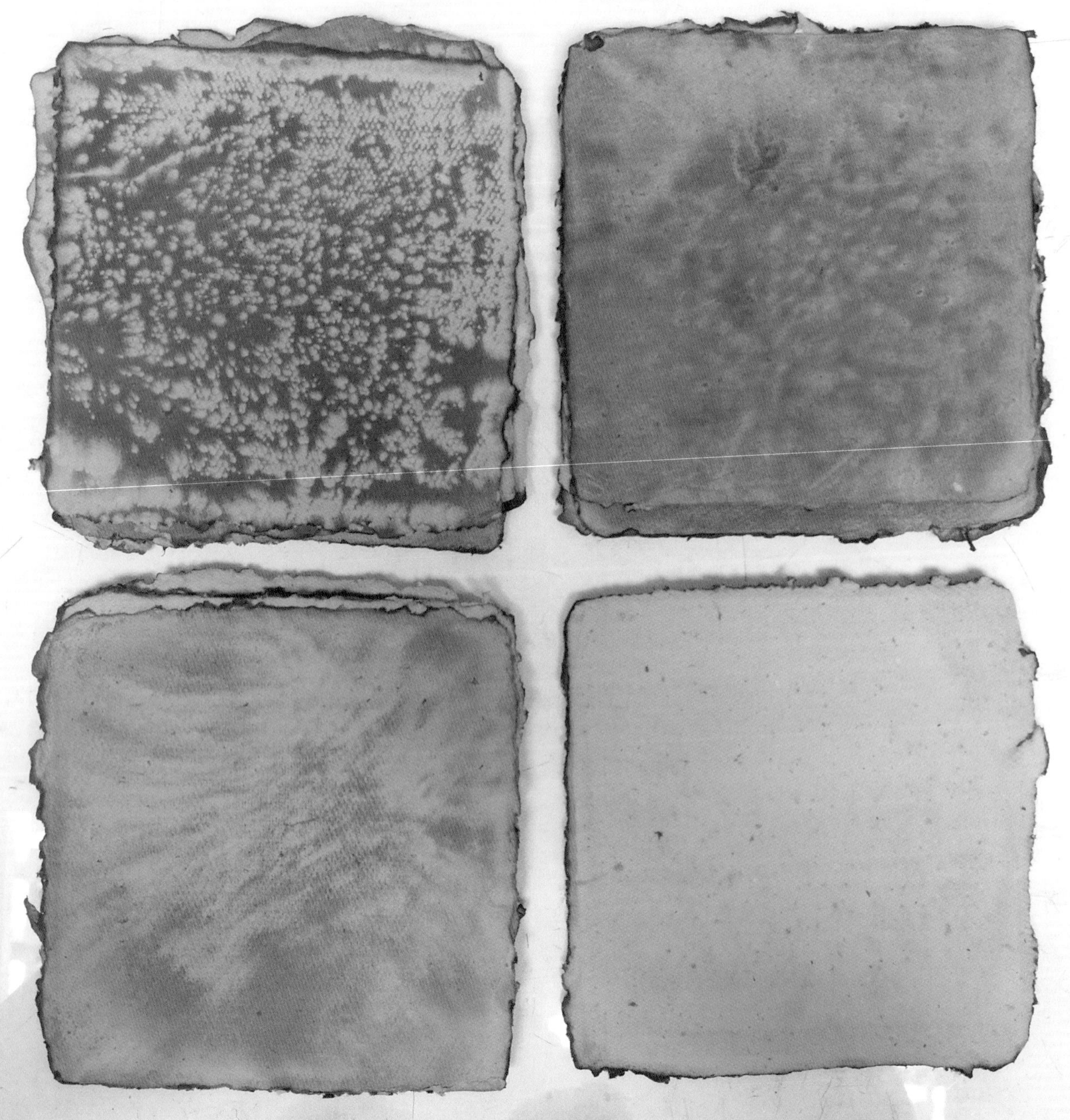

CHAPTER 2

SUBSTRATE

So we have our ink. Now we need a surface to receive it. This is referred to rather grandly as the substrate. This covers everything from the traditional paper through to anything that receives the inked impression – plaster, fabric, wood, concrete and anything else in between. Paper is the traditional and the most well-used substrate for printmakers, although there is evidence that fabric was receiving printed impressions long before the advent of paper. The substrate you use has a huge impact upon the end result of the print and is as much part of the artistic choice of the printmaker as the print design itself. The variety of paper available these days is huge and very ecological decisions can be made when buying commercial paper. Whilst also looking at a few alternative substrates, this chapter predominately focuses on paper, the choices to be made and of course how to make your own.

PAPER

Paper is used widely across the world. It has been with us as a surface for drawing, printing and making for millennia

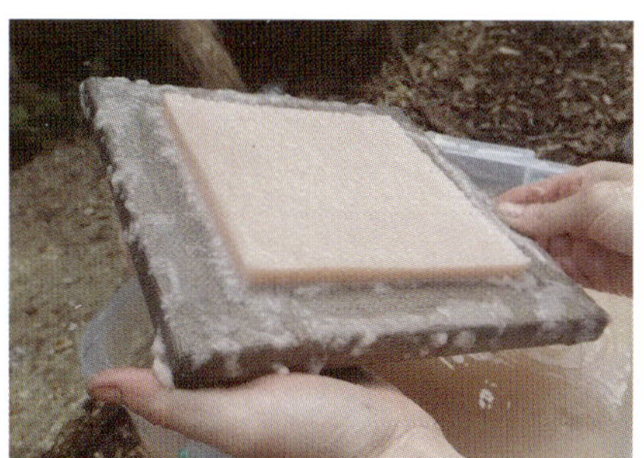

Pink paper pulled from the pulp vat ready to couch and press.

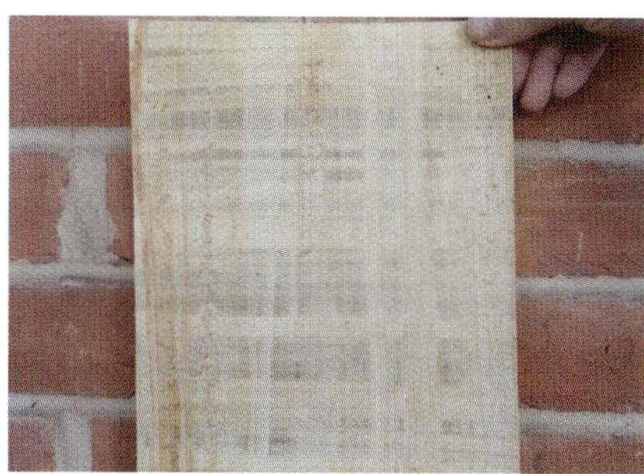

Papyrus paper is made from beating papyrus layers together.

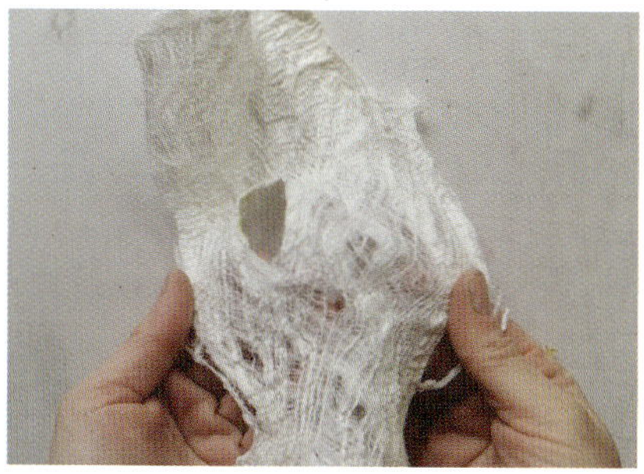

Dried and prepared kozo fibre ready for beating for paper.

and its uses are widespread. The majority of paper currently available on the market is made from a fibre pulp, be it tree, plant or rags (to name a few sources), which is then dispersed in a water bath. A form of wooden frame with a sieving screen stretched over is then dipped into the pulp bath, pulp is gathered on the frame surface, water left to drain and the pulp remains on the screen, forming the start of a sheet of paper. This wet pulp is then turned out from the frame, whilst its shape is kept intact and, depending on the style of paper, it will undergo pressing to remove excess water, bond the fibres together and form an even surface.

These are the basic principles of the majority of paper making methods, but of course not all. Some paper does not even require a pulp, such as birch bark. However, for the more commercial and widely used paper, the pulp basis is the most common and accessible. Across various regions of the world, different techniques have developed in relation to the different fibres used. For instance, in Japan, the long fibres of the inner bark of the paper mulberry tree are used to make a strong, highly prized printing paper. The paper pulp is drained over the surface of a bamboo mat, similar to a sushi rolling mat. In Europe, cotton and linen rag paper was developed and the paper-making frame known as a deckle came into being, made from specific wooden jointing and a woven wire mesh. In Egypt, beaten papyrus leaves were layered up to form papyrus paper, which did not even require a pulp bath.

Choices for printmaking

With so many approaches to paper production, we are fortunate that as artists, we can select the right paper for the specific need. Traditionally, printing methods were quite exact about the requirements of specific papers for specific needs, such as etching only being able to be printed on etching papers. However, although this is a useful guide, it is not the case that only certain papers will print certain print mediums. There are certainly some styles of paper that are more suited to some methods than others, but there are no set rules. Paper is there to be explored and to find the range that suits your methods, not the ones that people tell you suit your methods.

A great general guide to start off with is to ask yourself if you are hand printing or using a press. If hand printing, then the lighter the weight of the paper, the easier it will be for you to apply pressure to generate your impression. If printing under a press, bear in mind the paper needs to be strong enough to withstand the pressure of the press. Next, I would look at the methods you are wishing to explore. If you are making a lino cut, then ask yourself if a smooth surface paper would allow a better quality of ink transfer than a rough surface. Are you wanting a smooth result or a speckled one? The smoother the paper surface, the more even the result. If you are working intaglio or any other method that requires you use damp paper, make sure the paper you select can withstand getting wet without crumbling to a pulp or leaching a dye if you use coloured

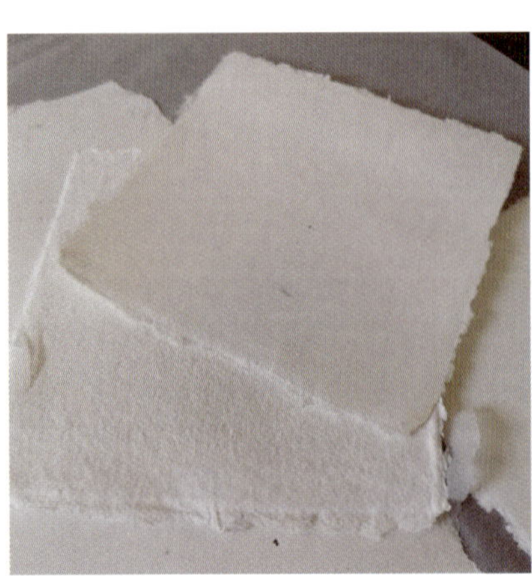

Selecting papers for print is a personal and important choice.

My general-use 'house paper' is made in different sizes and textures.

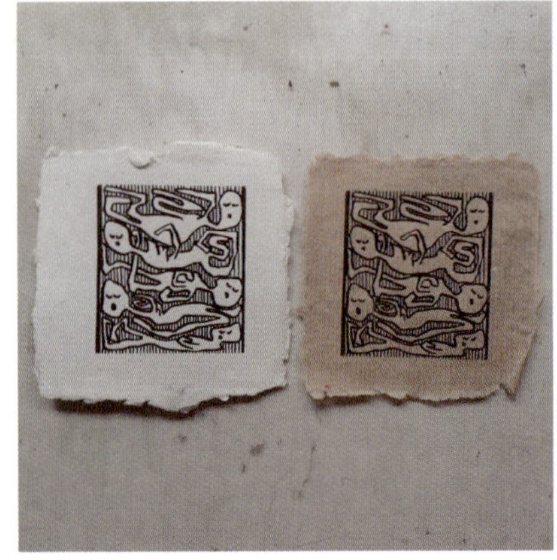

A lino can change in atmosphere when printed on different papers.

papers. Why not try a few samples first? If you wish to make some collage papers for work later, then you probably need a lightweight paper that allows you to glue and cut cleanly to allow for easy collaging. Perhaps this is where you would need to investigate washi papers. The questions and choices can be many, and we have not even delved into handmade or textured papers. I was trained using one type of paper, from one type of mill, and it has put me off using this mill again! Not because of the quality of paper, but because the lack of questioning and investigation I instigated at the time meant I was just working on the same paper all the time. Now I love to explore new papers and of course, I have found a good staple I use as my go-to paper and for teaching, but I also have a range of many other options for specific needs. And excitingly, I now make my own 'house' paper, which is great to print with and makes sure every print I do is truly unique.

Paper choice

Instead of buying a whole range of large sheets of paper each time you go to print, test a few sample sheets using the same print matrix to see how it affects the end result. This means when you go to make a print and select the paper, you have testers to help guide and inform your decision. You can usually purchase sample sheets or scavenge offcuts of a range of papers, allowing you to test smaller samples before investing in larger ones. It is a useful reference point for you to have when deciding on paper for a particular print.

The paper choice can make a huge difference in the atmosphere of the resulting impression, so it is nice to have a play.

MAKING YOUR OWN PAPER

Making paper at home can be a hugely rewarding experience. Not only does it allow you to trace the fibres used, but also allows artistic discretion and choices with regard to textures, weight, additives, colours and much more. To make a basic printable sheet you do not need much equipment and the quality of the paper will only improve the more you make it. You also have the chance to make custom moulds and thus

shapes of paper, which would be expensive or unavailable if looking commercially.

I have the wonderful luxury of having a garden, so I make my paper outside, using rainwater as my paper bath, topped up with tap water if I need to bulk out volumes. I have tested the pH of our water and it is neutral, and we are fortunate to live in an area of low pollution. In essence, I have had no issues with using rainwater apart from the sad demise of a few tiny worms in the paper pulp. Of course, I have not witnessed the effect of our rainwater on paper in 50 years' or even 100 years' time, but if the paper starts to degrade and only a trace element of my ink is left, then at least it has all gone back to the earth to feed the soil.

If you are working in a setting which has no access to outdoor space, make sure you have plenty of towels on flooring and your working areas to absorb spillage. Do not let it put you off, as it really is a magical artform and my first ever batch of paper was made at the kitchen table with many towels and two young children having a go.

Fibre: reclaimed

To make any paper, you will need to find a suitable fibre. The easiest at home to work with is probably reclaiming old paper scraps and reconstituting these to make paper. I collect all the offcuts from workshops I teach and turn this into my 'house' paper, a general mid-weight, pressed, smooth-surface printing paper. I make it in one batch when the water butt is full, and we are expecting more rain to fill it. So inevitably, I end up paper making in autumn or winter. I invested in a sturdy pond liner to act as a big pulp bath and I made a (very) crude deckle that makes sheets approximately 56cm × 76cm, or Imperial. I aim for this to be my paper for the year, give or take. As I sit here typing I have been procrastinating about the batch of paper I need to make very soon because I have used up all my last batch and I keep putting it off – not for lack of enjoyment, but because I make mine seasonally, I may end up with cold fingers! But the paper bath is calling me next week…

If you collect printmaking paper scraps, then you are guaranteed they are acid-free, which is a huge boost to starting out making paper. I avoid ones with ink on, although this can add a beautiful speckle to the paper which is also quite fun. The scraps of paper need to be soaked and then blended to a fine pulp. On a domestic scale the best machine to do this is a juicer or blender. The trick to using one of these successfully I have found is to not overfill the jug with scraps, add lots of water, and let it blend for a couple of minutes to get a beautiful pulp. If you are able, then the higher-quality the blender, the better it will cope with the paper pulp. If you get into paper making, then a professional set-up will more often than not involve a Hollander beater, which is a mechanised large machine that beats and crushes fibres as they are suspended in water. It can work with paper scraps and beyond, including old clothes, plant fibres and tree fibres.

Working with tree and plant fibres is a whole new level of paper making and often requires a lot more time. It is entirely possible, but patience and strong arms are needed! We will look at a basic process to integrate fibres into reclaimed cotton pulp paper later in this chapter.

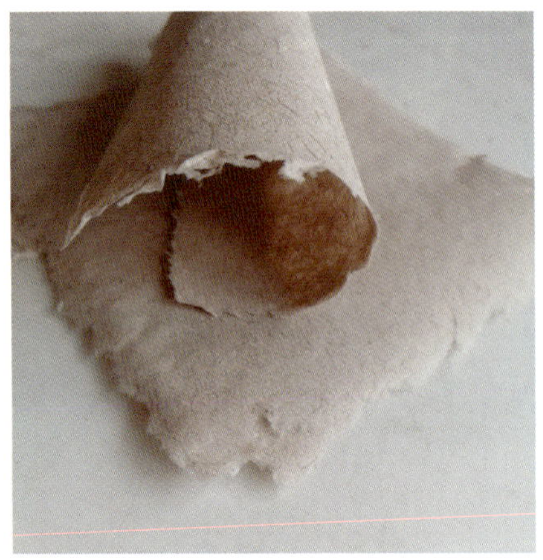

A sample of a homemade pink willow and linden bark paper.

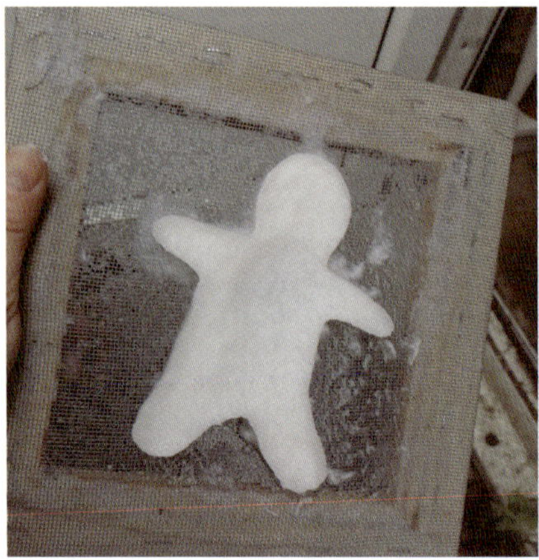

Making your own paper allows for many possibilities not commercially available.

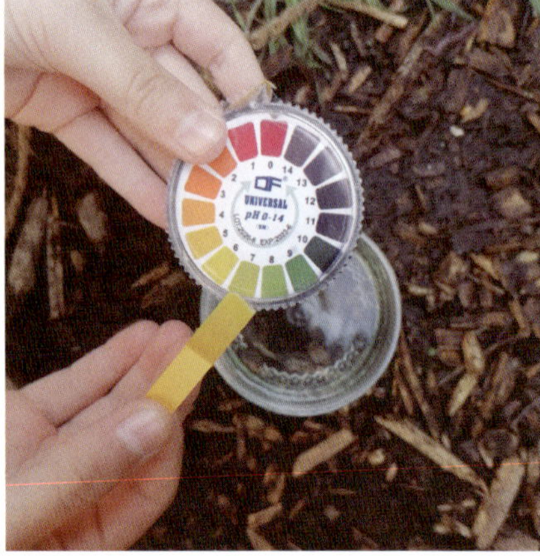

I test our rainwater pH to ensure it is neutral for use in paper making.

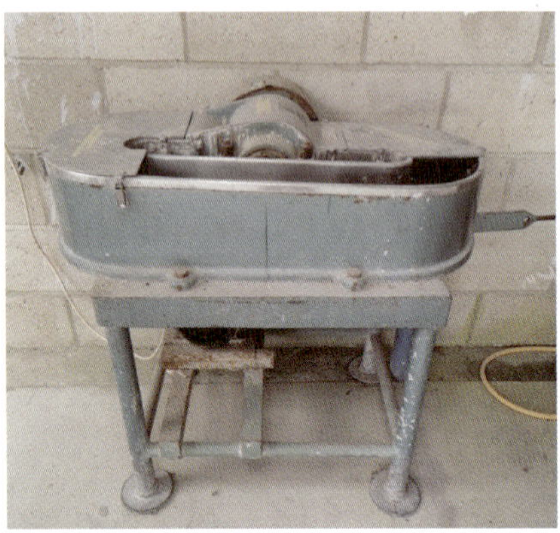

A Hollander beater is a professional pulp-making machine.

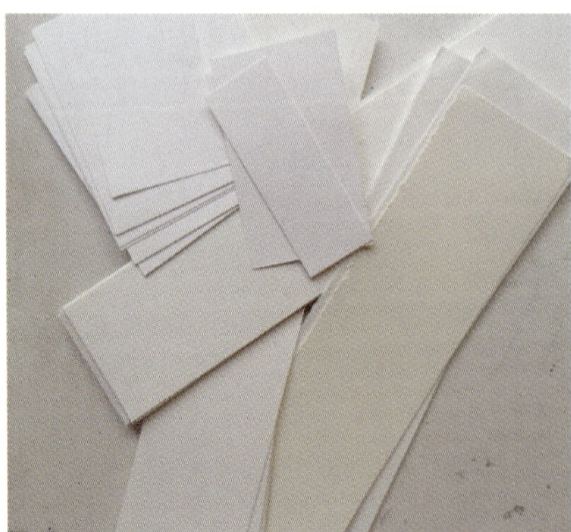

Reclaiming printing-quality paper offcuts makes beautiful re-made paper.

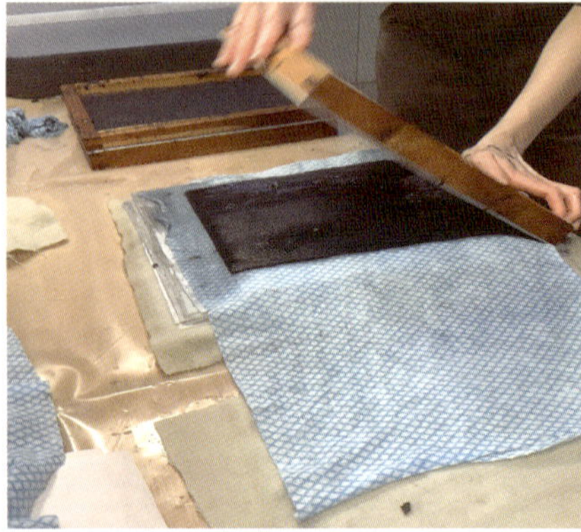

Alice Zakharenko couching beaten denim paper made from old jeans, using the workshop of artist and paper maker Jane Ponsford.

STAGE 1: MOULD AND DECKLE

The paper-making mould and deckle is a frame with mesh stretched over that allows you to separate the pulp from the water, forming a sheet of paper. Professional deckles are stunning and last generations and make a huge difference in making paper. I have taken the approach of trialling many a deckle to see which one works and how I can make them simply from materials around me. They are crude, but they do a job for now. In essence, you need two wooden frames. One frame has a mesh stretched over the top, the other frame sits on top of this frame, creating a raised edge so that when you gather the pulp it does not just float away, but is trapped on the mesh, in the form you wish. I use fine mosquito netting for the mesh, and on larger forms this is stretched over the top of some metal chicken wire to prevent sagging of the net in the middle. The materials I use are readily available and seem to do a good job in the set-up I have and for the requirements I have. You can invest is some stunning handmade mould and deckles and they would be worth every penny. Before you choose a size of frame, do make sure you have access to a deep plastic tub or sink that easily fits the frame. Old plastic storage boxes are great. This will hold your water paper pulp and you need your deckle to be able to fit in, with room to hold the side and pull out pulp.

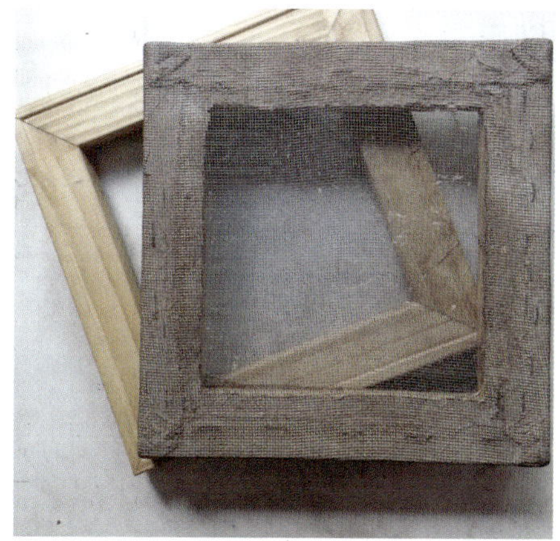

A mould and deckle made from an old canvas stretcher and frame.

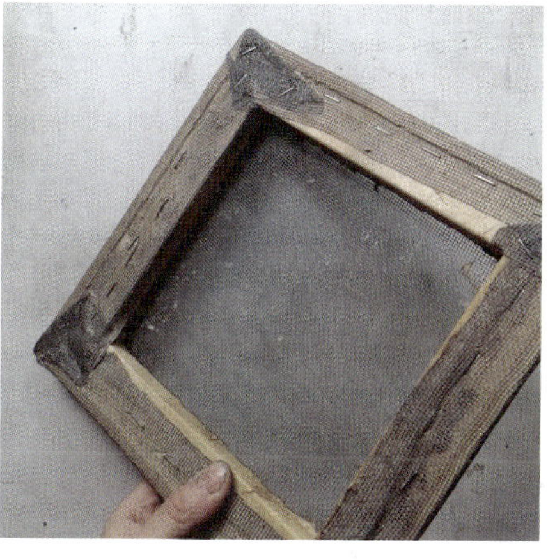

Mosquito net, or a similar metal grid, stapled tight at the back.

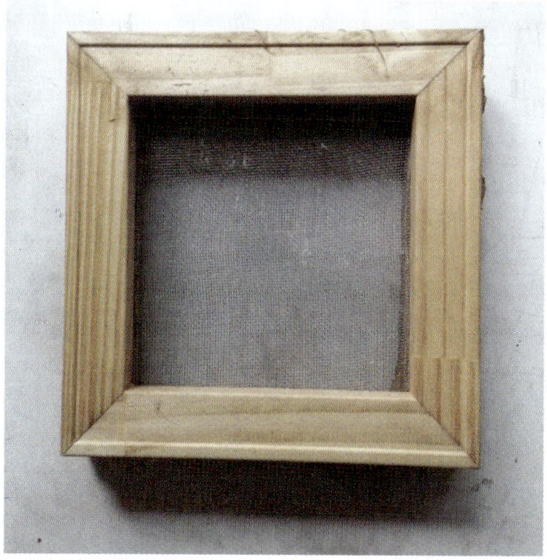

The basic mould and deckle for small paper making.

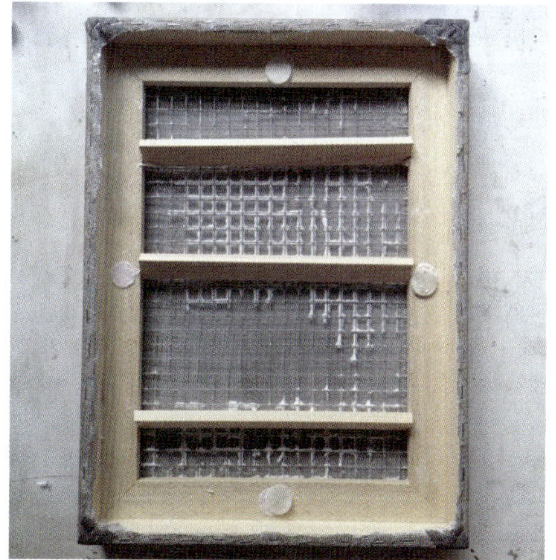

Larger mould and deckles benefit from cross bars on the back.

STAGE 2: PULP AND COUCHING

Now we have a basic mould and deckle, we can make paper. This project will guide you through a basic process that will get you a sheet of paper. You will need access to a blender and to make sure your work space is waterproofed or work outside, as I do. If you work outside, you may be open to added extras in your pulp bath like birch seeds or a few little flies! We will be looking at drying options following this process of couching the sheets.

You will need to make enough pulp concentrate for your needs. This depends on the size of your mould and deckle and how many sheets you want to make. You will need to top up your vat with a bit more pulp after each sheet, so make sure you have enough scraps pre-soaked and blended.

It is also really important that you do not add too many paper scraps to your blender at once. Not only could this overheat or damage the blender, but it produces a coarser pulp. I have a blender of capacity 2.5lt of water. I add 2lt of water and two small handfuls of pre-soaked paper scraps. You can also try using a stick blender.

Materials

Blender
Paper scraps and tub for soaking
Access to water supply
Mould and deckle
Vat about 40cm deep and big enough to take your mould and deckle. Old plastic storage tubs are good
Towels for floor protection if inside
Compressed felt blankets (I use old printing ones), interfacing or cloths for couching. They need to be pre-soaked so they are damp

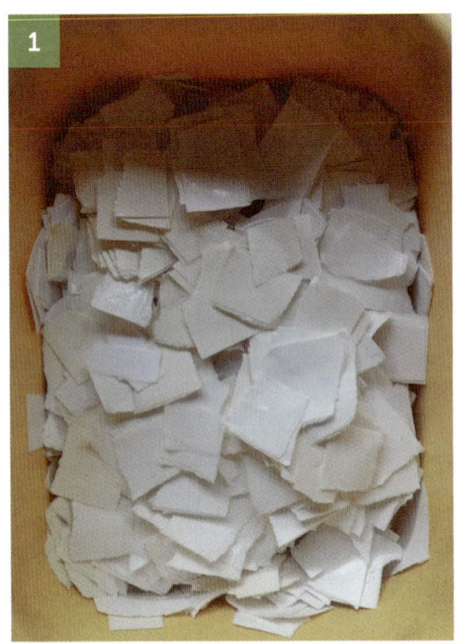

Tear up your scraps into small sections and cover with water. Soak overnight.

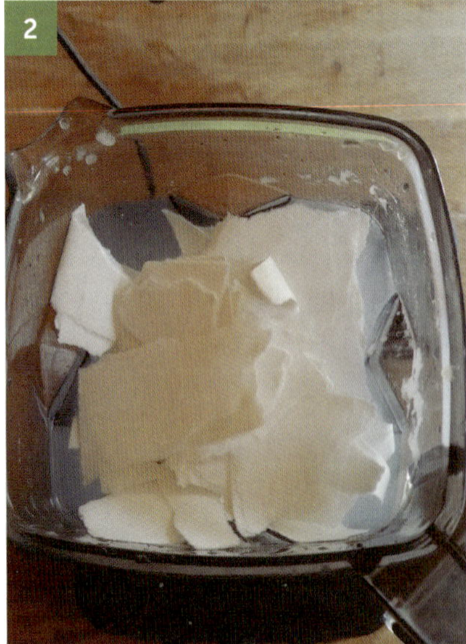

Fill the blender with water and a few paper scraps. Blend.

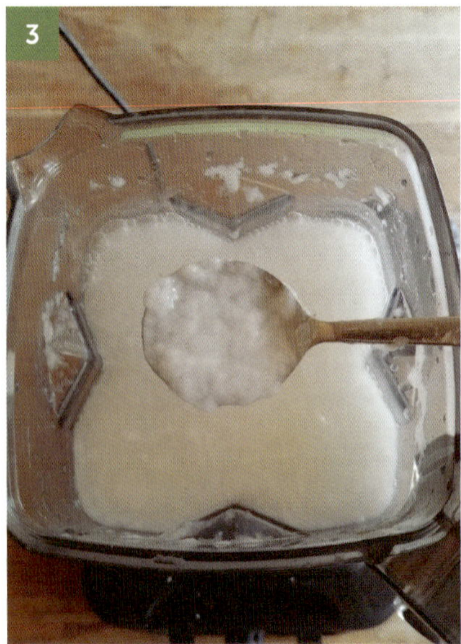

Check pulp is smooth, cleanly blended and soft to touch.

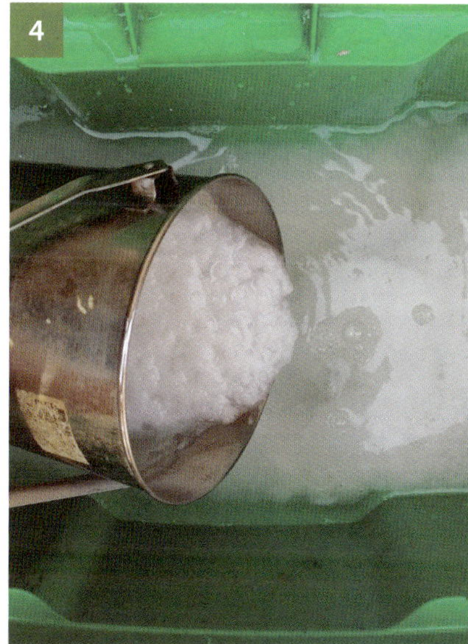

Fill vat with pulp and water until it looks like clouds.

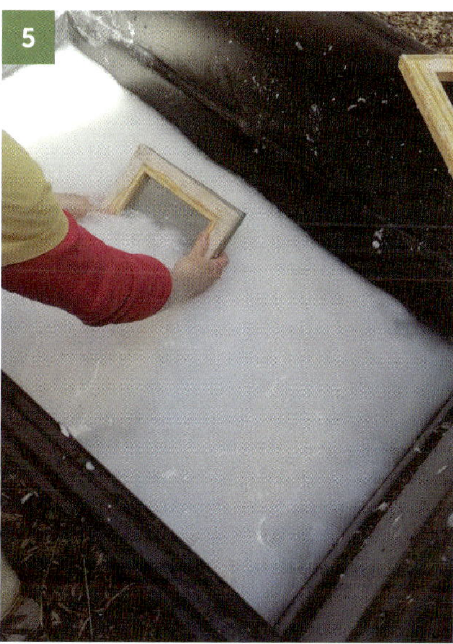

Using mould and deckle, take a deep scoop and gather pulp.

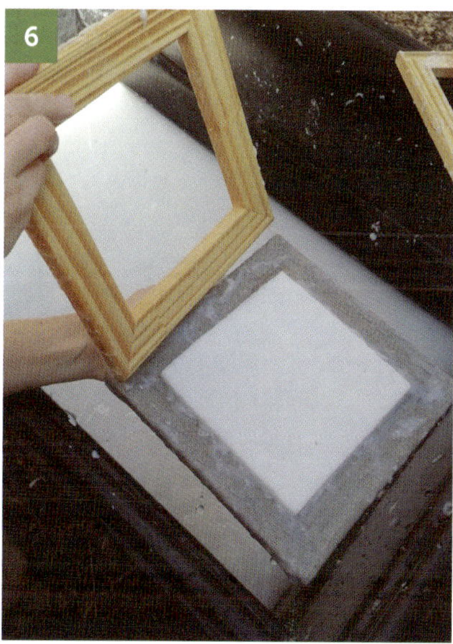

Gently rock to level the pulp. Let it drain. Remove mould.

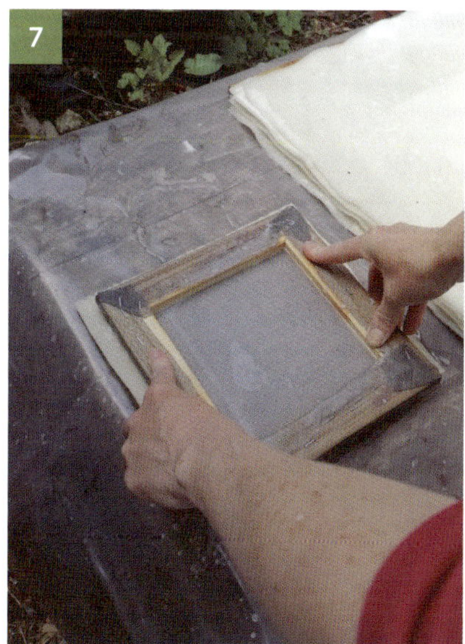

Couch the wet sheet onto damp felt. Press sides firmly releasing water.

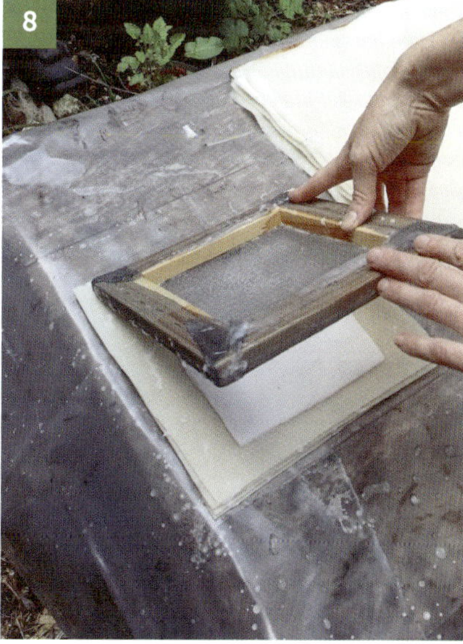

Carefully roll the deckle off, revealing a couched sheet of paper.

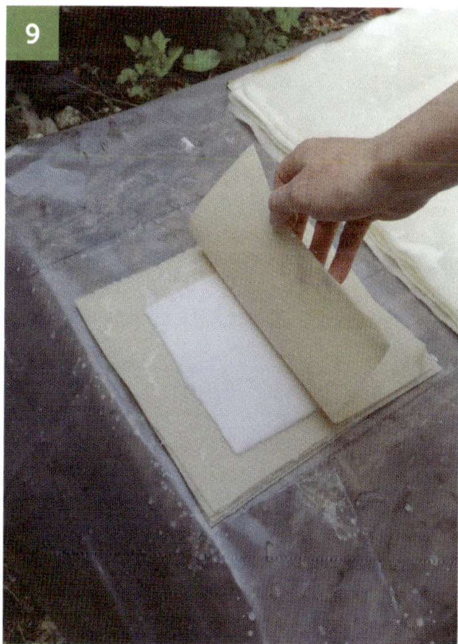

Place a clean damp felt on top, awaiting next sheet.

STAGE 3: PRESSING AND DRYING

We now have a lovely stack of freshly pulled, couched wet paper. Next, we need to press the paper to squeeze out excess moisture and help fuse the fibres together. Pressing basically involves applying pressure to your stack. In commercial operations, this is done with a hydraulic press. If you have access to a hydraulic press in your kitchen, this is the time to use it. If not, then you may have access to a nipping press or bookbinding press, which will also do a great job. You can also make your own system using G-clamps and some stretcher bars. It is a really important stage in helping the paper form, so it is worth investing some time to make a suitable system. Smaller-scale paper is easier to press than large sheets. Old nipping presses can be picked up second-hand for quite a good price. This is what I use for my small sheets. If using a clamping system, you will need to put your paper and felt sandwich between two clean boards and add clamps to the edges that you can incrementally tighten to increase pressure. With larger paper sheets, you will need to add some lengths of timber across the boards and clamp onto these so that pressure is distributed across the whole surface, not just the edges. It will not replicate a hydraulic press, but it will make them pressed enough to handle and thus remove for drying.

This basic paper-making method so far will result in a rougher textured paper that can be pressed flat and smooth under an etching press. We will look later at options to create a smooth surface at the drying stage.

Drying paper can be simply achieved by hanging groups of freshly pressed paper in a ball rack. The groups of paper are known as spurs and by hanging in a group, you minimise cockling as it dries. The marble rack leaves little imprint on the paper so works well. I have to use pegs in my marble rack to increase hanging space. These leave an indent but this flattens out when I press paper after drying. You can also drape the paper over old guttering and then press flat under boards after the initial drying stage.

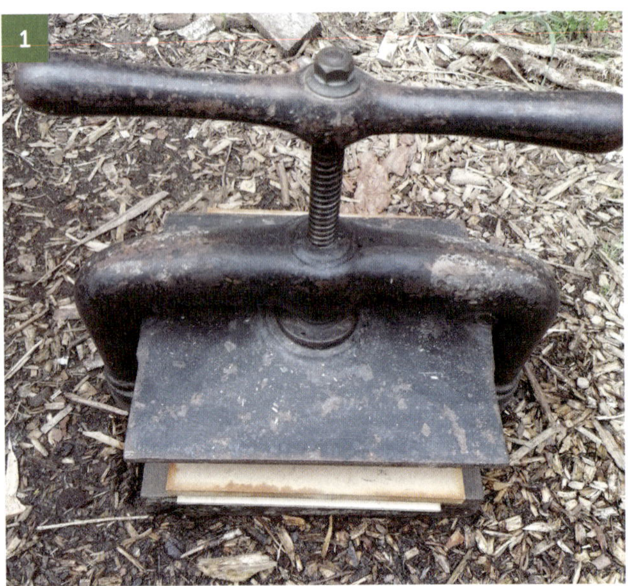

Tightly press couched paper and felt stack between two boards.

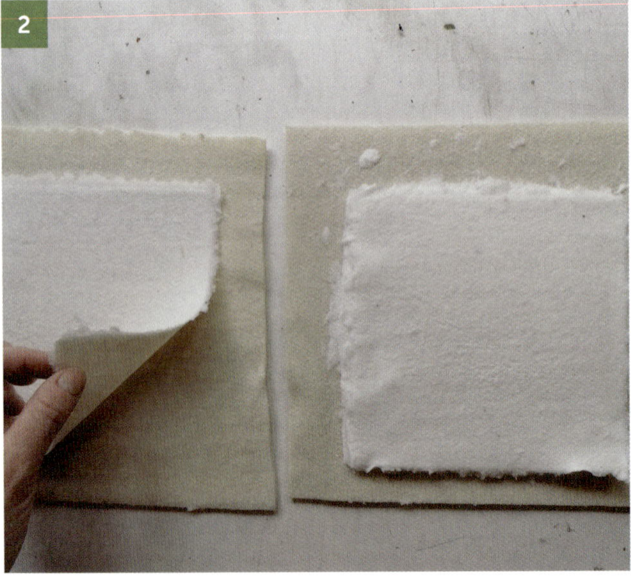

Peel off each sheet and stack in spurs, groups of four to five.

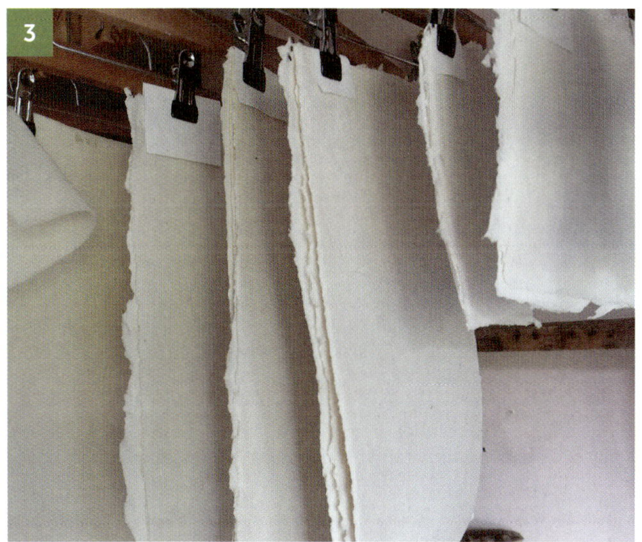

Hang spurs to dry using system as described.

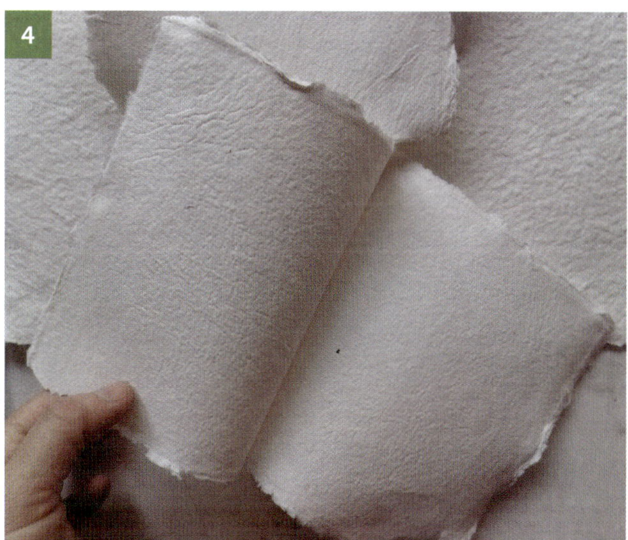

When dry, separate spurs in half, then individual sheets.

Sizing paper

A size is a substance that is added either as a surface size after the paper has been made, or it is added to the pulp bath, known as internal size. The size alters the absorbency of the paper, meaning that the ink will dry and sit on the surface of the paper rather than bleed into it. The majority of printmaking paper has a size added; if there is no size, it is known as waterleaf paper. I tend to internally size my paper as it is easier in the set-up I have. If you choose to size your paper, you will need to add the sizing mixture to the pulp bath before you pull the sheets of paper. Cornflour works as a great, simple and accessible size. For a pulp and water mixture in the blender that equates to 2.5l, I add 1 level tablespoon of cornflour. This ratio seems to work well, but again as with all papermaking you can adjust to your needs. Because I do not work with water-based media, I often don't add size to the paper as it is unnecessary with the oil-based inks and methods of printmaking I use.

Pressing and drying paper options

Commercially, printing paper is pressed between felt with a hydraulic press to remove excess water and then dried by air or in a drying box for a smoother surface. The pressure of the hydraulic press is very difficult to replicate at home. Yet in the hybrid techniques of printing that I use, it is better that the surface is as smooth as possible to allow for lithography, intaglio and relief to be printed upon the same surface. In my own cottage-scale paper making, I am happy to press each sheet individually under an etching press to achieve the smooth results I require. I give the sheet a quick spray with water and run under a very low-pressure setting between

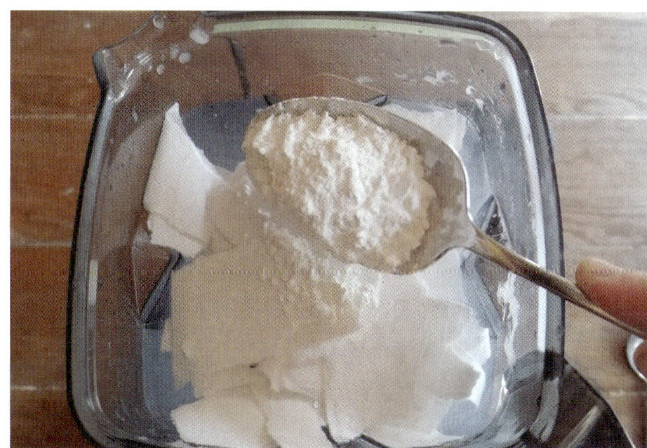

A basic cornflour size added to the pulp vat works well.

tissue sheets and gradually increase the pressure. It works really well. However, for larger batch production it may not be suitable to take so much time. There are a few methods that might be more viable to generate a smoother surface.

A method that is used commonly in Asian paper making is to allow each individual piece of paper to dry on a flat surface, such as glass. This happens after the paper pressing and generates one smooth, flat facing surface, which is the printing side. With the size and quantity I was making in my space, it was not practical to have multiple sheets of glass around, but it all depends on your own set-up.

Another method that is potentially viable in a domestic setting is to create a drying box. You will need to find some flat, clean sheets of corrugated cardboard all cut to a size marginally bigger than your paper sheets. The cardboard is layered up with clean blotters and your freshly pressed sheets. Pressure is added on top of the stack and ideally the whole stack is placed in front of a circulating heat source, such as a fan. The pressure applied to the top should be even, a bit like a flower press. It takes some practice to get the right layering and to avoid cardboard ripples on your paper. Layers of nice blotters and well-pressed paper seems to be key. The corrugated card must be stacked all in the same direction with the openings facing the circulating air source, so the air runs down the channels. The air gets circulated between the cardboard and moisture is wicked away from the damp sheets. It can take a day for the sheets to dry depending on humidity and air temperature, but if the pressure applied to the stack is correct, it will result in a smooth surface and quickly dried paper.

Making large sheets of paper

It is entirely possible to make small batch production of large paper sheets. I have made a very crude imperial mould and deckle and pull a couple of these every time I make paper. It takes a huge amount of pulp, so do be prepared for that. Because I do not have a hydraulic press in my kitchen, pressing the paper is tricky, so I have found a method that works in the situation I have. I couch my sheet and place a felt on top. I then place another board on top and jump up and down on it to squeeze out excess water. I then hang the whole felt up, with the pressed paper still attached and let it drip over a towel. It hangs like this for a couple of days and eventually the paper dries, allowing me to peel it off the felt. I then press this paper flat and smooth under an etching press.

Can the paper be soaked?

The handmade reclaimed paper prints beautifully on many methods of printing. The heavier-weight papers can be printed intaglio, but I do not soak them. Instead, I just spray with a fine water mist, blot off and away I go. They do work really well under a press and by hand. At the end of a paper-making session, I often pull a couple of sheets of the very fine residual pulp which will make a very lightweight paper. This is more delicate and it will go under a press, but not very many times, so I reserve it for hand printing. If you wish to make finer paper but with more strength, working with long plant and textile fibres may be the way.

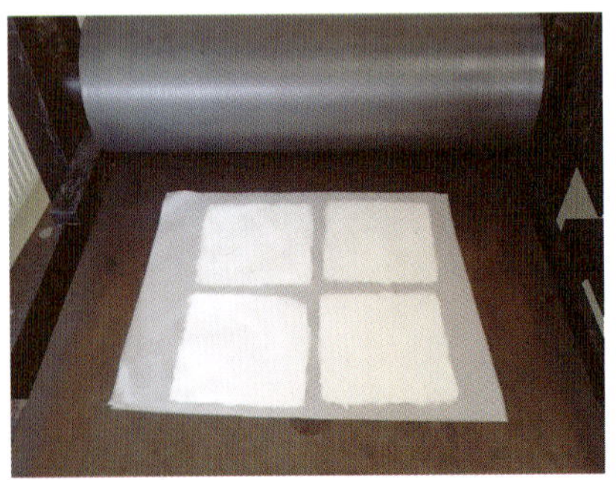

Running sheets under a press creating a smooth surface.

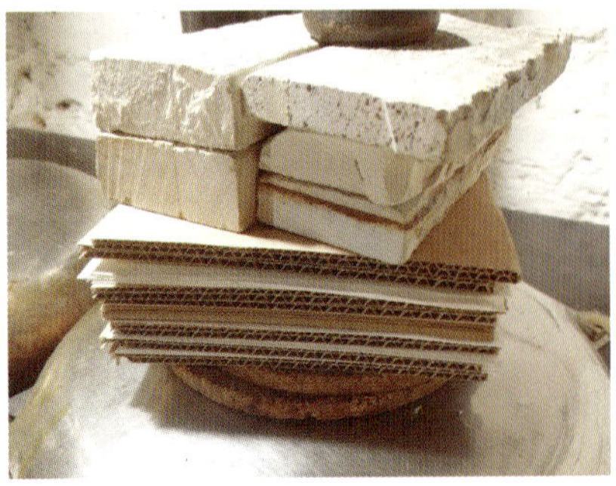

A simple homemade drying box helps speed up drying.

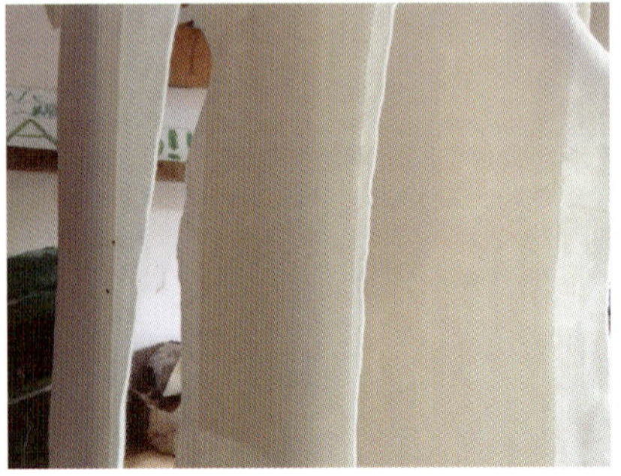

Drying large sheets of paper pressed on the couching felt.

FIBRE: PLANT AND TREE

Making paper can be hugely fun, rewarding and allows you to integrate whole new textures to the paper surface. If working at a domestic scale, the idea of beating denim or linen rags is not feasible, but you can have fun with various plant fibres. To make paper from 100 per cent plant fibre takes exploration into different plants and experimentation. Many of the natural fibre papers we use today have had the fibres beaten rather than blended. The beating allows the fibres to stay long, thus giving the paper its strength. If plant fibres get chopped in a blender, they risk getting cut up too small and thus the paper is very weak. It is possible to beat fibres at home using mallets or a pestle and mortar. Depending on the bark or fibre used it can be used as 100 per cent plant fibre paper or as an additive for strength, colour and texture to a reclaimed cotton pulp base. The latter is what we will explore for this book.

Many of the tree bark fibres will need softening before you use them and processing to use the inner white bark only. You can do this straight from the tree or I tend to let bark soak over winter, going rotten, allowing me to easily peel off the outer bark layers. In Japan, the inner bark of the paper mulberry tree has a very specific network of fibres that make the most prized paper. The artform of processing the mulberry tree to fibre is generations old and highly respected. The mulberry fibre, known as kozo, is unique, and many other tree fibres are not quite in the same league, but still worth incorporating or experimenting with.

Willow and cotton pulp paper

This paper is a good way to make a lightweight mixed-fibre paper. It does take time in processing the willow bark, but it does produce a beautiful paper that I use for relief work. Willow is indigenous to northern Europe, where I reside, so I like to use it. Always ask permission from the landowner before you collect samples of the bark. The bark collection is best in early spring, when you can peel great strips easily from clean poles. Once you have collected your bark, coil it up and place submerged in water for a few months to ret. If you wish to speed it up, the coil of fresh bark can be heated and boiled to soften. Retting works a lot better though. You would only need two big coils to produce enough fibres to add quality and effect to a couple of sheets of paper.

Materials

Two coils of pre-cooked or retted willow bark
Batch of ready-to-go blended paper pulp
Paper-making set-up
Smooth, sturdy table top
Knife
Pestle and mortar
Soda ash powder or washing soda

Tree fibres can be used to make interesting papers.

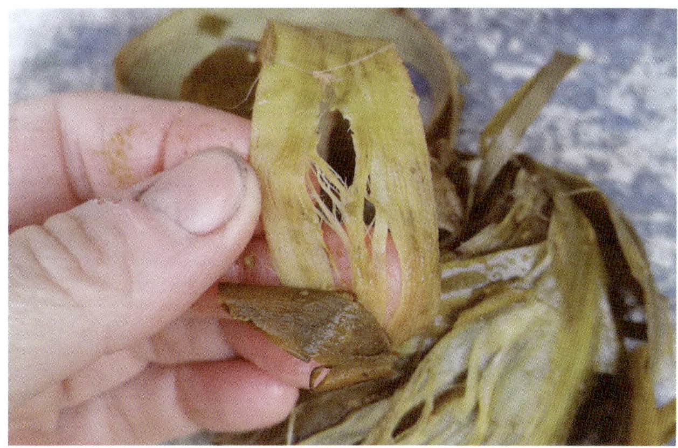

Assessing the fibres of retted inner willow bark.

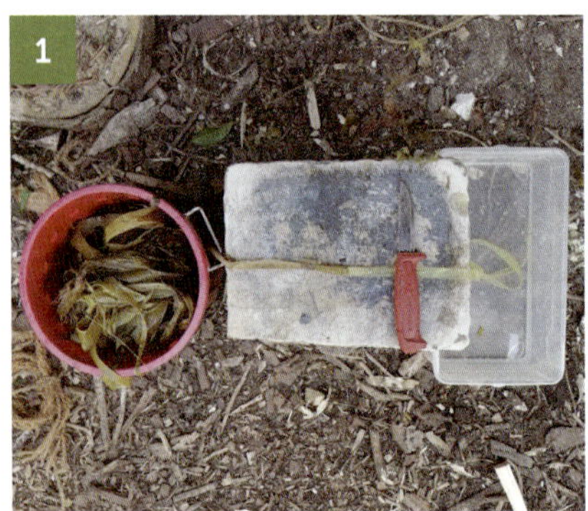

A good simple set-up ready to collect inner willow bark.

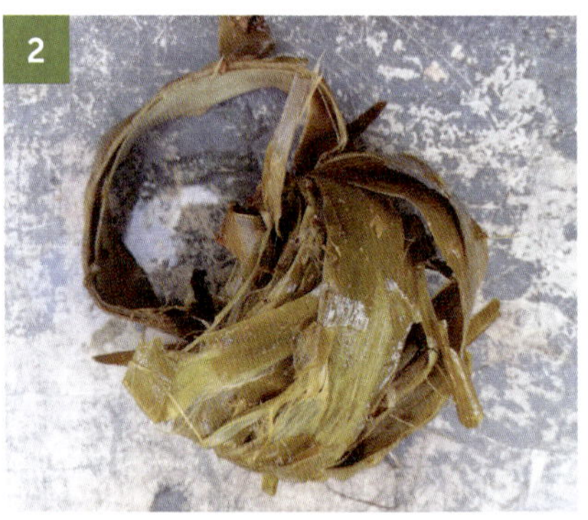

Start with a few softened strips of bark, gently washed.

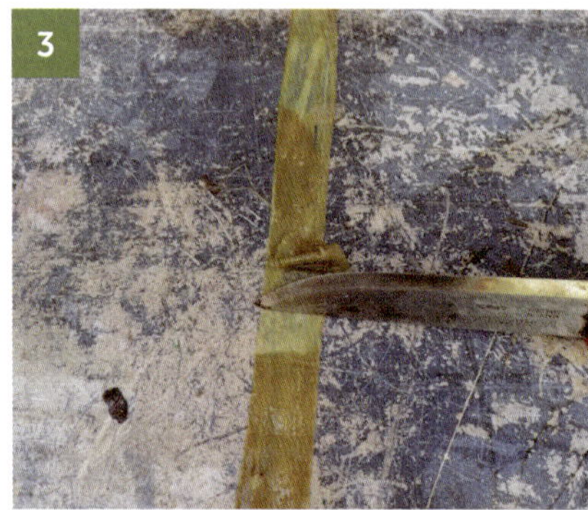

Using the back of a knife, gently scrape off the outer bark.

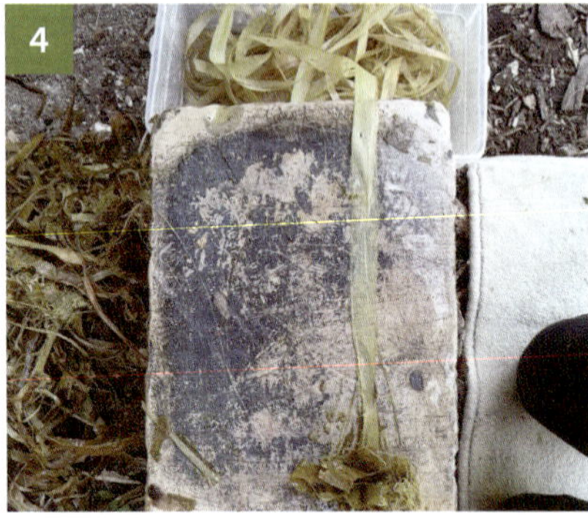

Store the white inner bark in water as you work.

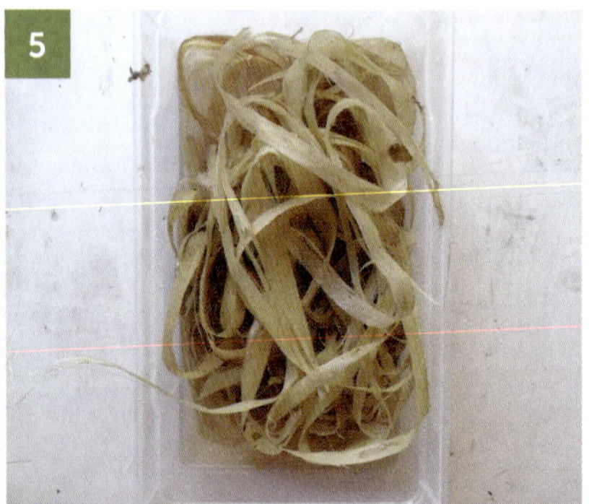

A tub full of strained damp inner willow bark ready to mash.

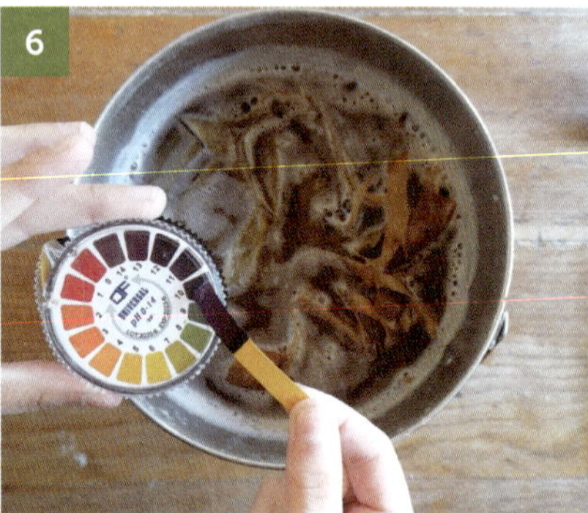

Add bark to a soda ash solution to pH 11. Boil for one hour.

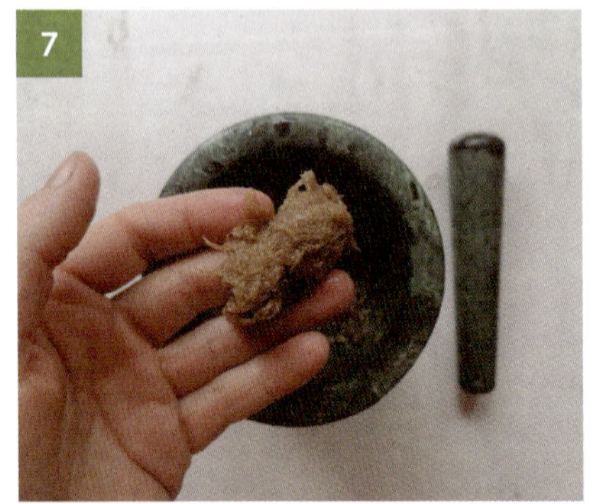

After boiling, smash a small amount with water until pulpy.

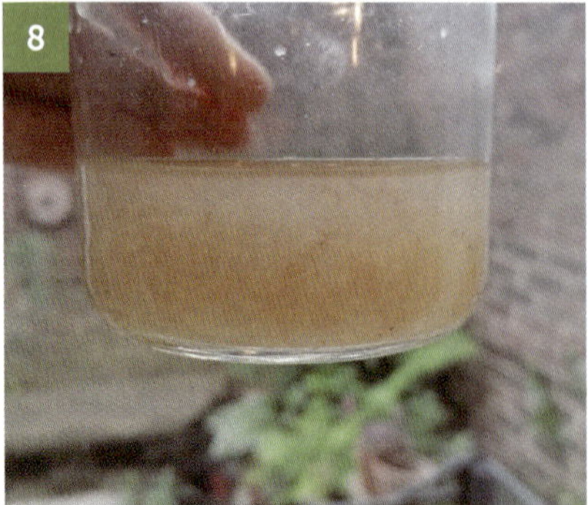

Test fibres in water to see if they suspend and separate.

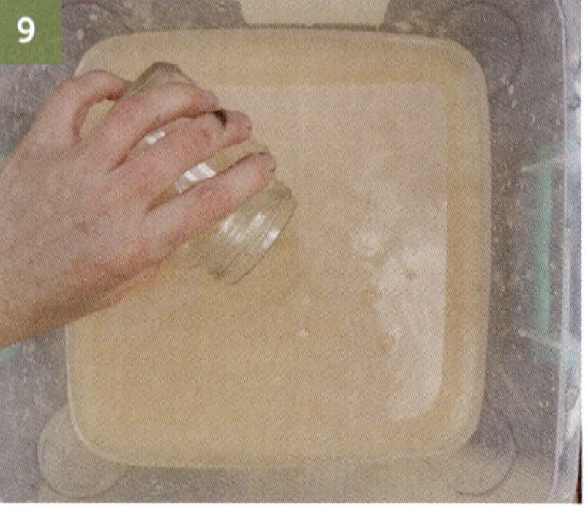

Add willow fibres to pulp vat, mix and pull paper.

COLOURING PAPER

You can of course dye paper pulp to make coloured paper, which opens up a realm of print possibilities. Any lightfast dye added to the pulp vat and left for a while will colour the pulp and produce a coloured paper. I only work with natural dyes, and often ones that are part of resource excess. Some of the commercial dyes used for clothing are not that great ecologically speaking, and may require a salt or other mordant to fix. This will inevitably effect the pH of your paper. The natural dyes I work with are lightfast so they do not require a mordant. One particular example is American black walnuts, which I collected in vast quantities one year. I removed the green husks, dried the nuts for later eating and then added all the husks into a giant bin and left for six months. Nature took its course and it naturally fermented, releasing a wonderful black liquor. This was then strained and added to a recycled paper pulp vat and left for a couple of hours to absorb. The resultant paper sheets not only were a beautiful brown, but they also had some wonderful speckles that the dye produced when pulling the sheets. I have also made blancmange pink paper from spent madder root taken from a compost bin after another educator's dying course. Have a play!

Re-using pulp

After you have made a batch of paper, the pulp that is left tends to be very fine. You can make very thin paper with practice, or you can sieve the pulp and squeeze out excess water with your hands. These pulp balls can be dried and stored and added to future pulp baths to increase the amount of finer pulp in the mix. They will need soaking ahead of time and re-blending to break up properly.

The remaining pulp left in the vat will need to be sorted. If you let the vat settle, the pulp sinks to the bottom and you can decant as much of the top water off as possible and feed plants. The residual slurry will need to be drained carefully over a sieve or cloth to separate pulp and water. Pulp can then be saved as we have looked at or recycled. You do not want to put pulp slurry down your sink in case it causes a blockage.

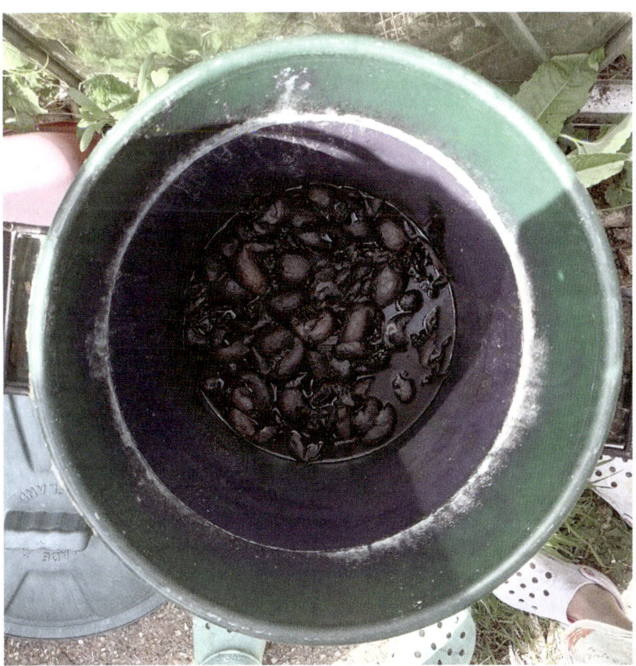

Fermented American black walnuts producing a rich brown dye.

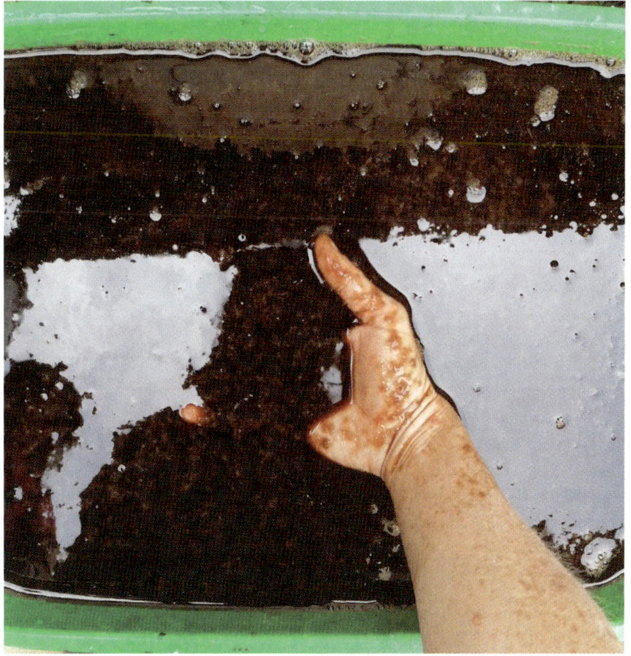

The pulp vat dyed brown with the walnut liquor.

Resulting dried and pressed walnut dyed paper.

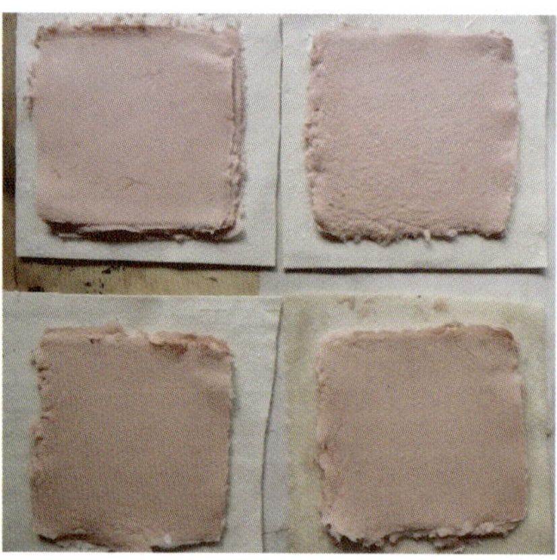

Madder-dyed paper drying in spurs.

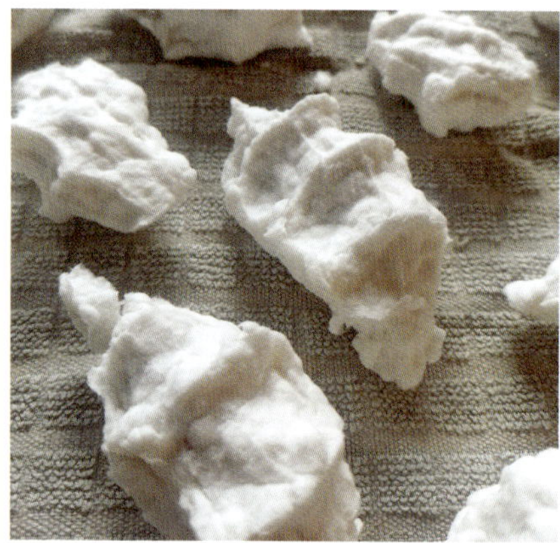

Sieved pulp drying out ready for next use.

WHERE TO TAKE PAPER AND RETHINKING EDITIONING

Paper is undeniably a very useful substrate for printmakers. Making your own paper suited for your own practice is also undeniably fun, interesting and useful. However, it is a big commitment which does require certain facilities. There are options for supporting handmade paper mills across the globe who make high-quality paper by hand, supporting a craft skill passed down through generations. Japan produces a stunning array of washi papers, made by hand using traditional techniques. Many of the traditional paper-making mills are keen on sustainability and their mulberry bark comes from coppice areas. Some factories introduce fibres from local bi-products (I remember seeing excess sweetcorn husks from the village harvest being added) and the skills of the paper makers are second to none. Here in the UK, a few commercial mills keep the art of paper making alive and many artists and hobbyists are producing small batches for sale.

Question editioning

Printmakers use a lot of paper, particularly because they are known to edition, creating more than one print from the same matrix. This will also involve dud prints, which usually get binned. A question to ask yourself, if you are really interested in ecological printing, is whether the edition is strictly necessary. Can a unique print say more for the moment being captured than a series of 50? It is such a fiddly debate. Printmaking stems from mass-produced works, a way to make 'things' available to the mass market for lower cost, even free. And this political side of print I love. In fact, the only time I edition on paper is when I produce prints that are given for free to a community, or as part of an event. I no longer edition my own work outside of this. I produce unique prints. Therefore, consumption is less, I can get away with making short runs of handmade paper, I use less ink, less material consumption in general, I do not waste, I do not work in excess and I have more space. The question of when editioning is relevant needs to be carefully considered.

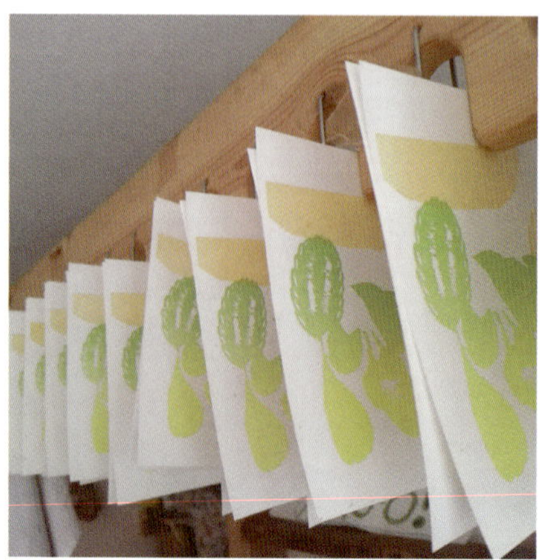

Is editioning relevant? Can we save paper by working on unique prints?

ALTERNATIVE SUBSTRATES: FABRIC

Printing onto fabric is most likely older than printing onto paper. Be it for clothing, books or decoration, printed fabrics are beautiful. Printing onto fabric is pretty much like working on paper. A good general rule of thumb is that the higher the thread count, and the finer the weave, the more detail the print will translate. Printing onto hessian will work less well than printing on a cotton poplin. The brief look into fabric printing in this chapter will be aimed at using the fabric print as an alternative to the paper and allowing for unique artwork to be made. Fabric printing for decorative, interior or dressmaking purposes is a whole new book and here we are merely touching the surface.

The ink sits on the top layer of the fabric rather than penetrating the fibres, as a paste for block printing might, which is commonly used for repeat interior or dressmaking block prints. I also print with fabric under a press and by hand, then use it as a construction piece for sewing and installation. The oil-based inks will not seep into the fabric, and I never bother to heat seal. They do take their time to dry, but once dry seem pretty indestructible. I have printed with oil-based inks onto cottons for dressmaking, which have gone into the wash (with a natural mild detergent) on a gentle warm cycle and they still seem fine. If you wish to use the oil-based inks on fabric destined for interior or dressmaking purposes, then it may require that you research and experiment, and perhaps look further into paste/dye block printing.

Fabric inks

I use the same inks for paper and fabric. This saves consumption, money and space. It works for my purposes.

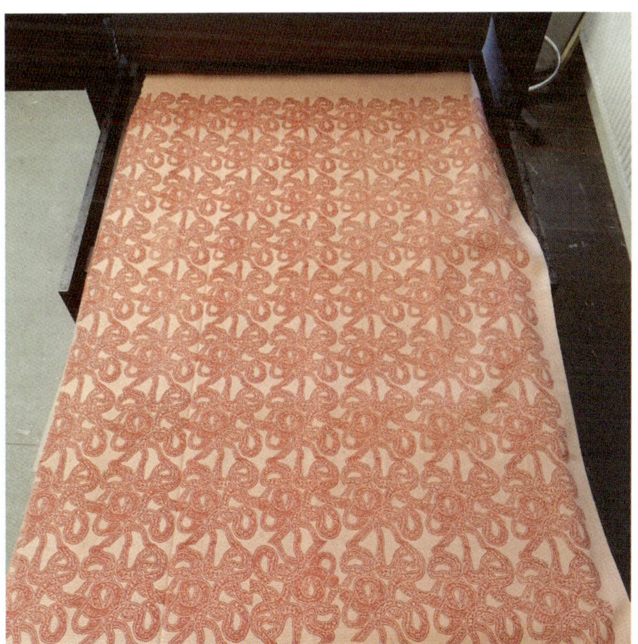

A lino block-printed piece of linen to be used in a print installation.

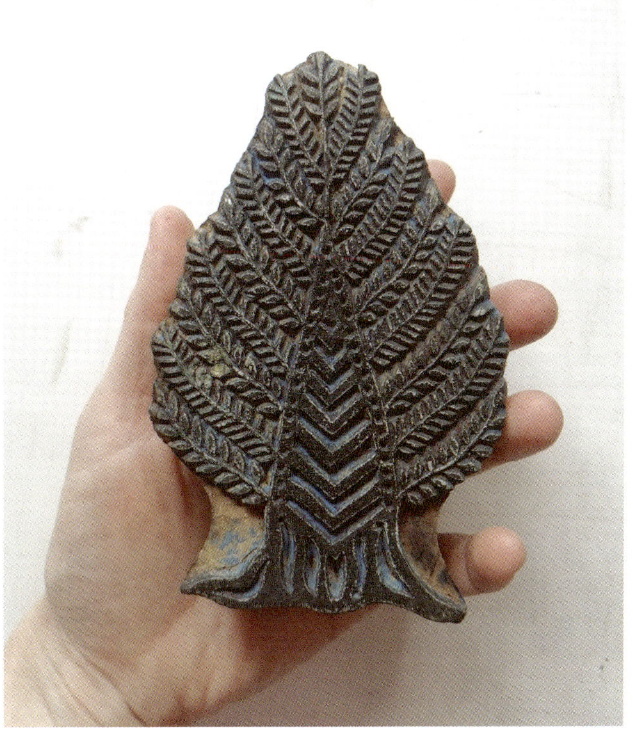

An Indian wooden block design to work with paste printing ink.

PRINTING INTAGLIO ONTO COTTON

In this demonstration, we will be printing some dry point onto a piece of fine weave cotton poplin. You can replace the paper dry point with any other intaglio method as explored in Chapter 5.

Materials

One piece of ironed cotton poplin (or old shirting) approximately 15cm × 15cm

Intaglio sample plate smaller than fabric

Inks and press set up to print intaglio

Water spray bottle

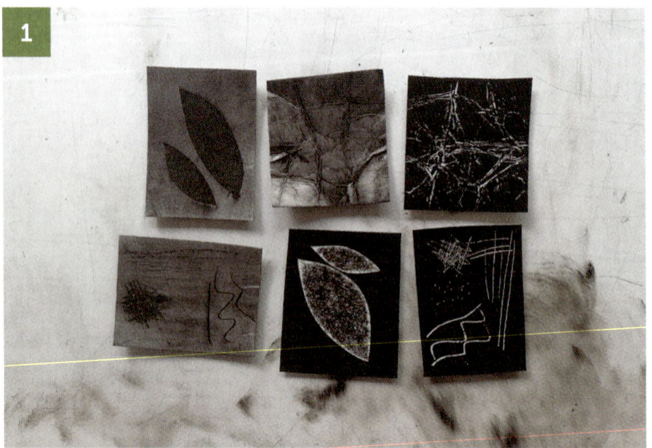

Six sample intaglio matrices inked up ready to print.

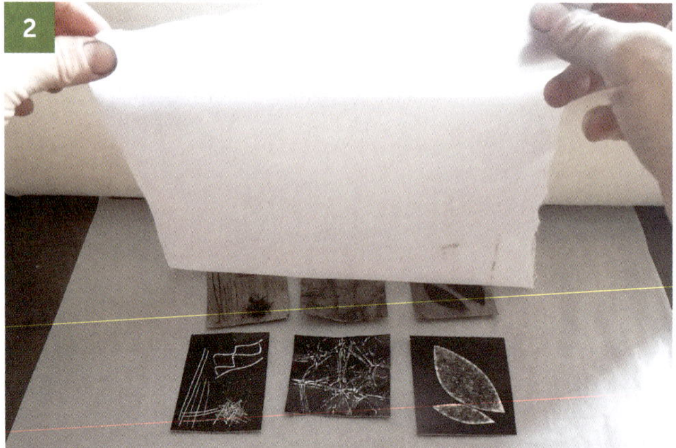

Lightly spray mist fabric with water and lay on top.

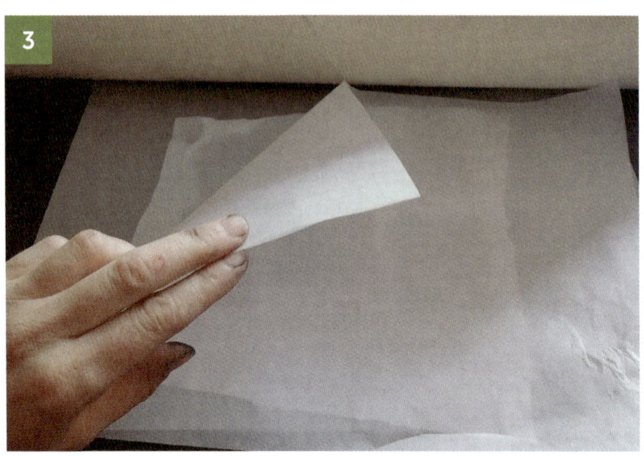

Place tissue paper on top and run through the press.

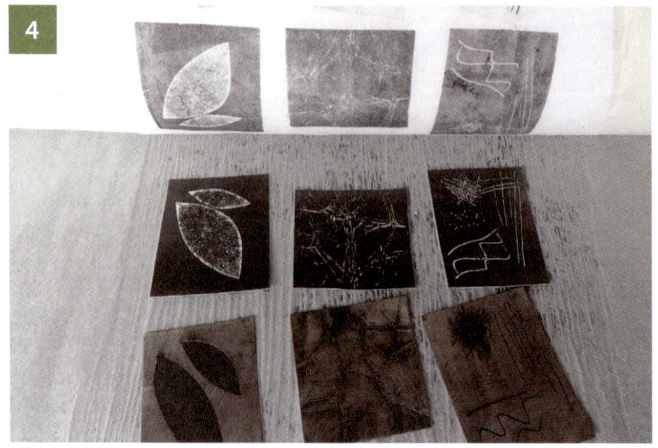

The completed print on cotton has a different quality to paper.

FABRIC CHOICE

Fabric can come in such an array of possibilities for print. You can get great fabric offcuts from second-hand shops, and some brilliant unbleached 100 per cent plant fibre fabrics from most haberdashers, which is an excellent ecological choice. Working with the pre-printed pattern on fabrics is fun and it offers a good way to introduce a background. Fabric also comes in a range of solid colours, so things need not be always white. Or, if you wish to be specific about the colour, you can print a flat solid onto the fabric first by rolling up your colour choice onto a sheet of Perspex and running this through a press with dampened fabric (using the spray bottle method). It works really well. Fabric has the distinct advantage that it can be folded under the press, so you can print on larger sheets than your press bed size. Remember to place tissue or newsprint between the folds of the layers to avoid double impressions on your fabric.

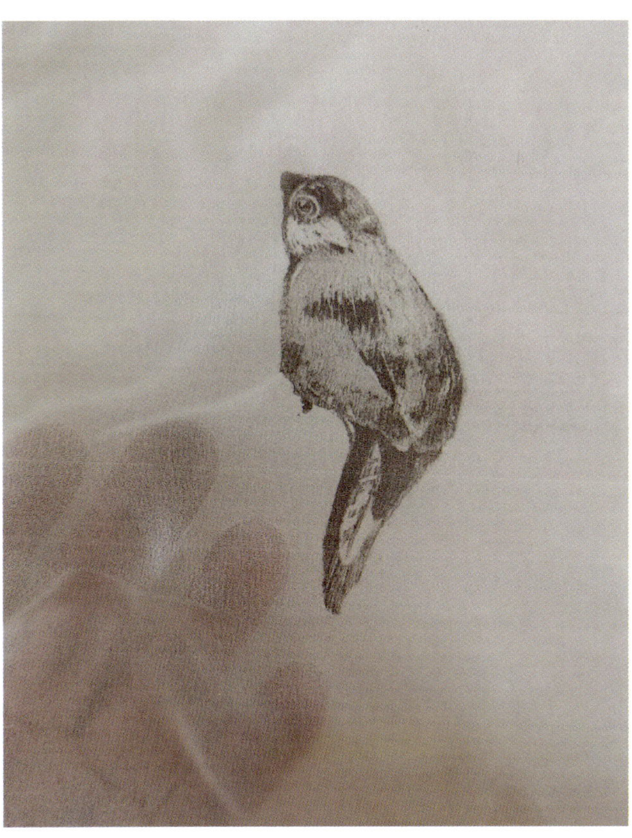

Fabric choice can change the quality of the print. A work in progress of printed birds by fine art student Twinky.

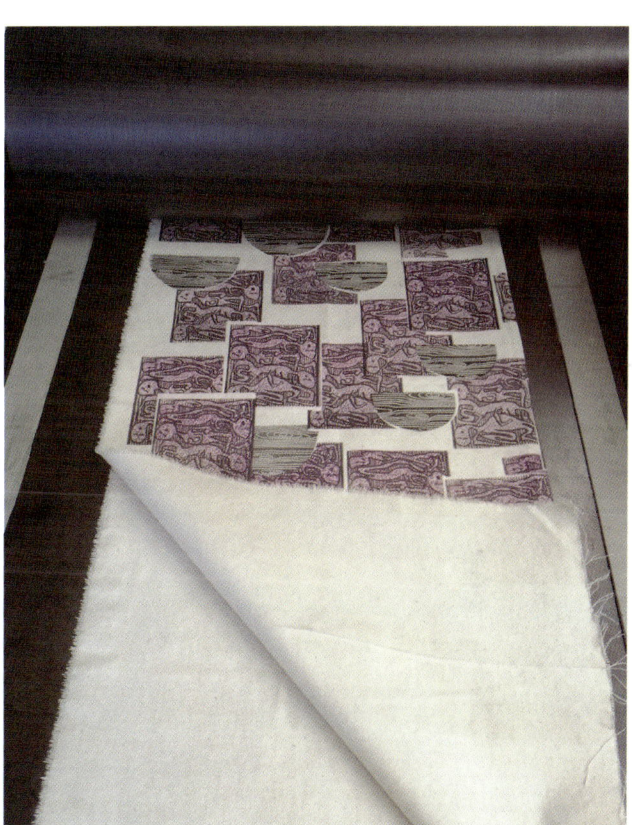

Fabric can be folded under a press so you can work large.

BLOCK PRINTING ON FABRIC

Because of the nature of the oil-based inks, block printing onto fabric by hand will only really work with smaller-scale blocks and a touch looser oil-based ink. If you are wishing to create a large repeat from smaller blocks by hand, it might be worth investing in specific block printing fabric inks, or investigating paste dying techniques. Here, we are printing under a press with a small-scale lino cut, celebrating the opportunity to work on fabric as an alternative substrate for unique printmaking. I have chosen to work with a cotton calico to illustrate a different fabric, but the printing principles apply to many fabrics.

Materials

Cotton calico, weave of your choice
Lino block to fit fabric sample
Sheet of Perspex approximately 3–8mm
Press set up for printing lino. Set to the depth of the lino, no blankets. Runners advised to raise roller
Oil-based inks and equipment for lino
Weak copperplate oil

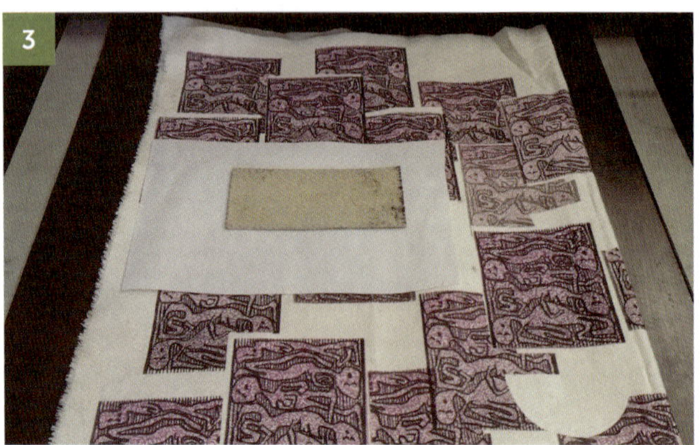

Add a few drops of weak copperplate oil to your ink mix to loosen.

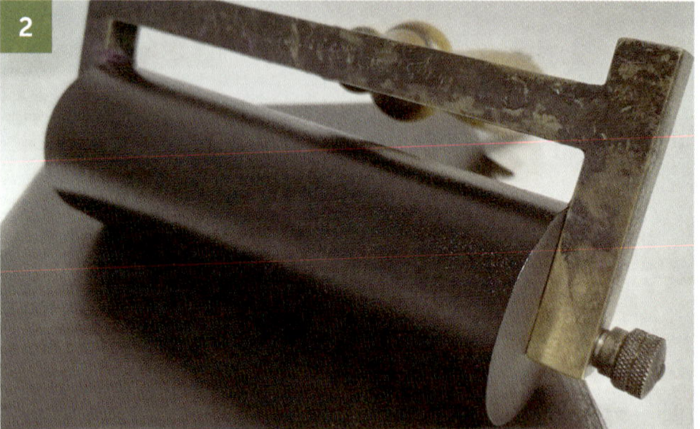

Roll out ink to a soft hiss and high gloss for fabric printing.

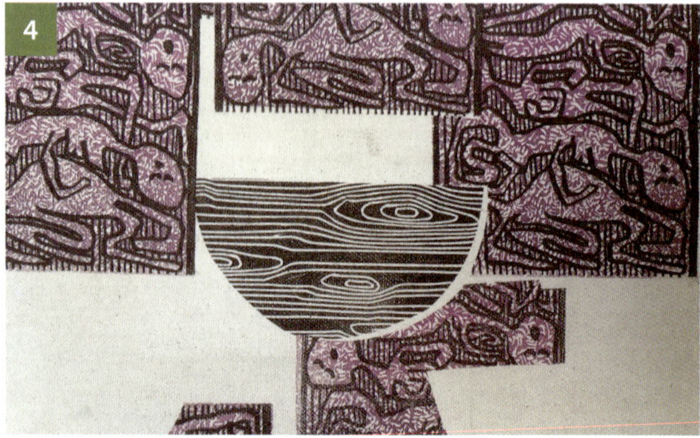

Lay your inked lino onto your chosen fabric on the press bed.

The resultant lino print on coarse calico has a textural quality.

ALTERNATIVE SUBSTRATE: PLASTER

Ecological artists and activists are constantly debating the effects of plaster. In recent times, there has been a large movement to ban idols made of plaster of Paris on the grounds that it is polluting aquatic life. It was found that this was less the plaster, but more the acrylic paint used on the idols that was actually the main pollutant. In many ways, plaster of Paris is made from materials that are of the earth. The problem that arises is that when they are activated into a solid state with water, they become insoluble and take a long time to degrade. During this time, they may break up into smaller and smaller particles, causing a pollutant effect. There are alternatives currently being developed on the market, one involving using post-consumer waste paper to make a paper-based plaster that degrades, leaching no harmful toxins.

The secondary ecological issue with plaster is of course the mining industry. It is not a renewable resource and the mining industry worldwide is over consuming. It is always a hugely tricky balance and one can only do so much. Many of the ecological issues stem back to over-consumption, particularly when digging up the ground. We have touched upon this in the pigment section. The choices are yours to make and I hope that the information is given to you to make them. Any change in practice to be more ecological and to advocate a reduction in consumption is a huge step, and step by step these changes add up to make leaps.

So I do include plaster here, because from a printmaking perspective plaster has the huge advantage that it can be cast into three-dimensional forms, whilst taking an impression. And in essence, the pure material is ecological and indeed very old; the process by which we now extract, process the waste and over consume is more questionable. But questions are there to be asked and considered, and this will inevitably form a positive balance.

Plaster of Paris, or casting plaster, is a great way to generate an impression. It can also be used as a printing plate, treating it as a carving block.

MAKING A SIMPLE PLASTER CAST

In this demonstration we will make a lino cast tile and a dry point cube. When I did this demonstration, the first attempt at the lino cast did not pick up a clear impression. I have included the results to showcase that it doesn't always go OK – and that is also OK! Try again and it will work. The reasons for the failure were most likely because I mixed the plaster too wet and I did not leave it to set for long enough in the mould. So I re-tried and included the results of the second successful one.

Materials

Plaster of Paris or fine art casting plaster
Lino that has been carved with textures, approximately 15cm × 15cm in total
Old Tetra Pak for dry point mark making (*see* Chapter 3 for guidance if new to it)
Stanley knife
Ruler
Oil-based black ink and equipment to ink up lino
Strong tape (I use the pre-gummed tape)
Mixing jug for plaster, water and stirring device (old spoon)
Dust mask and gloves

Further explorations

What I have shown you here is an insight into ecological approaches to impression surfaces. There is a whole world out there; there will be more ideas. I have seen prints printed onto giant sheets of bark, reclaimed corrugated cardboard, wood, scrap aluminium. There is so much potential that ecological approaches need not be boring. It does require a little sideways thinking (which is not as painful as it sounds), a bit of research and a big acceptance that the majority of the prints will be unique. Celebrate print as a unique artform, just as this planet is a unique system.

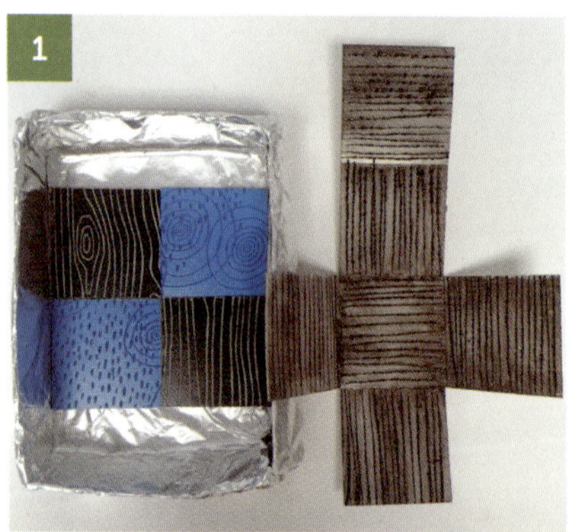

Some lino and a dry point cube inked-up and ready to cast.

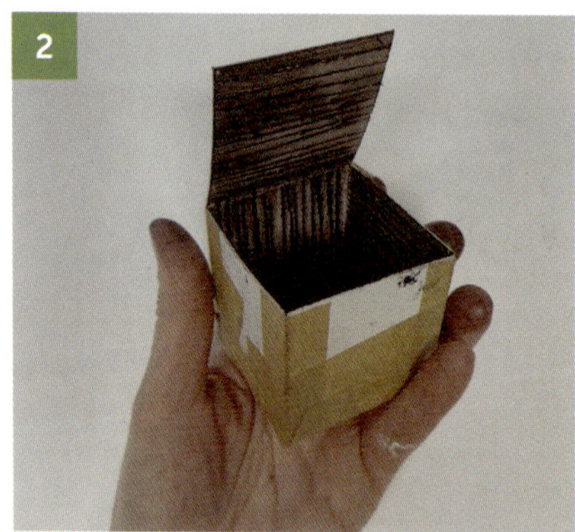

The dry point cube is folded up and edges sealed. Lid remains open.

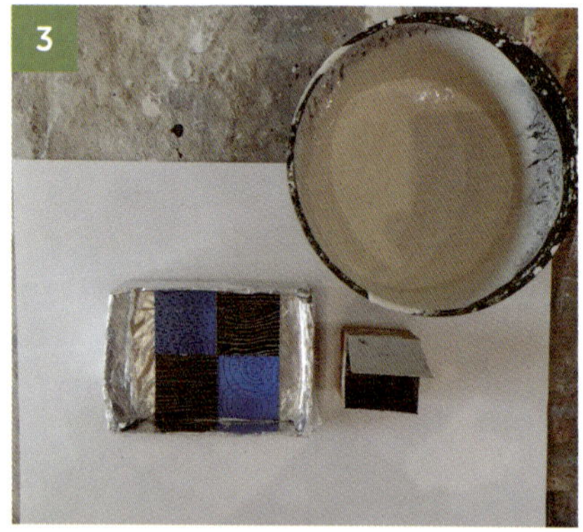

Plaster is mixed according to manufacturer's guidance.

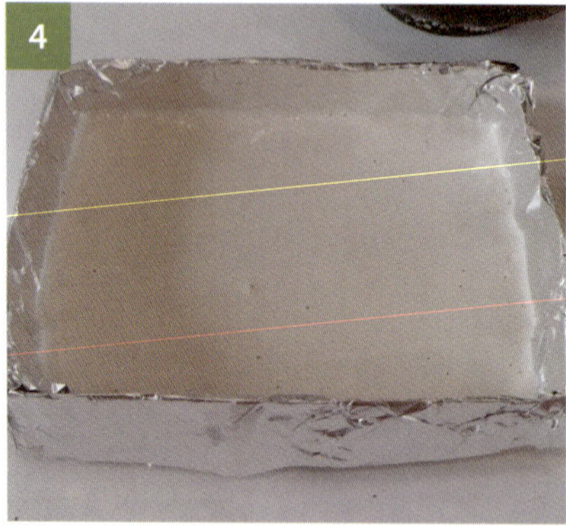

The plaster is poured into the moulds over the inked matrices.

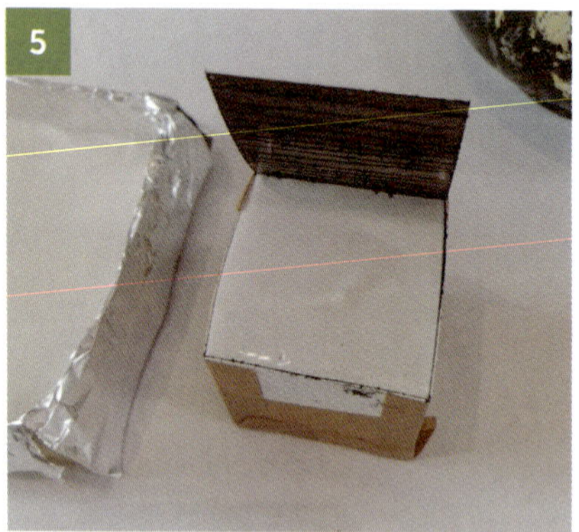

The cube is filled to the top with plaster, checking for leaks.

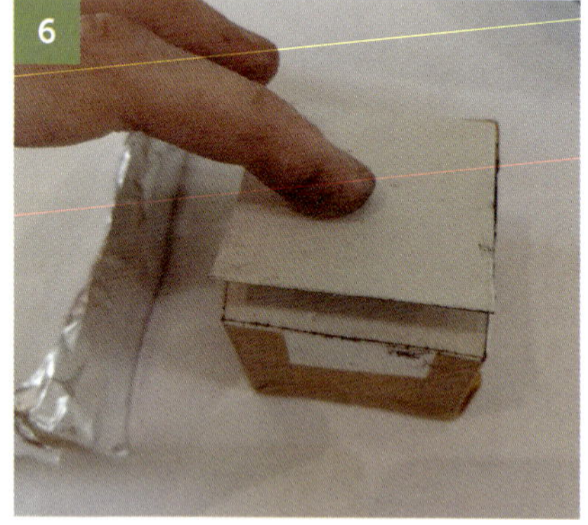

The lid of the cube is held down as the plaster initially sets.

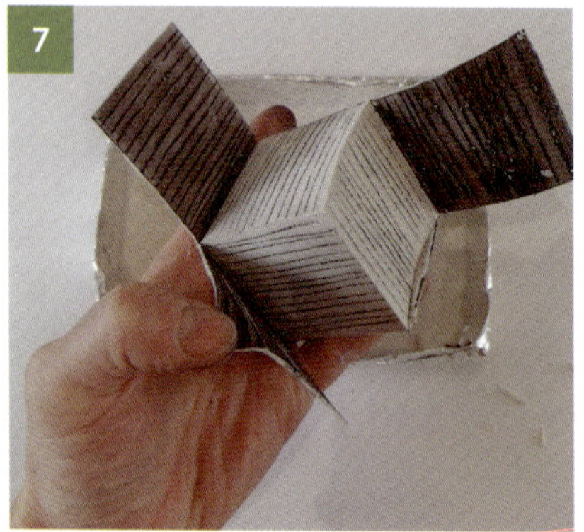

After curing time, the cube is demoulded revealing the print.

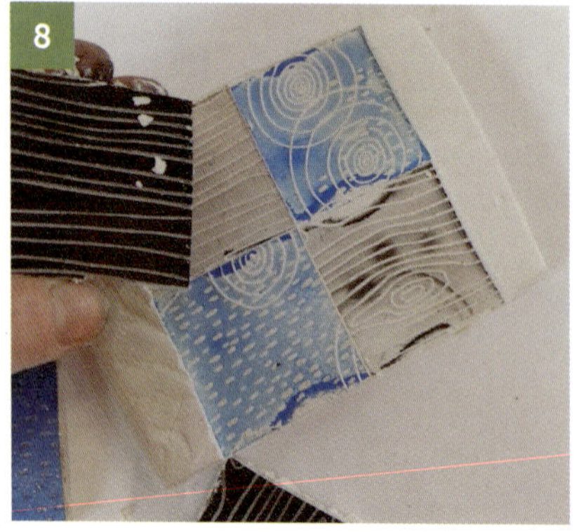

The lino peeled off. Ooops. This one didn't work that well. Why?

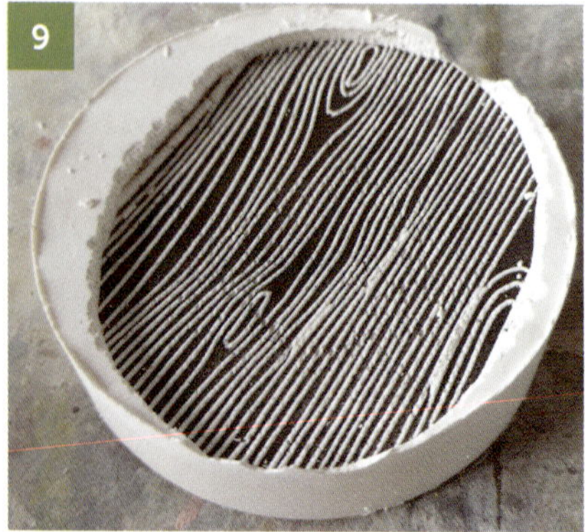

The lino test redone. Worked much better.

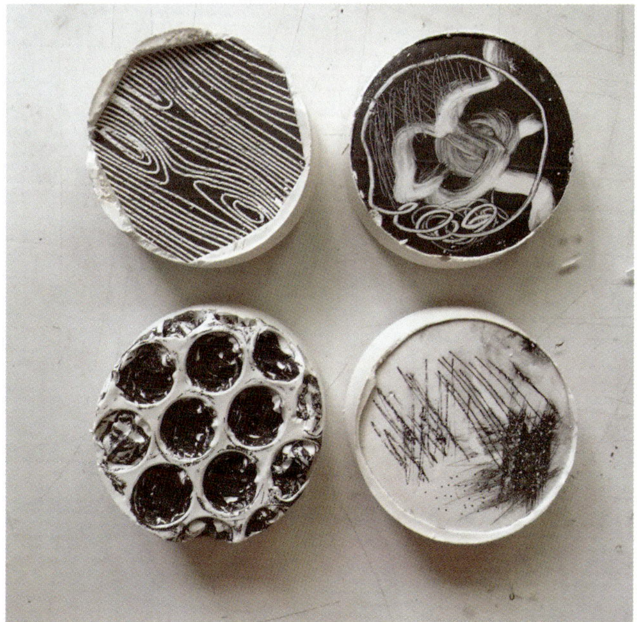

A selection of little plaster cast tester pieces.

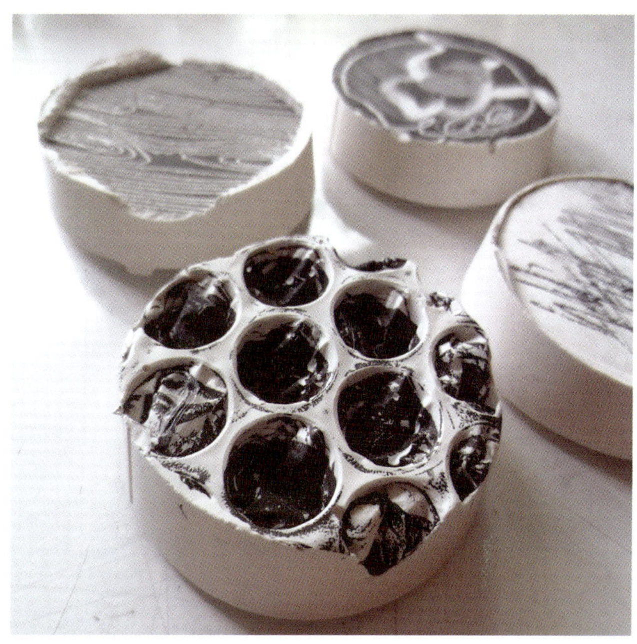

Plaster cast printing has amazing textural relief depths.

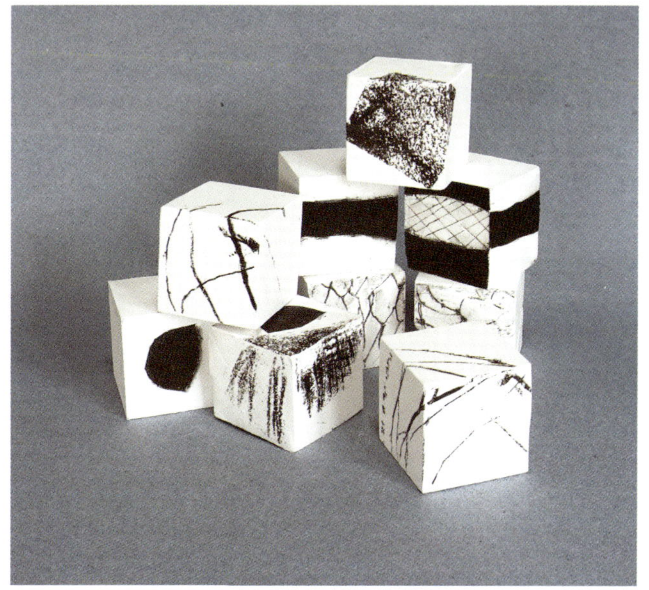

Turning print into object has a playfulness. *Trial and Error,* Consuelo Simpson.

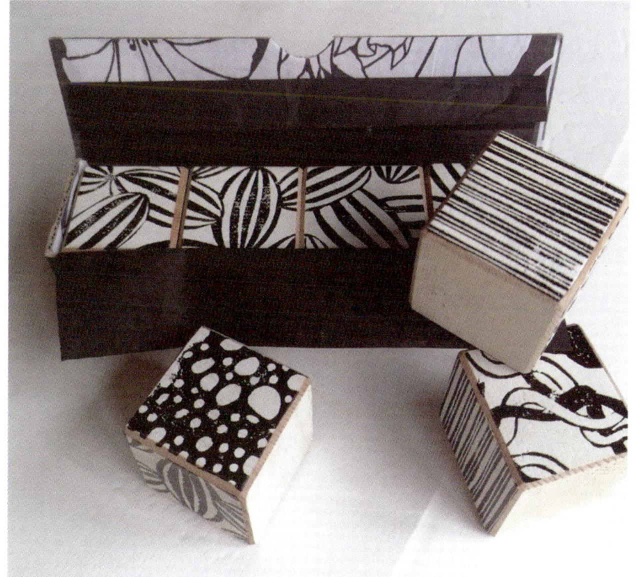

Print can come off paper! This is just the beginning…

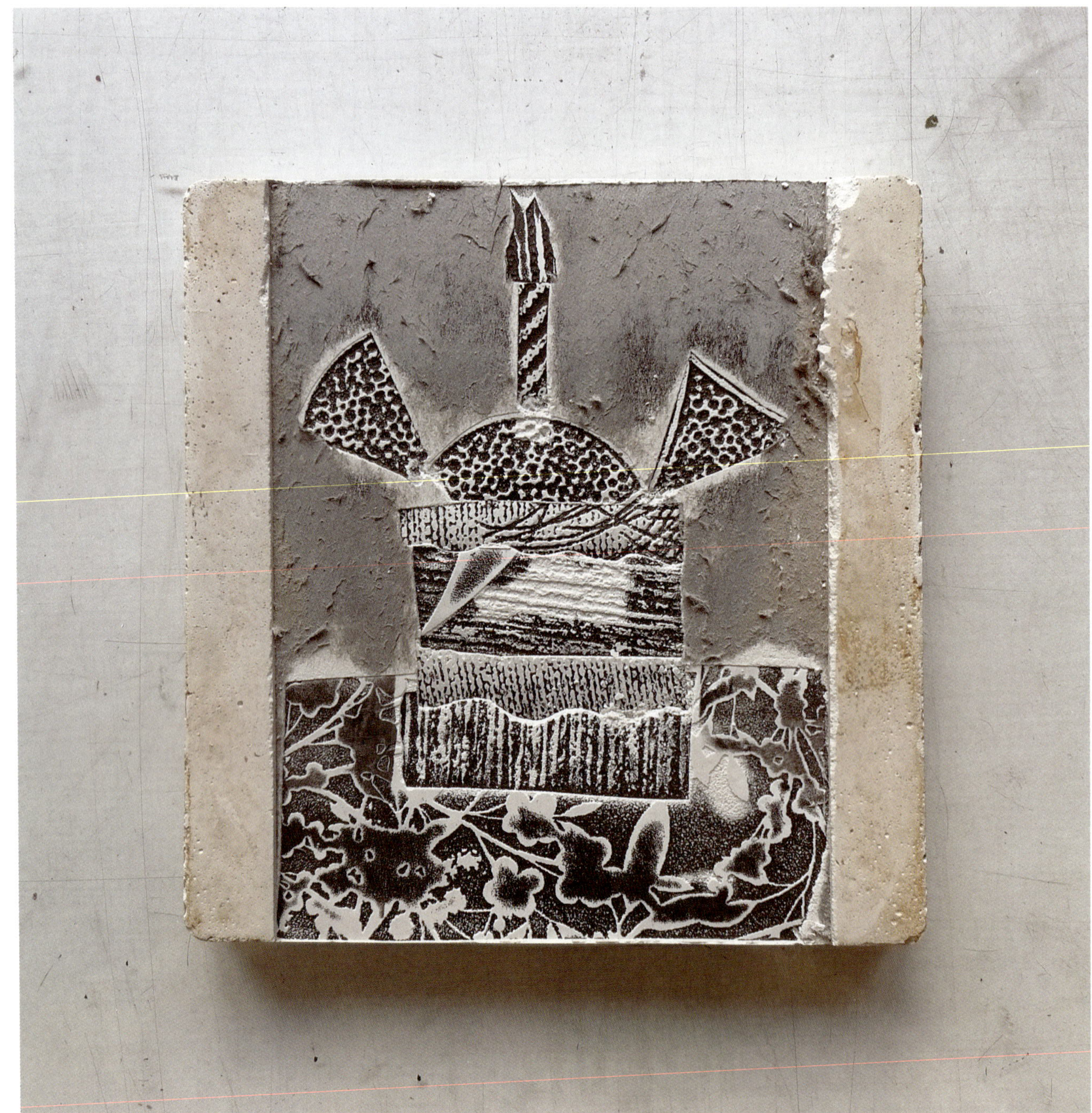

CHAPTER 3

THE MATRIX: RELIEF

How many opportunities will there be to reference an iconic film in the same sentence as the description of the surface that receives printing ink? So here we have 'The Matrix: Relief'. We are now looking at a breakdown of some of the options available for ecological printmaking. This chapter covers anything where the ink is sitting on top of a raised surface. I cannot possibly cover all options, so I have hopefully covered a good range to offer choice and exploration. We will be looking at both the common forms and the less common, the compostable and the biodegradable.

HOW TO APPROACH CHOICE

Printmakers have so many choices at their fingertips. Often too many, and the artform sings if you know when to choose and when to leave out. But in order to make the choice, you need to know what each option does, and how it works as a print. From an ecological standpoint, if there is a new method or matrix presented to me and I am intrigued as to the possibilities, the first bit of research I undertake is the MSDS. We looked at these in an earlier chapter; Material

Safety Data Sheets contain all the information you need to get your ecological investigations underway.

As an example, let us take a look at the MSDS for traditional lino. Every MSDS is structured marginally differently, but the information contained is principally the same. I will always

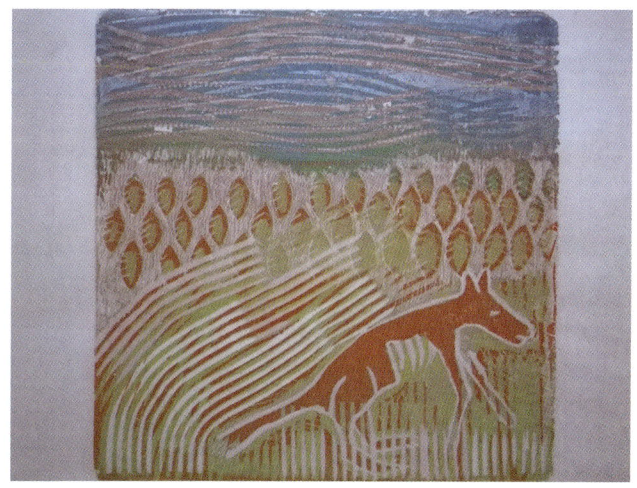

A plaster carved reduction print showcasing the stone-like texture. *Dead Fox*, Mary Dalton (2021).

get the MSDS from the manufacturer of the product in question, if I can. For lino it states in the first section 'Hazards Identification' that 'No particular hazard for persons and the environment known'. Brilliant. The next section states what the product is composed of. For lino, it says 'Linoleum based on a binder composed of vegetable drying oil and natural rosin, mixed with wood flour and limestone, pressed on a jute backing'. Again, this is all fantastic from an ecological perspective. Each ingredient is biodegradable and of the earth. Next, I will always look at the toxicological information, and for lino, 'no harmful effects have been reported to date'. This is as clean as you are going to get an MSDS. And for the ecological information it states 'product is biodegradable and can be composted'. With a glowing MSDS like this, you can see why I use traditional artist's lino so much in my work.

If your MSDS starts off a little less healthy, then further investigation of individual ingredients would be your next step. Depending on how deep you want to investigate, looking into research papers, blogs and books can help support your research. It is all dependent upon how far down the train you wish to walk. Sometimes it is obvious that one material is less ecological than another. Working

with lead white pigment comes with several health precautions before you even get to the MSDS. There is also an element of common sense and questioning with materials. The data is out there for you to take a look at; it is down to you how far you wish to investigate given your own set-up and lifestyle choices. Always be kind to yourself. Small steps of change are fundamental, and influence many more. So start with these.

LINO AS A MATRIX

Lino, as we have just found out, is just wonderful stuff. We will be dedicating a large chapter in this book to it, and the wonders of what it can offer the printmaker beyond the relief print. In this section we will look at lino in its most known form, the relief carving. Lino can be composted. The little carving scraps can just go straight into a compost as they degrade very easily. The large spent sheets and offcuts need to be cut up into smaller sections and mixed with other compostable materials to distribute. So do collect up the little carvings and add to a compost if you can access one, or even council green bin collections. The rate of degradation of the lino bits will depend on your composting system, but it is entirely feasible.

Many artists will colour their lino with an acrylic wash or Indian ink. I never bother, I would avoid acrylic washes because of the micro plastics issue, and it seems another process that just makes an inherently simple process more complex. If you want to draw out your image on the lino, a chinagraph pencil works brilliantly. Just give it a little wipe off with a clean rag to remove loose particles before printing, to prevent the pencil mark transferring to the impression. You also need to be aware with nearly all print methods that what you create on the matrix is actually mirrored when you print, so utilise tracing paper to make sure your specific orientation of the impression is mirrored for the actual lino surface. Or don't bother and just start drawing, which is my general approach.

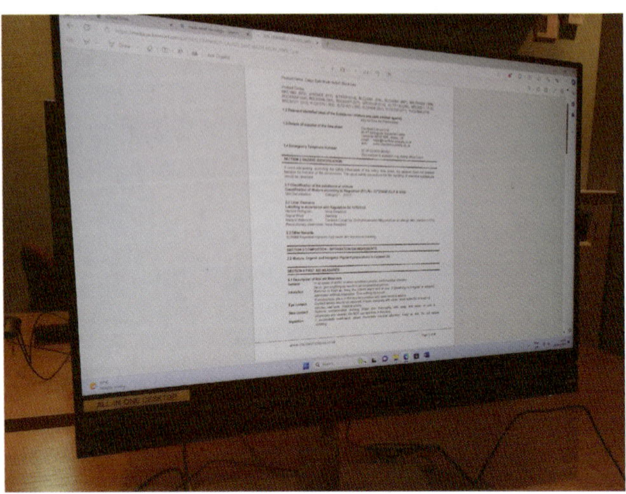

Individual research on materials is key to understanding more.

A MONOCHROME LINO CUT

This is a demonstration on how to print a monochrome lino cut using homemade soot black ink, printed onto handmade paper and all cuttings composted. So I suppose a bit more than your standard lino cut then…

Keep an eye on the ink thickness on your roll-out surface. Too thick and little details in-fill on the lino; too little and you won't be able to hand print the rich blacks. Remember the image you are to draw on the lino will print in reverse, so if it is essential to have a certain orientation, make sure you draw the mirror image onto the lino. Everything you carve away will be the paper colour, or white.

Materials

A5 sheet of traditional artist's lino
Chinagraph pencil
Lino cutting tools
Paper suitable for hand printing, about the weight of print-out paper (I'm printing on the mallow and willow paper made in Chapter 2)
Black ink (I'm using the vine black ink made in Chapter 1)
Roller and set-up to ink up lino
Printing baren to handprint (a wooden spoon works really well)
Oil and rag to clean up

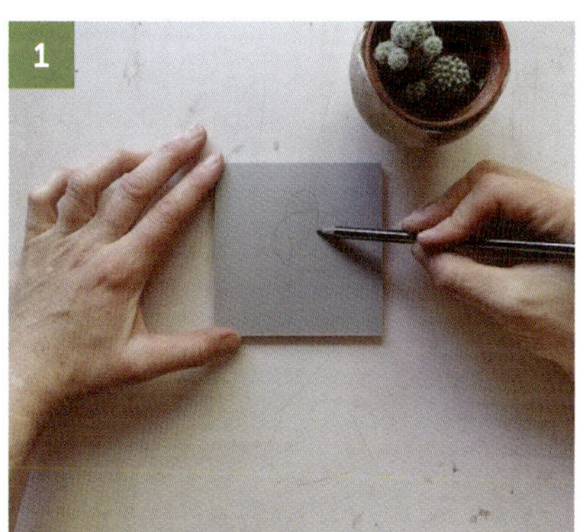

Draw out your design onto the surface of the lino with a pencil.

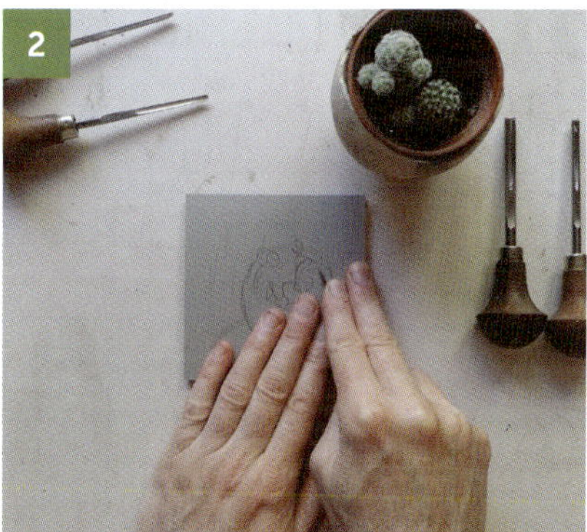

Carve away areas to remain white – ink only sits on the top surface.

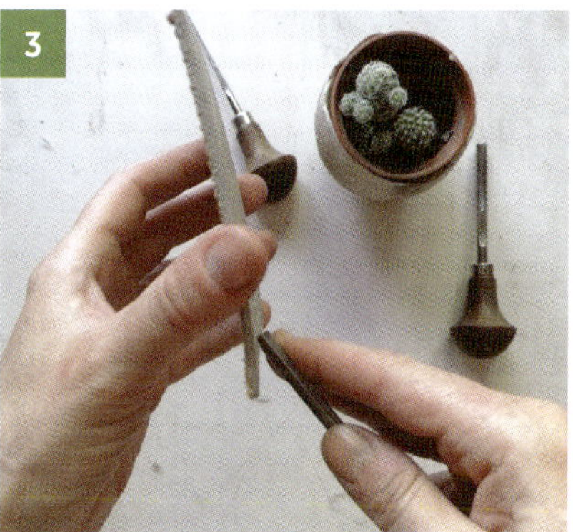

Keep a good cutting angle and carve away from yourself.

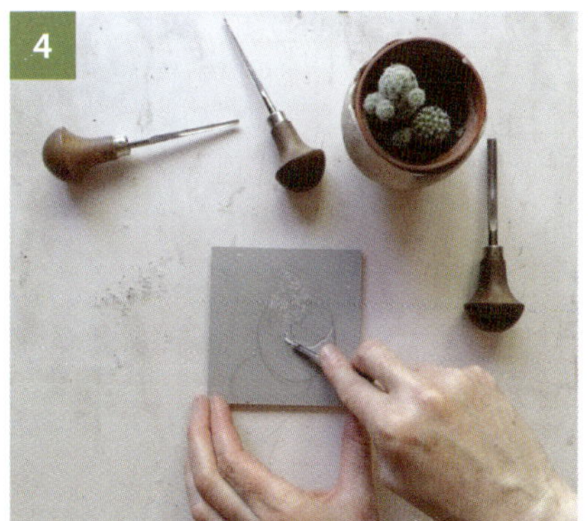

Play with mark making with the tools for different effects.

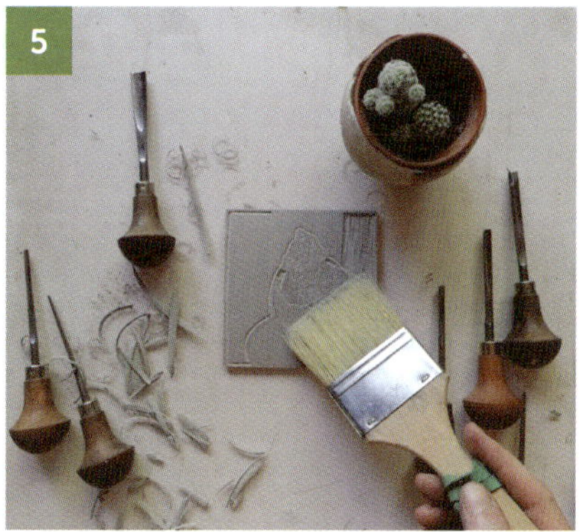

Before printing, brush off loose detritus from the surface.

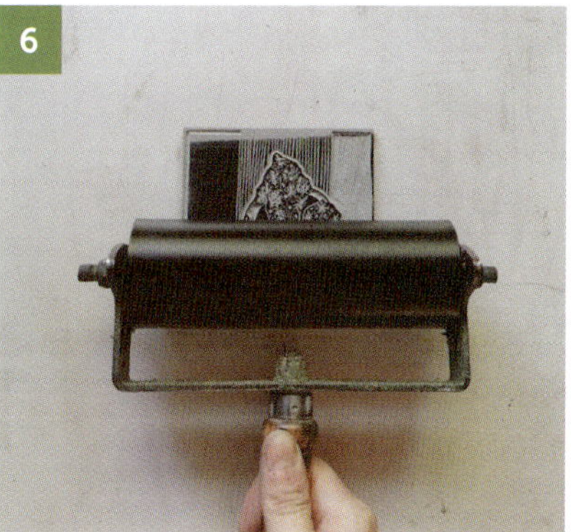

Roll the top surface with a light gloss layer of black ink.

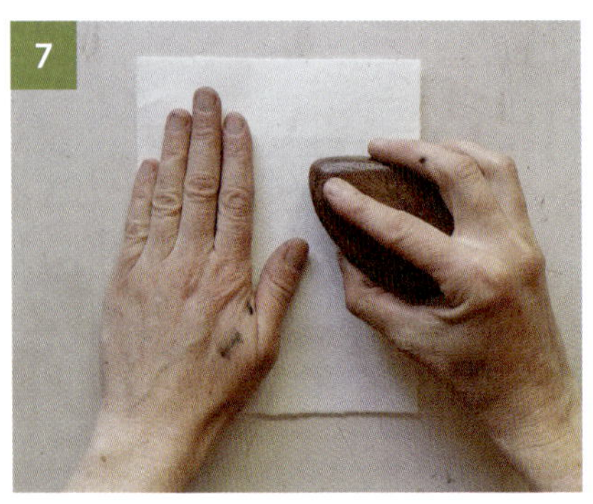

Place paper on top and apply pressure with the baren.

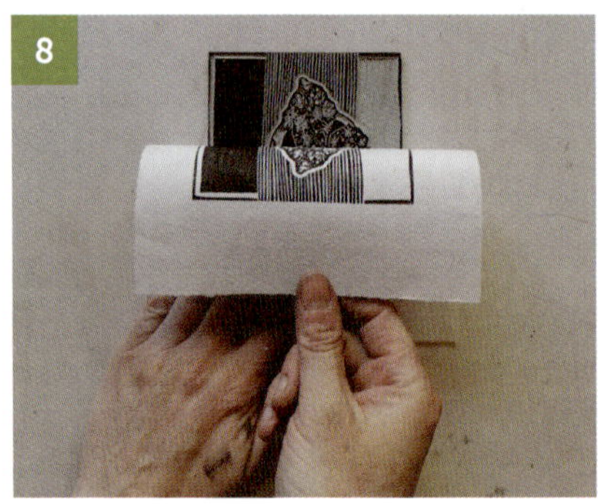

Gently check pressure and image before peeling away paper.

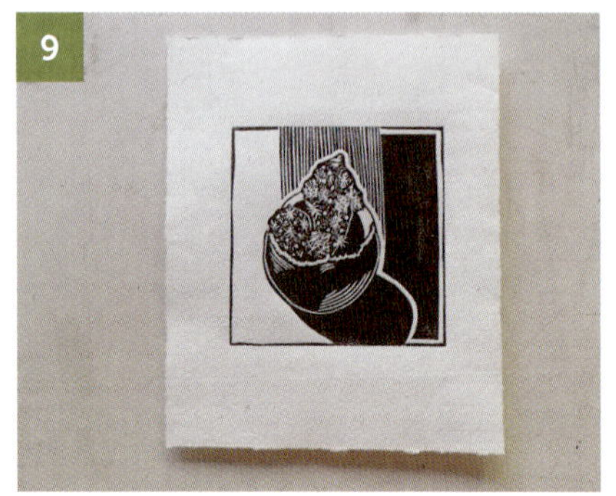

The completed monochrome lino cut on handmade paper.

Lino beyond relief printing

At various point in this book, we will be exploring lino more than just as a relief. Lino can be printed as lithography, monoprint and intaglio. It can be drawn on with tools other than the graphic carving ones. It is truly a wondrous substance, so be prepared to be amazed. And, as mentioned earlier, it is completely biodegradable. A natural product that creates phenomenal prints.

Oiled stencil card

Oiled stencil card is, as its name suggests, a card that has been treated with linseed oil and used for making stencils. It cuts very cleanly, is incredibly tough and withstands much inking and pressing, is waterproof (to an extent) and is made up of recycled manilla board and linseed oil. In essence it is a great ecological choice for making stencil work. From my understanding it is also biodegradable, but please do research for your own purposes.

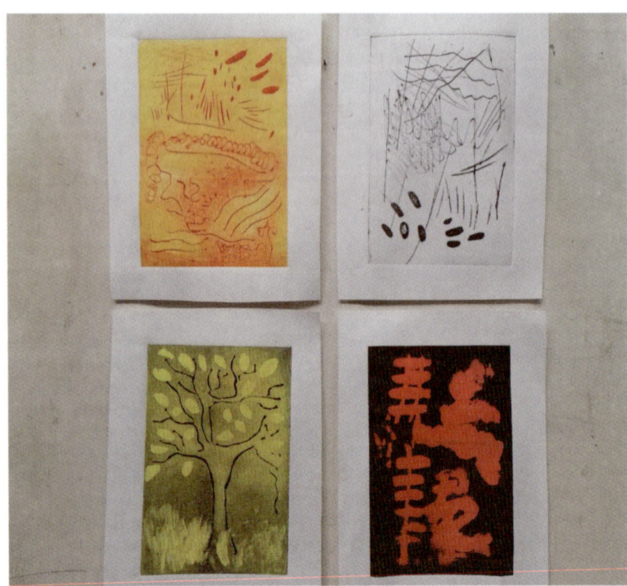

Lino does not have to be just relief as seen in these lino prints.

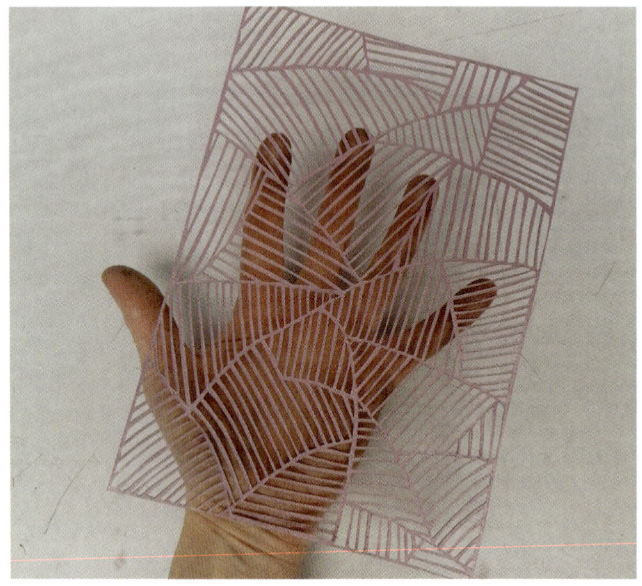

Oiled stencil card is capable of very fine detail.

STENCIL CARD PRINT

For this project we will be using stencil card as a way to create a simple black-and-white cut. Do keep an eye on the sharpness of your cutting blade. If you want clean lines and detailed cutting with ease, then replace the blade regularly. You can get scalpel handles with disposable metal blades of different styles or ones with blades that snap off to reveal a fresh edge. Both work great on stencil card. With a sharp blade you should only need to cut through once.

The card can be hand printed, but you must watch for slippage of the paper on any fine areas of cutting. If you have an etching press, it prints beautifully under the press at medium pressure with or without blankets.

Materials

Piece of oiled stencil card approximately A5
Scalpel or craft knife
Cutting mat
Black ink and set-up to roll a relief print
Press or printing baren to hand print

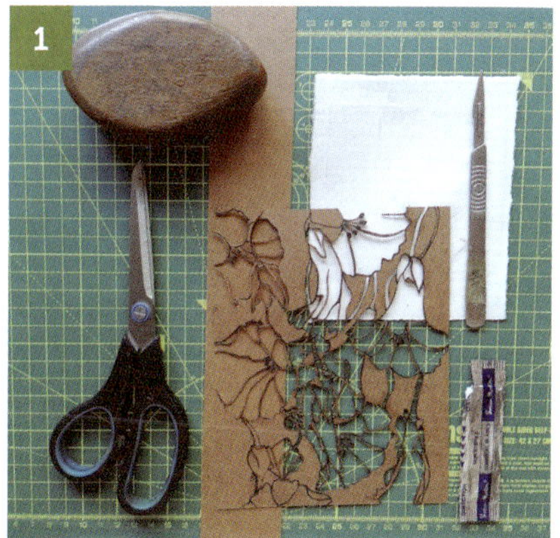

The materials needed to make a basic oiled card print.

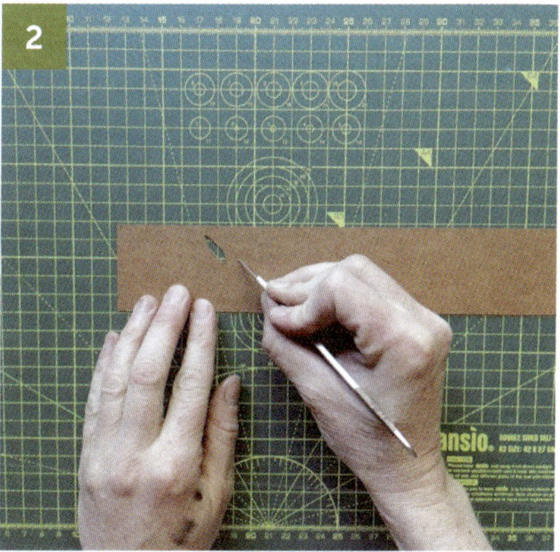

Using a sharp knife, carefully cut away areas not to print.

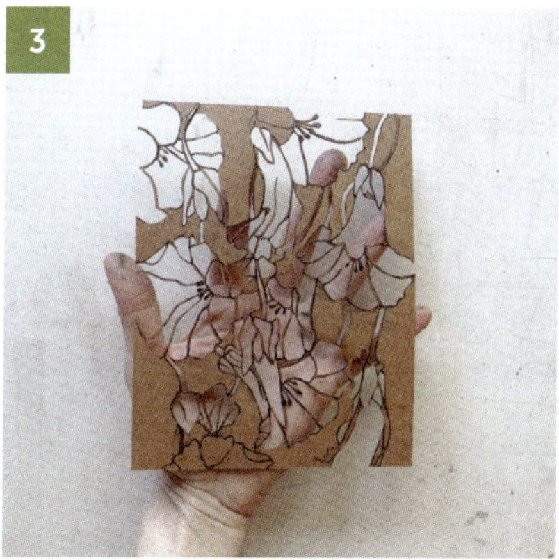

The completed stencil is cut and ready to print.

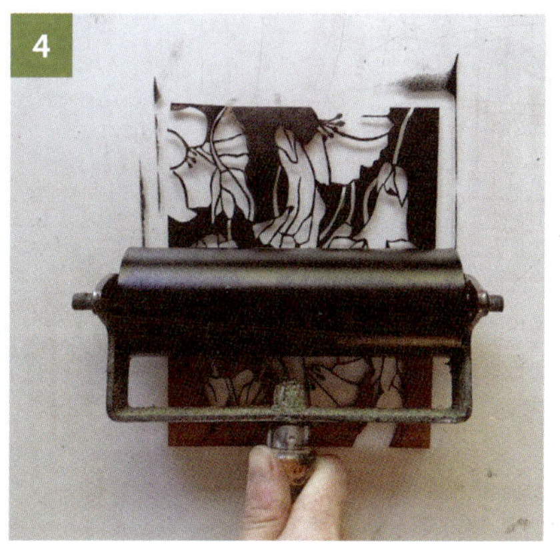

Very gently roll up the stencil with black ink.

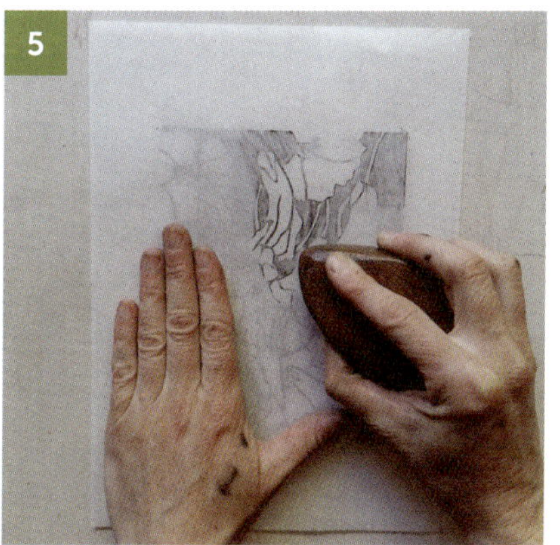

Hand print the stencil making sure to hold it firmly in place.

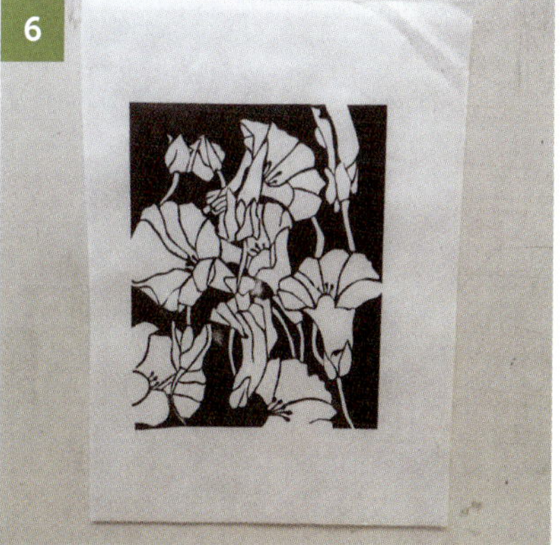

The completed monochrome oiled stencil card print.

STENCIL CARD AS REDUCTION

The stencil card can be used as a means to edition. Even under a press, it will last a significantly long time before it starts to fall apart. I've used stencil motifs 25 times and more under an etching press before the edges start to fail and tear. Noting that the stencil card is tough, it can be treated as a reduction matrix. In essence, you cut away the first stencil and print, then let the ink dry on the surface of the oiled card. Cut away more and print in register again on top of the first impression. This process, as with any reduction print, is repeated until the desired result, or nothing more of the matrix is left. To have a go at this, the same materials as the previous project are required, plus a selection of coloured inks. I am using yellow, red and dark brown.

Oiled card does not like to be cleaned up with vegetable oil, so if you are working this reduction live then cut away on the back of the card onto a scrap of paper on top of your craft mat. This way you avoid getting ink all over yourself. If you work in a reduction manner or wish to reprint with a stencil card over more time, then after printing I run the card through a press to remove excess ink and just let the ink dry on the surface. This doesn't take too much time and after a few days, the stencil card is all dry and ready to re-use.

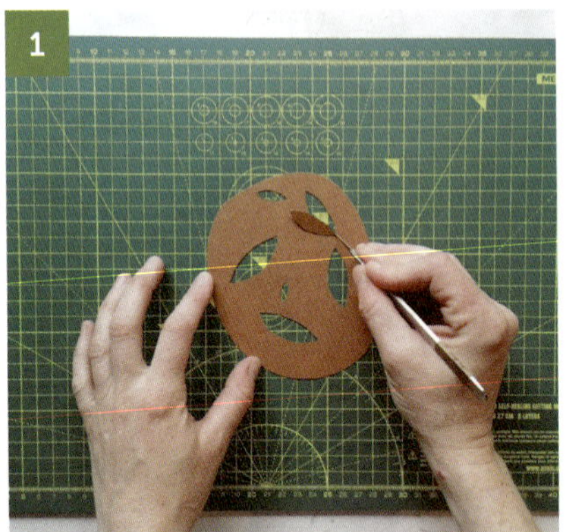

Cut away your first layer into the stencil card.

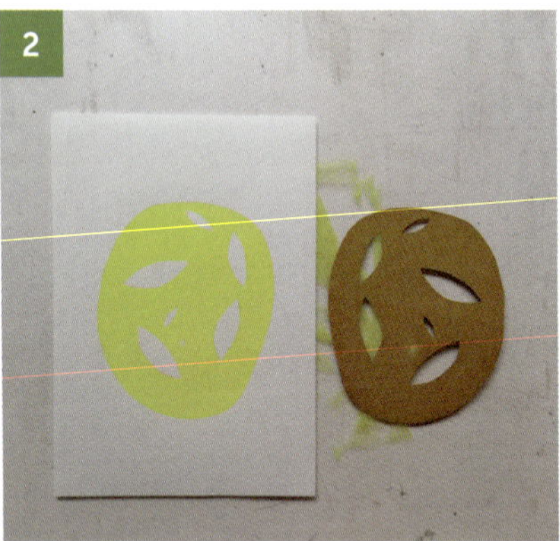

Ink up in yellow and print onto paper.

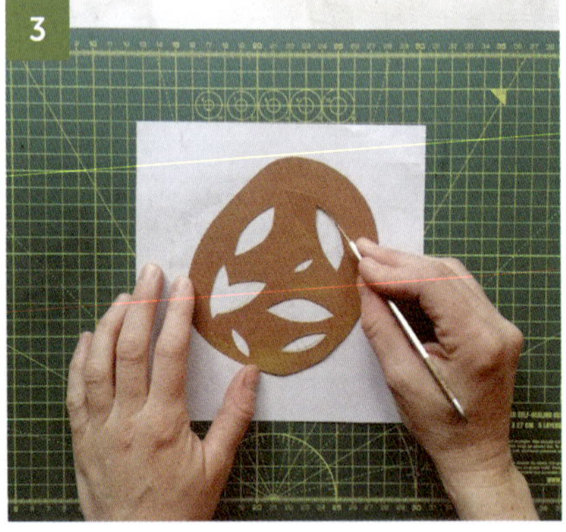

On the back, cut away more card into the same matrix.

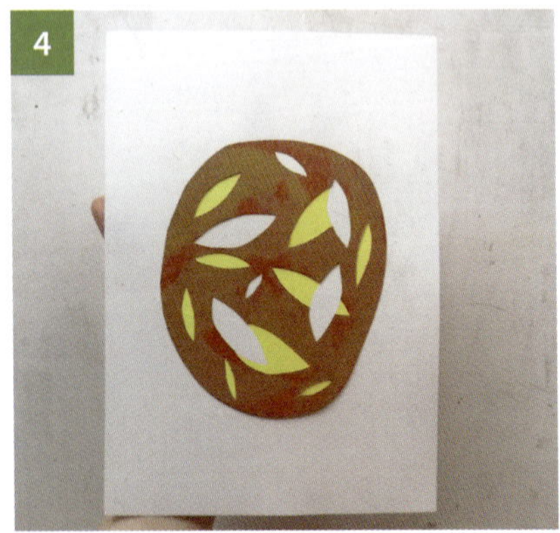

Place in register on top of the yellow impression and print.

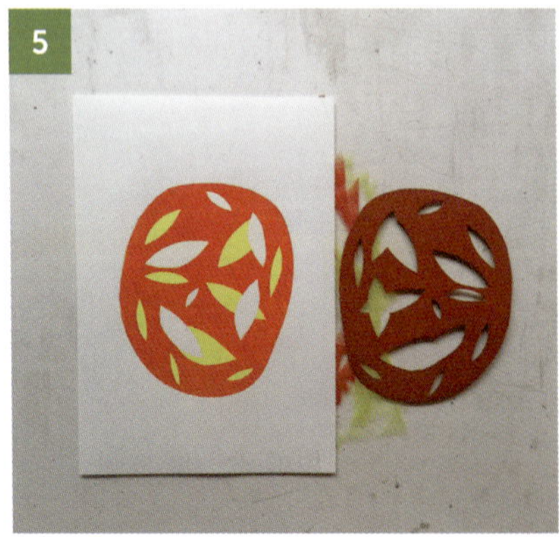

The red and yellow impression thus far.

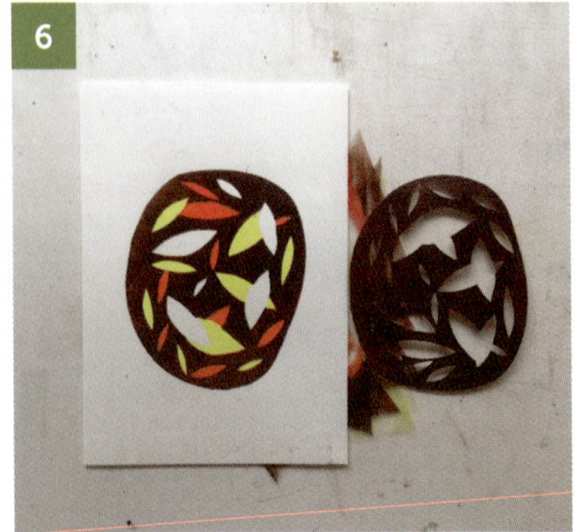

The same steps are repeated and printed in dark brown.

REDUCTION PRINTING FOR LINO AND FURTHER RELIEF EXPLORATIONS

The reduction print principle can be applied to a lino matrix as well. Simply carve away, print, carve, print, carve, print and repeat all in register on the same impression. It is a great way to maximise material resources and gives some beautiful results. If working on many layers, it is best if you let the first ink layer dry before printing the next, as this allows for a cleaner colour. You will also have to have a little think about colour theory, because as you get further down the layers then the colours on top of one another influence each other. So a blue sitting on top of a red may be slightly purple. You could add a bit of homemade extender to your blue to make it more transparent and then this would exaggerate the purple further.

Multi-plate printing is a further method to explore with stencil card and lino. In essence, you have multiple matrices inked up in different colours and you print them on the same impression. This allows for colour and shape overlap. You do need more material resources than reduction, but the effects are different.

Jigsaw printing involves cutting up the one matrix, inking the pieces separately, reconfiguring before printing and away you go. You work with the same matrix, but it allows you to cut it up into different sections that might have completely different textures or colours. And further to this, you can treat each jigsaw piece as a reduction to add further complexities in the impression. Cutting stencil card is easy enough, but lino is trickier. It likes to have larger jigsaw pieces with not many detailed outlines. You use a sharp knife to carefully score the top surface and then gently open up the cut and run the knife steadily and repeatedly through the cut. Eventually you get through the lino surface. It takes a bit of patience, but it is worth it.

Plaster of Paris

We looked at the ecological questions regarding plaster of Paris earlier in Chapter 2. As I highlighted, one of the key roles of this book is to present information as far as I have researched thus far, allowing you to make informed decisions. So here, we see the return of plaster one last time. In this instance, we are going to carve it and treat it as a reduction print. The quality of a plaster reduction print is quite extraordinary. The ink picks up on tiny particles of plaster dust when printing and it gives the quality of stone. Plaster also has the distinct advantage that you can carve it using tools other than traditional lino carvers. You can scratch, sand, flick or chip away at it using many semi-sharp tools. This offers the artist much freedom in carving expression.

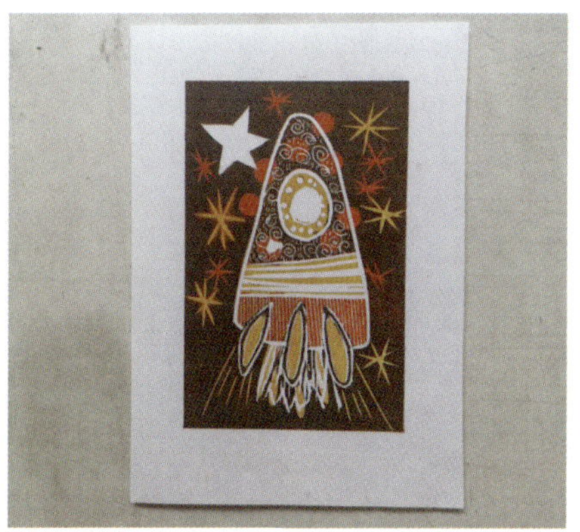

A reduction lino – yellow, red and blue – note blue appears brown on top of previous layers.

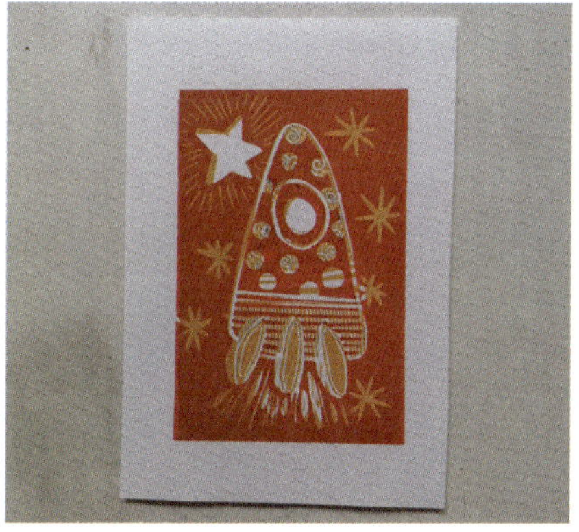

A two-layer multi-plate rocket – yellow and red – note the overlays.

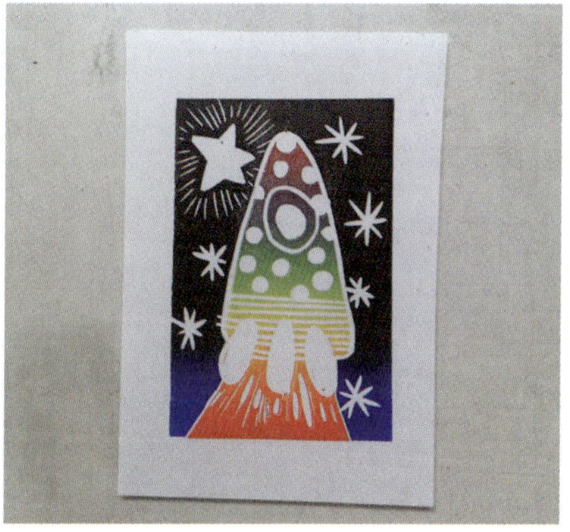

A two-section jigsaw lino allowing rocket to be rainbow and sky black.

ALTERNATIVE MATRICES

Sawdust

When approaching the choices of matrix, it is always advisable to think outside of the box. Take inspiration from culture around the world – how have different peoples made substances that have the potential to receive ink? Does it involve looking at printmaking specifically, or perhaps a broader approach to materiality? Material research can often bring about inspiration that was not the initial research topic, and indeed this often allows for much exploration and eureka moments. Much of my own research stems firstly from looking at and understanding a material that is biodegradable and that I have in abundance. For instance, sawdust. We have a lot of it as a bi-product from sawing timber. Further, I use a carpentry workshop several times a month and a bag of sawdust from the power sanders or sawdust sucker (aka Hoover) is much appreciated.

Once I have a material I have ready access to, I start to research through books and online resources, as well as playing with the material, to see how and if I can utilise it. Sawdust is a great example. I knew wood flour was already a key component in lino, so sawdust seemed like it might have a use. As I researched, I found it had been used across many cultures to make a modelling paste mixed with glues and oils, and indeed it was used to make the textured patterns on Anaglypta wallpapers. I print with these quite a bit to add brilliant relief texture and so I got playing. I managed to get to a good consistency of paste that allowed me to generate a biodegradable substance that I could mould-make from (for the toy making) and also to make a textured matrix that I could print from to create pattern. Bingo. There was my use for sawdust.

Sawdust prints

In this example we will look at how we can create a patterned block. This block can be used to apply texture directly to a print or as a way to create texture on a lithino matrix (*see* Chapter 6). The block will last a fair amount of time and after that, the sawdust can be scraped off and composted and you can go again. Always wear a face covering when dealing with sawdust, even if it comes from genuine solid timbers.

Materials

Sawdust of the finest grade you can get
Mixing pot
Linseed oil
Rice paste (nori) or wheat paste glue
Piece of backing card or thin timber
Mark making tool (I am using the end of a paintbrush)
Oil-based ink
Face covering

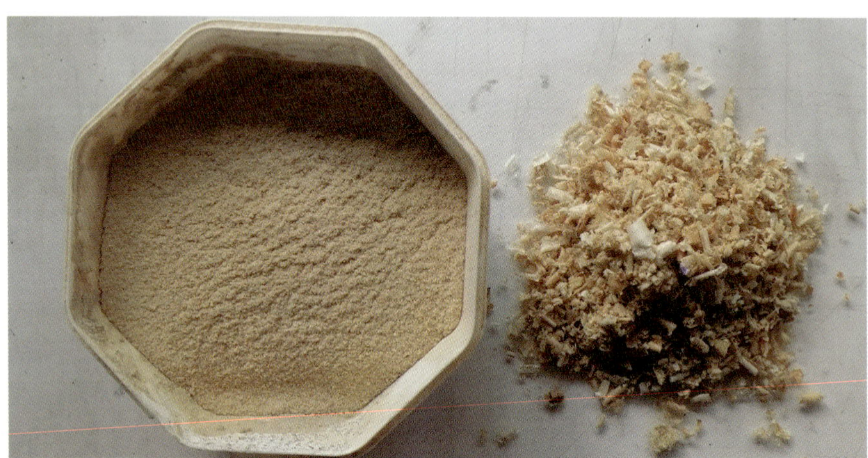

Hardwood sawdust was a resource I had in abundance.

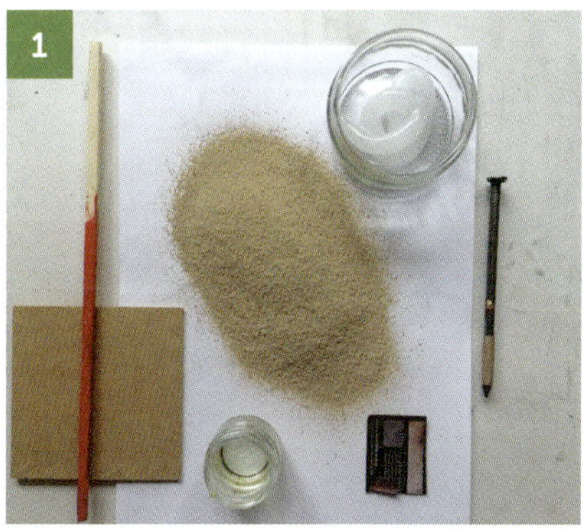

Materials needed to make a sawdust relief print.

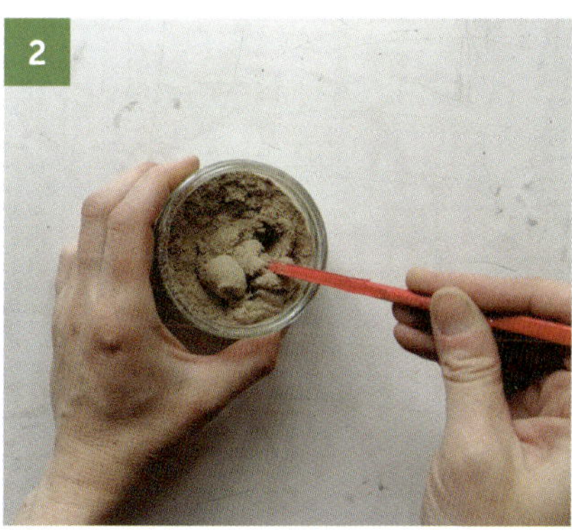

In a pot, mix rice paste glue with the sawdust. Wear a face mask.

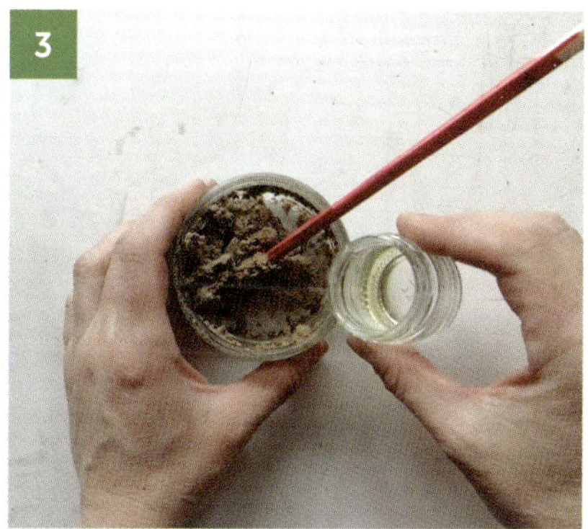

Add a few drops of linseed oil and mix until smooth.

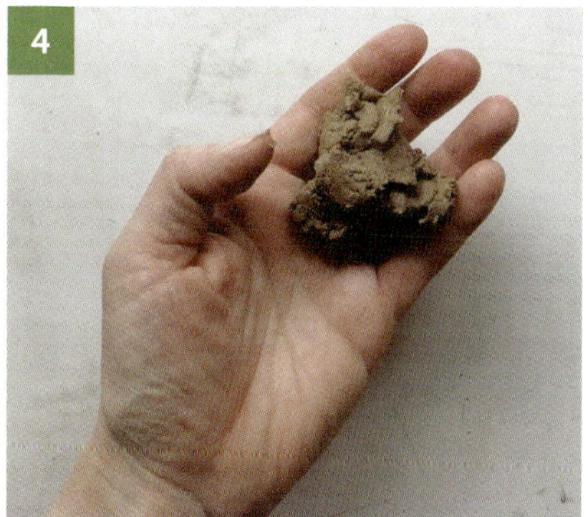

Add more glue and oil drops until the mixture is smooth.

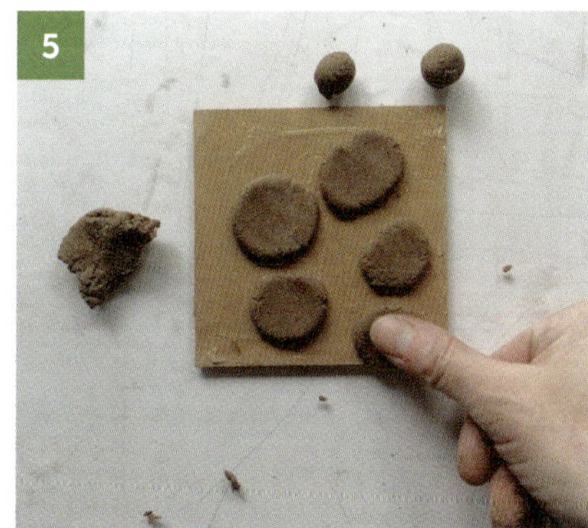

Cover a backing board with rice glue and add sawdust areas.

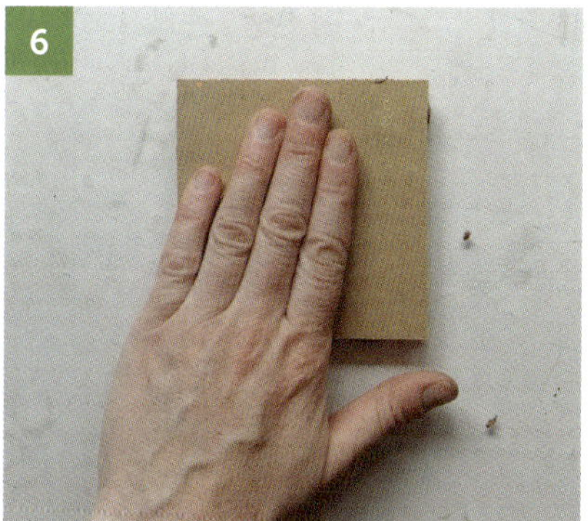

Place a secondary board on top and press sawdust level.

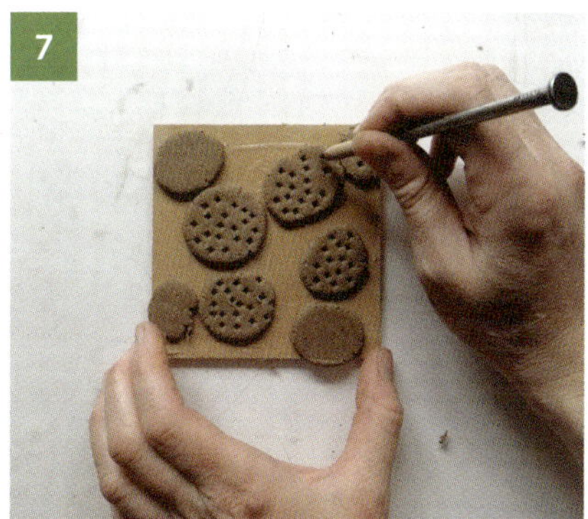

Use tools to add texture to the sawdust areas. Leave to dry.

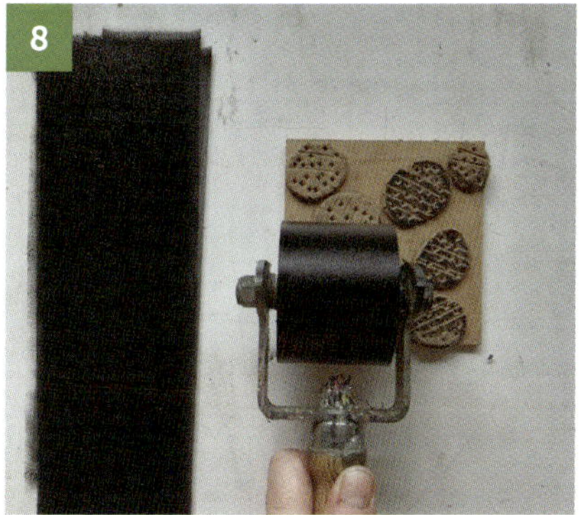

Ink up the dry sawdust relief with loose ink. Hand print.

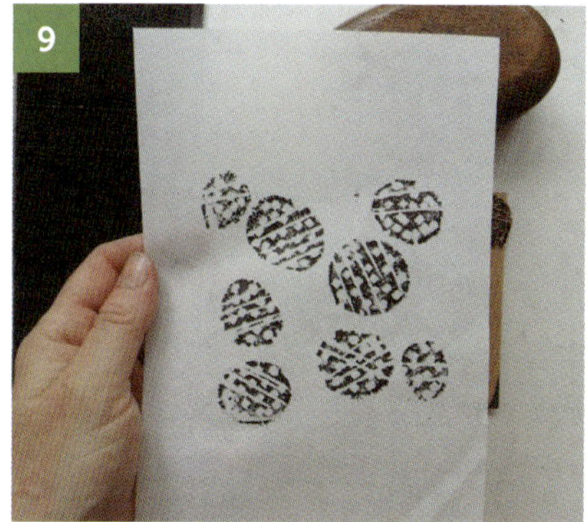

The completed sawdust relief print with beautiful textures.

BEESWAX

I am fortunate that my uncle is a beekeeper. He has my late father's bee hives and nurtures them lovingly. And because of this, I get much beautiful beeswax sent my way throughout the year. Beeswax is a thing of wonder. So many uses, including in printmaking.

After researching encaustic painting and the consistencies it generates for wax, I was intrigued as to whether this wax-based substance could be used as a method of generating texture in print. And after much exploration and mess and beautiful-smelling kitchens, I found a great ratio of beeswax and resin that allows you to generate some stunning and unusual effects. As with many of the techniques explored in this book, the beeswax prints are aimed at supporting unique printmaking. The beeswax matrix will last you a few prints before it gets squashed a bit. It is great fun to make and very expressive. I have found it works really well as a key line in black on top of some under-printing or collage. The trick to making this work well is to not layer up too much beeswax texture. Keep the textures to one layer and nice and distinct.

Materials

Beeswax 50g
Damar varnish resin 10g
Scales
Non-food pan (it is best to set a pan aside for beeswax only)
Heat source
Tools to 'draw' with (such as old brushes, batik Tjanting tool, nails or scrapers)
A few pieces of grey board 1–3mm for backing, approximately 15cm × 15cm
Ink and set-up for relief printing
Washi paper between 29gsm and 60gsm for hand printing
Printing baren (wooden spoon)
Face covering

Beeswax samples

The beeswax prints are best hand printed, but under a loose pressure and with nice damp paper, they can be press printed. The paper must be damp so it does not stick to the wax mixture. The brush marks that are available are stunning and I have even re-used the beeswax after printing by scraping off and remelting, ink and all. Beeswax offers very exciting potentials in relief printmaking.

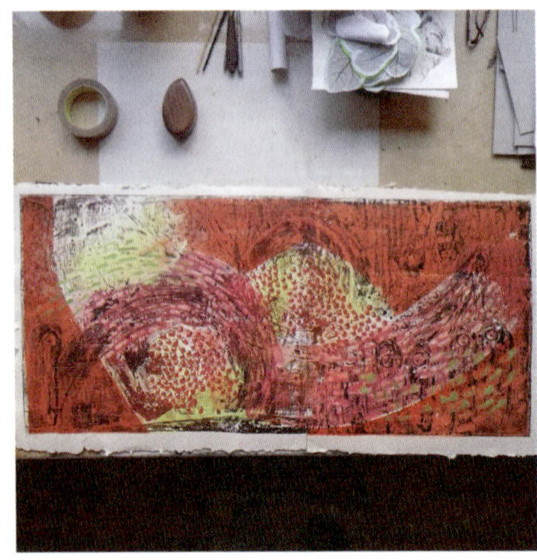

A large-scale wax relief print in progress upon a monoprint background.

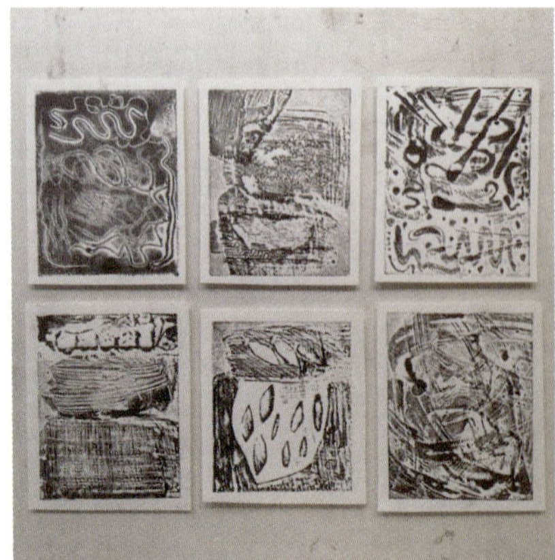

A range of tester pieces showcasing the range of marks.

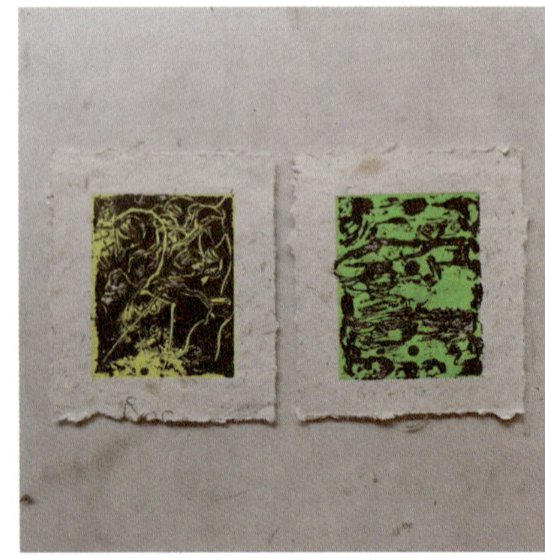

Two wax prints made by Rose, aged five (left) and Guiwenneth, aged nine.

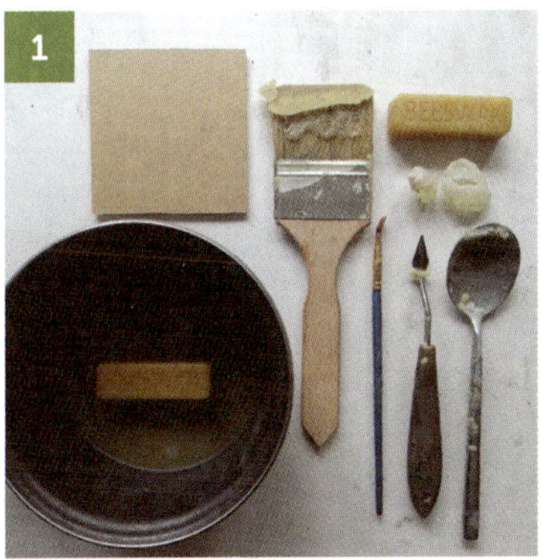

Materials needed for making a beeswax relief print.

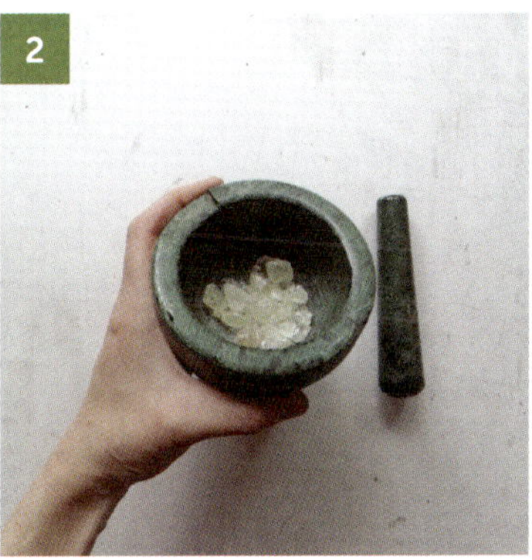

Break up the damar resin to a coarse powder. Wear a face covering.

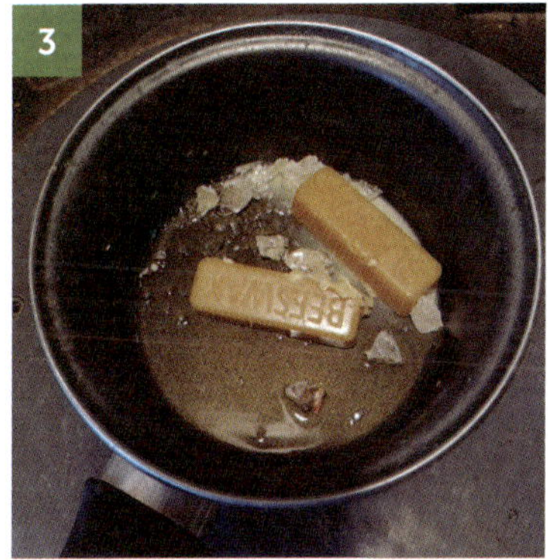

Melt the beeswax and resin together on a medium heat.

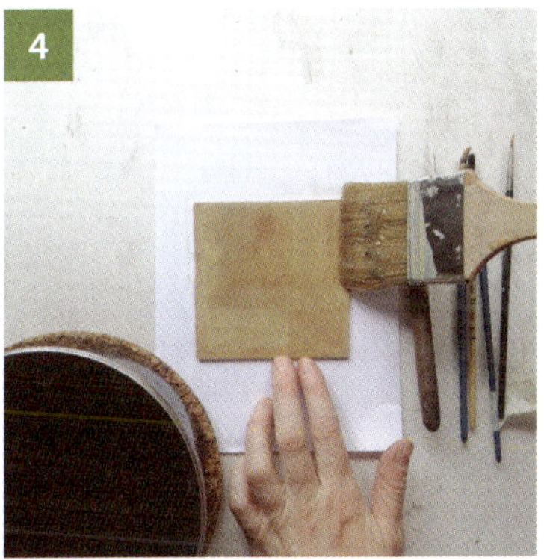

Brush on the beeswax mixture onto a backing board.

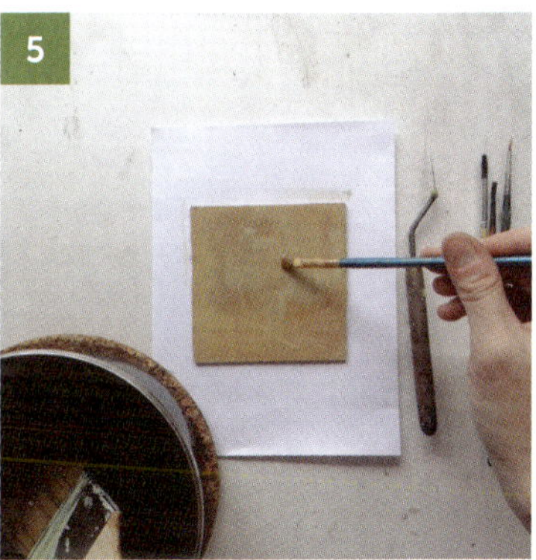

Use other tools to 'paint' with the wax for gestural texture.

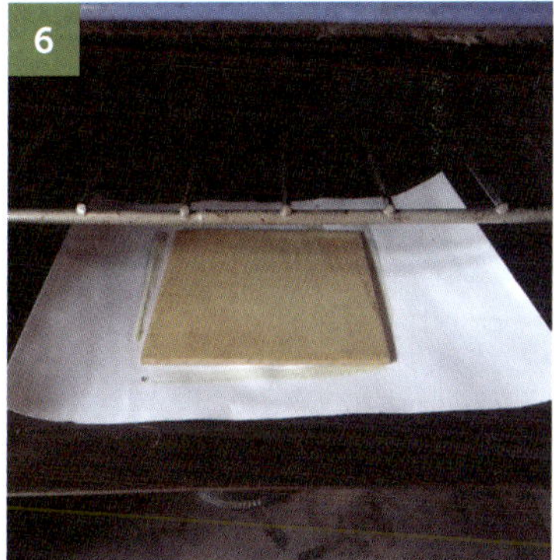

If a smooth surface is needed, heat beeswax on a board in a low oven.

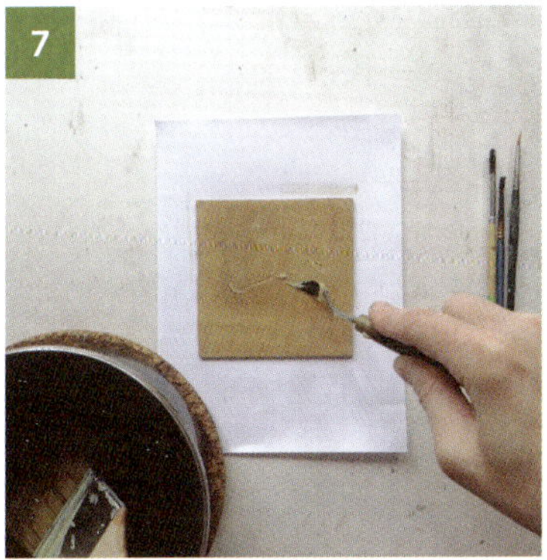

Play with tools to mark make in the wax.

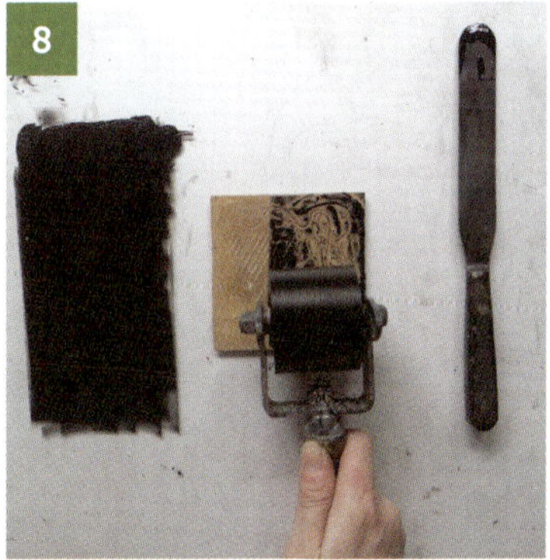

Roll up with a light gloss ink and light pressure.

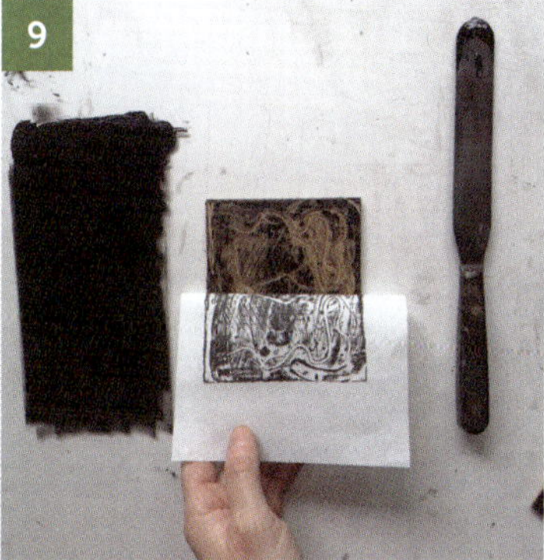

Carefully hand print onto slightly damp paper and peel off.

FISH, VEGETABLES AND MORE COMPOSTABLE ITEMS

The matrix you print from does not have to be of permanence. It can be a completely disposable item, or a compostable item. In Japan, a tradition called *gyotaku* exists, in which a print of a fish is created by applying sumi ink directly to a dead fish and hand printing the image onto washi paper. Originally for fishermen to record their catches, it has become an art form and representation of the fish's beauty. Printing with vegetables and other food items is a great way to integrate pattern. You can also of course hand stamp any item with relief texture. When used in conjunction with a mask, it can be highly effective.

Printing directly from leaves and other organic items is hugely satisfying and can produce prints that are beautiful in their own right or in conjunction with a larger composition. There are a few tricks that will enable a beautiful print of such clarity that it looks like a graphite drawing. In the following demonstration, I am working with a fig leaf that was picked in late summer/early autumn. The fig leaf has strong veins and is robust, so does not fall apart too readily on the roller. Any leaf that is gathered is printable, just be aware the more squashable the leaf the more likely it is to fall apart under the pressure of the press. Also be careful not to print anything that is really thick, like pine needle branches, twigs or similar as it can damage your press. Ginkgo, oak, hawthorn, holly, hazel and birch leaves all work well, as do hydrangea heads. This process really does work best with the traditional oil-based printing inks because they allow you to roll out even the thinnest amount of ink evenly, which is what we are after.

Materials

Oil-based printing ink
Fig leaf
Etching press set up with a facing blanket and finger-tight pressure
Roller and printing set-up
Smooth surfaced paper, such as Somerset Satin

How to develop further

Relief printing is hugely accessible at home with or without a press. Have a play with hand printing lino cuts with different pressure from your baren. What happens if you use the pointy end of a wooden spoon to print instead of the flat area? Plaster cast prints can also develop combining the information in this chapter and Chapter 2 to become complex and detailed reliefs. The world truly is your oyster.

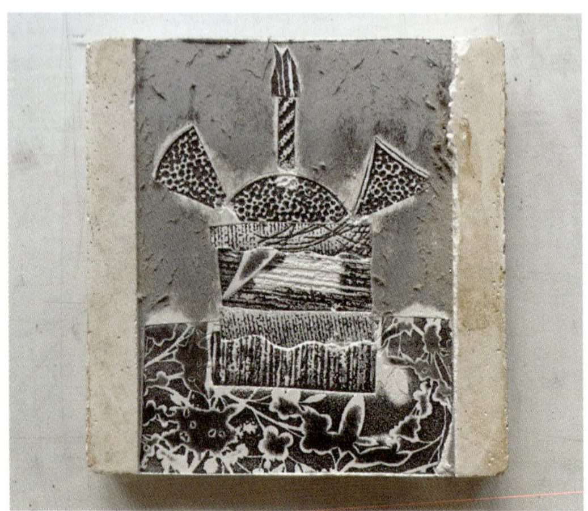

Plaster cast print by Guiwenneth Street aged eight. Look at that cake!

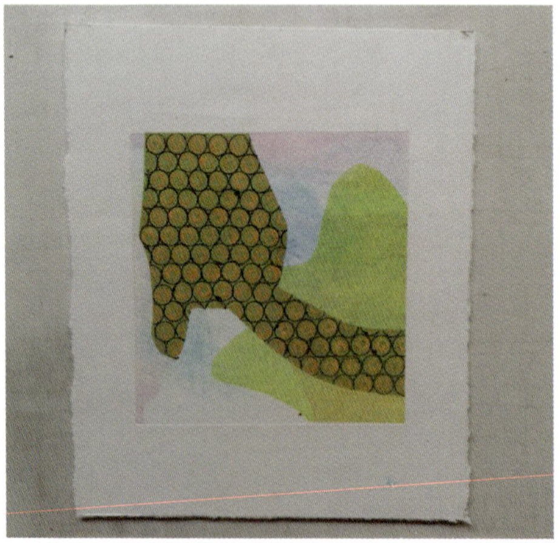

Print showing hand stamped copper piping and nails.

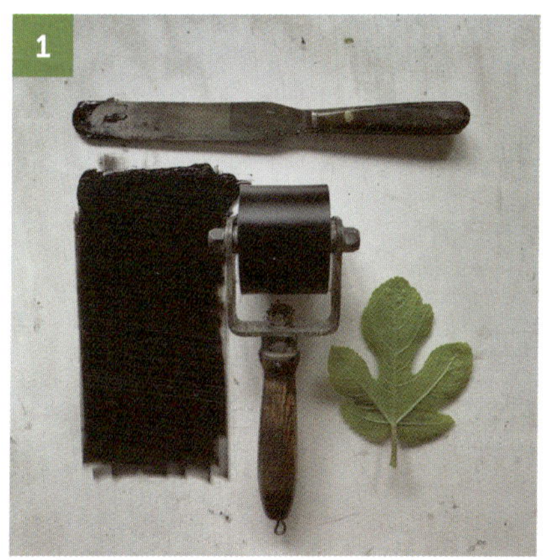

Materials need for a fig leaf relief print under a press.

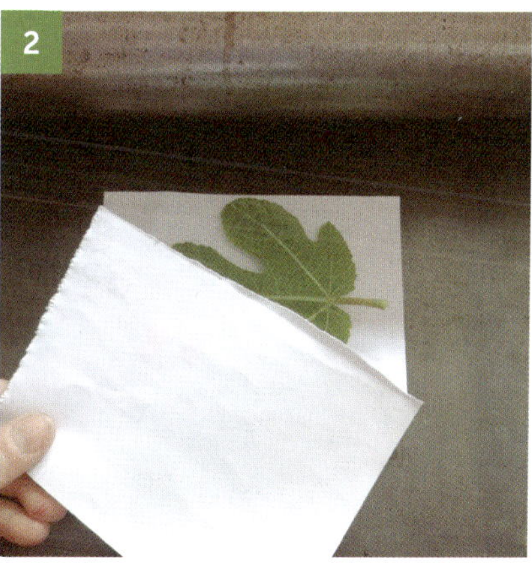

On loose pressure, press excess juice out of the leaf onto paper.

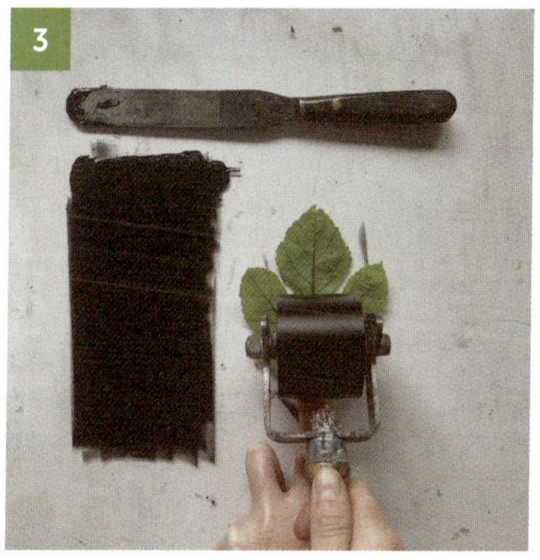

With very thin ink, carefully ink up the leaf.

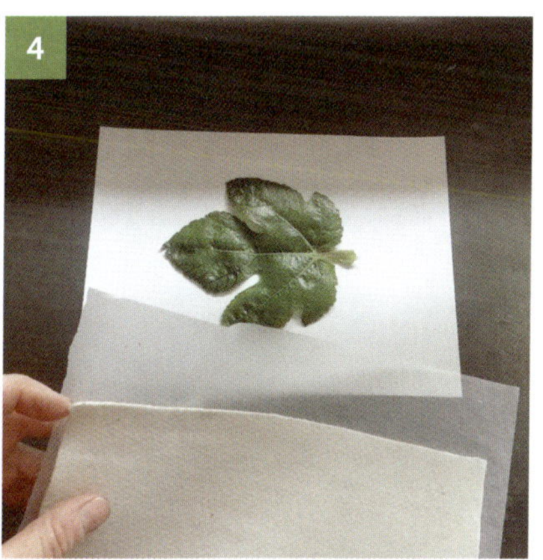

Print on loose pressure, no blanket, ink side down.

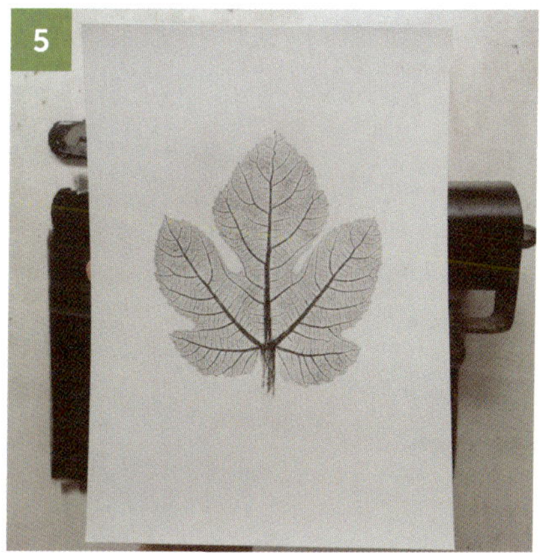

The completed fig leaf print in stunning detail.

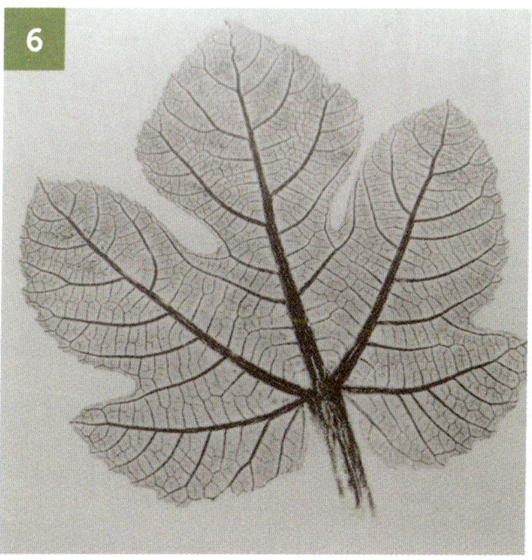

The quality and depth of detail in the veins is exquisite.

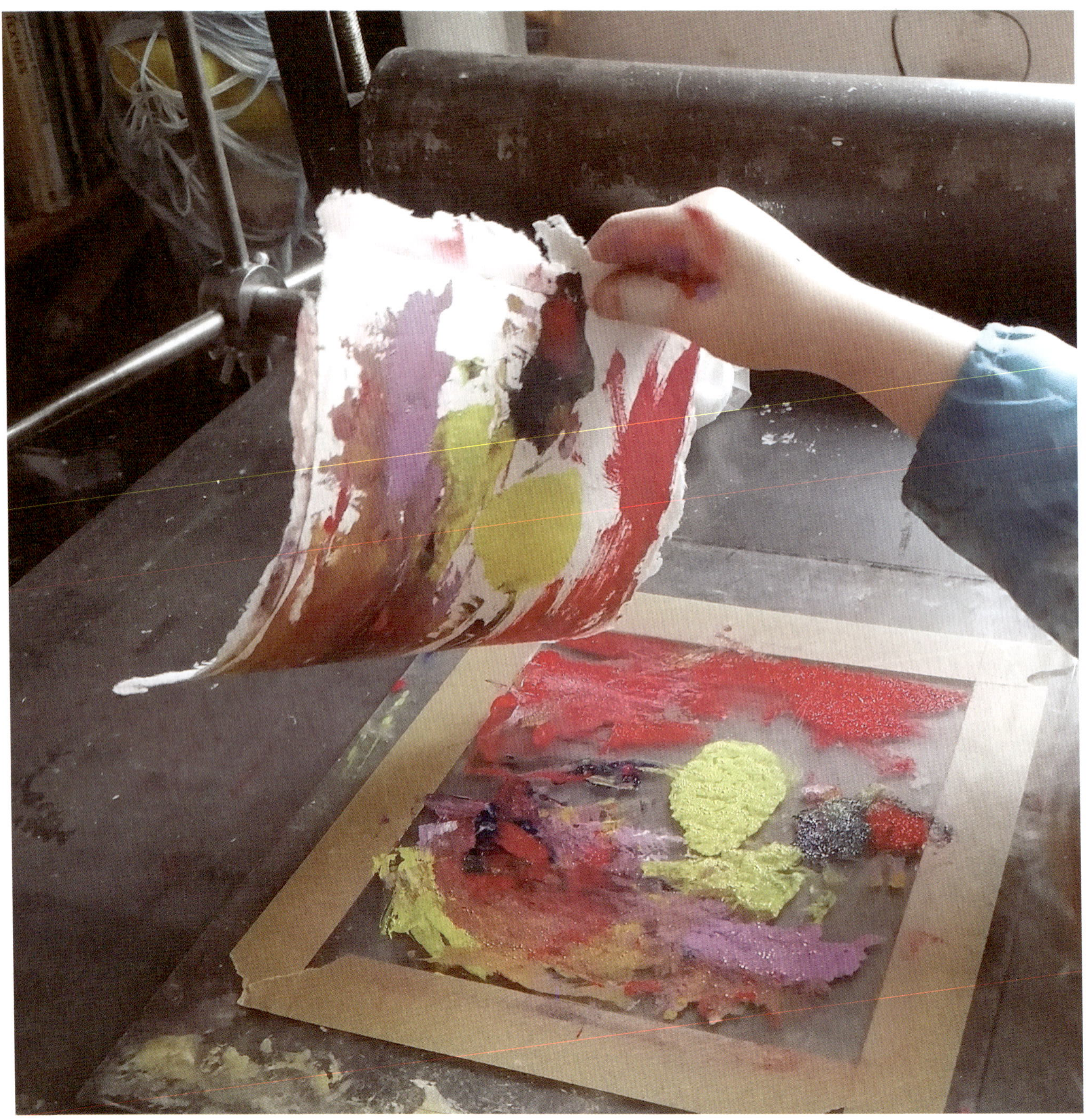

THE MATRIX: PLANOGRAPHIC

Monoprint is describing a singular (mono) print, one that cannot be editioned. In essence, nearly all the prints described or shown in this book are monoprints, including the sumi ink fish. Therefore it is a very generalised term to cover many a print. However, in the printing tree of terms if you referred to a monoprint to most printmakers, they would associate it with printing directly from the ink without the use of another matrix to generate the impression. And this is how we shall approach it. And ecologically, it is fantastic because all you are using is ink and paper. Without a repeatable matrix, you have cut back materials and processes to a very sustainable core. In this chapter we will look at the potentials of single plate, multi plate, colour and monochrome monoprints with an array of techniques for texture and bold graphics in between.

SURFACE

To create a monoprint, you will require a surface to apply ink to. If you are printing under a press, then this surface needs to be flat and smooth. I always go with aluminium sheets because I can use them for many a year without having to dispose of them. The majority of aluminium is generated from recycled aluminium because in theory the metal is

infinitely recyclable. Recycling is certainly not the answer to ecological issues because in itself it requires a huge amount of processing energy, but it does mean the metal is not a virgin metal from the earth. As a monoprint surface, if well looked after it can be used and re-used multiple times and stored for years without the need to purchase more.

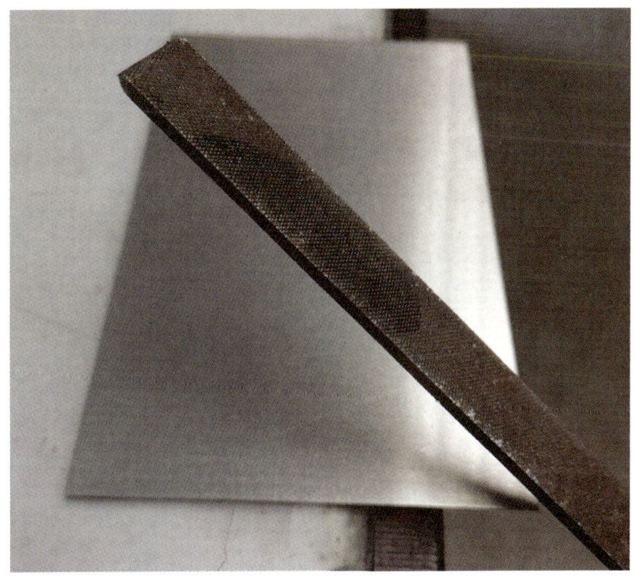

If using an aluminium sheet, the edges will need to be filed.

Aluminium sheet can be ordered cut to specific size and of a certain depth. I tend to use 2mm sheet metal, and it seems to be sturdy enough even for large-scale sheets. This also prints beautifully under a heavy top-roller etching press without having to adjust any pressure. When you order in the aluminium, you will need to file the edges to remove cutting burrs that risk slicing up your blankets.

LARGE-SCALE REDUCTIVE PRINT

Monochrome monoprints are a fantastic way to loosen up and enjoy the process of drawing and mark making. I sincerely suggest you go as big as your press bed and paper allow for this project because allowing yourself to have a full arm's swoosh across a page creates a fantastic flow of energy. In this instance, the sheet of aluminium I am working on is 45cm × 60cm. We are going to be trapping the paper in the press after the first turn to allow another ghost print to be printed in register on the same impression. This can be repeated multiple times to get a monochrome variance.

Again, I would fully advise working with oil-based inks because they will give you the viscosity to smear, smudge and wipe as well as staying open, or wet, for a long period. This gives you a long working time without worrying if your monoprint is going to dry before you have even printed it.

This type of working lends itself to a series, and more often than not when you are really tired and all you want to do is stop, make one more print and that will be the one that is the most successful. If working in a series, then give yourself as much time as you can permit to generate a number of images. This type of monoprint works significantly better under an etching press with damp paper. We will be looking at methods of hand-printing monoprints, but to get the contrast of the rich blacks, the fine line details and the midtones, an etching press is your tool of choice.

Materials
Aluminium sheet, edges bevelled
Oil-based black ink
Roller and print set-up
Damp paper to fit your aluminium sheet
Rags, paintbrushes, knitting needles, other such blunt items to mark make
Vegetable oil

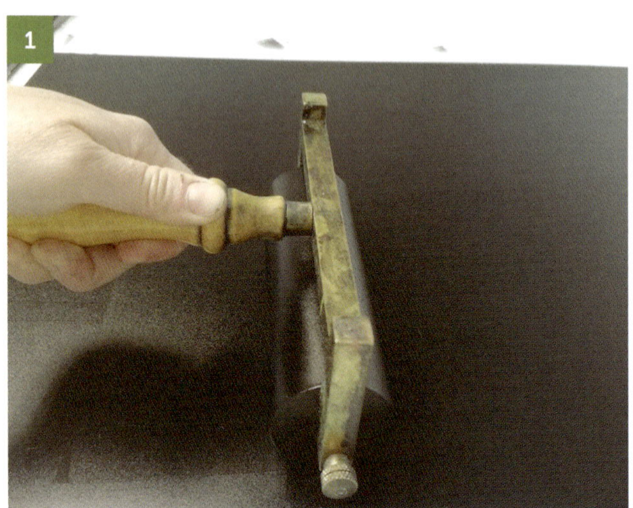

Cover your entire aluminium plate with an even film of ink.

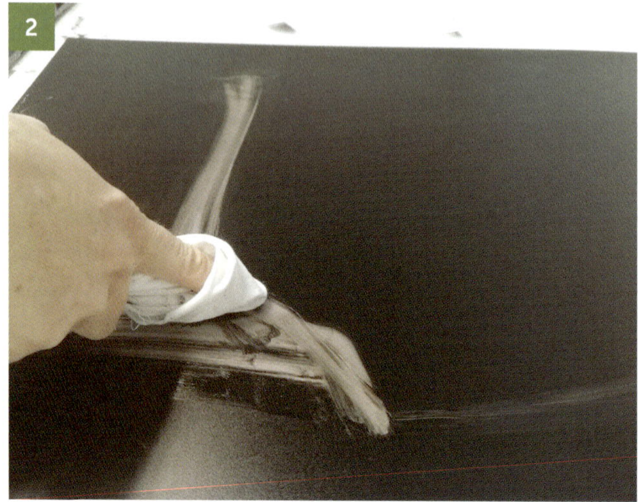

Using a rag, wipe away any areas where you want no ink, or rag texture.

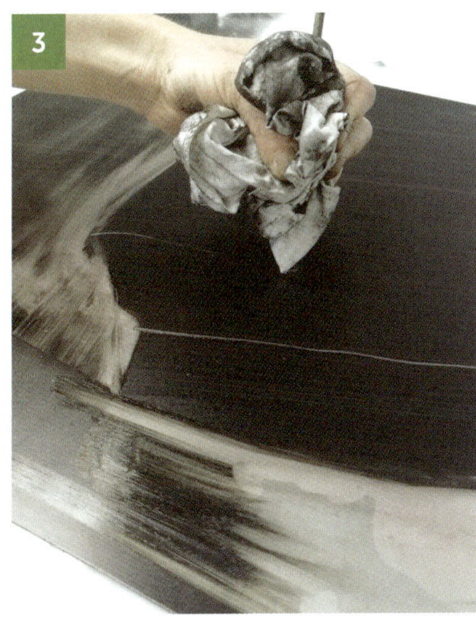

A rag wrapped around a stick makes a great ink removal tool.

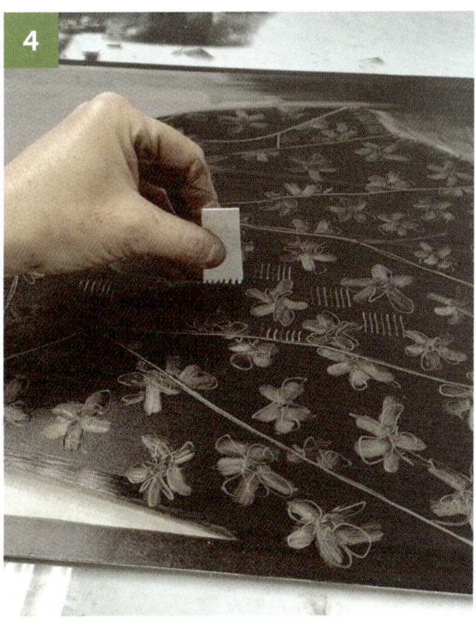

Making custom card scrapers produces an effective texture.

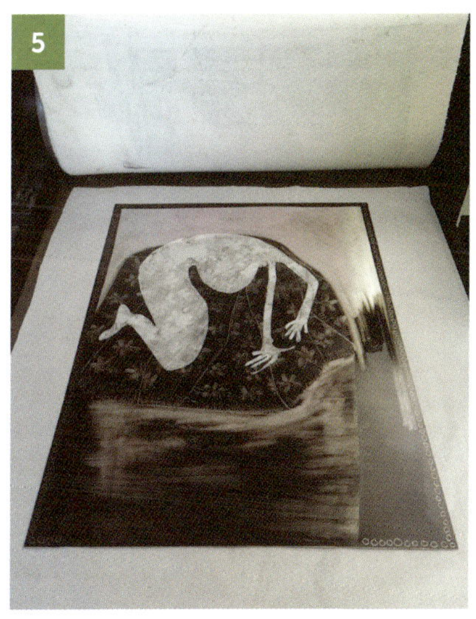

Place any tissue paper masks before printing to stop ink transfer.

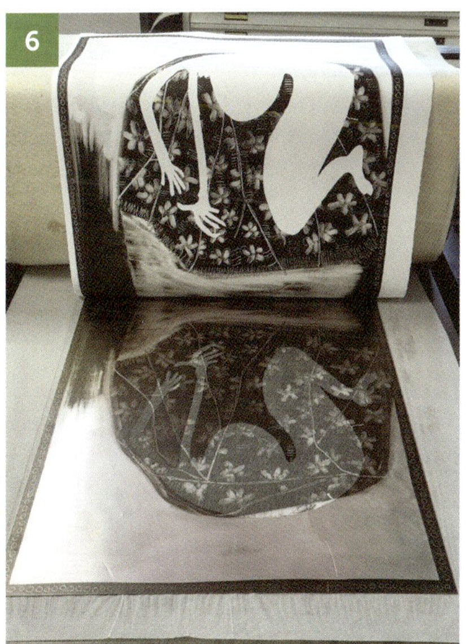

The first layer of the monoprint produces rich blacks.

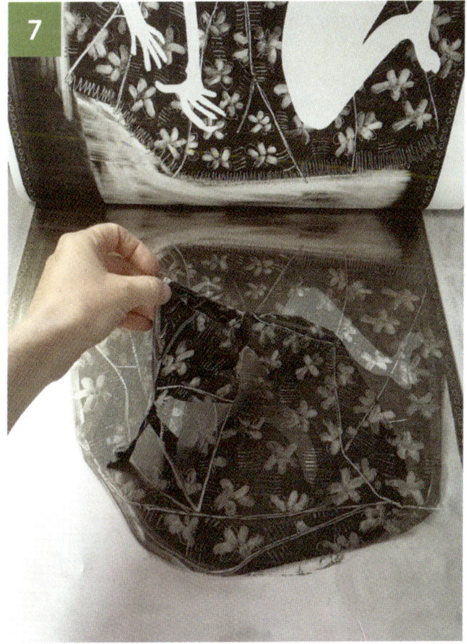

With paper trapped, peel away tissue mask without moving aluminium print.

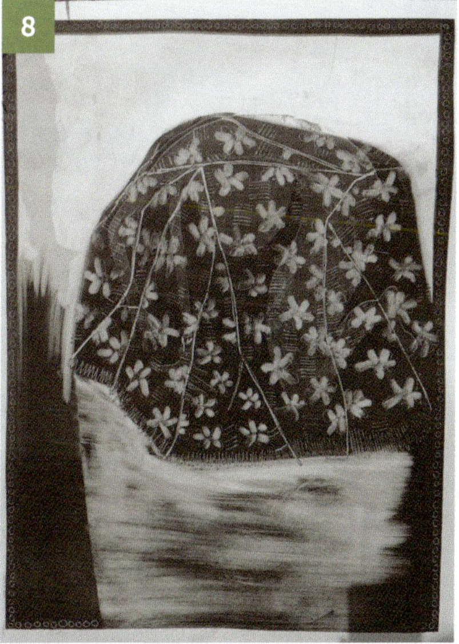

The black and ghost area clearly visible on the completed print.

HAND PRINTING A MONOPRINT

Using an etching press certainly makes for ease of printing a large-scale print, as well as creating a full range of tonal values from the ghost to the rich black. However, as we all work in different circumstances, a press is not always possible to access. You can hand print a monoprint to a good level of detail, and in fact add some effects that are not achievable under a press. It becomes harder to hand print the ghost impressions purely because there is less ink on the matrix and so the pressure required to transfer this onto an impression is a lot higher. Not impossible, but just requires more strength. Hand printing a monoprint as used in the reductive monoprint example will work better if you use a lighter weight paper. In essence there is less fibre for you to have to force the pressure through to generate an impression. Asia makes some beautiful lightweight washi papers that are also supremely strong and can withstand the rubbing of a printing baren on the back. A nice range of weight to start with is between 30gsm and 80gsm. Washi papers have a 'correct' printing side, which is the smoother side by feel. This does not mean that you cannot print on the other, rougher, side, it is just something to note if you wish to use the side made for printing on. When printing using the lightweight papers, you do not need to dampen them. You should get a good impression dry. If wishing to work on a heavier weight European paper, you can hand print onto pre-soaked and blotted paper. It will help with lifting more detail from your matrix but you do need to work with a little haste to avoid the paper drying.

You will also need to add a piece of greaseproof or tissue paper between the baren and the damp print. This prevents the damp impression paper from rucking up.

Adding relief textures

A monoprint can also integrate surface texture from other materials. Anything that can hold a relief layer of ink can transfer a mark. This relates back to the hand stamping in Chapter 3, but you can also ink up surfaces and run them

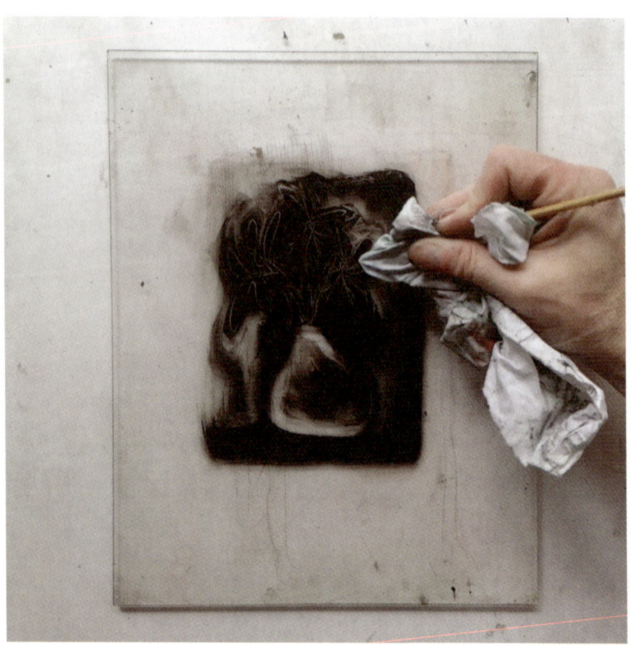

Using a variety of tools to remove ink from the surface.

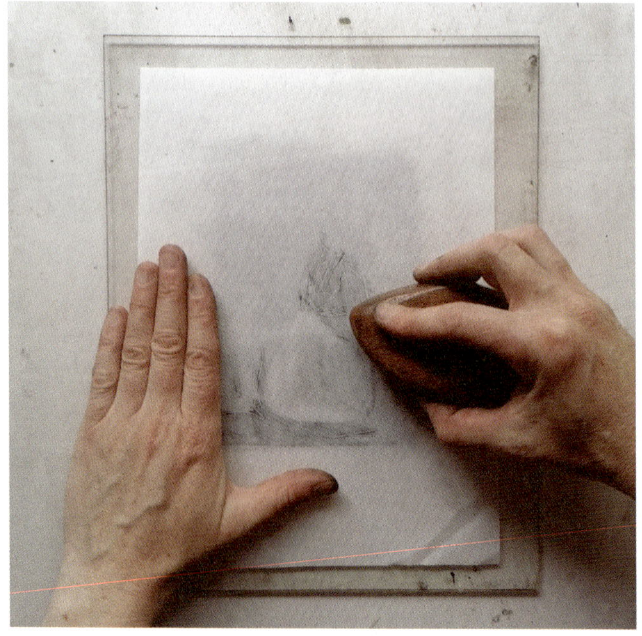

Using a wooden baren to hand print from the back.

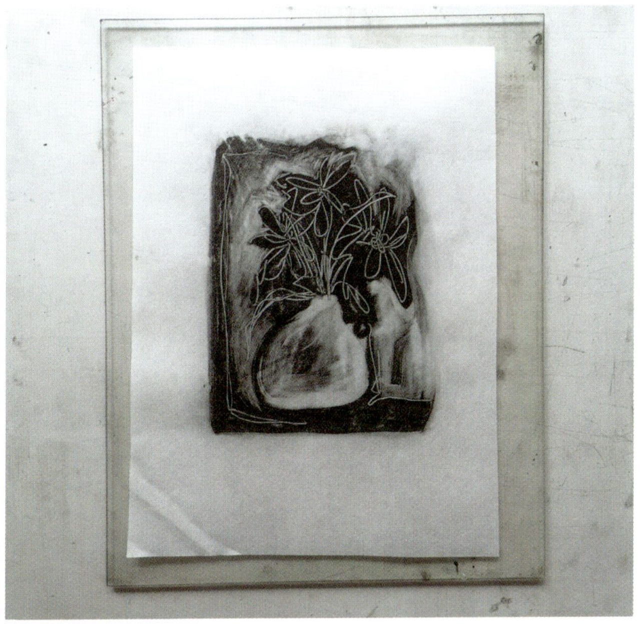

The completed hand-printed monoprint has wonderful energy.

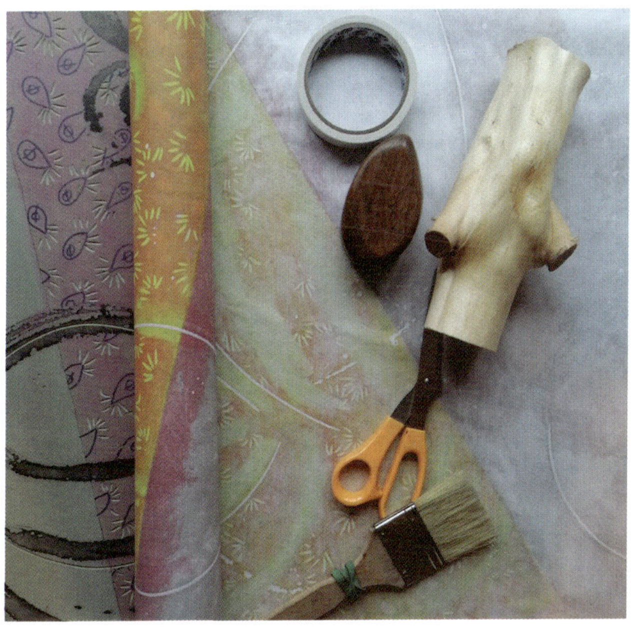

Hand printing barens can range from the traditional to the unusual such as logs, scissors or tape roll edges.

through an etching press to great effect. Do always make sure that the materials contain no metal and that the press is set to the correct pressure for their depth. It is a very intuitive and free way of adding texture and expression to a print. You can always start with the black background we have been looking at, add some reductive marks and then add in some inked relief textures before printing. Inked up corrugated card, textured wallpaper, thin thread all work really well and allow you to place them directly onto the printing matrix before creating the impression.

Baren choice

The tool you choose to transfer pressure with is unique in its own right. Every baren will create a different type of mark and texture. Some will print flats better than others. Some will be able to generate super high pressure for ghost printing, others will have a particular nook that makes a particular nooky mark. When hand printing, the baren should be seen like the paintbrush, just as getting to know and use a press is the tool of a printer's trade. Anything that transfers pressure is seen as a baren. This could be a traditional printing baren or it could be a stone. It could be a handmade wooden baren or it could be a metal teaspoon. It is worth trying out some different ones to see how they affect the impression. A great way to explore this is to roll up an area of very thin black ink (I mean barely there), lay paper on top and use the baren to apply pressure to the back. You will be able to fully explore the mark-making potentials this way.

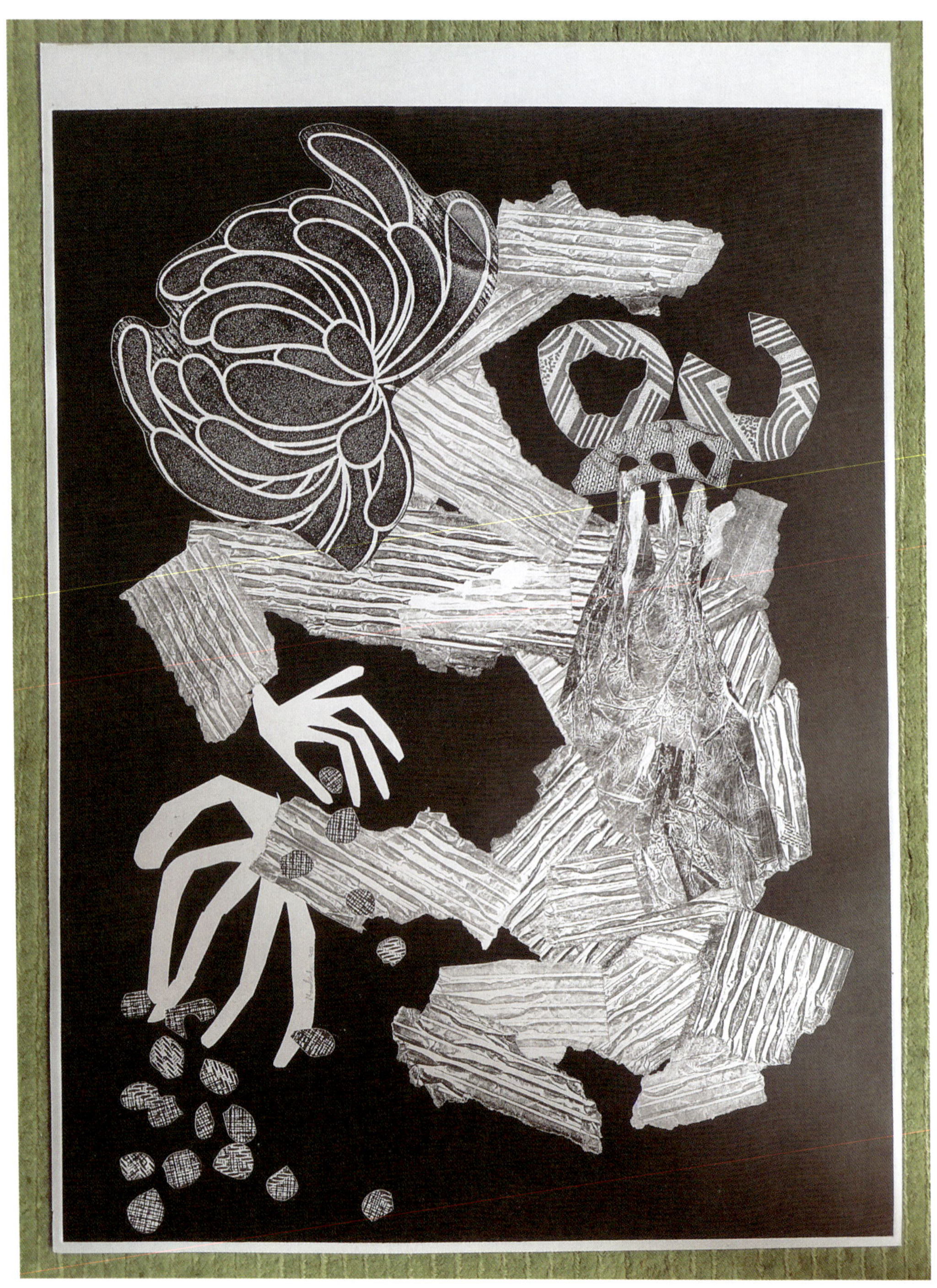

A monoprint with relief textures of wallpaper and card. *Greed* (2023), Mary Dalton.

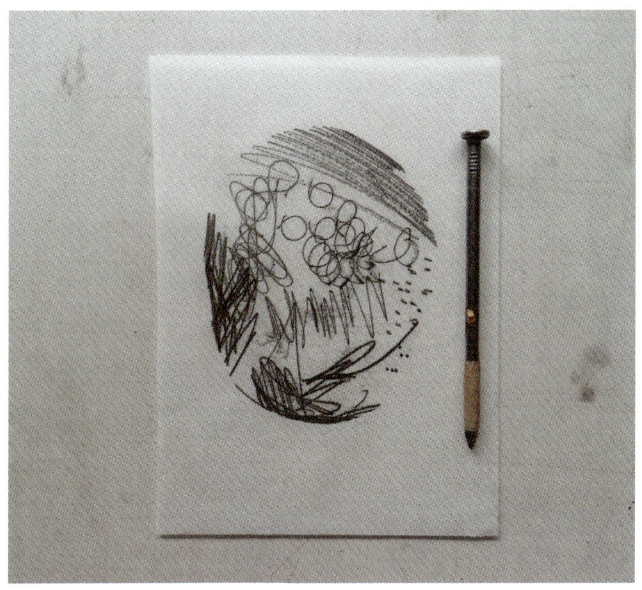

Fine line effects achieved by hand printing with a nail.

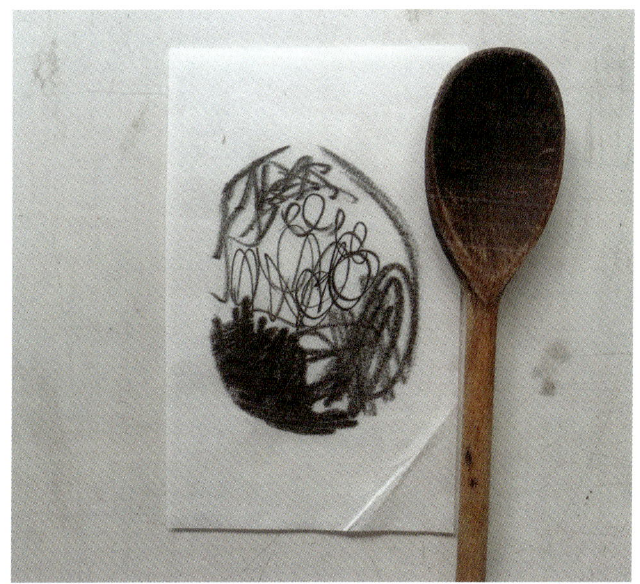

A lovely range of marks made with a wooden spoon.

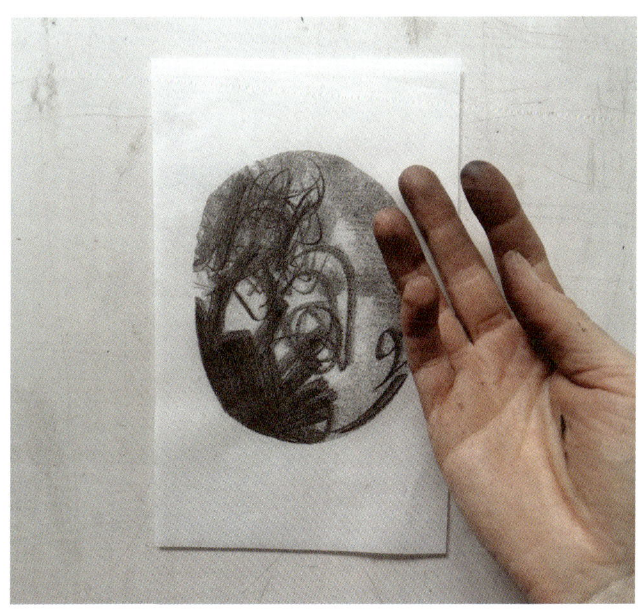

Your hands can make some wonderful ephemeral marks.

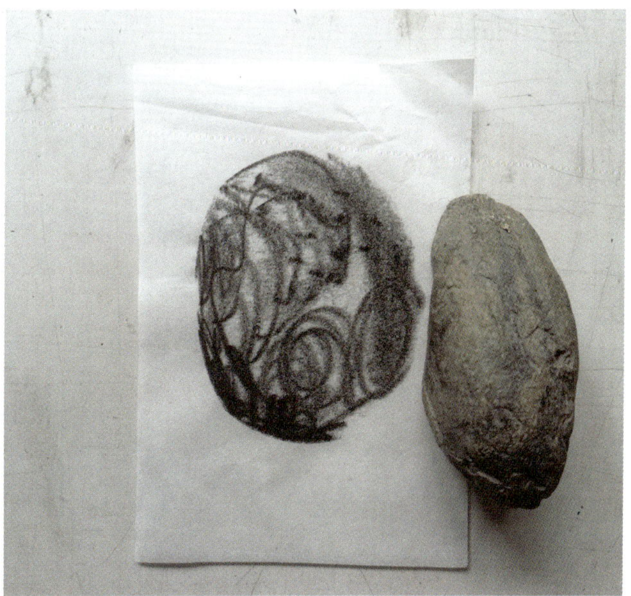

Printing with a textured rock is always interesting.

HAND-PRINTED MULTI-LAYERED MONOCHROME MONOPRINT

I could not think of a better way to describe the following demonstration, so I thought the tongue twister of a title would create intrigue! In this demonstration we will be creating an impression over multiple layers of monochrome monoprint. We will be hand printing all layers over the top of each other, creating an impression of depth and intrigue. I would strongly advise working with a Japanese washi to ease off on the shoulder work required for the heavyweight paper.

Materials
Aluminium sheet or equivalent for monoprint
Washi paper (I am working with a 39gsm paper)
Printing barens of choice
Black ink and inking-up surface
Mark-making tools for the monoprint

Single-pull monoprint in colour
Working on from the reductive monochrome print, we are going to look at creating a technicolour single-pull monoprint. This technique often appeals to painters because of the directness of colour application. In essence, it is as simple as applying coloured ink to the aluminium surface where you want it and building up your image using tools to create texture and surface design. Many monoprint artists will resort to solvents to dilute their inks to create thinner washes. I use thin or weak copperplate oil to increase the flow of the inks to allow for a smoother painting process. This contrasts beautifully when used with a more viscous sticky ink that is harder to manipulate. Playing with the ink texture is a fun way to generate life and energy on the flat plane of a printed image. It is also

important to note that when adding colours to your aluminium plate, your layering is backwards. What you as the artist see in the plate will actually be the layer that is in contact with the paper first, and thus at the back. The first ink that was laid down is actually the ink that will be sitting at the front of the paper. Do bear this in mind in layering up colour. Some artists will resort back to a piece of clear plastic at this stage for their monoprint surface, enabling them to lift it up and look at the underside to see a true reflection of how it will print. I like to live life on the edge a little, as much as is possible in monoprinting, working using skill, technique and an acceptance of the beauty of imperfection, and stick with the aluminium which will not allow me to do this.

Secondly, a single-pull colour monoprint works at its finest when the colours and forms are kept bold and distinct. Too much mixing on the palette of oil-based printing inks and they can readily muddy, losing that beautiful clarity that they are renowned for.

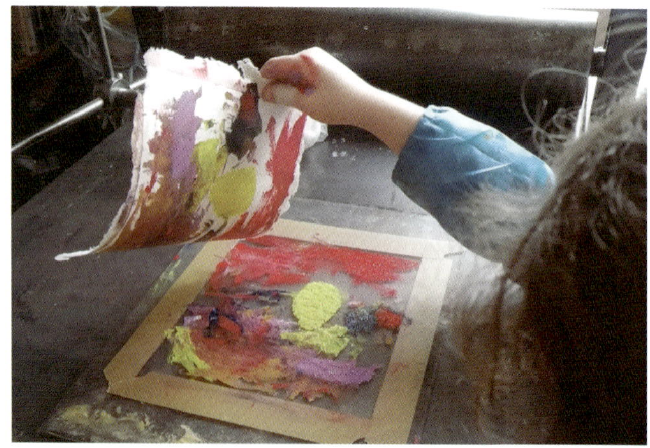

Rose pulling a grand reveal of her beautiful colour monoprint.

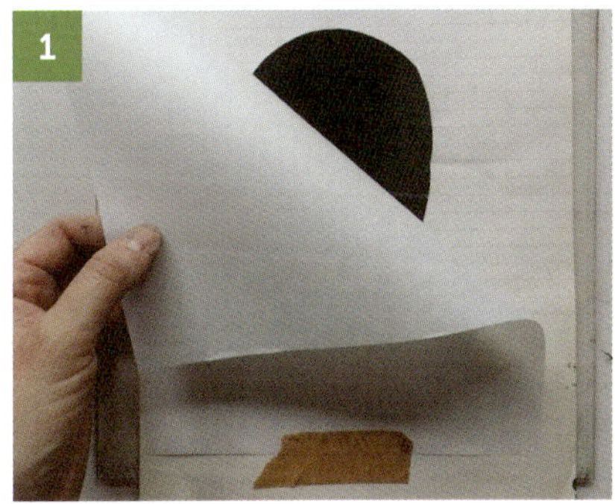

Make a mask to lay over your black ink and tape paper on top.

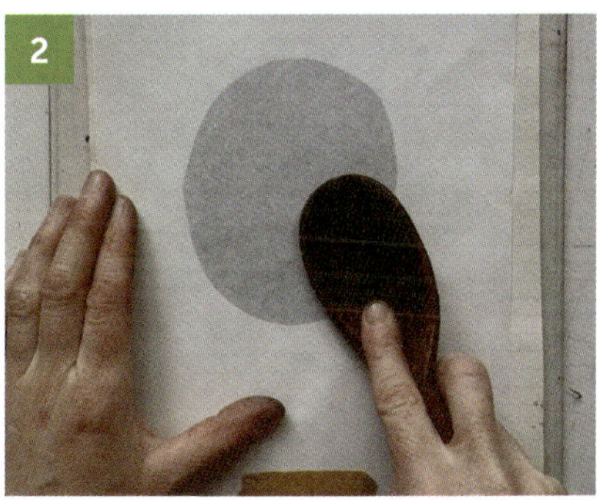

Using a baren of choice, make the first marks very lightly.

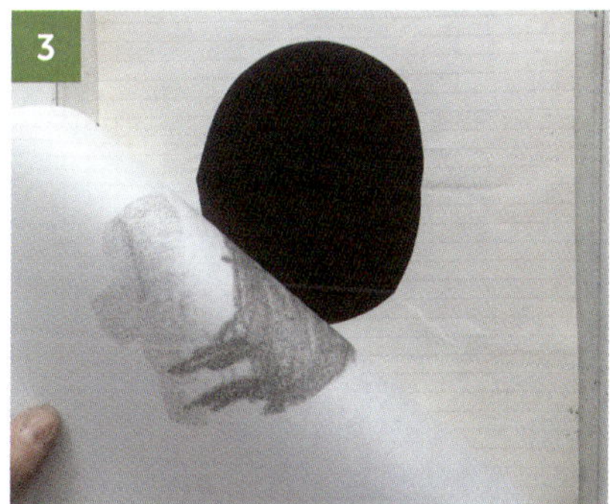

Keeping paper taped in place, carefully peel paper and mask off.

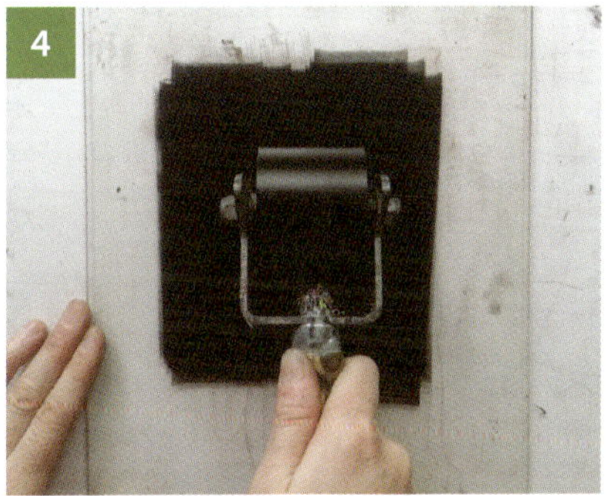

Re-apply a thin layer of black ink to the surface.

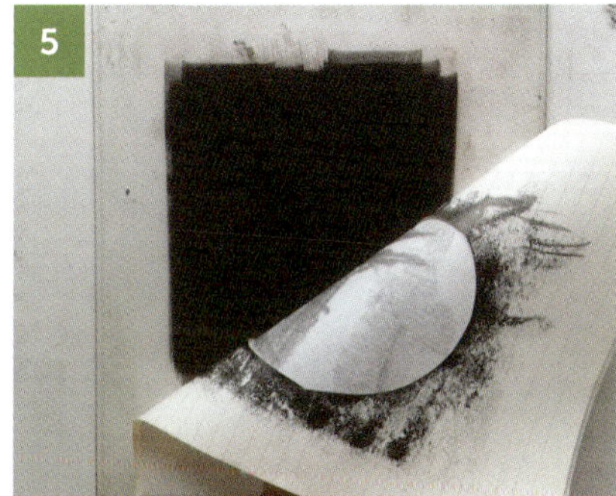

Place the mask and paper back on top of the ink.

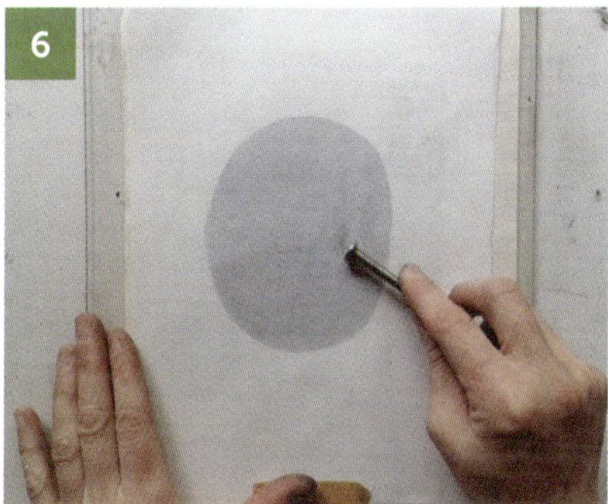

Use a secondary baren to make stronger, denser black marks.

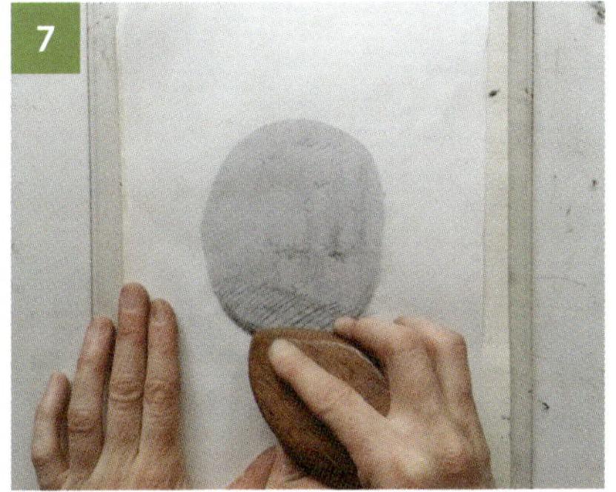

Repeat mask removal, ink and hand printing with third baren.

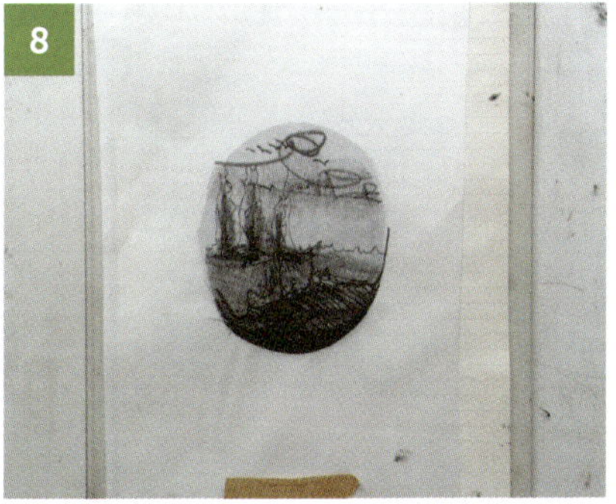

The completed hand-layered monoprint with tonal variance.

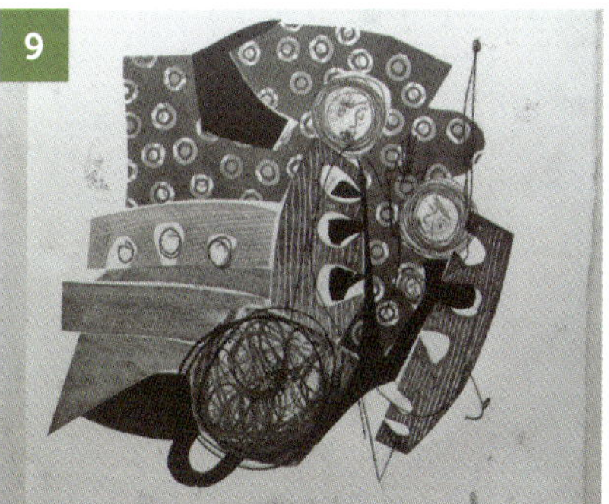

A further example of a multi-layered monoprint utilising the ghost and baren pressure. *Sea Harvest*, Mary Dalton.

WATERCOLOUR COLOUR MONOPRINT

Working with oil-based printing inks is a wonderful layering process, enabling you to print and build up transparent and overlapping layers. However, if you are wishing to generate bold impressions of a single layer, then there is another way that is equally vivid and dynamic. If you create a drawing with water-soluble media, and then print this onto dampened paper, the drawing is re-ignited under the pressure of the press to create a sumptuous impression. This is really a single-pull print because you are unable to re-dampen the paper to print subsequent layers without the water-based media running everywhere. However, it is a great way of working. Furthermore, from an ecological perspective, you can readily trace and track the pigments used in water-based media as with oil-based inks, and it is even easier to make your own watercolours or goauche from pigments. Water-based pencils and crayons are pretty ecologically clean, depending on the pigments used. Key to this method of working is to create your drawing on draughting film, or True-Grain. This is a piece of plastic that has a textured side made up of a microscopic grain. The grain allows you to draw with crayons, pencils and even watercolour washes without it pooling too much. Although plastic, this surface can be re-used again and again by just cleaning and drying. Although you cannot re-dampen the paper, this water-based monoprint creates some beautiful effects that could be used as an under print for techniques that print onto dry paper, such as lino or other relief work. The draughting film can simply be washed clean after use and re-used.

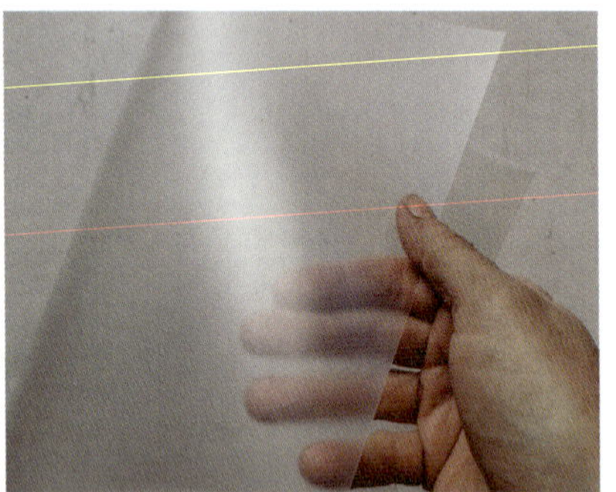

Draughting film allows for wet washes be replicated.

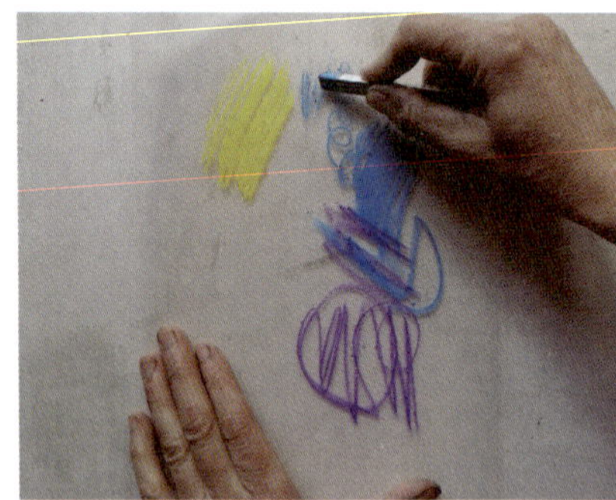

Draw with watercolour pencils or crayons onto the grained surface.

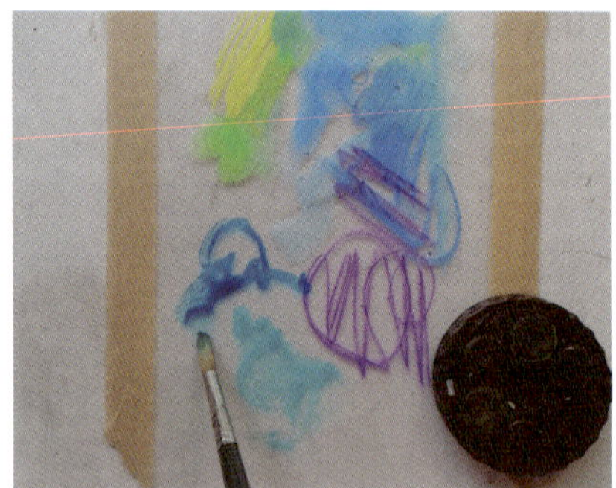

Add tape at edges to flatten and add any wet washes.

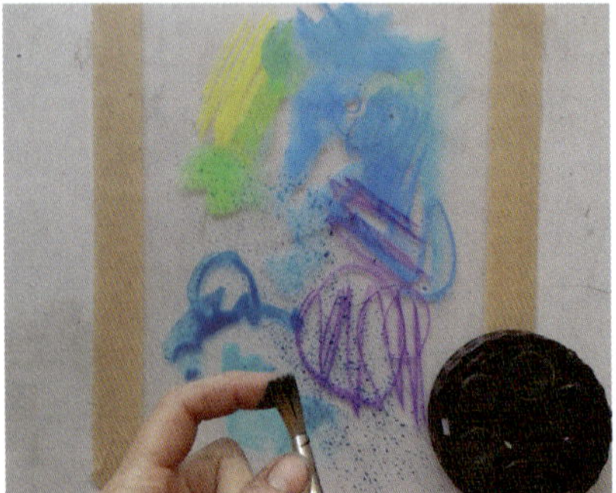

Have fun with splatters and other watery marks.

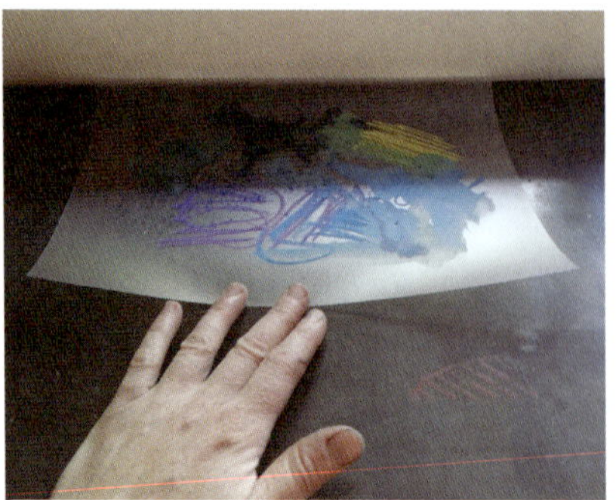

Marks side up, print on *damp* paper and at high pressure.

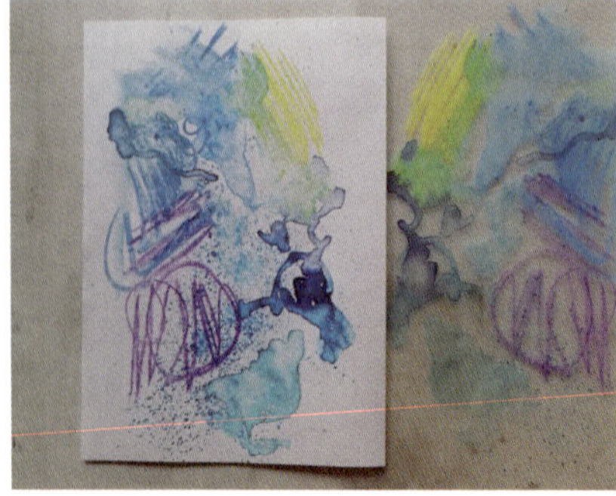

The completed vibrant single-pull watercolour monoprint.

VISCOSITY ROLLS

Viscosity rolls are a bit like sushi rolls. Really, they are – you layer them, you mix them and then you put them all together in a single print and all the ingredients work together to make a beautiful end result. Viscosity printing is a wonder to printmaking that allows the artist to apply layers of fine colour to build an image that gets printed in a single pull. Viscosity printing takes its name from the change in viscosity, or oiliness and thus texture, of the inks you are using. The altered viscosity of each layer means that when applying the new ink with altered viscosity, it will not mix and muddy the previous layer of ink when you roll over the top, because the two viscosities repel each other rather than mix together. For instance, if you did a black reductive monoprint on a sheet of aluminium and then wished to apply a yellow background, you can use viscosity printing. The yellow ink used will need a few drops of copperplate oil added to alter its viscosity when compared to the black you have used. This yellow then gets rolled out in a thin layer and rolled directly over the top of the black monoprint created on the aluminium plate. If the viscosity mix has worked well, then none of the black ink will pick up on the yellow roller, and the yellow will sit cleanly on top of the black allowing for a yellow background with black monoprint.

The viscosity technique is fantastic for adding a single-colour roll over as we have just explored, but it can also be used to add multiple layers of colour on the same print. As long as each ink is adjusted to alter its viscosity from your previous layer, you can in theory get many a beautiful layer of colour building up. It works very well for monoprinting when used in conjunction with masks or direct ink application between each layer. Viscosity printing is a method of print you have to do rather than read about, as it makes far more sense when feeling and looking at the inks. It really is very much like cooking!

VISCOSITY ROLL TARGET PRINT

A fun exercise to get used to adjusting ink viscosity and rolling clean layers. Printing under a press will give you the best result, but as with a lot of printing methods, you may also hand print this.

Materials
Yellow, red, blue and black ink
Roller and inking set up
Thin/weak copperplate oil
Paper suitable for mask making, such as thin cartridge
Damp printing paper
Aluminium sheet for monoprint

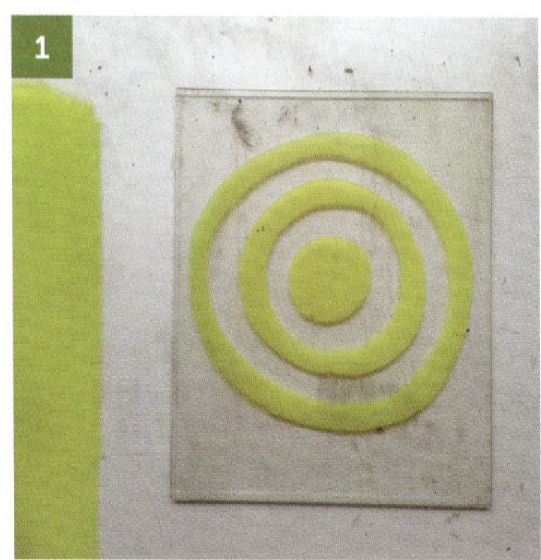

Roll on Perspex with a thin yellow and remove ink as described.

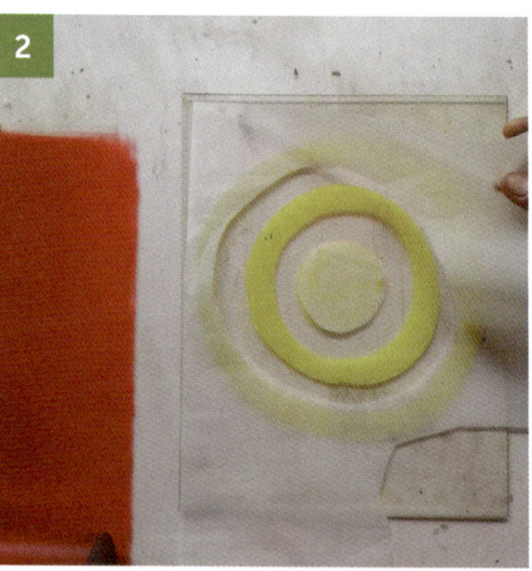

Place tissue paper masks as positioned to protect yellow.

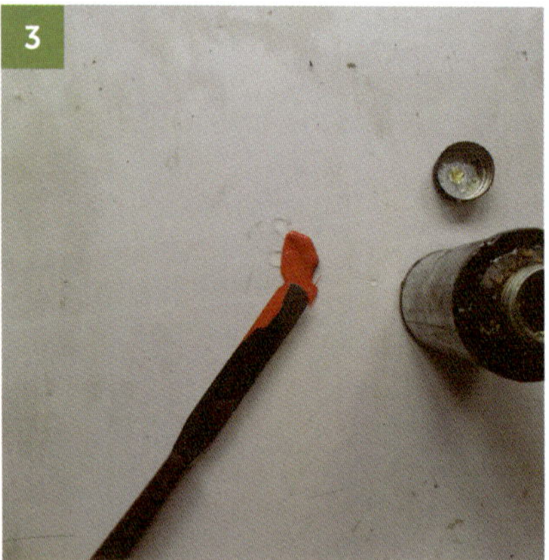

Add two drops of weak copperplate oil to the red and roll out.

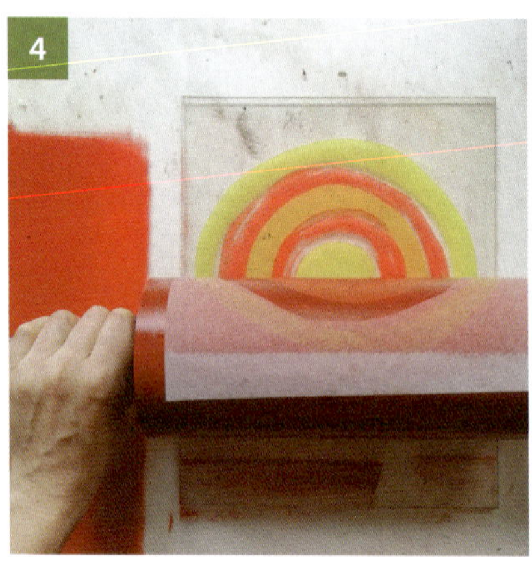

Firmly and slowly roll over with red once, pulling masks off.

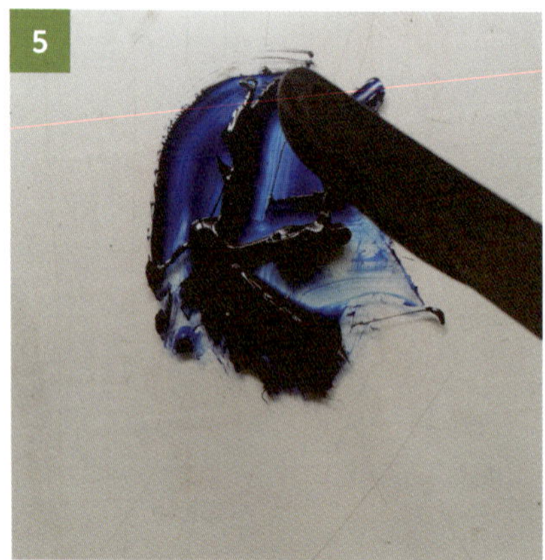

Loosen the blue with four drops of weak copperplate oil.

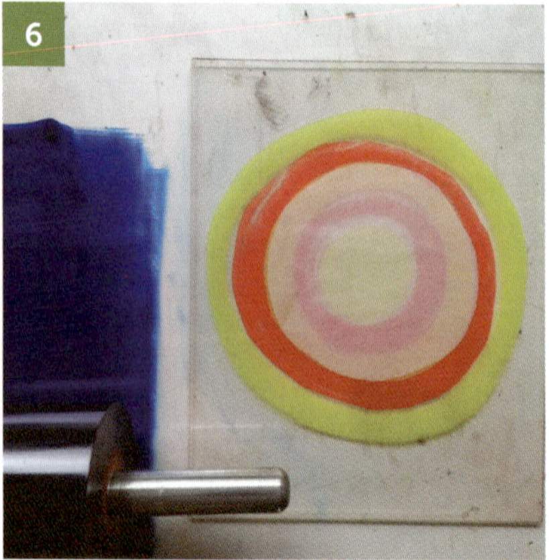

Add masks to the matrix as described.

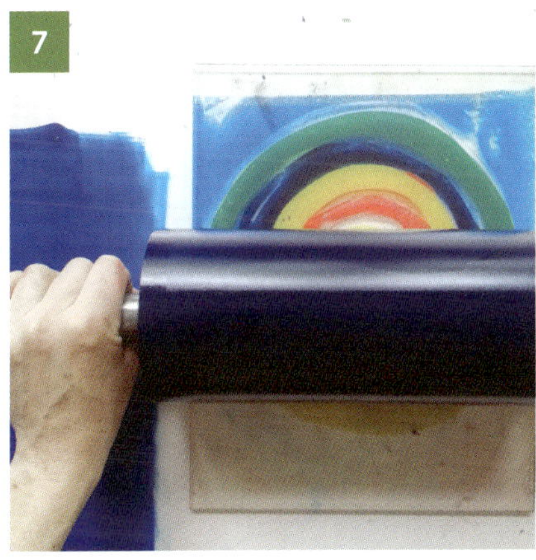

Roll over once with the blue ink.

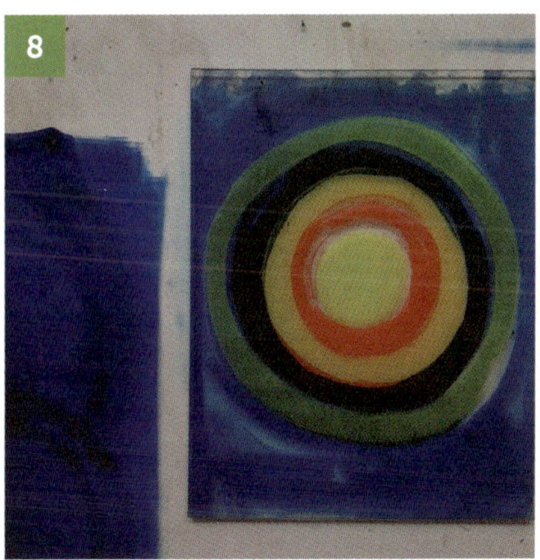

Ahead of printing, remove any blue background with a rag.

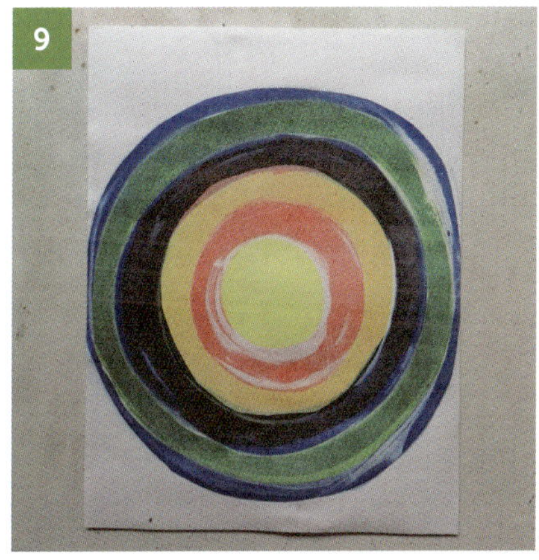

The completed viscosity target print showing colour overlays.

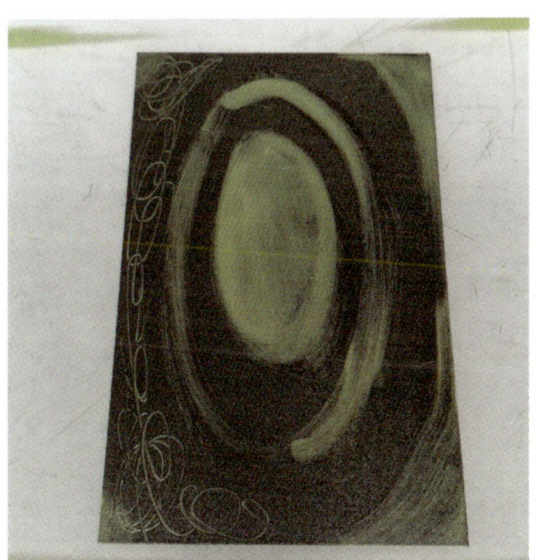

A black monoprint with a clean yellow roll over, ready for printing.

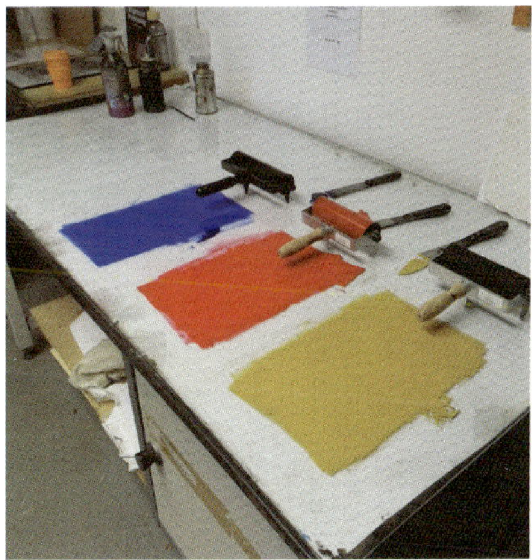

A set-up of four different viscosity rolls in preparation to roll.

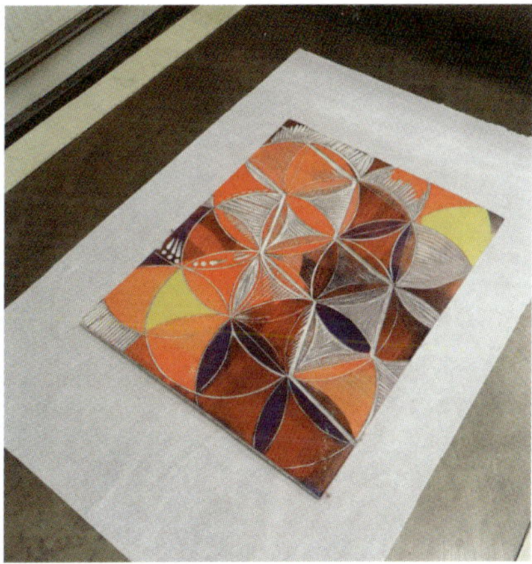

Viscosity rolls applied on the surface of lino cut. Rags used in between each layer to remove ink.

MULTI-PLATE MONOPRINT

Printing a single-pull monoprint with all the tools and tricks available to you is incredibly satisfying. Nothing quite like achieving a result in a singular pull. But we can also have a lot of fun with multiple plates, which all get printed on top of each other on the same impression to generate a multi-plate monoprint. This is really exciting and allows for more shapes and forms to overlap cleanly without the colours mixing on the aluminium plate. It does require a little bit of thought to ascertain which plates are going to affect which other plates, and which colours are going to overlap, generating another colour. But once you get into the swing of multi-plate work, it is very dynamic.

As with all the previous monoprints, I am going to work on aluminium plates. It does pose challenging questions with regards to registration because I am working without a guide drawing which ordinarily would be on the back of a piece of plastic to allow the artist to know where to add colours and shapes in relationship to the overall image. I like to think of this as a benefit because I am working more fluidly, using instinct and my judgement to build up the layers. If something is not pinpoint registered, I feel this is actually a benefit and adds life to an otherwise

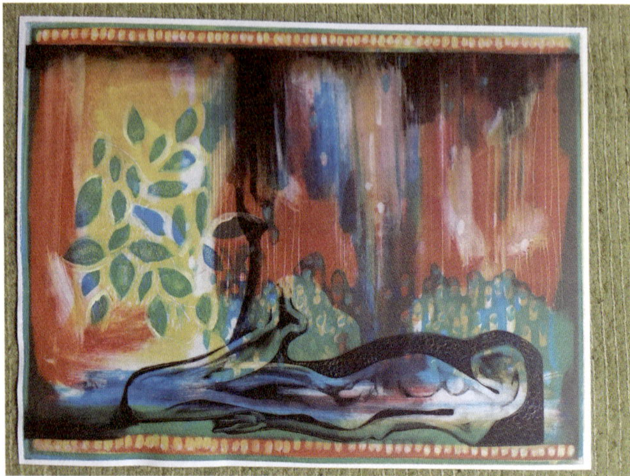

A four-colour multi-plate monoprint is exciting and dynamic. *In the Rain Again* (2022), Mary Dalton.

very controlled and static print. It allows for the human element of chance.

The paper must remain trapped under the rollers between each pull, to prevent slippage and mis-registration. Thus, if working on damp paper, you must be speedy during printing to prevent paper drying and have all your plates prepared ahead of printing.

Alternative registration

If you get really interested in the multi-plate monoprint technique and wish to register to a more precise level, there is an alternative. A sheet of clear plastic or thin acetate will enable you to see precisely what you are drawing and what areas you are removing. Albeit a sheet of plastic, if you re-use it numerous times and look after it well it should last a lifetime. I suppose one of the many balancing acts that an ecologically aware artist has to make is the weighing up of the material used over the shelf life for any given material. If you were to dispose of a sheet of acrylic each time you used it, that would certainly be a negligent approach to any care for the planet. However, if you invest in one sheet of acrylic or draughting film and clean and re-use this multiple times, that is a great use of a material.

I would invest in draughting film because the grain would enable fine work that acrylic may not. It can go under a heavy top-roller etching press without having to reset any pressure or add runners. You can purchase it in a larger sheet enabling work at scale, and if cleaned up well you can also use it for the watercolour techniques. You are able to hold it over your master drawing or layout plan to enable you to see where you are to add ink information, or you can draw directly onto the back with chinagraph pencils so that you always have a reference layout for your work.

If you wish to work on a colour layered monoprint but without the multi-plate registration troubles, you can use the viscosity rolling technique to produce multiple colours in a single pull. Instead of the very gestural painting style monoprint, this works with clean layer building on top of one another, a bit like layers of acetate. We will look at this as a step-by-step example.

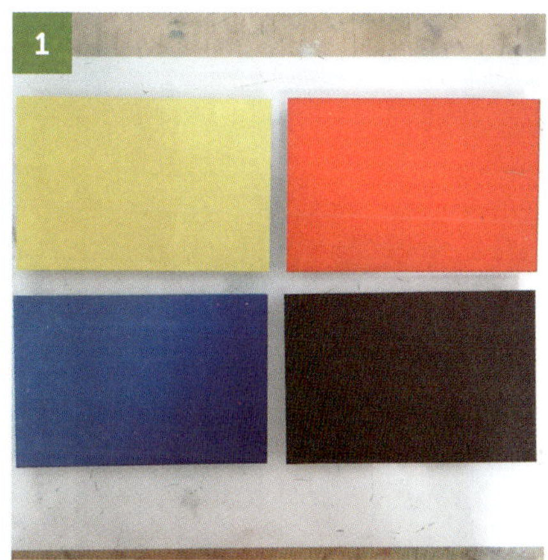

All the colours to be worked with, inked up on aluminium.

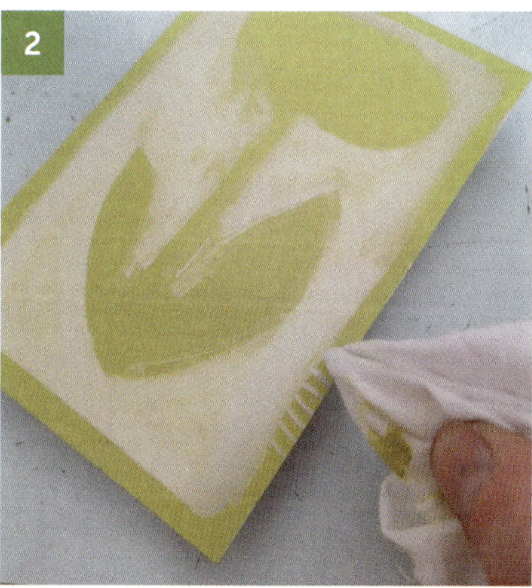

Each plate is worked separately, thinking ahead of colour overlays.

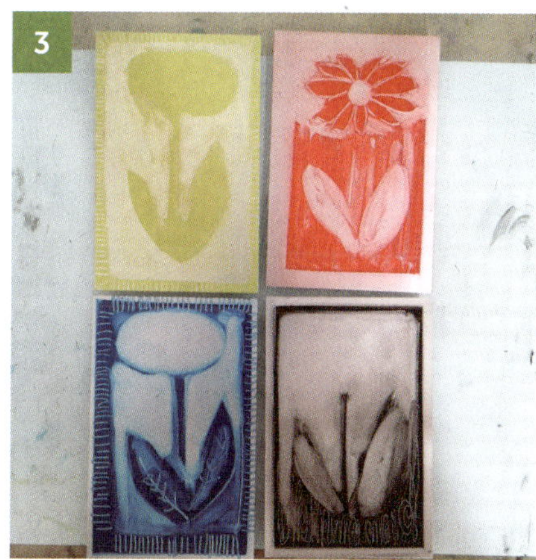

The completed matrices ready for printing.

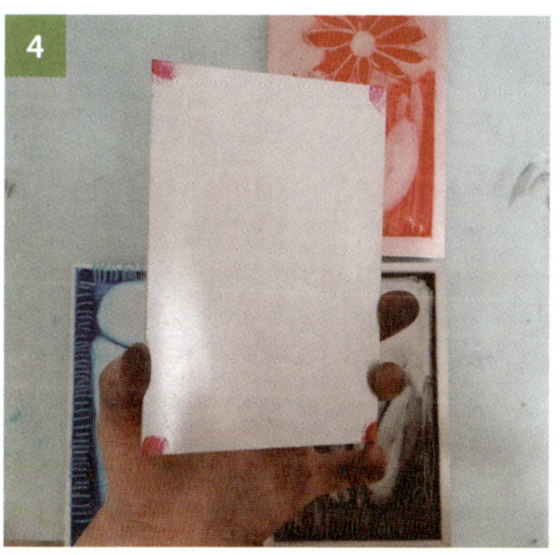

Adding thin finger marks to plate corners for registration.

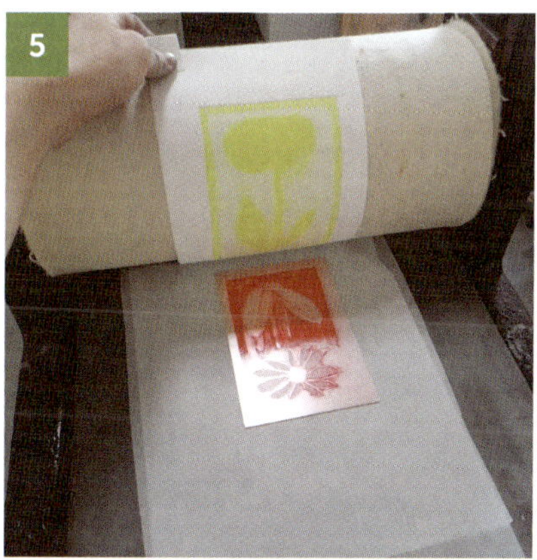

Yellow printed, add red plate in register on finger marks, print.

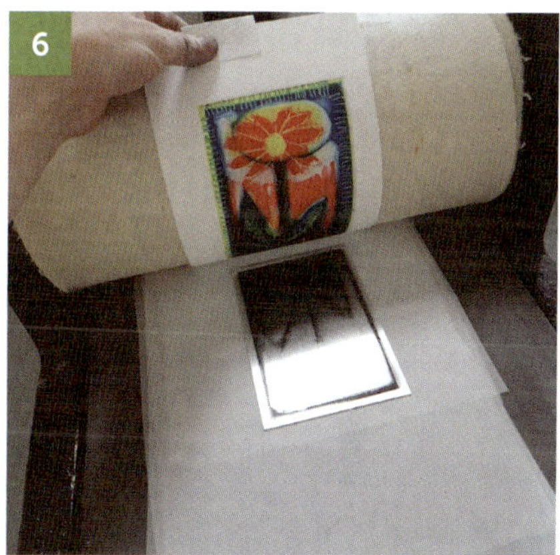

Repeat this process with remaining two plates to reveal print.

SINGLE-PULL COLOUR MONOPRINT

Materials

Sheet of A5 aluminium
Yellow, red, blue, black oil-based inks
Roller and set-up for rolling up
Rags and similar reductive monoprint items
Weak copperplate oil
Palette knives
Paper
Etching press

Having a play with colour monoprint layering techniques is great training in understanding colour theory and the nature of printing ink layers. The colour that you mix may be true to form on white paper, but when added on top of the other impression layers it can change dramatically. This is the beauty of oil-based printing ink, allowing for all that richness and colour strength.

Incorporating monoprint

Monoprint does not always have to be a stand-alone method. The wonderful thing about a monoprint is that it can be incorporated into many other methods of printmaking. If we are to look at the monoprint from a technical perspective, then in essence pretty much all the works and techniques demonstrated in this book are monoprints. They are singular (mono) prints that, due to the complex nature and expressive qualities, are not able to be editioned. This may even include some of the lino work in Chapter 3. However, this could get very confusing and would promptly stop any printmaking family tree discussions with fellow printmakers. Thus, the way I tend to approach it is that, for instance, lino is capable of editioning hundreds of times, but the artist has chosen not to, so it is a unique lino cut. The processes of monoprint as discussed in this chapter are incapable of ever being editioned, thus purely is a monoprint. It prevents arguments!

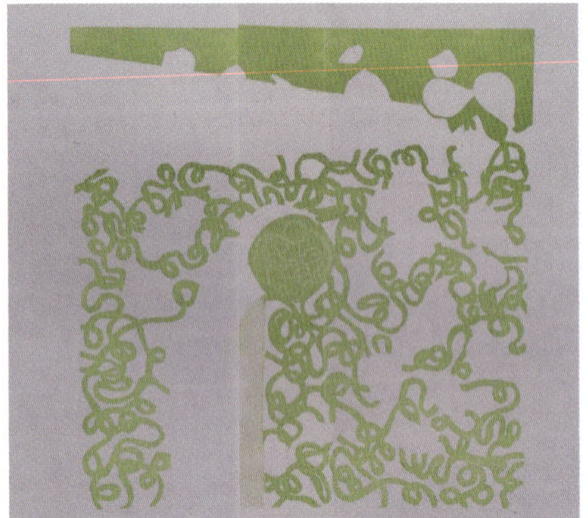

A green layer lino cut for a hybrid print, shown on white paper.

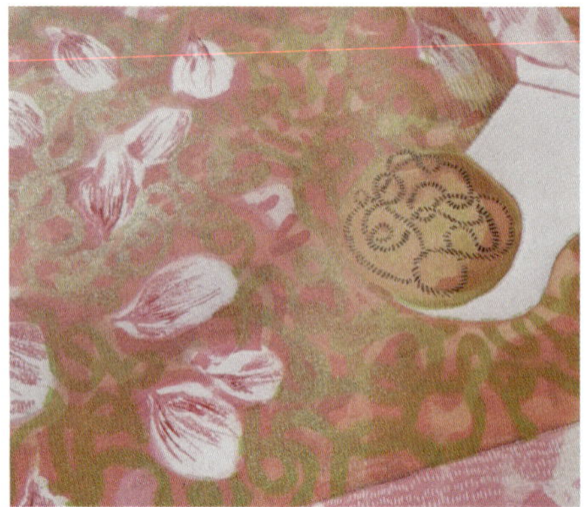

The same green layer printed on the pink impression has changed in colour.

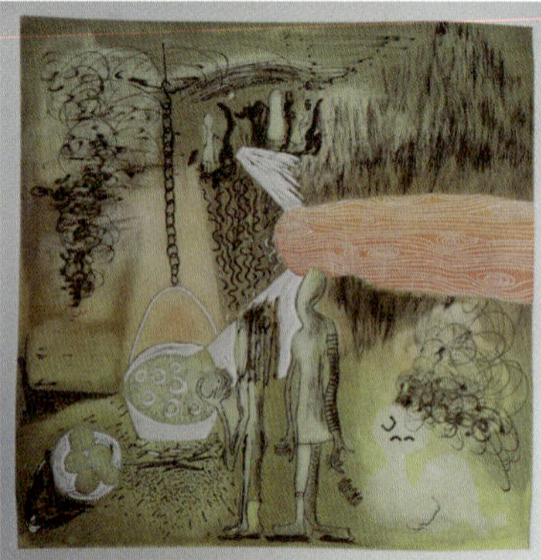

A complex lithino, lino intaglio print with monoprint viscosity rolls.

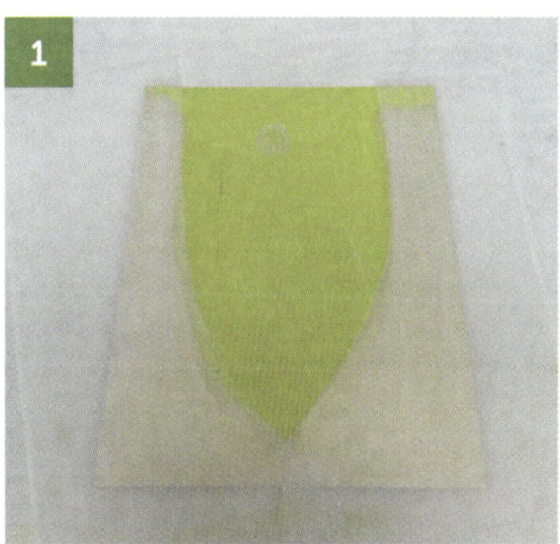

Make a yellow shape on your aluminium with roller and rags.

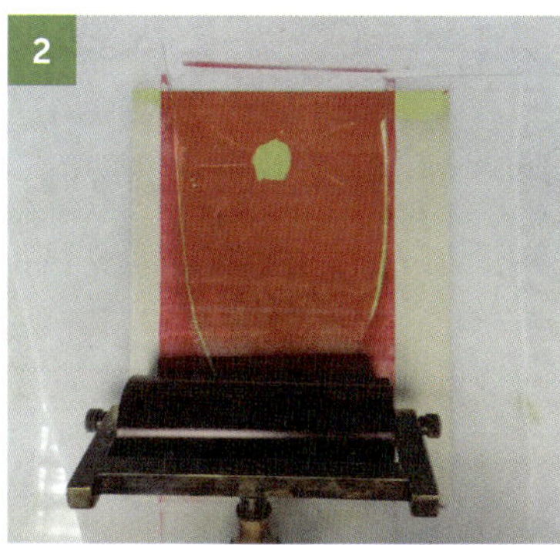

Mask off areas of the yellow and roll over a looser red.

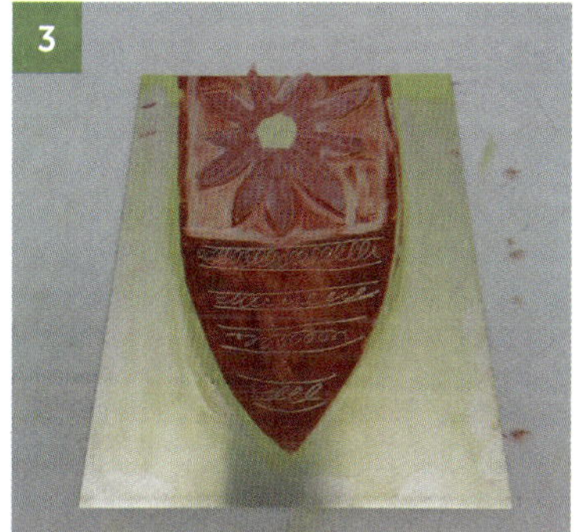

Remove tissue masks, remove areas of ink and add new masks.

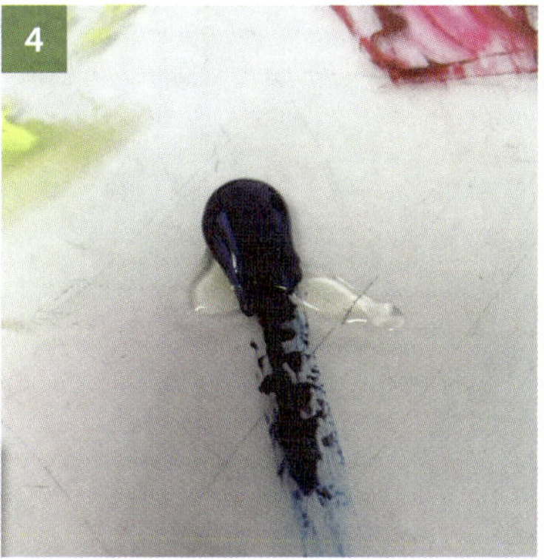

Change the viscosity of blue ink with weak plate oil.

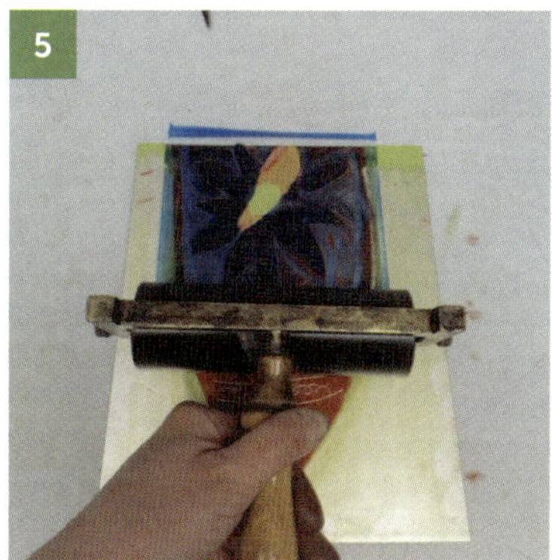

The completed single-pull viscosity print. Note clean colour overlay.

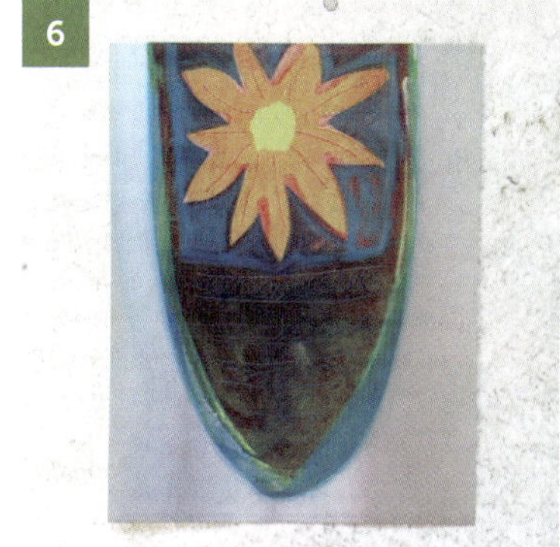

The matrix so far showcasing the colour overlays.

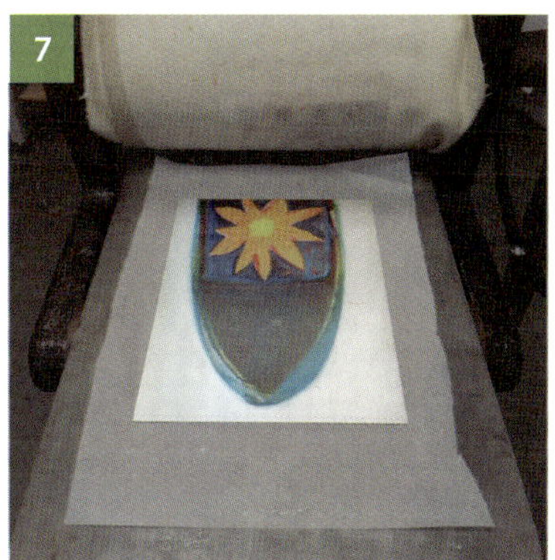

Print the matrix under an etching press with damp paper.

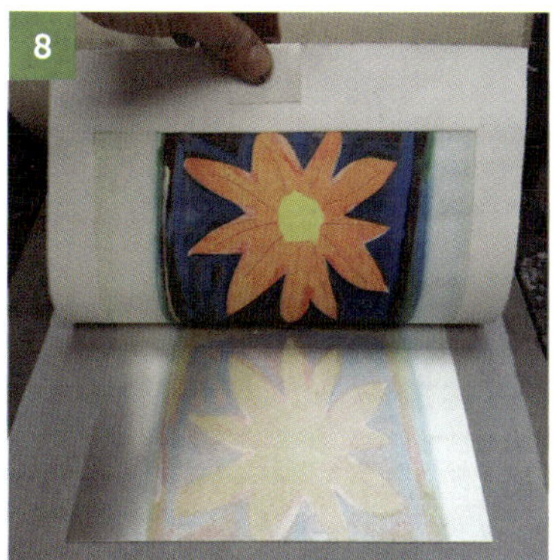

Carefully peel the impression off.

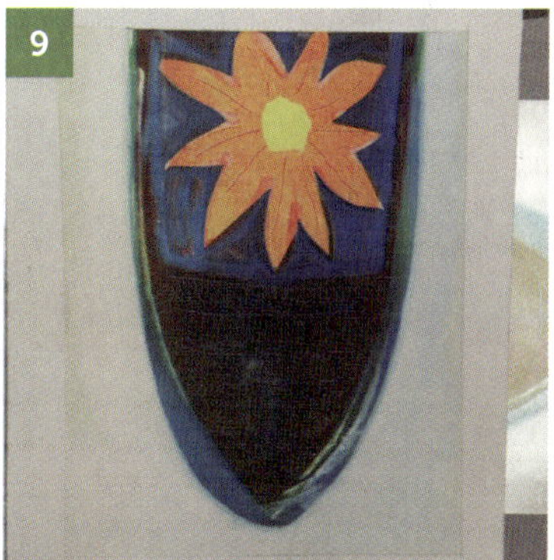

Roll over matrix in blue, revealing new colour overlays.

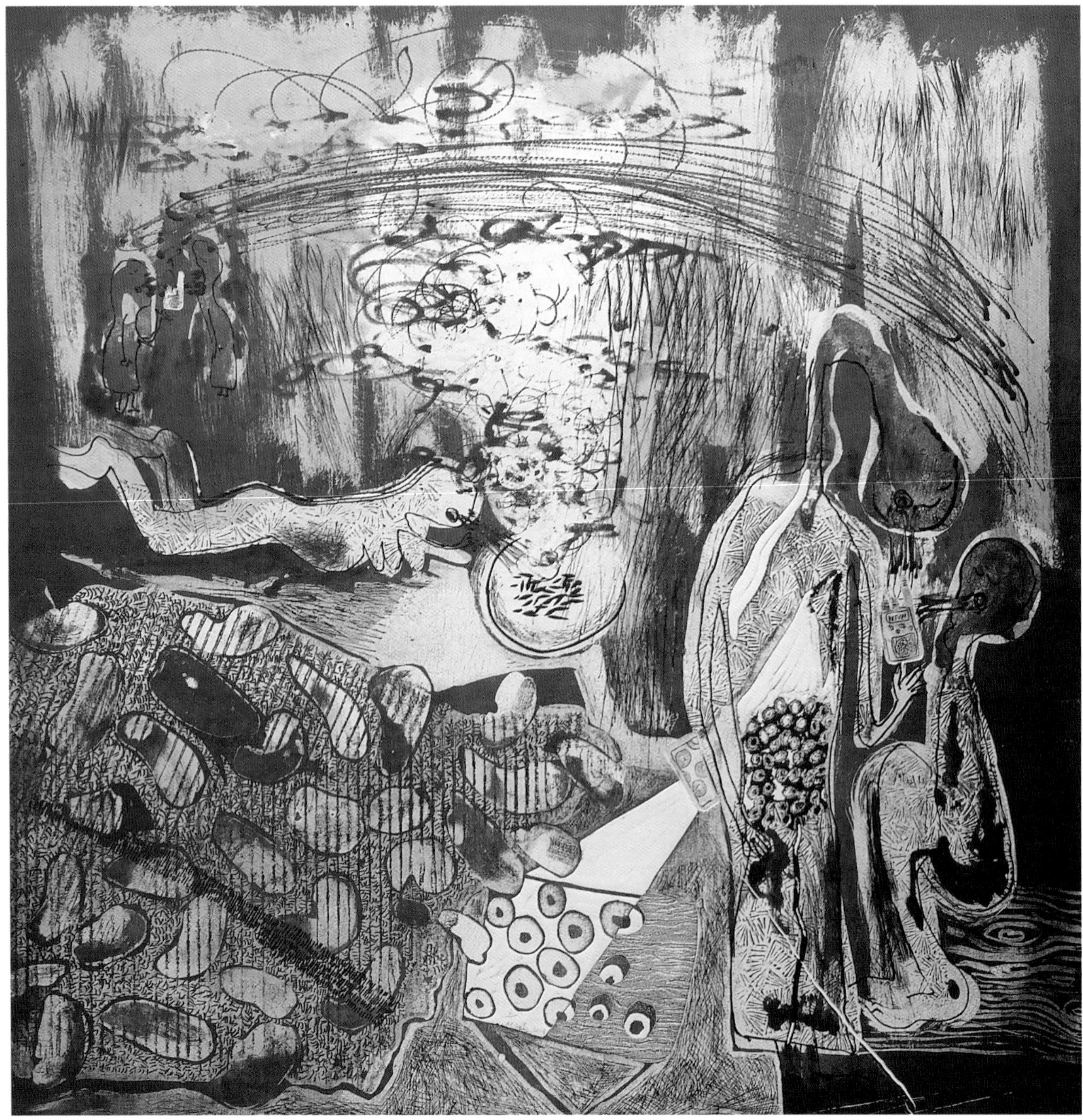

CHAPTER 5

THE MATRIX: ECOLOGICAL INTAGLIO

This chapter is a big one. Not necessarily in volume, but more so to try and emulate the effects that intaglio printmakers love so dearly, and indeed are so distinctive, but without all the hazards of many a toxic chemical. I hasten to add that to try to replicate the effects of a sugar lift, a steel plate etching black or a fine copper aquatint is impossible and indeed pointless; however, there are some intaglio approaches that can produce something that is worthwhile pursuing and investigating. Not only do these alternative methods generate some stunning results, they do so at no harm to the planet, do not involve digging up copper from mines around the world, and encourage the artist to explore, express and protect the planet.

COPPER MINING

I love etching and I love the beautiful results. The notion it can be editioned is neither here nor there from my perspective, but the effects of a sugar lift, a fine misty aquatint, or a deep scratchy line appeal to me immensely.

It took up years of my first training in print and years and years after to pursue until I was unable to work with the chemicals because of no adequate ventilation. So I started looking for alternatives. I always worked on steel because I liked the black you could achieve without an aquatint, but that stopped pretty much as soon as I could not work safely with nitric acid and I began questioning things more. However, many intaglio etchers choose copper, and the less toxic salts associated with it, and now as well aluminium for the apparently even less toxic approaches. Two major events happened that made me question both.

The first was a random discussion one day when having breakfast at a teaching residential. A hugely tall and broad gentleman came and sat with me over breakfast. He turned out to be the owner of a series of South African copper mines. He had recently given up his business because of the conditions of not only the land involved in the mining, but the treatment of the workers that were being sent to the mines. I will not go into details as they were pretty harrowing human rights violations. He may have been telling a series of falsities, and you should always investigate on your own terms. But the conversation got me thinking, researching and looking into the situation. After a series of a few weeks and months pondering the use of metal in etching and copper mining particularly, I decided I would endeavour to limit the amount of virgin metal I would use and so first off the list was etching. And I am sure there are many things that if you trace back to their roots are not entirely satisfactory, and so it is finding a balance and finding ways to move forward with a sensitive approach that works in your practice. But sometimes we also have to take bold moves to find completely different alternatives.

The second scenario was when I forayed and pondered the less toxic aluminium etching that is currently being used. Fantastic, I thought, etching! I got as far as the salt room door before I was met with the warning sign regarding copper sulphate and the effect it can potentially have on the reproductive system of females. As a mother, I did not even bother trying it out. For all the masks, gloves, ventilation, it is just not worth it in my mind. There must be other methods of expression that are less harmful. So I started to look into a far more sustainable and gentle approach to creating intaglio works that avoided all of this. Sure, they do not replicate an aquatint, or a fine etched line, I am deeply aware of this, but they are not to be compared. The methods present an option in printed expression that is akin to etching, and while certainly not the same in effect they are – from my research with an ecological perspective – kinder to the planet.

Intaglio printmaking is like the stealthy beast of the printmaking world. I always imagine lithographers to look like a hairy monster (perhaps deep purple with some primrose yellow tinges) with stubby claws and big strong arms, whereas intaglio printmakers are kind of a tall beast with birds' claws and dark eyes and perhaps a few hairy feathers… This is of course complete madness because if like me, you do both and more in between, then the beast hybrid will be completely hilarious and worth a good fancy dress outfit. The principle being, however you approach ecological printmaking, and expression in general, determination and investigation and joy will be your friends. I am very pleased to say I print on the kitchen floor, at night, with a cider. It works.

And intaglio printmaking is a wonderful expressive artform, despite the stealthy beast lurking in acid rooms. It is also pronounced with a silent 'G'. My poor pronunciation was keenly corrected by a fluent Italian speaker in a workshop of mine who made the word 'intaglio' sound like a breeze on a summer's day wafting through a wheat field. From that moment on, in all my classes I make a point of attempting to replicate the silent 'G'.

Intaglio is primarily describing the method of inking up the print matrix, rather than the material used for the matrix or the end impression. The method of inking involves forcing ink into pre-made scratches, grooves or marks that hold ink. After ink has been forced into these incisions, ink remaining on the surface is wiped away, leaving ink only in the scratches. This is then printed. There is of course a huge amount of wondrous artistry involved in the process, and the above is purely the base level of description of intaglio. Metal plate etching is the traditional intaglio example, but in this chapter we will be looking at intaglio on lino and various dry point methods. The methods explored are significantly less harmful to the planet and to the animals, including humans, that reside upon it. The lino method is rarely explored, and at the time of publication, I am the leading artist pioneering this new venture and it is taking off fast. It is truly very exciting. And completely biodegradable.

INTAGLIO ON LINO

Lino is classically known as a relief print. This means that you carve away into the surface of the lino, removing areas that you wish not to print. Ink is rolled upon the surface of the remaining areas and an impression is taken. This is the classic way to approach lino and indeed one that works, has a huge number of possibilities and is also looked at in this book. And of course this is all lino has to offer, right? Think again…

Lino can also be printed intaglio. This makes for some beautiful results that are quite unlike any of the other intaglio methods. Again, the question needs to be asked; why do intaglio on lino? Well, it allows for the fine scratching, sanding, spontaneous mark making that the relief work often struggles with. It will pick up on the finest of marks on the surface, allows for a small edition and can be combined with a relief print as well. And of course, working with traditional lino you know that the matrix you are using is completely biodegradable.

As with nearly all intaglio work, this will need to be printed under an etching press. Because of the depth of the lino, you will need to raise and support your top roller by inserting runners. Runners are strips of lino that sit at the edges of the press bed, underneath the roller. The pressure of the press is set with blankets and the runners inserted, thus supporting the roller to raise up to the depth of the lino smoothly rather than clunking up and jumping down. I print with an old facing blanket (the finest felt blanket) and a swanskin (the fluffy one). The pressure is high and the emboss with the intaglio lino cut marks is deep, so to avoid damaging a set of fine intaglio blankets, I switch to an old facing blanket that I use for collograph.

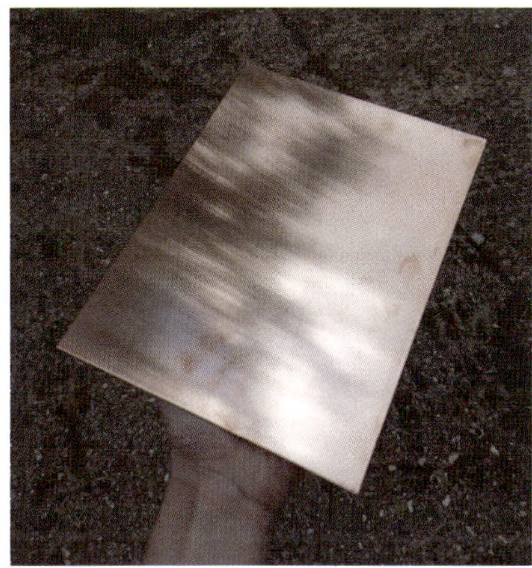

Research into metal mining and processing led me to question it in print.

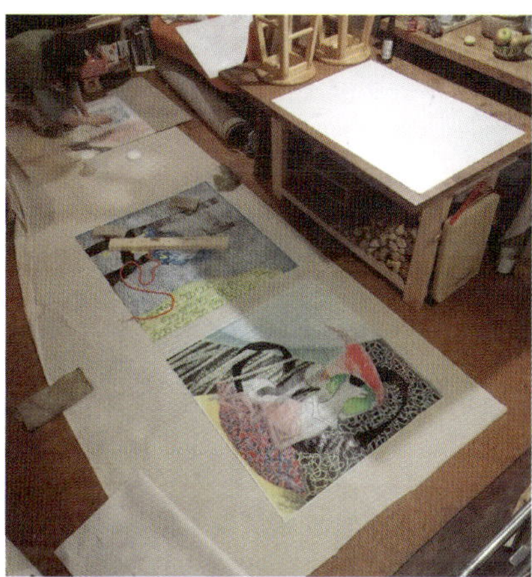

Printmaking can happen in all locations at all times of the day.

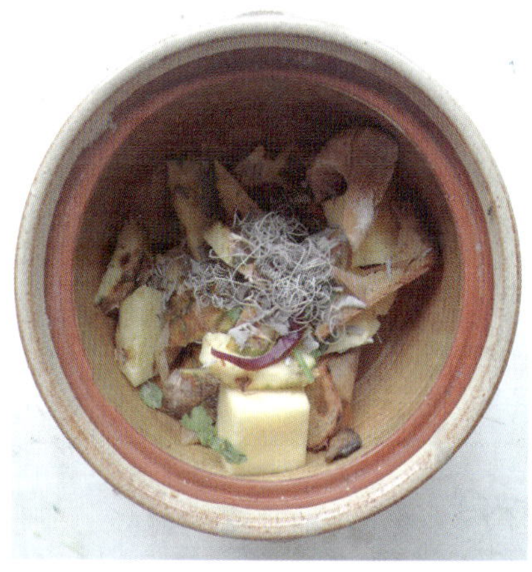

Traditional lino is biodegradable and the scraps can be composted.

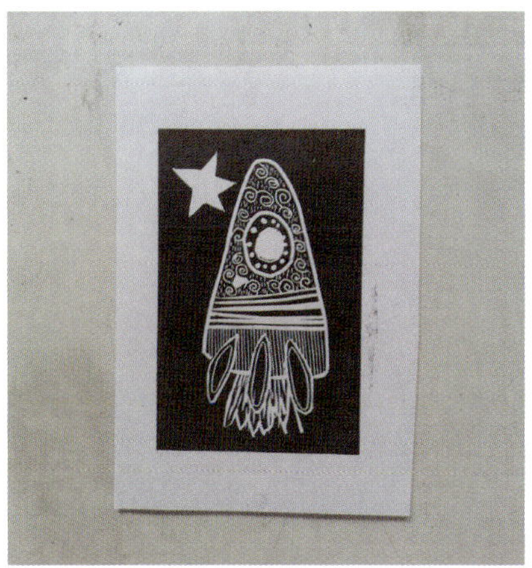

Lino is only good for relief space rockets right? Think again.

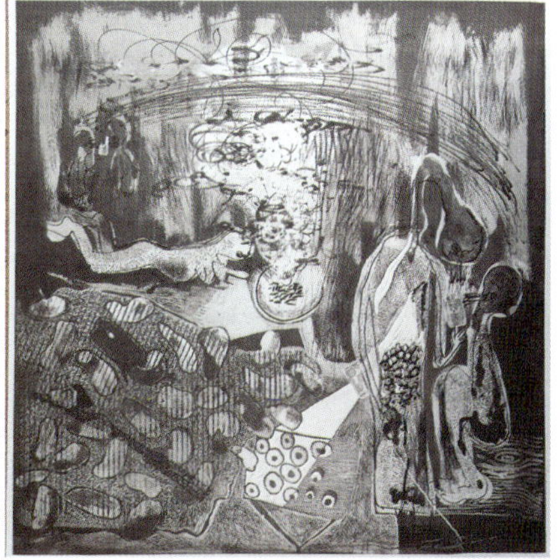

Winter Solstice II, Mary Dalton. A monochrome intaglio on lino showcasing the energetic marks.

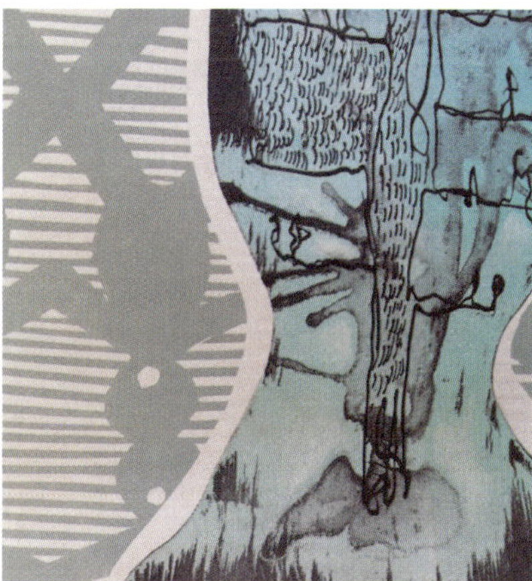

Lino intaglio can be combined with other methods for intrigue.

MONOCHROME INTAGLIO ON LINO

This lino exercise will introduce you to the possibilities of the marks and the process of printing. It does need to be printed under an etching press to achieve the high pressure needed for intaglio. You will need to make sure lino runners are inserted to raise the roller of the etching press. You will need to do a blind test of the press on your lino. This means without any ink added, run your lino with a spare sheet of paper under the press. Check there is an emboss and paper is being forced into carved marks. Next check the lino has not stretched by measuring one side of your actual lino with the correlating side on the paper emboss. If they are the same, you're good to go. It the paper emboss is longer, your press pressure is too high. Re-set and go again. A medium to heavyweight printing paper is ideal for this process, and it will need to be soaked or surface dampened. In this exercise we will surface dampen using a spray bottle (a sponge can also be used) as it is quick and fine for learning pieces. Pre-dampening paper will give a marginally crisper and more detailed result. I would also fully advise to switch to an intaglio etching ink for this method. You can use a relief ink for this process, but you will be wiping down the excess for a very long time, whereas an etching ink is designed to be easier to wipe down and produces beautiful results.

Materials

A5 sheet of traditional artist's lino
Lino cutting tools
Other sharp items that have the potential to mark make on the lino surface – graters, sandpaper, hand engraving tools, roulettes
Black oil-based intaglio ink
Old credit card or similar stiff loyalty card
Cotton rags
Workspace set up for inking up your lino and etching press to print with runners to raise the roller
Paper 180gsm–250gsm
Spray bottle or clean sponge
Etching press set up with lino runners and blankets

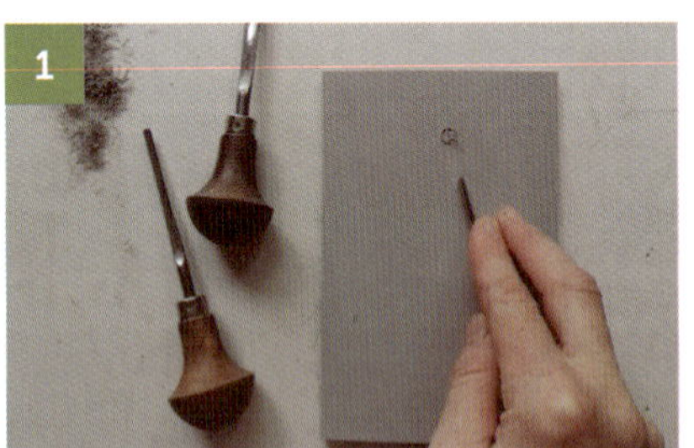

Carve into the lino with traditional tools, making shallow gauges.

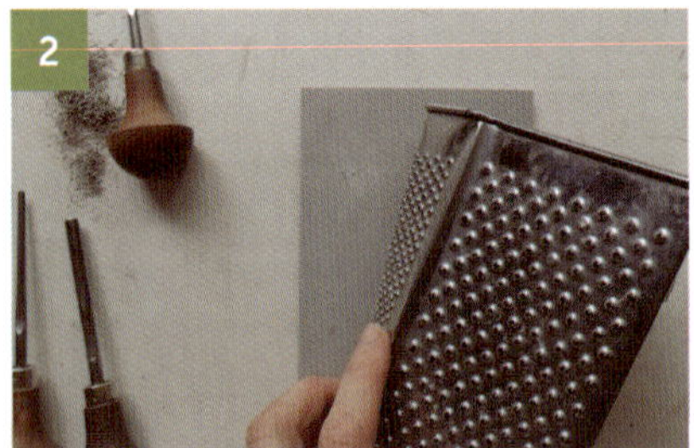

Explore other tools even if they only leave a shallow mark.

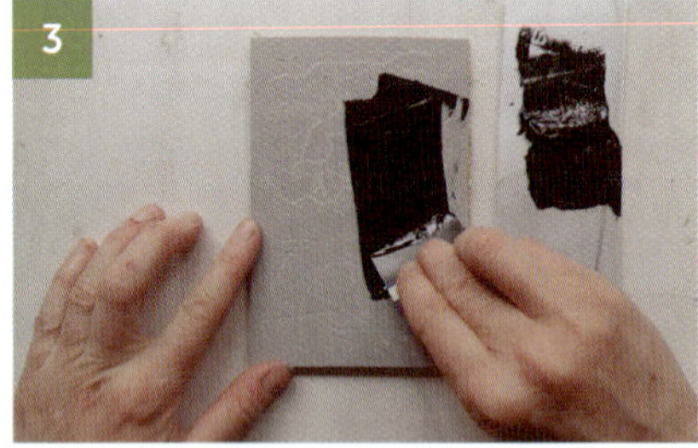

Scrape ink across the surface of your pre-carved lino.

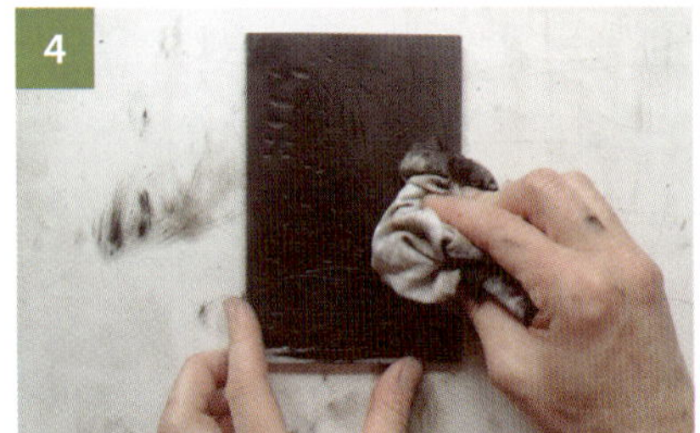

Using a cotton rag, wipe off excess ink from the top surface.

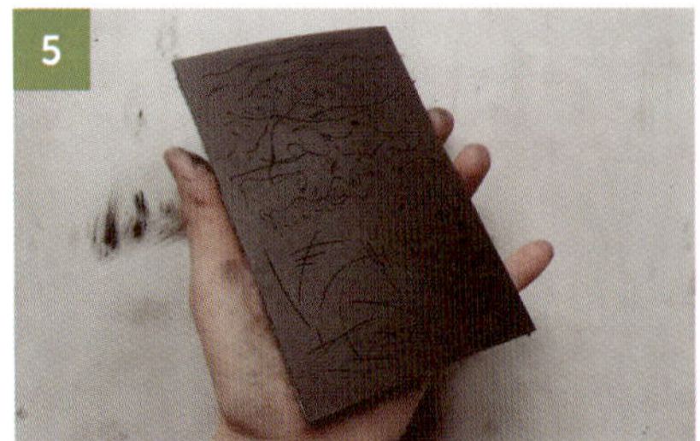

You can see the black ink staying in the carved marks.

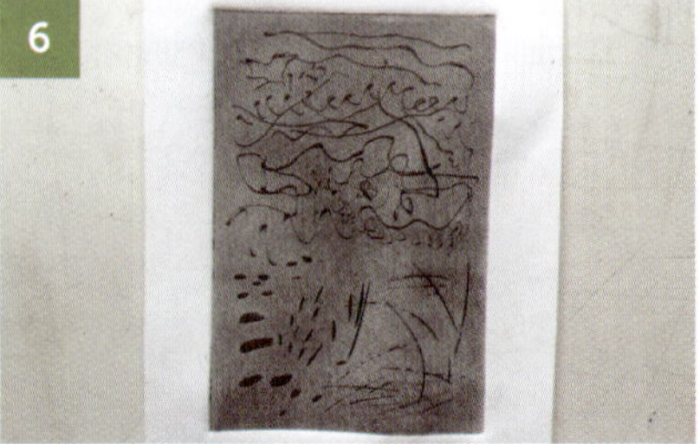

Print with damp paper under your etching press set-up.

PLATE TONE

You will have noticed that the lino surface holds onto a small amount of ink in the background. This prints as a pale grey on the print, referred to as a plate tone. In metal plate etching, metal plate will wipe down clean, leaving no plate tone, so non-image areas are white on the impression. The lino has a slight surface texture which will always hold a small amount of ink and create a plate tone. If you ink up in black this appears pale grey on the impression; if you ink up in red, it will appear pink on the impression. The two main options that present to the artist are working with the plate tone or fully/partially removing it. Both can be done.

WORKING WITH PLATE TONE

The plate tone allows for some atmospheric effects and can be partially removed in non-image areas, but left around the inked-up marks. Using a rag, the residual ink can be carefully wiped away leaving areas of cleaner white on the impression. This process is freeform and intuitive, but you will still be left with residual plate tone around the inked-up intaglio marks. If you follow this wipe-down method for plate tone, you can actually work with it further to make it into a positive effect on the impression. By applying the principles of a viscosity roll over upon the inked surface of the lino, you get to play with areas of colour blending. For instance, if you

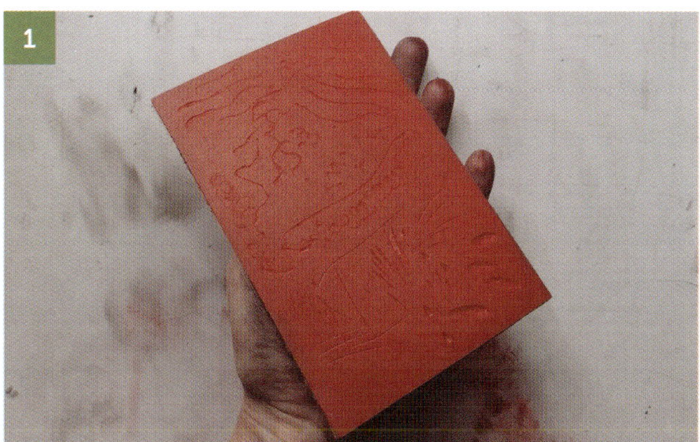

A lino plate inked up and wiped intaglio in red ink.

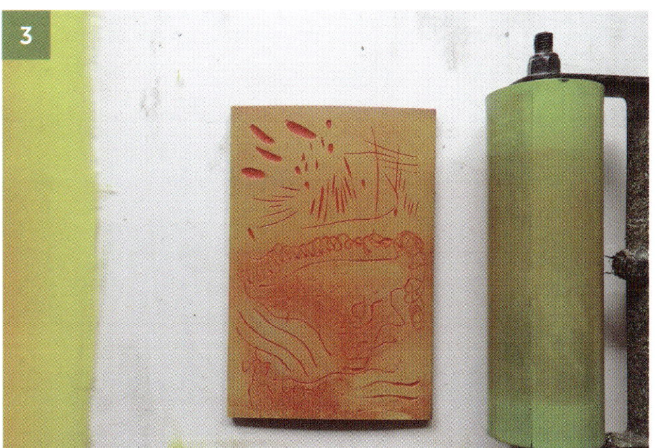

Using a rag to remove plate tone from select areas.

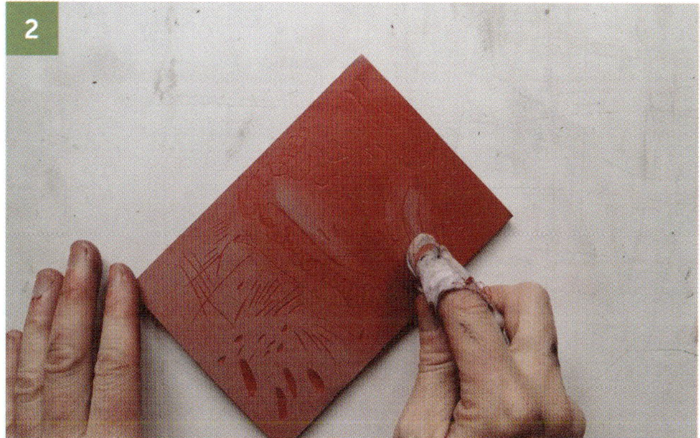

A loose yellow roll over applied to the lino.

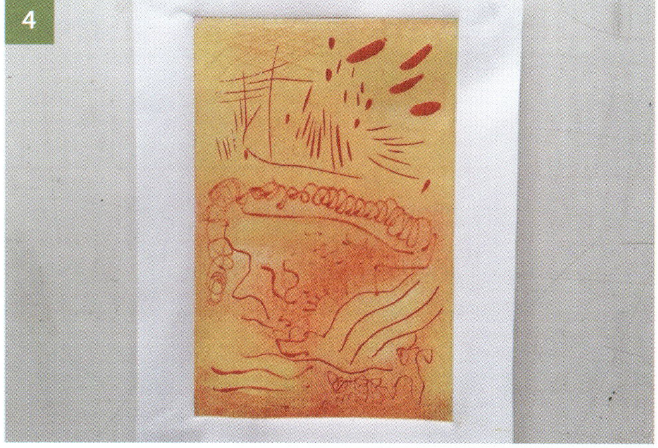

The completed vibrant lino intaglio print.

were to ink up the intaglio lino in red and then wipe areas of plate tone away you would be left with a red line impression with areas of pink plate tone and areas of white where plate tone has been removed. Before you printed this plate, if you rolled over a thin layer of yellow ink you would have areas where there is no plate tone printing yellow, areas where you have pink plate tone printing orange (as the pink and yellow mix) and the intaglio marks still a strong red. It gets rather exciting.

The plate tone can be used to the advantage of the artist to great effect, and is certainly something that can be repeated in an addition. The viscosity roll over technique can even extend to several colours integrating the use of wipe down and masks as played with in Chapter 4. With this, you are able to achieve some quite phenomenal prints that have the incredible line detail of an intaglio mark, as well as some marks reminiscent of lino cutting but in the positive rather than the negative.

CAN WE REMOVE PLATE TONE?

Yes we can. We have looked at the manual method of removing the plate tone, by wiping down before we print. This gives a lovely generalised effect, but we are unable to wipe near to the intaglio marks without the risk of wiping ink out of grooves themselves. But if you wish for a clean black line against a white background, then yes, there are

ways. The method I have started using is not one that is readily editionable. However, for the first unique print it is absolutely brilliant and it uses the concepts taken from lithography that I brought over into the intaglio to make sure that there are options to remove plate tone all over, or in specific places. And, as with nearly all things I am finding out, gum Arabic is the key, as are the principles of oil and water resist. In principle, we are using gum Arabic as a protective layer on the surface of the lino. You need to give your lino a light sand with wire wool and then give it a thin layer of gum Arabic all over. The intaglio marks are inked up and wiped down as usual, but before printing, the gum Arabic is removed with a wet sponge, taking with it the plate tone, leaving only the ink in the intaglio areas. This method will only work if you use traditional oil-based ink; because of the use of water in the process, you cannot use a water-washable ink. The result is the clean lines of the intaglio and no plate tone.

Incredible results for this technique. As we know, the principles of this book so far are to encourage unique prints and this is no exception. And what I find exciting is that once you have the intaglio lino print, you still have the original lino matrix available to introduce lino cut relief into the impression. Your lines are there from the intaglio mark making, so if you were to then treat the rest of it as standard relief lino work, your intaglio marks would not get covered over because they are already carved away from the matrix. So it opens up possibilities that are endless when combining the intaglio and relief.

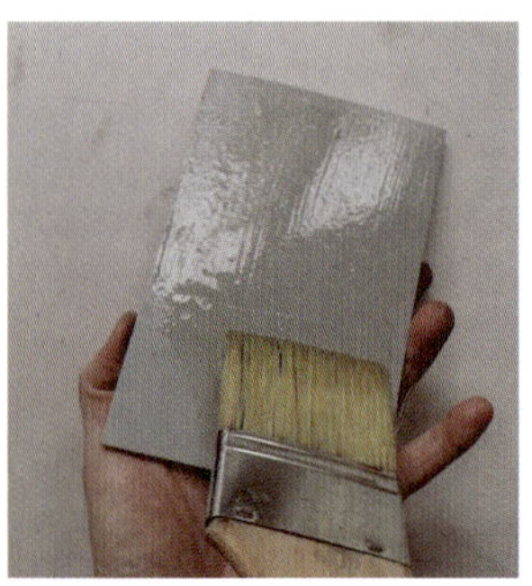

Covering a sanded lino plate with a thin layer of gum. Dry.

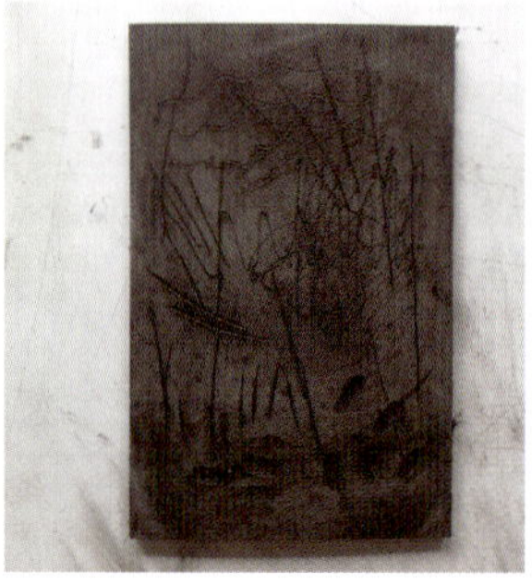

Carved marks added and inked up intaglio over gum.

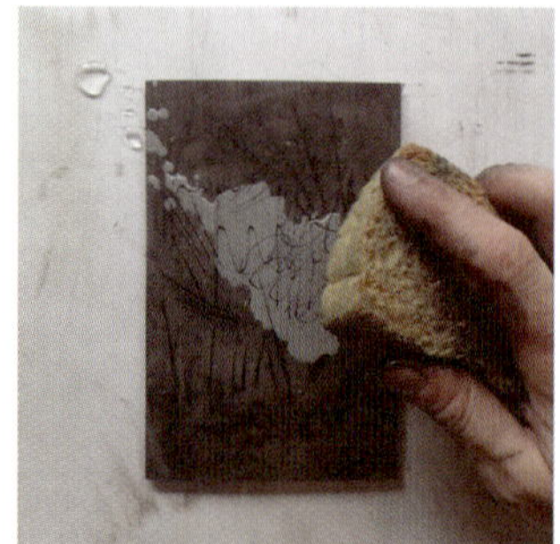

Water being added and gum layer being washed off.

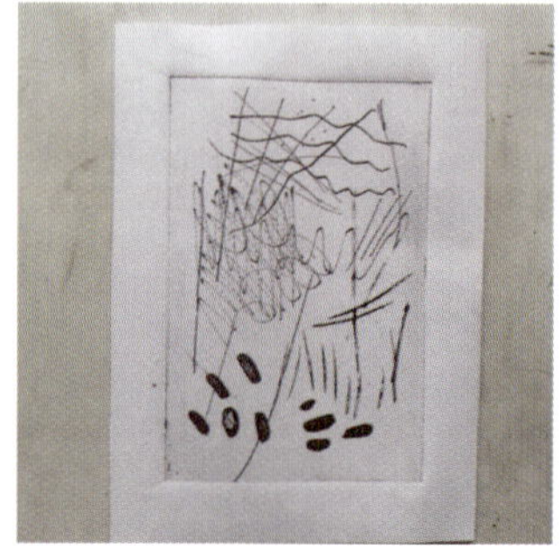

The completed print with no background plate tone.

PAPER SHRINKAGE

If you were to print intaglio and then wish to work back into the same matrix as a lino relief, you need to make sure that your paper does not shrink after the moisture required for the intaglio printing. When working with damp paper, the fibres are relaxed and open. After you have printed the intaglio lino onto the damp paper, even under drying boards and weights, the paper fibres tighten and contract as they dry and thus the paper can shrink. This causes major problems when you want to register your original lino matrix with the impression and you realise that the impression has shrunk by a couple of millimetres. To solve this, as soon as your damp paper has been run under the press for the intaglio layer, you will need to stretch the paper on a board. This means that as the paper dries, the paper fibres cannot constrict and tighten because the impression paper is taped down. Therefore, your paper does not shrink, allowing for further layers to be added in perfect register.

STRETCHING PRINTS

Stretching paper is easy, and it has the added advantage that it dries really quickly and beautifully flat. The world is then your oyster as to how you incorporate the original matrix back into the print.

Materials

Wooden board bigger than your impression paper
Traditional gum tape that requires to be wetted
Water
Sponge

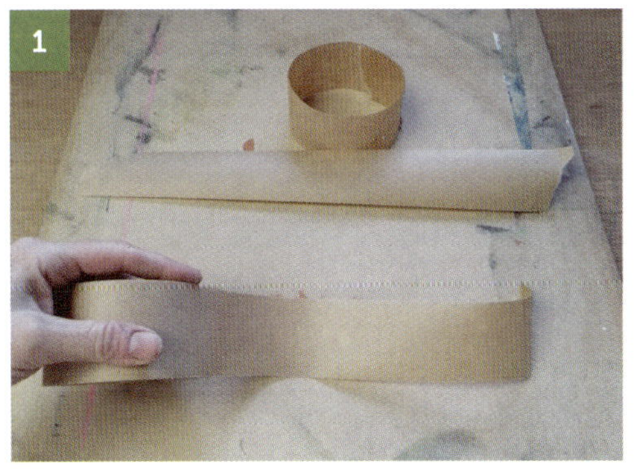

Prepare lengths of gum tape longer than your paper sides.

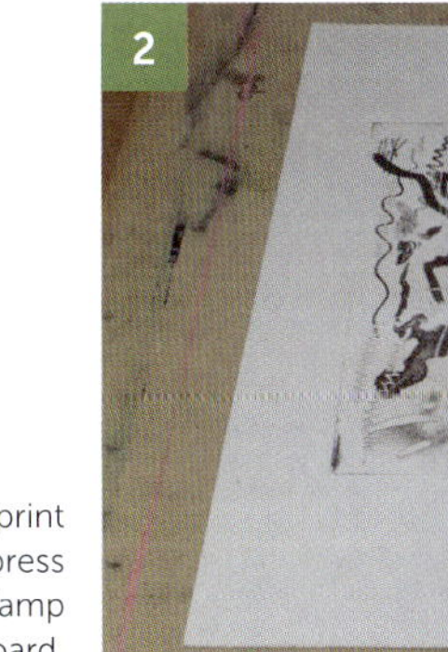

When your print is off the press bed, lay damp onto the board.

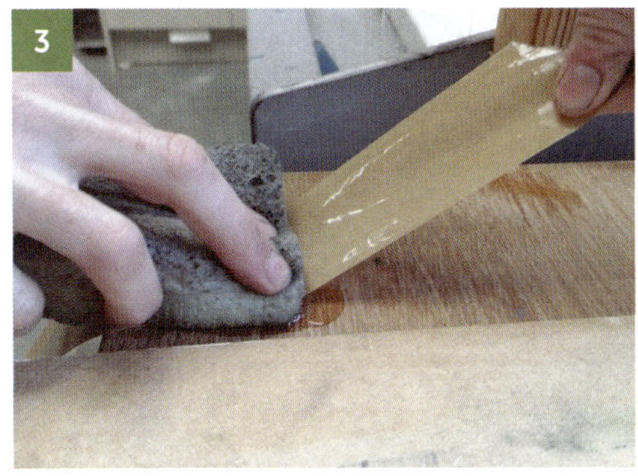

Using a wet sponge, apply water liberally to the shiny side of the tape.

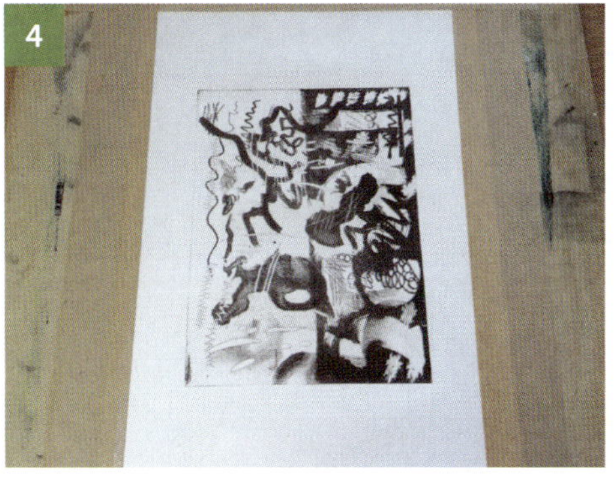

Stick gum tape to sides and let dry. Cut off when flat.

PARTIAL GUM APPLICATION

Following on from the all-over application of gum Arabic to the plate, I wondered if you could apply gum to partial areas of the plate so that they wash off the plate tone, and have areas of no gum, so that they print with a plate tone. This would open up an array of possibilities when combined with viscosity rolling. The following project is a good way to demonstrate this. Again, it is crucial to use oil-based inks and also to let your lino plate dry after washing off the gum and before applying the viscosity roll. Any residual water from the gum wash will repel the oil-based viscosity roll. I am working with a black etching ink for the intaglio lines, knowing that the majority of shop-mixed blacks have a slight green base, which works well in the following demonstration with plate tone.

The potentials of intaglio on lino

From the projects and examples, you can see how the intaglio on lino can have huge expressive potentials. It is also remarkably stable to re-ink and edition. Some of the finer marks such as sanding may flatten, but the deeper marks will ink up happily again. If you are doing the gum Arabic technique for plate tone, this is something that only works for the first time around, as a one-off.

The wonders of this technique are quite astonishing and it certainly is one to pursue by itself or in conjunction with another medium.

Dry point on aluminium and card

Dry point printing is a method of intaglio work that does not involve the use of the acid, salts or other wet solutions to

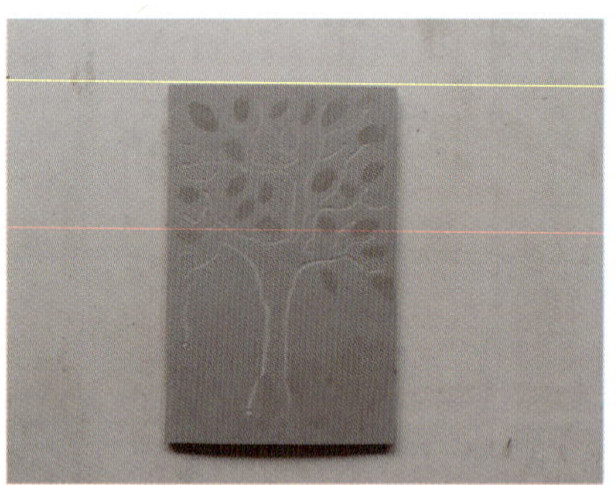

A lino plate with intaglio lino and some gum applied.

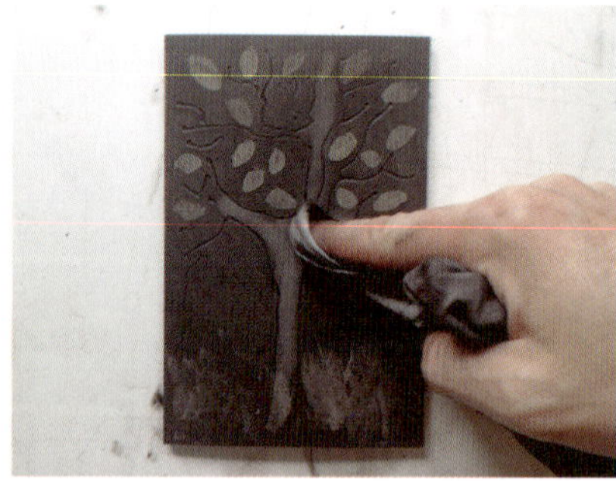

After inking intaglio, a rag is used to remove plate tone.

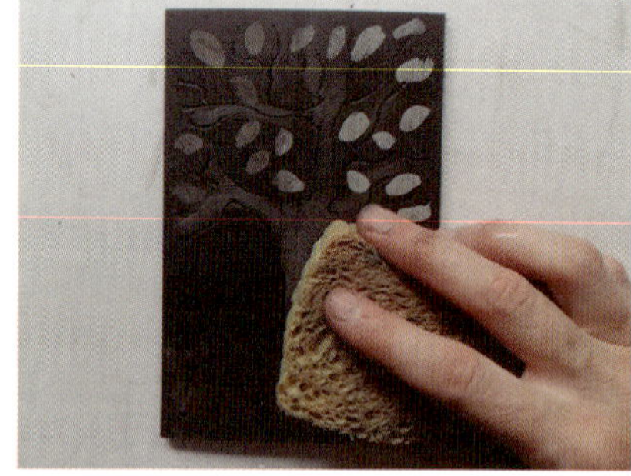

Water and a sponge are used to wash off the gum.

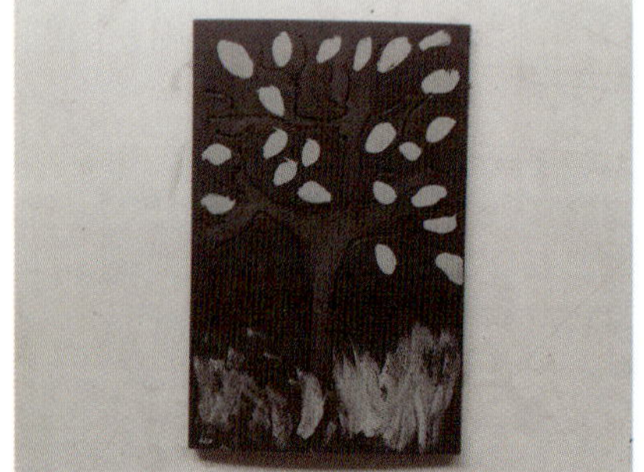

The monochrome plate dry and ready for a roll over.

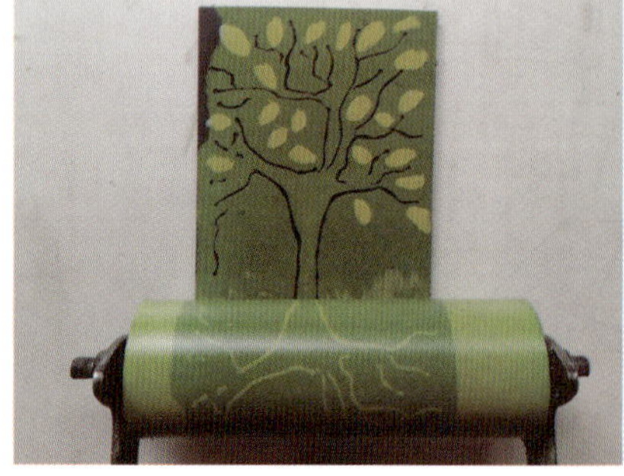

Rolling over the lino plate with a loose yellow roll over.

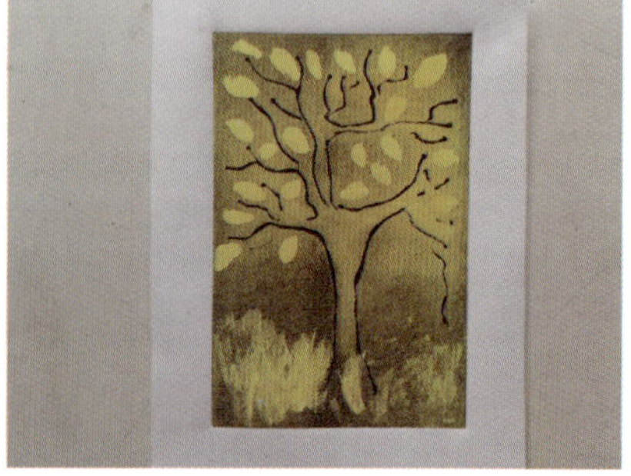

The completed print showing areas where gum has removed plate tone.

generate the mark making. It can be done on the surface of anything that allows you to scratch into the matrix. Dry point on metal has a characteristic fuzzy line which is created when the ink is forced into the groove, wiped from the background plate and printed. The fuzziness happens because the ink is actually sitting in the tiny burr either side of the line that is kicked up when the sharp tool scratches the metal. These two burrs either side of the drawn line hold the ink and create the slightly fuzzy line on the impression. This is of course if you generate a clean line; there are many approaches to dry point that are not based on using a fine etching needle.

Dry point is a very accessible medium and great results can be achieved directly and predictably. We will look at examples and demonstrations on how to do dry point on aluminium and on dry point card. From a sustainability perspective, aluminium is one of the most readily available metals that is continually recycled. As we have considered before, recycling is not always the answer because it does require large energy inputs to create the output. However, as metal plates in printmaking go, it certainly seems better to use a metal that can be re-used rather than a newly mined one. You can also re-use old aluminium sheeting or if you know of any lithographers, then their aluminium photo litho plates are supreme dry point plates, so that is a great use of reclaimed resources. You can buy aluminium sheeting from printmaking specialists or from sheet metal companies.

Dry point on card primarily focuses on using plastic-coated card, also known as Tetra Pak. Now, this is certainly questionable from a sustainability perspective, because the plastic coating on the bought dry point card sheets prevents the recycling of the material. But nowadays, many companies are using plant-based plastics, which is an exciting step in the right direction. However, if you wish to make smaller scale dry points, then the use of reclaimed Tetra Pak from long-life 'juices' and plant-based milk cartons works beautifully. We will be making prints using these in this chapter. We will also be looking at options as to how to make your own basic alternative to dry point card using grey board and hard wax oils. The results are different, but do allow custom scale and matrix and from an ecological approach, it may well be a better alternative to buying large sheets of plastic-coated dry point card.

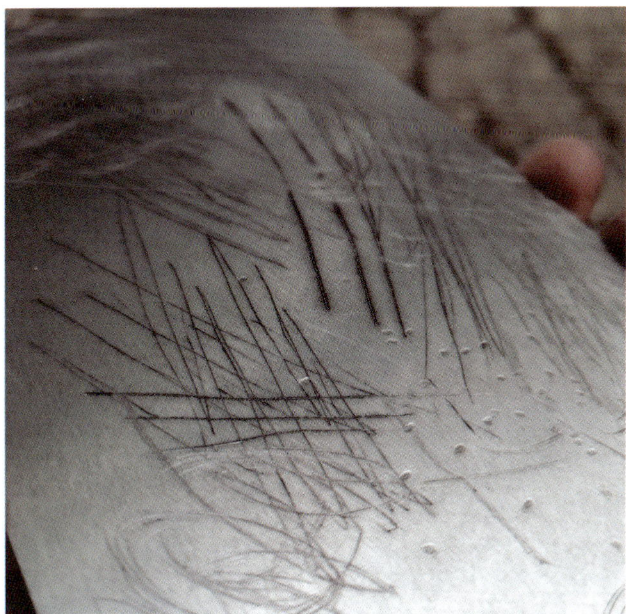

Still Life With Green Walnuts, Mary Dalton. In intaglio on lino piece with viscosity colour rolls.

The burr kicked up on an aluminium plate holds the ink.

ALUMINIUM DRY POINT

This step-by-step project will involve the use of an etching press to ensure full printed detail. We will be looking at hand-printing methods further on in the chapter. This is a simple monochrome dry point exploring mark making.

Materials

Aluminium sheet approximately A4 in size
Black oil-based etching ink
Cotton rags
Paper around 200gsm–280gsm
Water spray bottle, or paper sink to allow for pre-dampening paper
Old loyalty card
Various sharp tools for mark making. Anything that will dent or scratch the surface will work, for example etching needles, sandpaper, graters
Etching press with set of three blankets set to intaglio pressure (high)

Where to take aluminium dry point

Dry point on aluminium is a fantastic and accessible way to generate dynamic prints that have a mixture of fine line and textural value. They have a low edition rate because every time the print is printed under a high-pressure etching press, the aluminium burr and marks get flattened, thus they hold less ink. The aluminium matrix can be inked up in colours other than black, and in fact it can be inked up in more than one colour on the surface of the same matrix. They can also be printed as a multi plate or with chine collé. Multi-plate printing with the aluminium dry point is very similar to the multi-plate monoprint example in Chapter 4, and indeed you can combine monoprint techniques onto the surface of the inked-up intaglio plate for added extra zing.

If you know of someone who uses photo litho aluminium plates, then do use the back of the spent ones as dry point plates. The commercial variety are particularly good because the aluminium is thicker than the grade supplied for individual artists. They are easy to mark with tools and can take a great battering for beautiful effects. The thin sheets of aluminium are also fantastic because you can cut them with a pair of snips or strong scissors to take the print away from the square. You can have such fun playing with cut-out aluminium shapes that can be inked and moved around the press bed. It is liberating to cut up the print matrix from beyond the square.

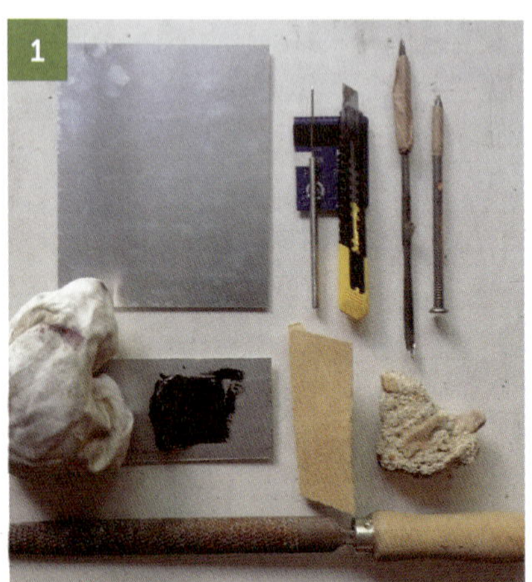

Materials needed to make a simple aluminium dry point print.

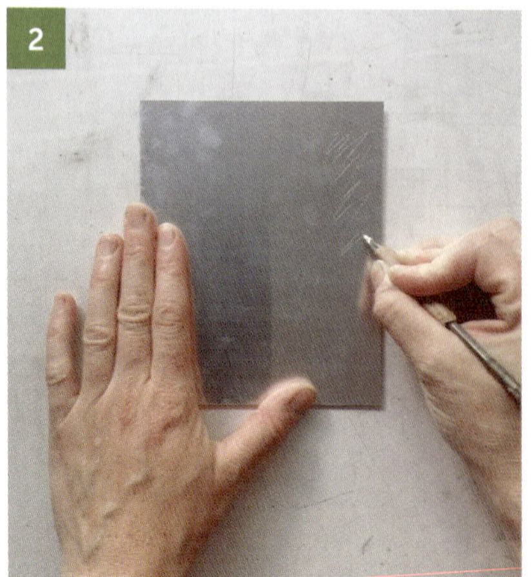

Using sharp pointy tools will create fine scratch lines.

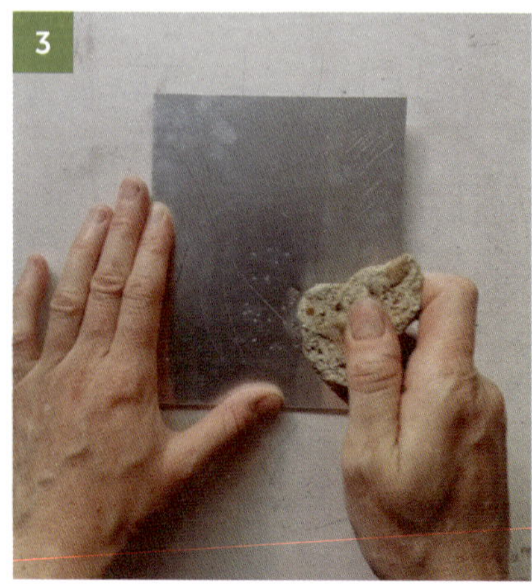

Use alternative tools; the deeper the mark, the more ink it holds.

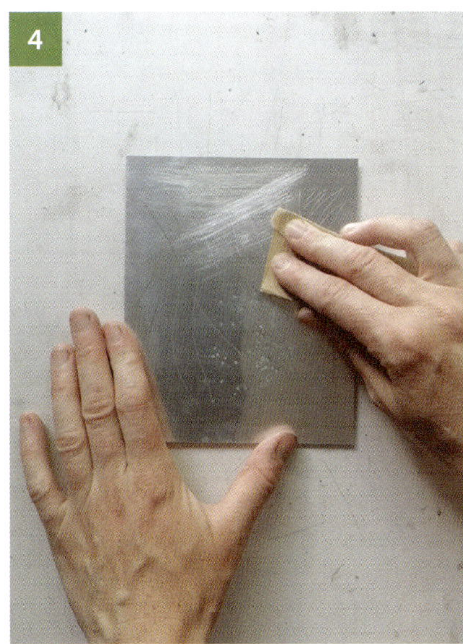

Sandpaper or wire wool generate tonal areas.

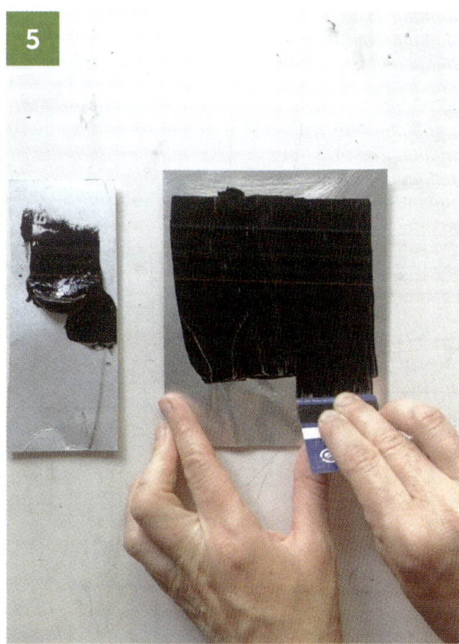

Ink up gently with your scraper covering the whole plate.

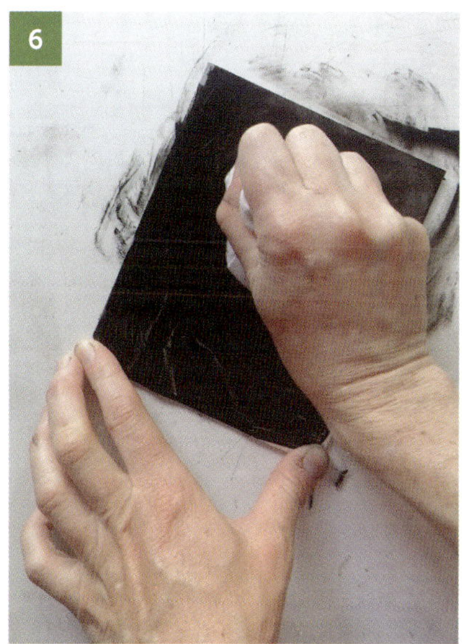

Using a cotton rag, wipe off excess ink gently.

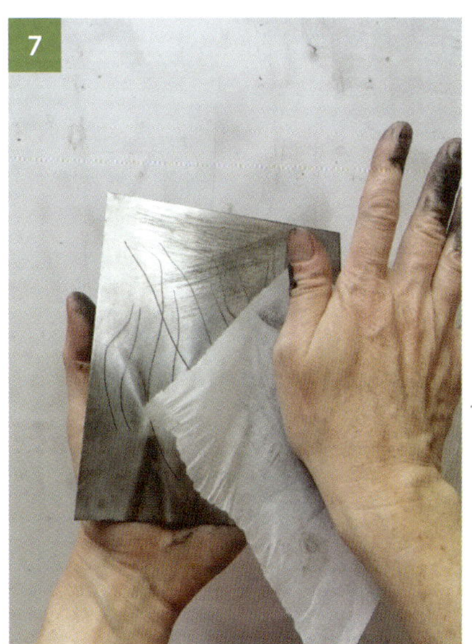

Gently polish the plate with clean tissue to crisp marks.

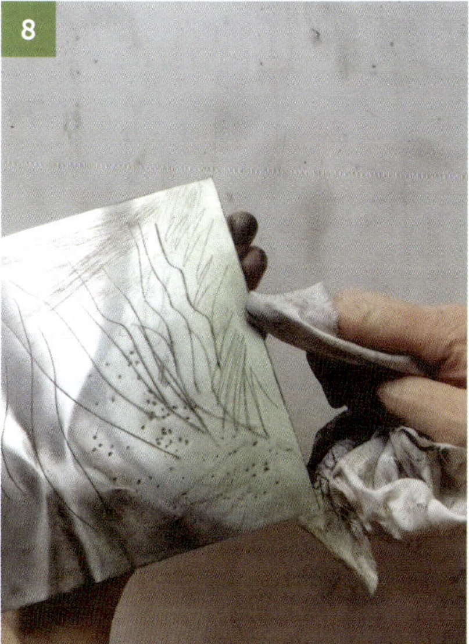

Wipe excess ink from edges, particularly checking the back.

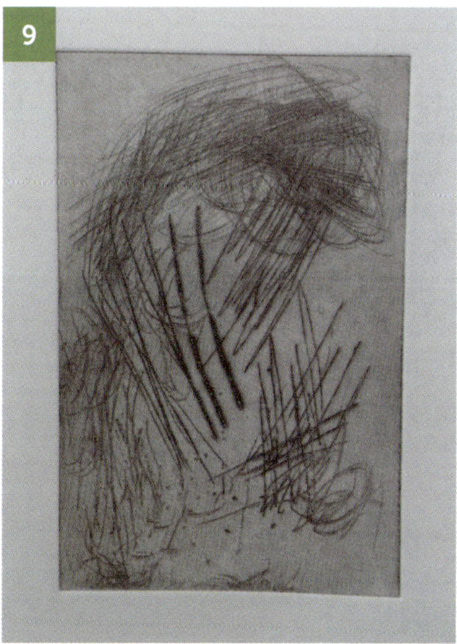

The completed print, printed under a press on damp paper.

PAPER DRY POINT

Paper dry point operates in a very similar way of expression as aluminium dry point. You make marks that adulterate the top surface of your matrix and these marks are inked up using the intaglio method, leaving varying amounts of ink within the surface undulations. If you go onto a printmaking or arts supply website and look to buy paper dry point, it will come up as a plastic-coated thin card. In principle, this is very much like Tetra Pak, the material used to make long-life milk cartons or similar items. Tetra Pak and other manufacturers are now using plant-based plastics for this surface, which improves the sustainability credentials. When using it for a dry point surface, it is highly sensitive and under the pressure of a press you can get a small print run before the marks get squashed. Re-using the plant-based packaging is a fantastic alternative to buying in the plastic-coated card, and even if you don't use the long-life milks or equivalent yourself, a local cafe will have loads of the cartons. Mark making and inking up is the same process as the aluminium dry point, and it is all about having a play with the tools you find. One advantage of the paper over the metal is that you can peel away the top coating to reveal the fluffy card underneath. This fluffy card will hold onto a lot of ink and print dark. An effect well worth having a play with. The card is also softer and more pliable than the metal, so you can mark the surface with tools that are not sharp, such as a knitting needle or even scrunch up the card for a crinkly effect.

Old photo litho plates make brilliant dry point surfaces.

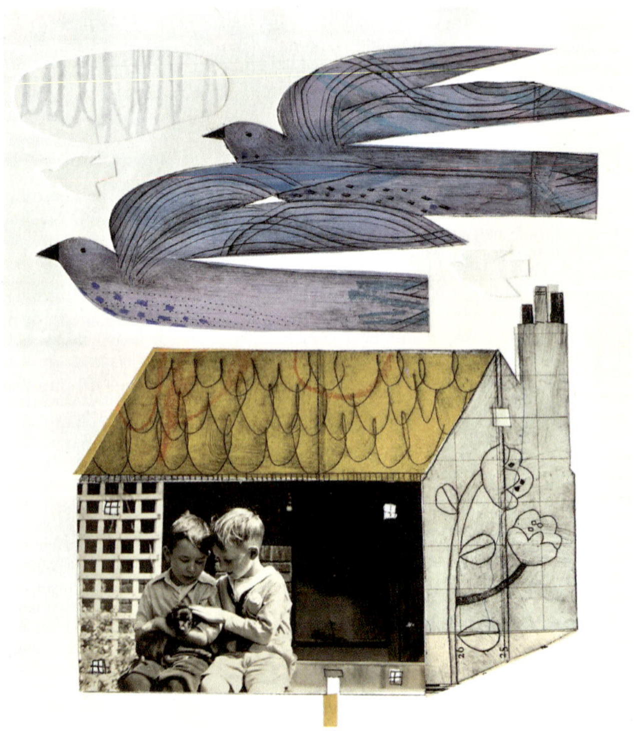

A wonderful example of a print made from packaging and some chine collé (*see* Chapter 7). The quality of the print is outstanding and showcases how if used well, packaging seams are integrated without an issue. *New Friends*, Lisa Stubbs.

FREEFORM TETRA PAK PRINT

This step-by-step project will allow you to explore re-using old packaging and illustrate how easy it is to cut and manipulate.

Materials

Tetra Pak carton (such as soy milk or orange juice)
Black oil-based etching ink
Cotton rags
Scissors and/or craft knife
Paper around 200–280gsm
Water spray bottle, or paper sink to allow for pre-dampening paper
Old loyalty card
Various sharp tools for mark making. Anything that will dent or scratch the surface will work (such as etching needles, sandpaper or graters)
Etching press with set of three blankets set to intaglio pressure (high)

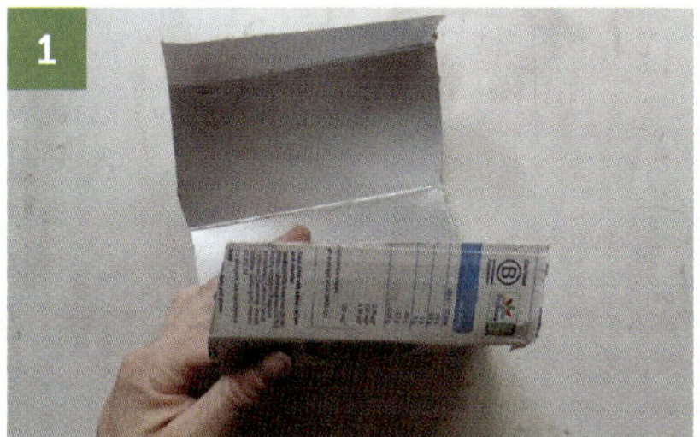

Clean and dry your packaging and open out.

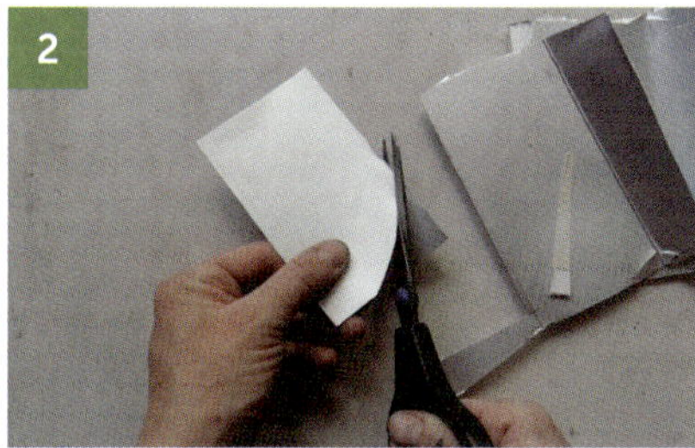

Apply marks to all the pieces of cut-up packaging.

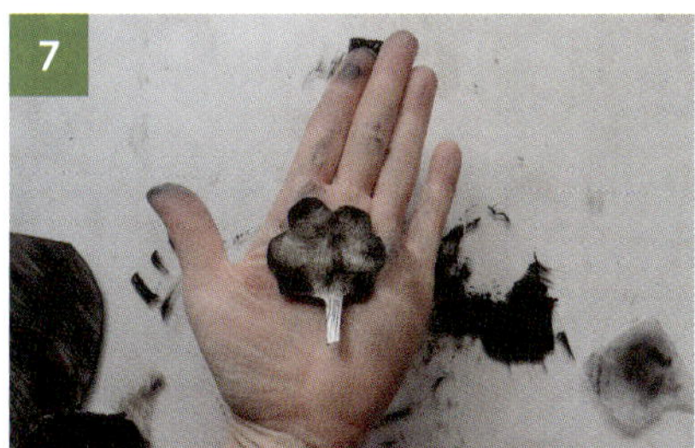

Leave ink on in areas to add textural effects.

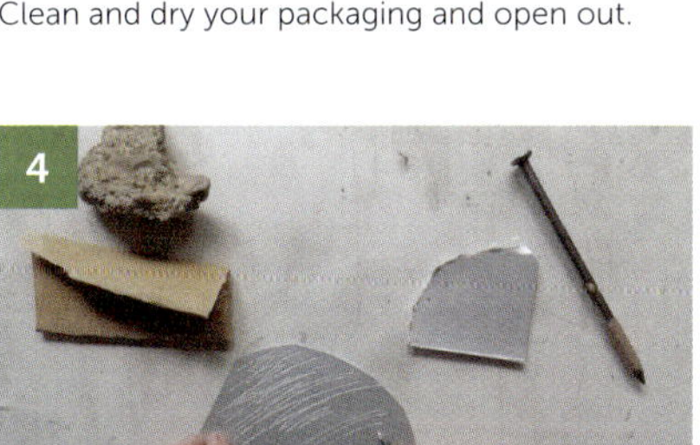

Cut out shapes using scissors or a knife for a clean edge.

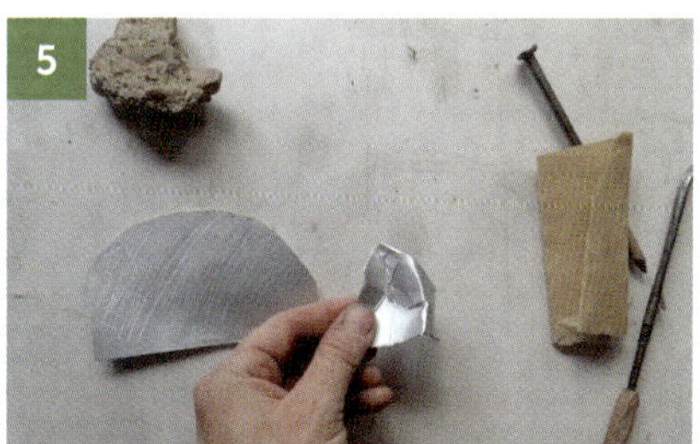

Remember packing can also be crumpled, sanded and torn.

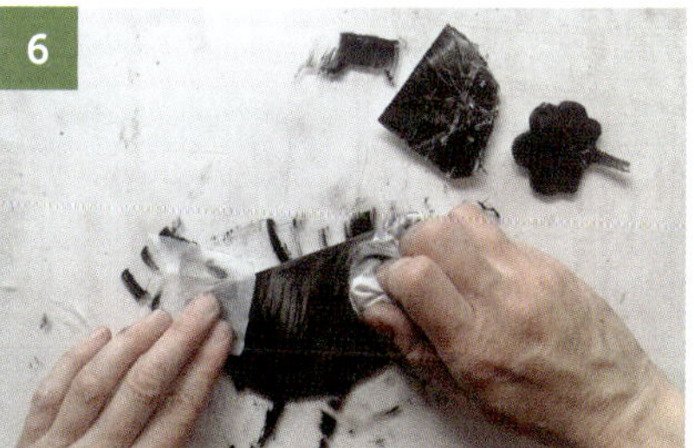

Polish with tissue areas where you wish to highlight whites.

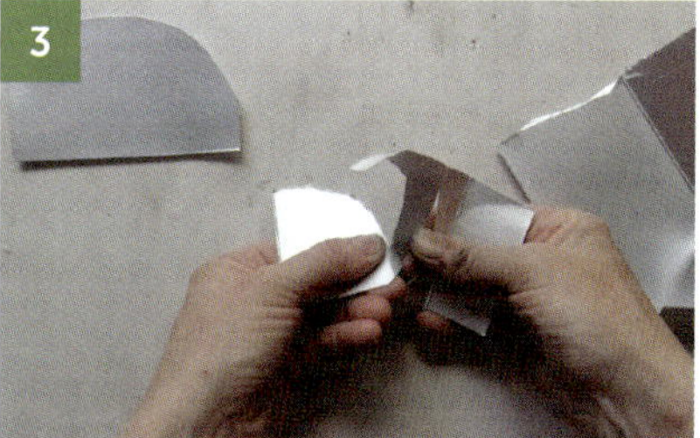

Tear out other shapes for a bumpier textured edge.

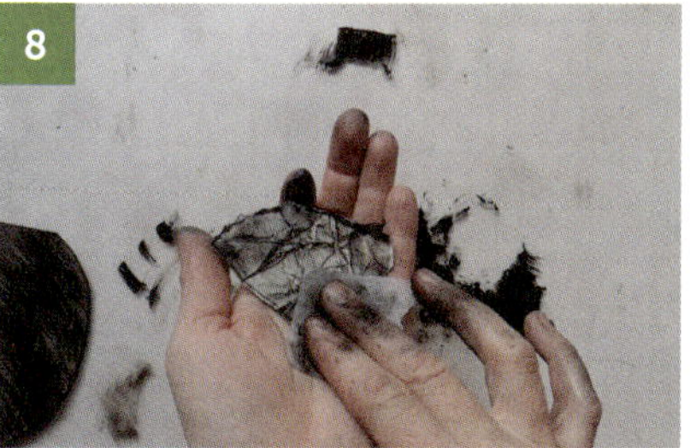

Ink up and wipe down as in aluminium dry point.

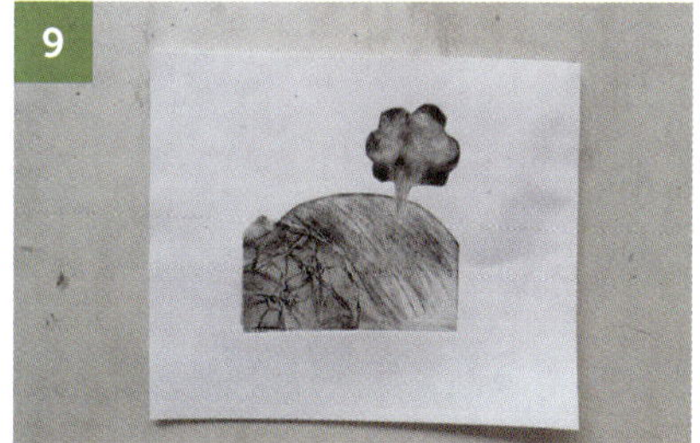

Lay inked pieces on press bed and print onto damp paper.

Beyond the packaging

Re-using old packaging is a great way to generate paper drypoint prints from a waste product, which in turn is certainly kinder to the planet. You are, however, restricted by the size and shape of the impressions you can make. One of the beauties of the paper drypoint method of printing is that it is so liberating and easy to make marks, which in turn would be beautiful to scale up so that the marks can be more dynamic and gestural. In my research, and this is ongoing, I have been attempting to develop a varnish or coating that you can make safely at home to coat standard grey board that enables a similar effect to the packaging. I have gone through many variations, and I am still falling back on a hard wax oil. Now, from an ecological perspective, I am still not entirely happy with this. As with many varnishes, they are diluted with turpentine or methylated spirits, including hard wax oil. So I am still continuing my journey to make and develop a completely biodegradable varnish that works. The hard wax oil worked well because it is tough and smooth, so allows for wiping down, but has enough give to allow for incising and mark making. By making your own grey-board coated sheets, you can go larger than packaging, which you would otherwise have to buy as a plastic-coated dry point card. In that sense, the hard wax oil probably wins out ecologically, but it is still most definitely research in progress. However, these research in progress projects are always important to include to showcase that ecological printmaking is ever developing.

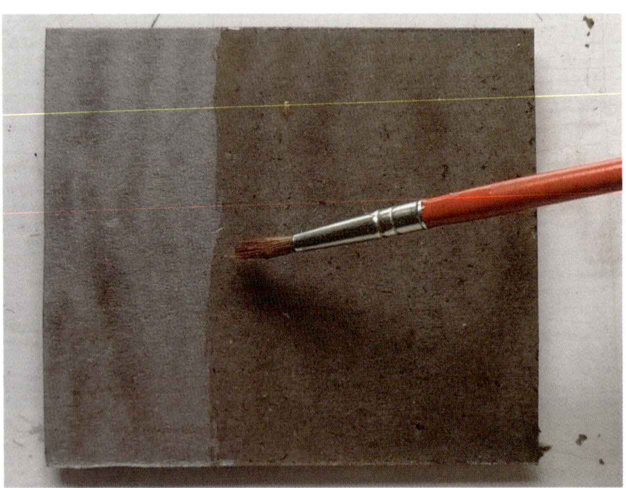

Brush on four layers of hard wax oil. Treat as paper dry point.

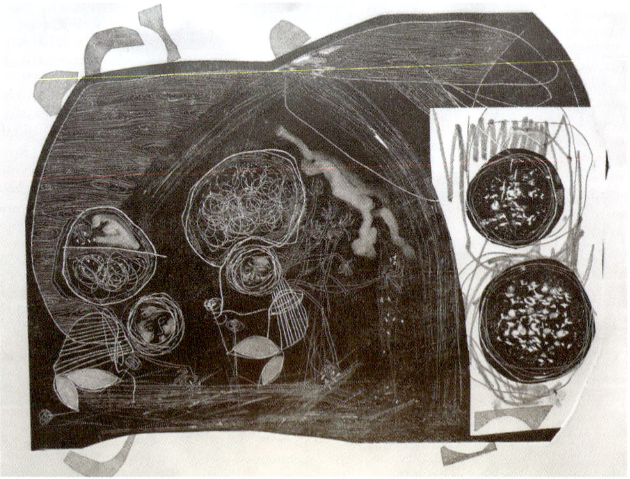

Picking Purslane (2022), Mary Dalton. A print made using a large sheet of grey homemade dry point.

CAN YOU HAND PRINT INTAGLIO?

Up until this point, we have been using the high pressure of an etching press in conjunction with damp paper to achieve the look we are after. This is the ideal way to print an intaglio impression. However, with some elbow grease, you can print them by hand. There are also some other sneaky effects that you can try with your intaglio plate that are easier to print by hand and offer you a different result.

When printing an intaglio dry point plate by hand, you do need to work with slightly damp paper. This means that working large scale proves tricky because the paper will dry before you manage to hand print all of the impression. Thus, working smaller scale, for instance on old packaging, is the best option. You will also need to apply high pressure using a metal spoon or similar hard printing baren. A metal teaspoon is brilliant because it applies direct high-pressure points and is readily available. You can print on heavy printing paper, and in fact this takes the dampening stage better, so is ideal.

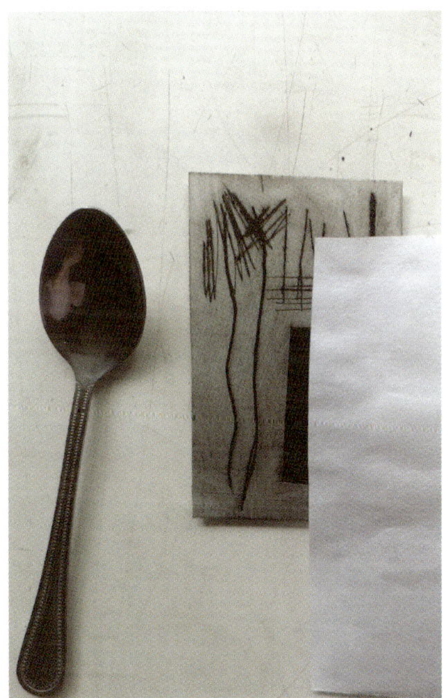

A paper dry point inked and ready to hand print.

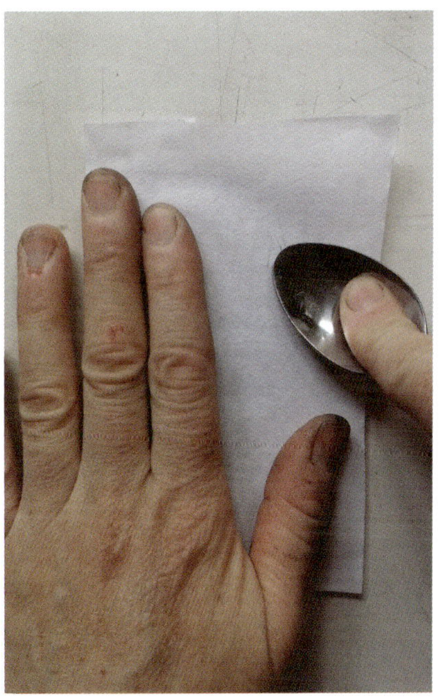

Carefully apply pressure with metal spoon on damp paper.

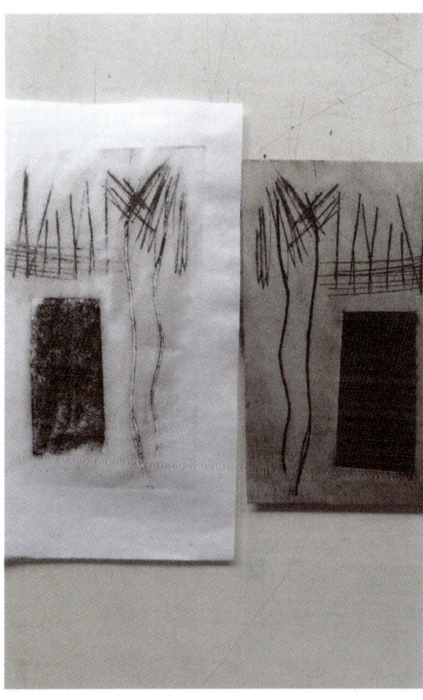

The resulting intaglio marks show how it is better under a press.

SPECIFIC DRY POINT EFFECTS

Paper dry point does allow for some specific effects, which are useful to know when composing an image. You can treat the surface not just as intaglio, but as relief, thus the incised marks become white. Here I have highlighted some, all made on reclaimed packaging and printed on damp paper under an etching press.

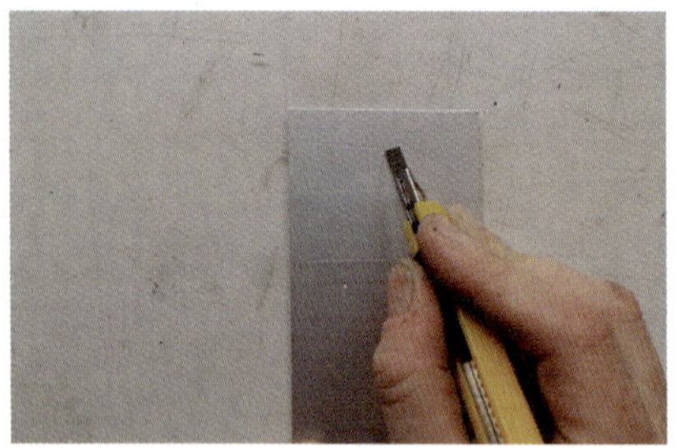

Score the top surface of the Tetra Pak. Do not go through.

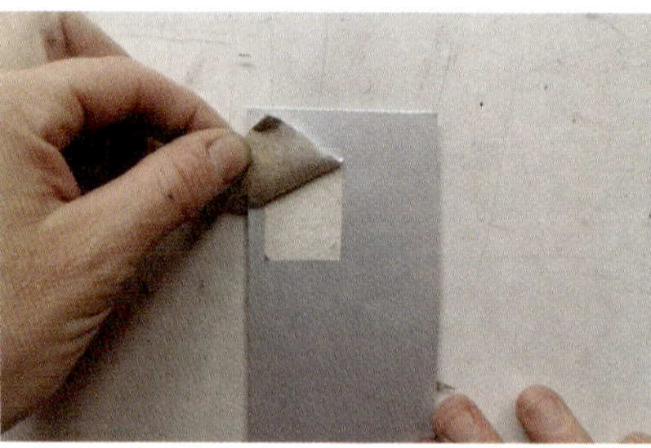

Carefully peel away the top layer only, revealing card underneath.

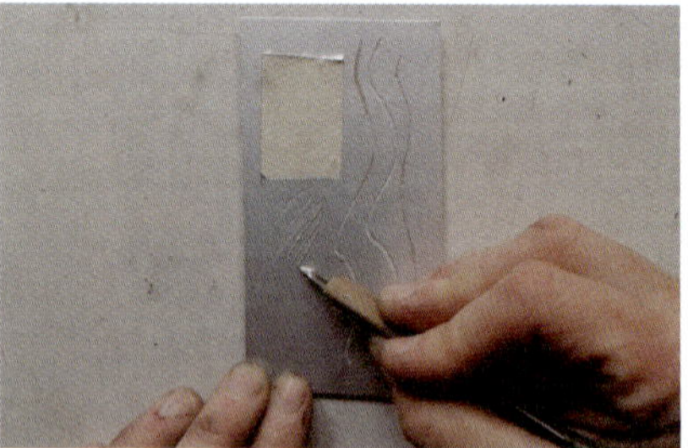

Add other marks using a variety of different tools.

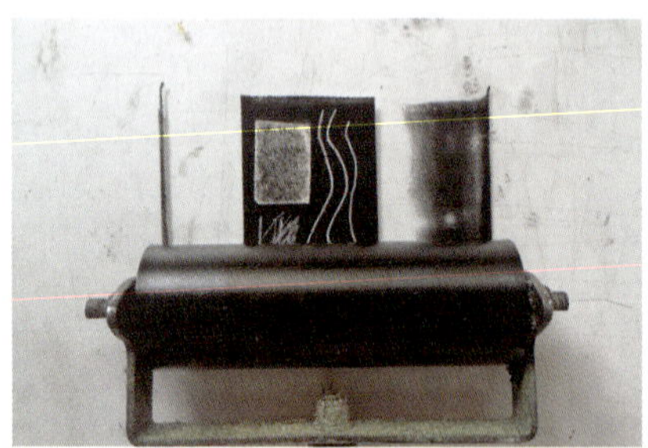

Treat card as relief and roll over the top surface with ink.

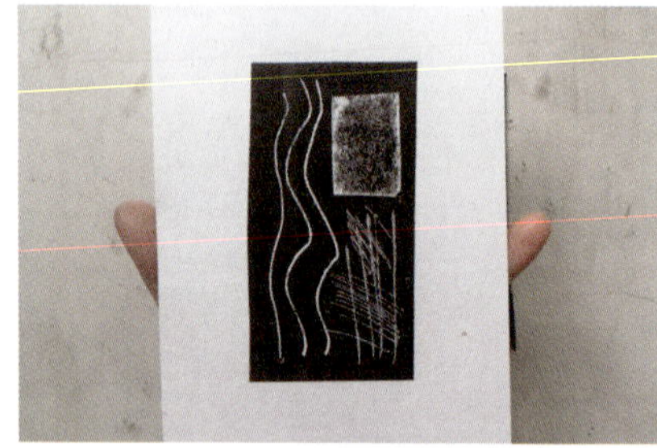

The completed impression with incised lines as white.

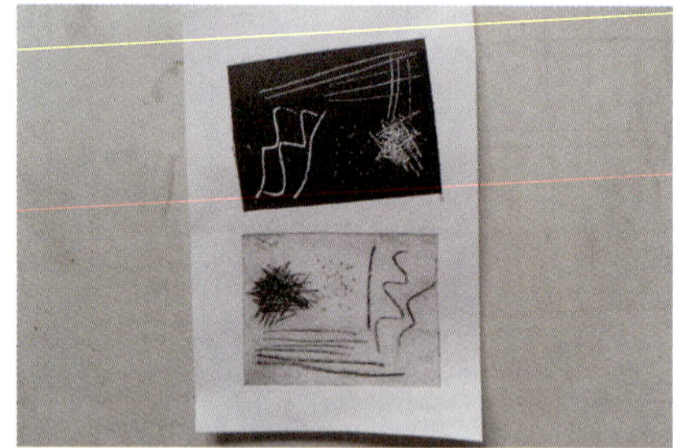

A similar dry point card printed relief and intaglio.

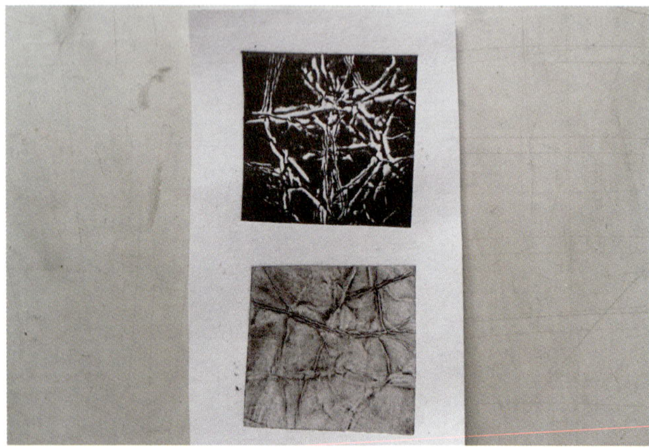

Crumpled inked-up intaglio and in relief.

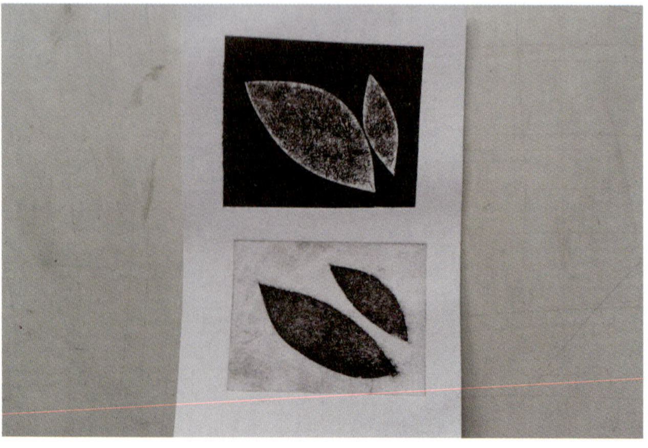

Card peeling inked-up intaglio and relief.

HAND PRINTING AN ENVIRONMOUNT BOARD MATRIX

Environmount board is a completely card surface that allows for similar methods to the dry point card, but it does leave more plate tone. Thus it is best approached as a method to make a card relief print, rather than using the intaglio method. I could have included this in Chapter 3, The Matrix: Relief, but I felt for continuity it should sit here. In this step-by-step project we will showcase how it can be hand printed well.

Materials

Piece of Environmount board, approximately A5
Various mark making tools, including craft knife
Black etching ink
Roller and roll-out area
Washi printing paper around 40gsm
Wooden printing baren

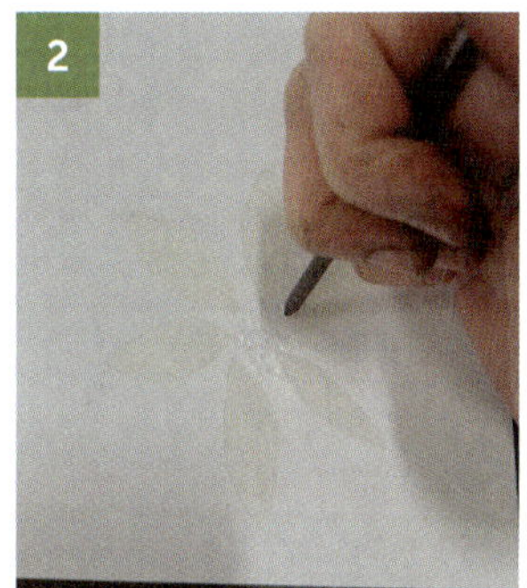

Score and peel away areas of the top layer of card.

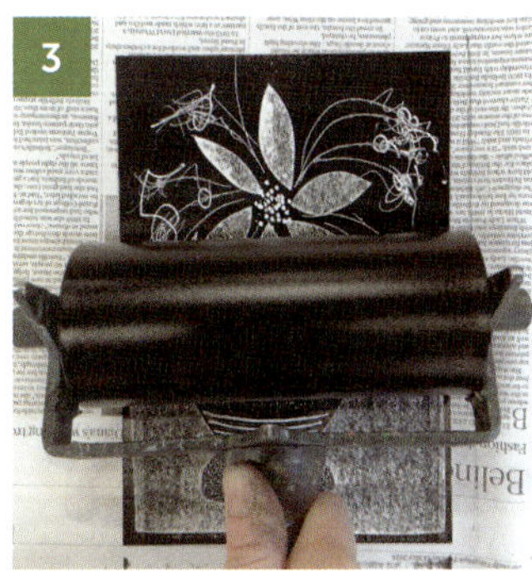

Add any incised scoring marks with sharp tools.

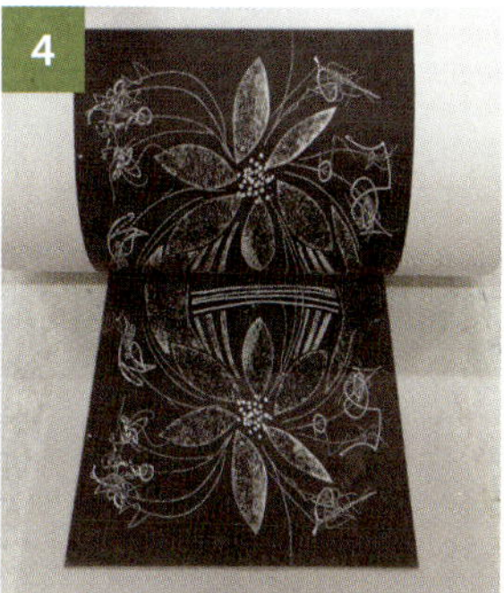

Roll over with a medium layer of black ink.

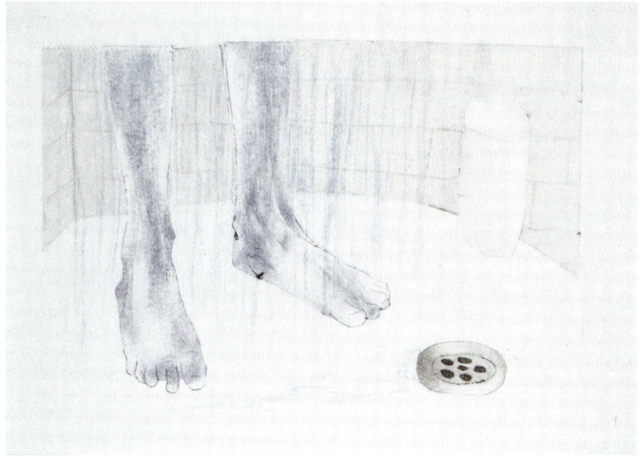

Hand print with wooden baren and lightweight paper.

Where to take dry point

Dry point is a highly versatile printing medium. The mark making is expressive and engaging. However, it can risk losing spontaneity and becoming very tight, producing images full of fine line that lose a sense of breath. The key is to remember to open up, to be bold and unpredictable with the mark making and to avoid using it as a medium to replicate a drawing or photograph. I often suggest that students hide away all previous works and sketchbooks and devices and just draw. If the images and stories that are a part of your work are strong enough, then they will naturally appear on the card. It takes many unlearning attempts to loosen up and to allow the marks to become a story in themselves rather than replication. Keep pursuing and playing and soon a language of its own will emerge, by which point the dry point impressions are already well worth the time investment.

An evocative use of paper dry point, letting the marks tell the story. *Your Sparkly Shampoo Taunts Me* (2022), Nina Gross.

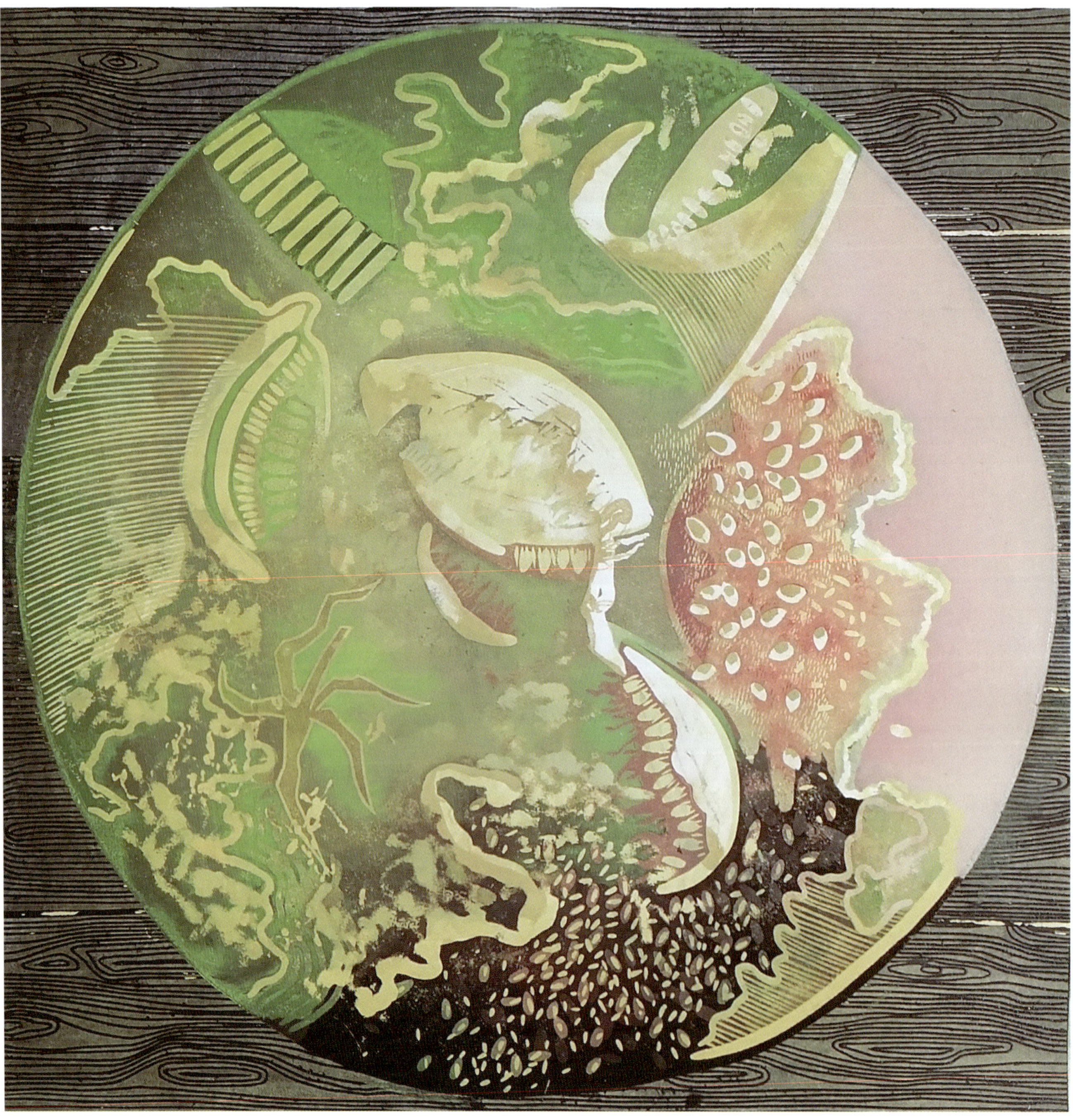

CHAPTER 6

THE MATRIX: LITHINO

Lithino. Lithography on lino. This process is relatively newly developed by myself since 2022. It is extremely versatile, expressive and exciting. The research into the results and the endless possibilities are still ongoing and every time it gets written about, I keep adding more wonders. It works on the surface of traditional grey biodegradable lino, which is one of the most sustainable, if not the most sustainable, printing matrix out there. It combines expressive lino marks with graphic lino cuts, allows for re-use of the matrix, re-stabilisation mid printing, ink marks, crayon marks, carved marks, crackles, crazing, drips, splodges, scrapes, dip pens, pencils, smears, smudges, dremmels, engraving, sanding, sgraffito…

Let's go.

LITHOGRAPHY

Lithography is absolutely beautiful. Apart from one woodcut done on my foundation course in Art and Design, stone litho was the first bit of taught printing I ever experienced. I first came across it when I wandered (I do a lot of opening of doors I technically shouldn't) up the corridors of the Slade School of Fine Art. I was studying a course in Architecture at University College London at the time and was feeling a little disillusioned by the ever smaller lines I was drawing. On my wanderings I ended up on the top floor, where little did I know was the stone litho and printing room. As I wandered in, I saw these giant slabs of limestone and caught a student who was grinding one. I got chatting and it made no sense whatsoever but I liked the idea of drawing on stone. Then the technician asked who I was, because he didn't recognise me and he was less friendly. I was super-intrigued and that was the start of my printing journey. I have been fortunate to get training from some of the finest lithographers, which I hope I do justice to and attempt to break as many of the breakable rules as possible.

However beautiful stone litho is, it does require a stone press and stones. So in a home studio of a mini house that we occupy, this was not entirely feasible. Neither was zinc plate litho because of the use of prepasol and other chemicals that I choose not to use. Photo litho became a mainstay for a long period because I could make my own photo developer, and it seemed a little more sustainable and manageable as I could print it under an etching press that I have access to. But I still was missing the direct drawing onto the matrix – the risk and the intuition associated with this appeals to me hugely. Whilst I was delving deeper into ecological printmaking and my journey ended up frequently landing upon lino, I started musing how to change lino into a surface receptive to the lithographic process. And the solution was so unbelievably simple I couldn't understand why it had not been explored before. But it hadn't, and so the journey started.

What is litho? Is it magic?

In principle lithography is not magic; it is actually incredibly logical and scientific. However, if we wish to describe magic as something that produces wonder, joy and a sense of awe, then yes, litho is *magic*. All lithography has one underlying principle. Oil and water resist. The artist draws directly onto the matrix using tools that contain an element of grease. The artist is drawing in the positive, so if you draw a tree, the tree will print. Once a drawing has been completed it undergoes a stabilisation process underneath a film of gum Arabic. When ready to print, the gum is washed off and the matrix is kept slightly damp. The non-image areas (which do not have greasy drawing on) will absorb a thin film of water. The greasy drawn image areas repel the thin film of water. When oil-based ink is rolled upon the surface, the greasy drawing attracts the oil-based ink and the damp non-image areas repel the oil-based ink, thus remain clean. And a print is taken.

Lithino works on exactly the same principle. The key with working on the lino is to make sure that the surface of the lino is able to remain damp. Lino is derived from flooring, which inherently is designed to be water repellent. The trick

to changing the top layer of the lino surface to accept the thin film of water evenly in non-image areas is to add a plate grain. Adding a plate grain is actually common practice in all lithographic methods, from grinding a stone to chemically treating a lithographic zinc plate. The grain allows for the artist's drawing to be true to the marks such as washes and dip pens, whilst also allowing a thin film of water to stay evenly across the surface of the non-image areas without pooling. To grain the lino we sand it. Simple. In fact, the more research I do, the more I see it is absolutely essential this process is done well to ensure a good stable print. Just as with grinding a stone or preparing a zinc plate, the first stage of this plate graining on lino is the most crucial for the whole process.

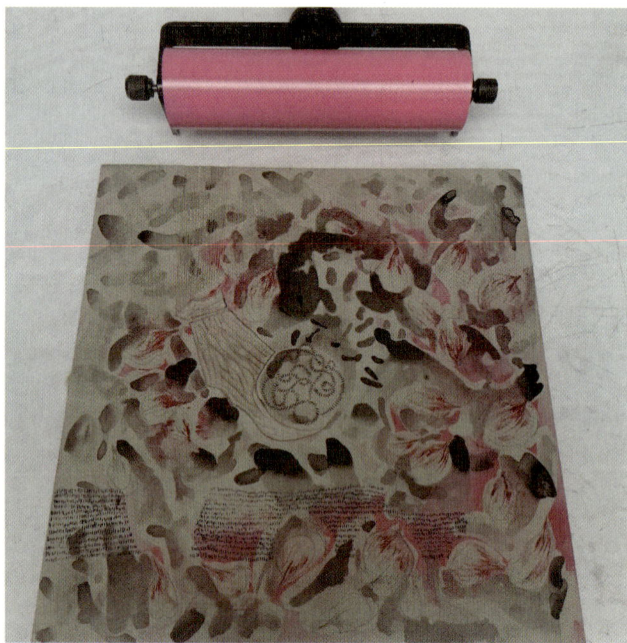

Non-image areas staying clean as this pink lithino gets inked.

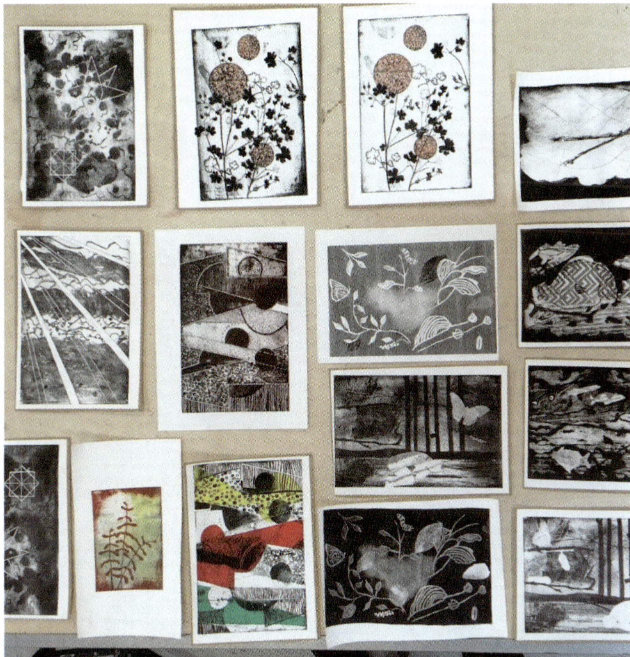
A range of beginners' lithino prints showcasing the versatility.

Preparing your lino

Work with the freshest lino you can. Lino has a shelf life. The natural materials in it eventually cure and harden, making fantastically durable flooring, but a very difficult surface to draw on. Fresh lino is flexible and is not hard. You will need to sand the surface of the lino before you commence any drawing. I highly recommend using a medium-grade wire wool as opposed to sandpaper or a power sander. The sandpaper clogs very readily with lino dust and ends up polishing the lino as opposed to sanding and creating a tooth on the surface. Likewise with a power sander, the sandpaper clogs and you end up polishing rather than sanding. Wire wool can be opened out and used in different aspects and it creates a great grain. Please do wear a face covering and/or work outside when sanding to prevent inhalation of dust. I sand methodically up and down the lino, working from left to right, then rotate the lino 90 degrees and repeat. I make a minimum of seven rotations. You cannot over sand the lino with the wire wool; the more sanding the better the print. Once fully sanded, it is ready to receive the drawing materials. If you are not working on the lino immediately, wrap it in some clean tissue paper or newsprint and place drawing surface side down to avoid any contamination of the lino surface from grease in the atmosphere.

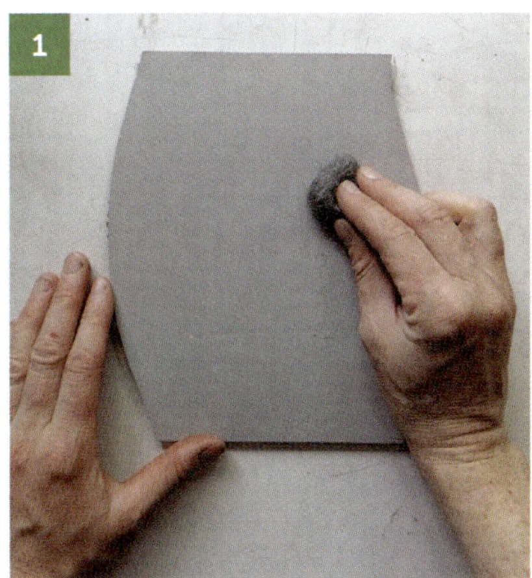
Using medium-grade wire wool, sand the lino in one direction.

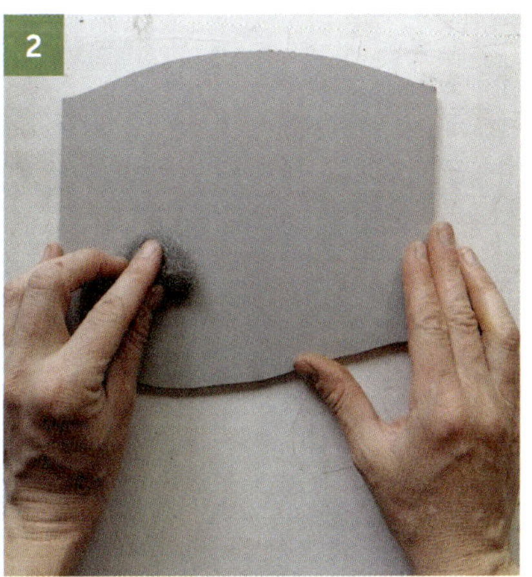
Rotate the lino 90 degrees and sand in the other direction.

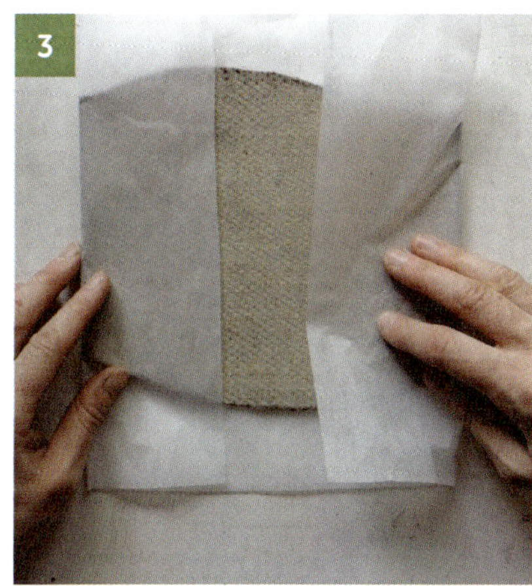
If not using immediately, wrap carefully and store face down.

DRAWING MATERIALS

As with all litho, there are traditional drawing tools and there are the alternatives. Traditional tools are more predictable and more stable because they are designed for the process. However, you can of course experiment with non-traditional tools that may contain an element of grease. For instance, lipstick or greasy croissant crumbs. The alternatives require you to experiment and document which you like. The traditional litho materials seem expensive at first, but they do last a very, very long time, so they are worth the investment.

Litho crayon

Lithographic crayon comes in a square profile or in a more pencil-like variety. Both types have gradings of the amount of grease. The crayons can be bought in soft form or hard form and anything in between. The soft variety are really grease heavy and lay down a thick black mark. They are great for expressive drawing, but less good for detailed delicate areas. The hard variety are more sensitive to allow for cross hatching, tone building and so on. The round pencil-like crayons come with a paper holder or as the separate core, which you need to insert into a clutch pencil holder.

The traditional litho crayons with a black paper outer have a special way to reveal a new amount of crayon nib.

Use the crayons to create cross hatching, tonal areas, bold expressive squiggles and the like. They can be overlaid, smudged and played with, as with all the tools.

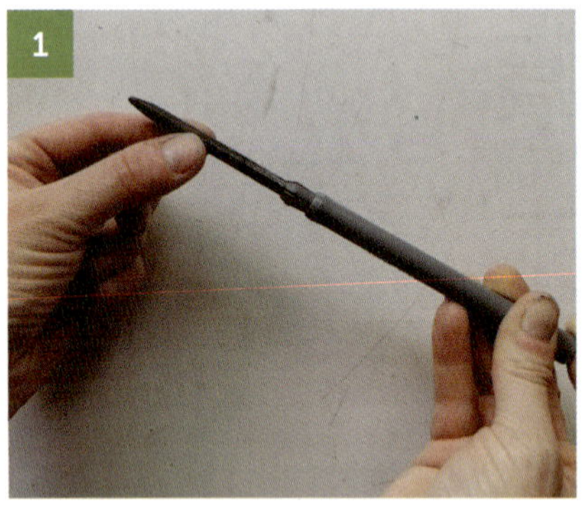

Place the crayon core into a clutch pencil holder to use.

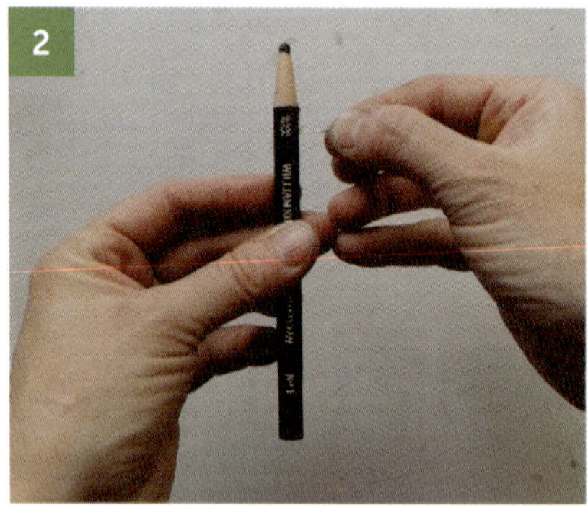

Pull string downwards by about 0.5cm, or markings on pencil.

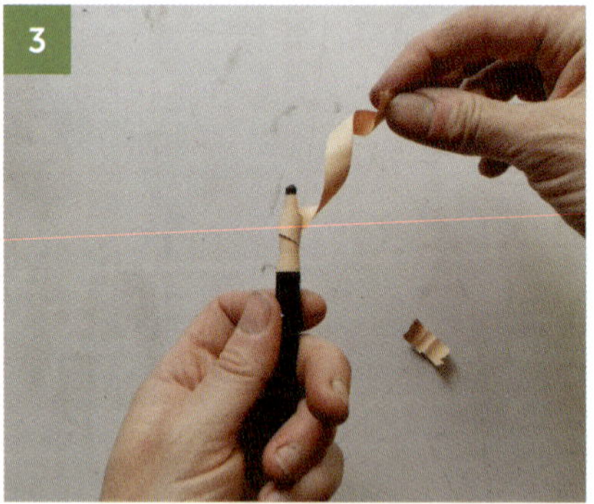

Peel away paper from string torn edge and off the end.

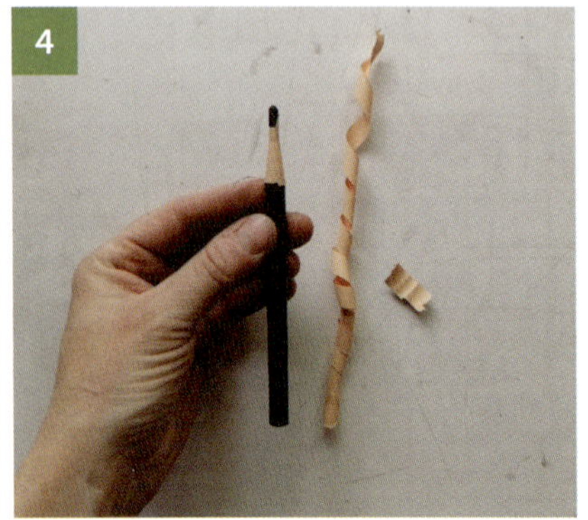

A new section of crayon is revealed. It can be sharpened.

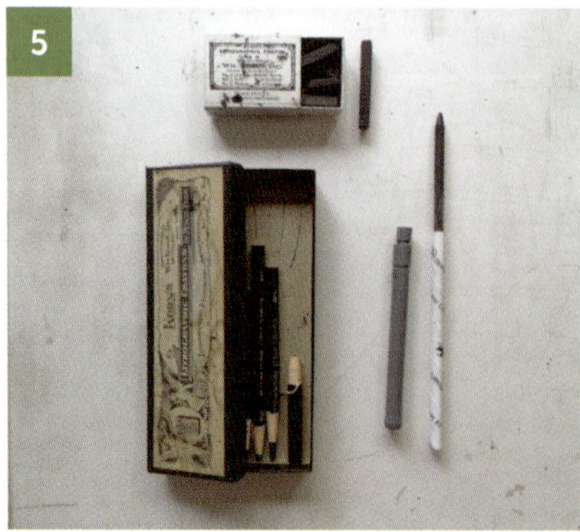

The range of lithographic crayons is exciting.

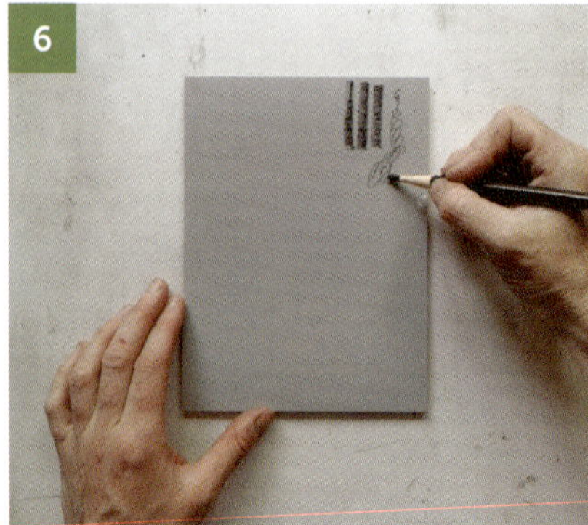

Draw with different grades of crayon to change the marks.

Autographic ink or drawing ink

Lithographic drawing ink is brown in appearance and it prints quite dark, pretty much black depending on how it is applied. Use it like any drawing ink and apply with a dip pen for fine lines, brushes, twigs, feathers and anything in between. It will print dark so is a useful medium to use. It does evaporate if stored without a lid on the container, so do decant a little bit from the main jar and work from that. If you have an old jar of litho ink it can start to congeal and go sticky or even start to separate. Sometimes with a good shake with some warm water you can reinvigorate it, or it might be worth treating yourself to a new fresh bottle.

Rubbing ink or rubbing tablet

Rubbing ink is a solid grease block which is applied to the matrix to give smeary or charcoal-like effects. As with the litho crayon, it comes in varying degrees of hardness – the soft one is sticky and very strong, and the hard one is more delicate. Be warned. It is incredibly grease heavy, so you may think there is nothing on your lino when you smear it on, but when you go to ink it up black, it will fill in heavy black readily. Apply lightly, sparingly and with a sensitive approach and it can be a beautiful medium to use. You tend to use your finger to gather some grease from the block and then smear this onto your matrix. It works beautifully in conjunction with a stencil to create a defined edge. You can overlay smudges and smears, just be aware the more layers you apply the more grease is being laid down onto the surface and thus the darker it will print. The hard rubbing ink is fantastic at building up subtle layers or smudges.

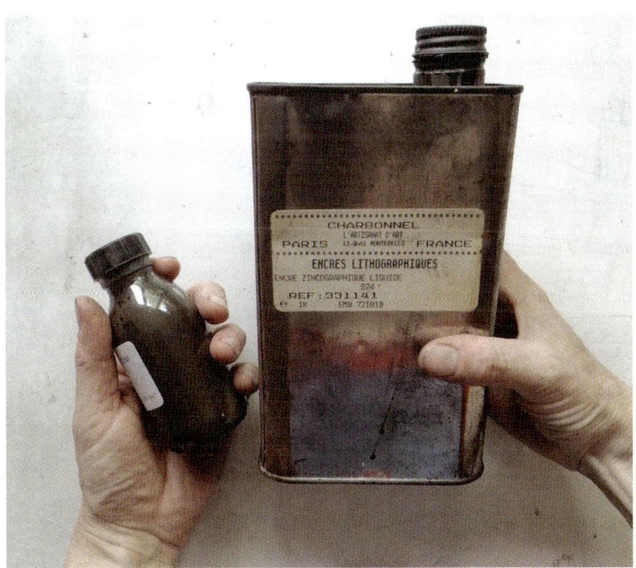

Lithographic drawing ink made by different companies.

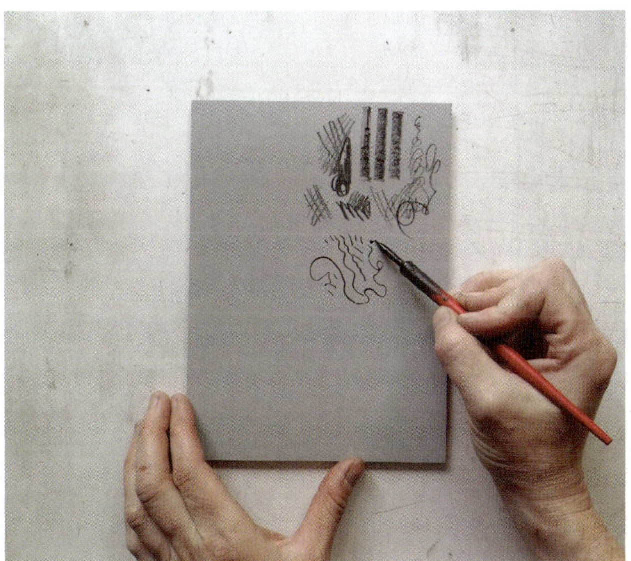

Treat like ink and use dip pens, sticks and brushes to draw.

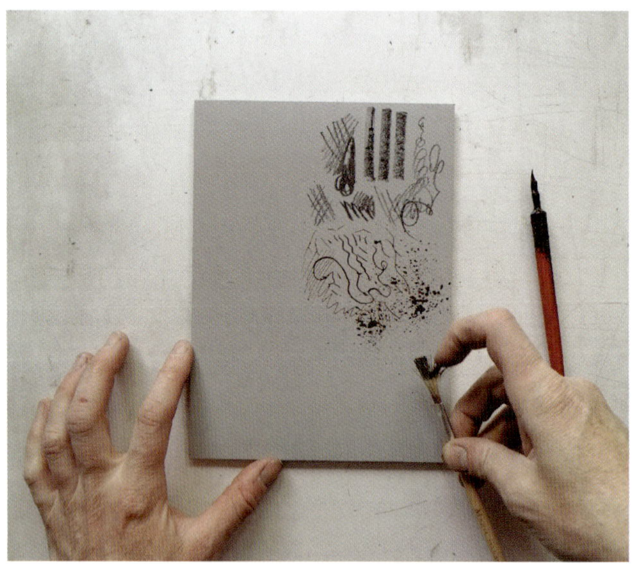

You can also create gestural marks like splatters.

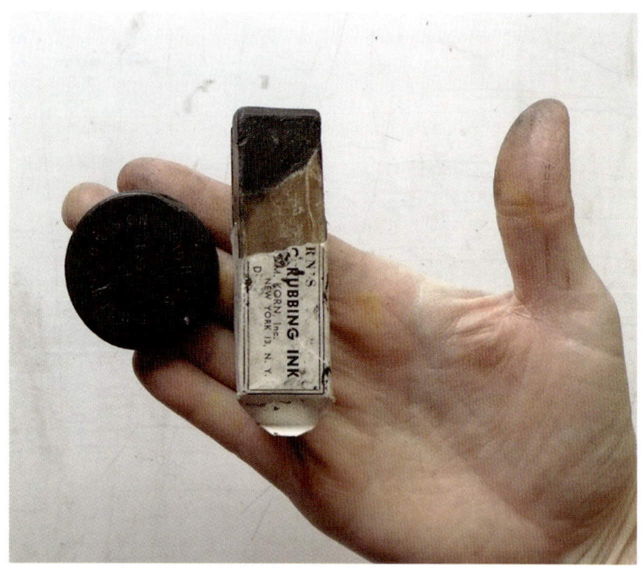

Rubbing ink or tablets come in different grades and makes.

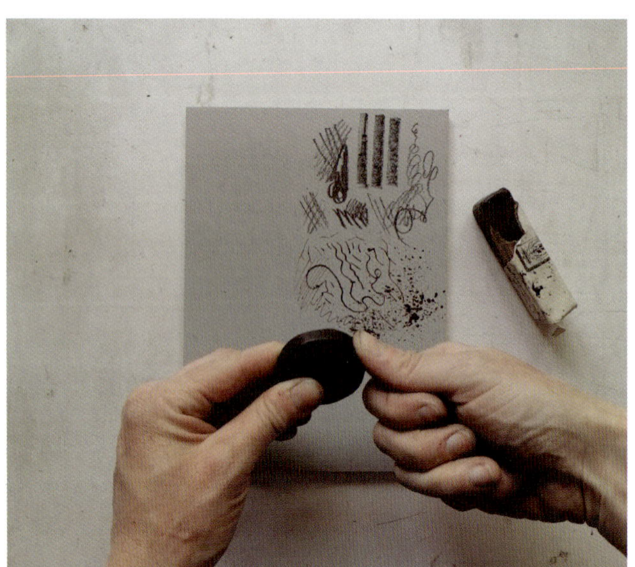

Warm up with a thumb or rag and rub on the lino, like charcoal.

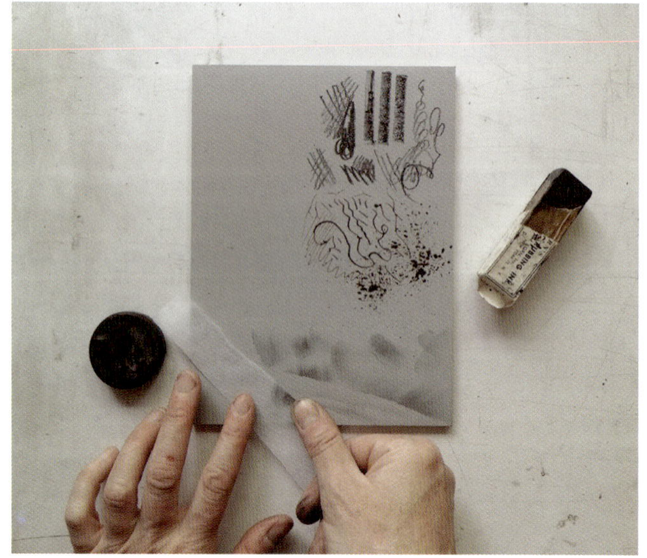

Use masks to create crisp edges in contrast to swoosh marks.

LITHOGRAPHIC TUSCHE

Tusche is a liquid drawing ink that is fantastic at creating tonal washes. The drawing ink is better at creating black and used in conjunction with drawing tools such as dip pens, tusche is the medium for gradient washes and tonal areas of wash. It comes in a tablet form or pre-mixed. The tablet form requires that you dissolve the stick in water to make up a tusche solution. Once you have a strong tusche solution, be it made up or pre-bought, you can then take from this to dilute further with water to create washes of different grades. Tusche is something that is specific to litho and the washes are characteristic to the process. They do some wonderful things as they dry, called reticulation. This is where the grease particles pool and gather at the water's edges as the water in the wash evaporates. It creates characteristic ripples and speckles with the washes. Rather beautiful and a giveaway that a print is a lithograph. Lino

produces and prints reticulation very well for the first few prints and I have been able to get reticulation still present in prints over edition ten. Once a wash is dry, you are able to overlay another wash on top. Just be careful with how many washes you overlay. On the matrix it will look all tonal and beautiful, when you go to print the lithino, the lino will just read too many overlay washes as layer upon layer of grease build up and ink up black. If you wish to keep your washes clean and distinct, then I advise working with a very pale wash, a medium tone and a dark tone and keep the contrast of the washes tidy and clean. Working with tusche is hours of fun and experimentation to understand its lovely nature and how it will print.

I always work with the stick tusche because it will store for years, and I find I can make up my own strength of wash. It takes a little practice to make a good tusche solution from the stick, but it is satisfying and well worth the patience in learning.

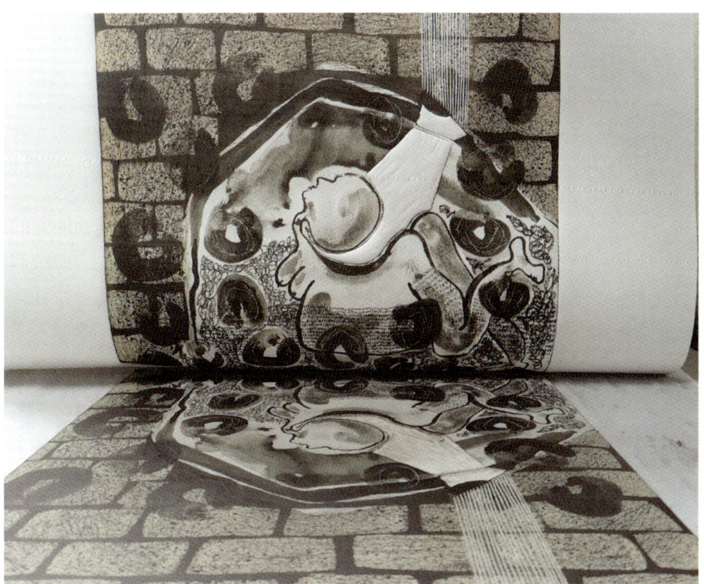

Pulling a lithino from the press, with a beautiful array of marks.

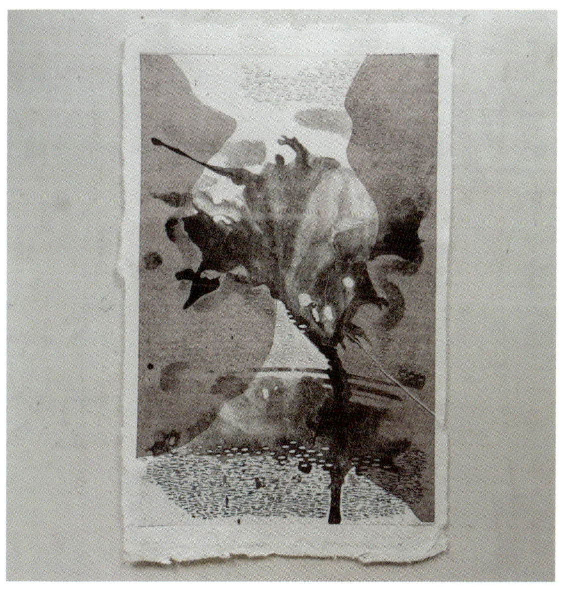

Tusche can give some beautiful ink wash effects, giving the lino a fluidity in expression. *Storm*, Mary Dalton.

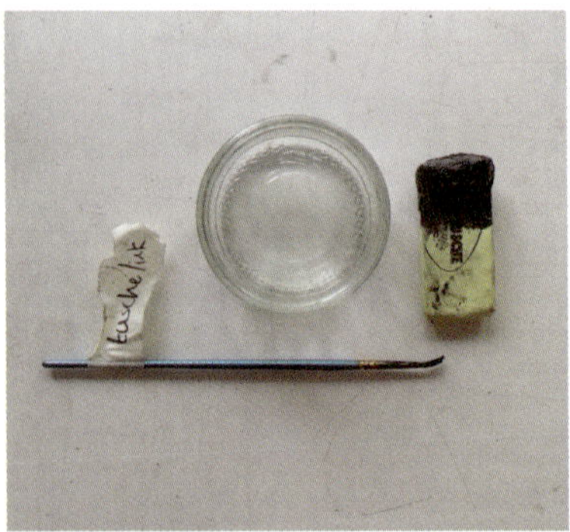

Lithographic tusche in stick form. It can be bought in solution.

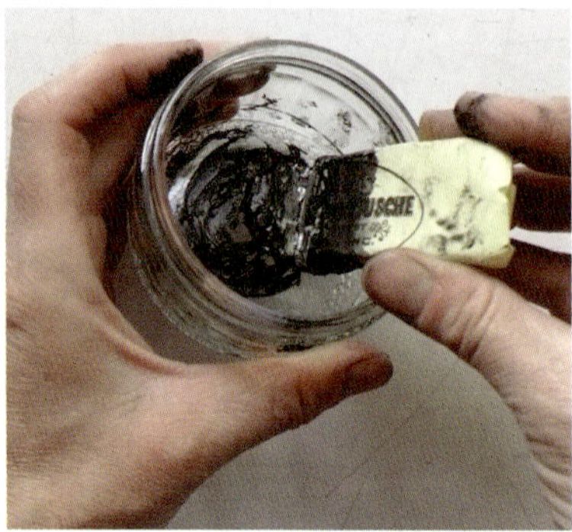

Rub the stick on the bottom of a heatproof dish to cover.

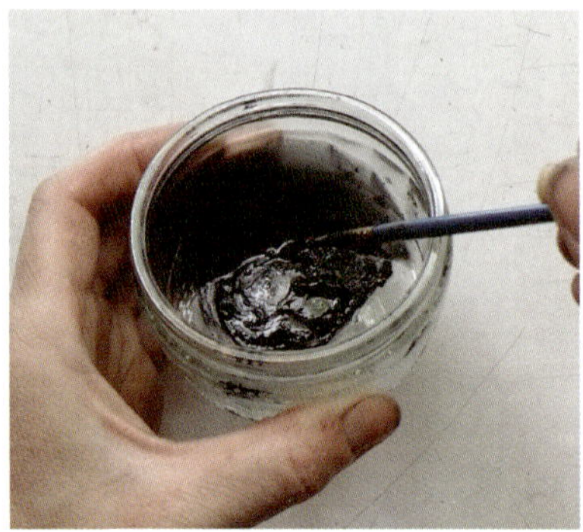

Add small amounts of hot water and mix with a brush until dissolved.

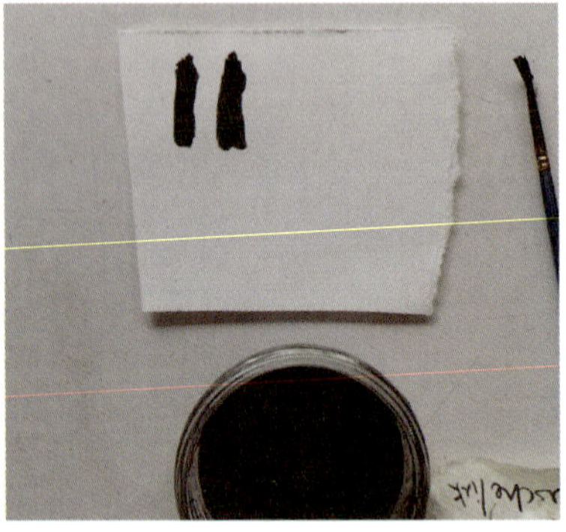

Test the depth of the neat tusche solution on paper. It should be black.

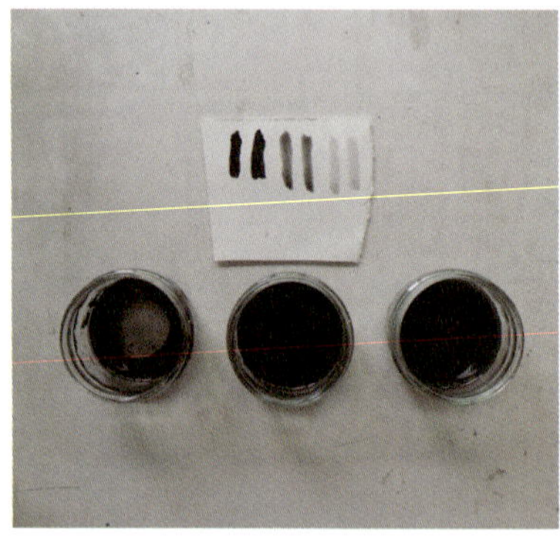

Mix neat solution with water for different concentrations. Test.

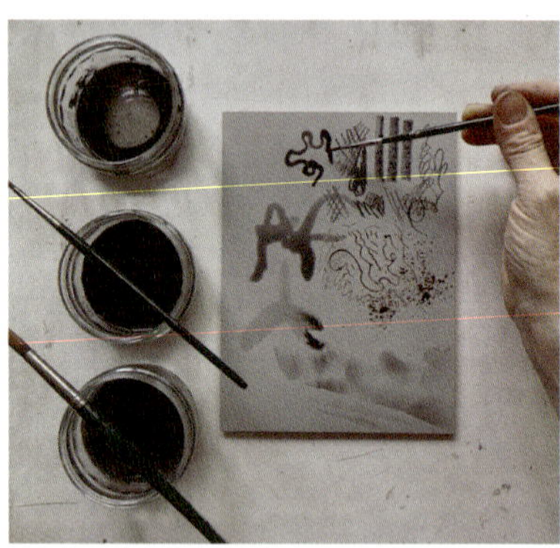

Paint directly with the tusche concentrations on the lino.

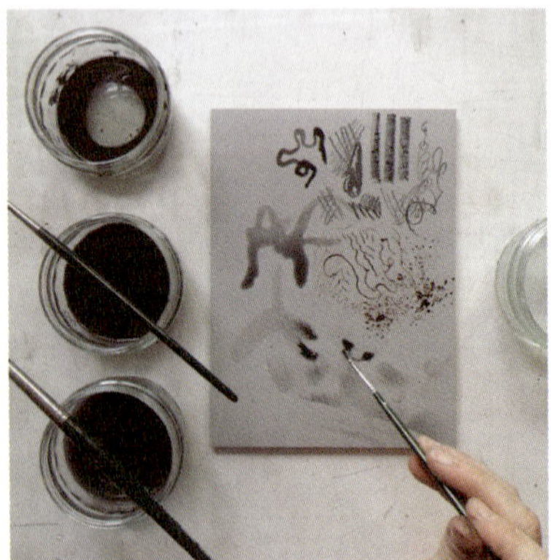

Let the tusche washes dry undisturbed to achieve the reticulation.

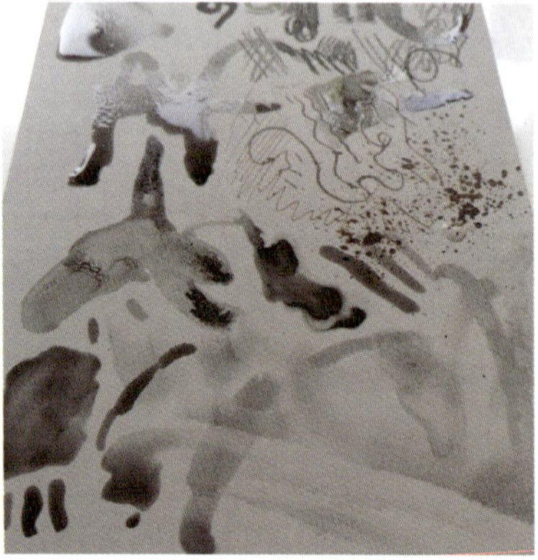

Let some tusche bleed into pools of water on the lino.

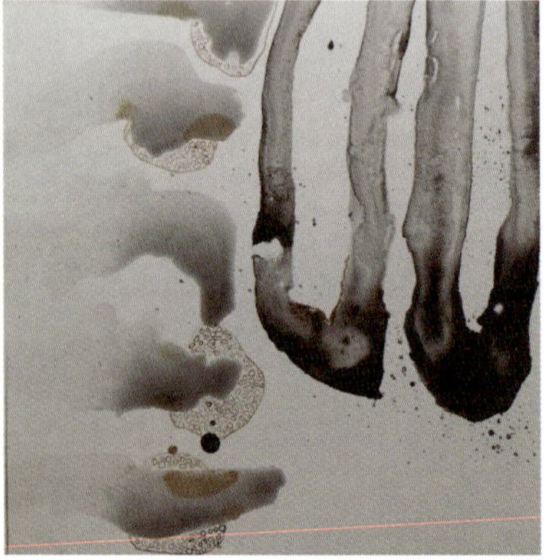

An example of liberally tusche washes.

OIL-BASED PRINTING INK

Using traditional oil-based ink as a drawing medium is a fantastic way of working. You can transfer monoprints onto the surface of the lino, use it to stamp pattern and create ink transfer drawings. The oil-based ink naturally attracts the oil-based lithography ink upon rolling up and so you can create a very stable, dark mark. You will need to let the black oil-based ink dry on the lino before you print it, otherwise you risk transferring black ink if you are rolling up in colour.

Transferring a monoprint is easy enough. You will need to make your monoprint on a sheet of dry point card or a re-usable sheet of thin plastic film, then print this onto the surface of lino as opposed to the surface of paper. This will require an etching press with the roller raised to accommodate the depth of the plastic and lino. You could also hand transfer it with a baren, but the intensity of the black will be less strong.

Stamping textures with oil-based ink is a great way to introduce pattern. It is very direct and can also remove the artist from the burden of creating imagery, instead focusing on direct communication.

To make an ink transfer drawing, you will need to create a sheet of paper similar to carbon paper by applying layers of oil-based printing ink onto the surface. I tend to use a smooth-surfaced layout paper, or even photocopy paper. The smooth texture allows for a clean transfer of your drawing onto the lino. The trick is to build up the ink application layers very thinly. Too thick ink will result in splodging rather than a clean drawing. Be patient, keep rolling on thin layers and it works beautifully. If rolling up your lithino for printing in any colour other than black, you must let the black oil-based ink dry. This will take a week or so.

Alternative materials

Any material that contains an element of grease can be experimented with. For example face creams, greasy takeaway papers or lipstick could be drawn with to create a mark. These marks are experimental and less predictable and this needs to be taken into consideration when printing. Also remember that using alternative materials that are quite liquid and do not dry/get absorbed by the lino can cause issues further down the line. The material that you experiment with needs to not pool or stay wet, as this will smudge when we apply the gum Arabic etch, so drawing with vegetable oil would not work, but perhaps stamping the lino with a greasy takeaway wrapper would generate an impression.

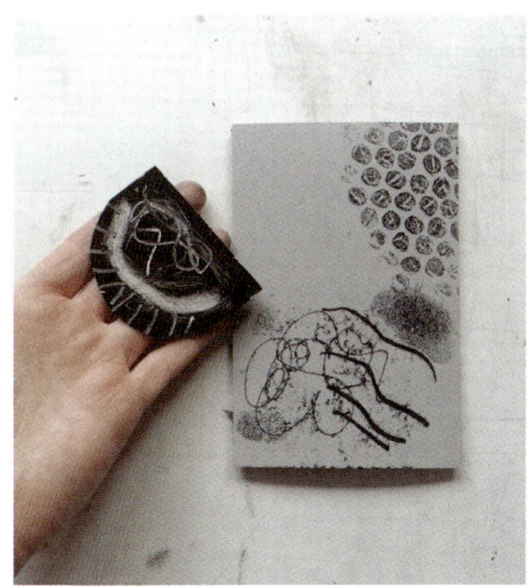

A monoprint created with oil-based ink on a scrap of Tetra Pak.

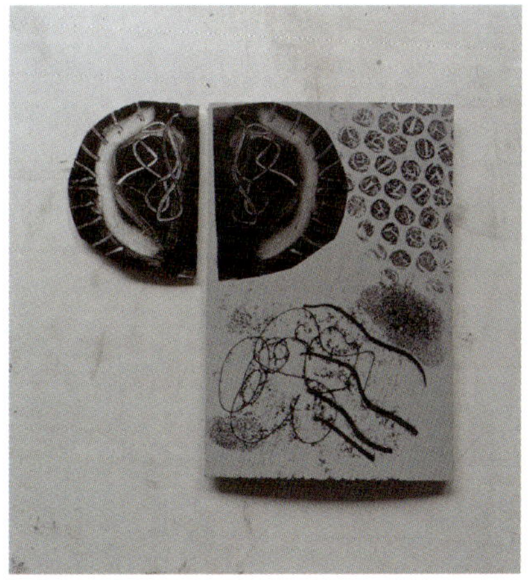

The monoprint transferred to the lino surface under a press.

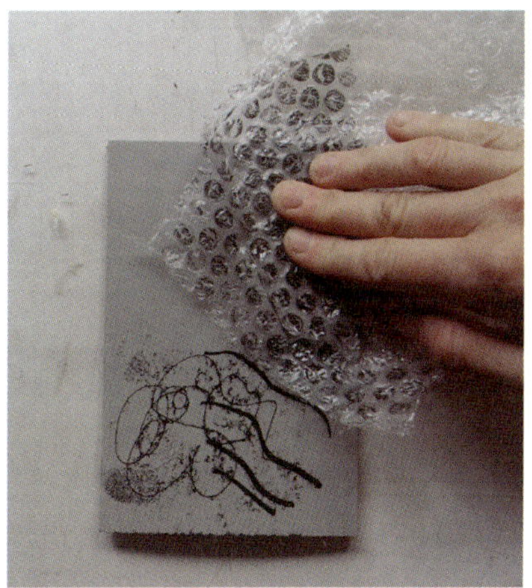

Hand stamping some bubble wrap inked up with oil-based ink.

Layering materials

Lithographic materials can be successfully layered on top of one another. Just be aware, the more layering you do, and thus the more grease you lay down, the more likely the print will just roll up black rather than reading as separate layers. Imagine each layer is a grey sheet of acetate. The more grey acetates you stack upon one another, the more it will just read as black rather than separate grey layers. I tend to advise a maximum of three layers on top of one another. If working with tusche washes, keep your washes clean and distinct. The more muddying of washes through layering, the higher the chance it will just ink up black.

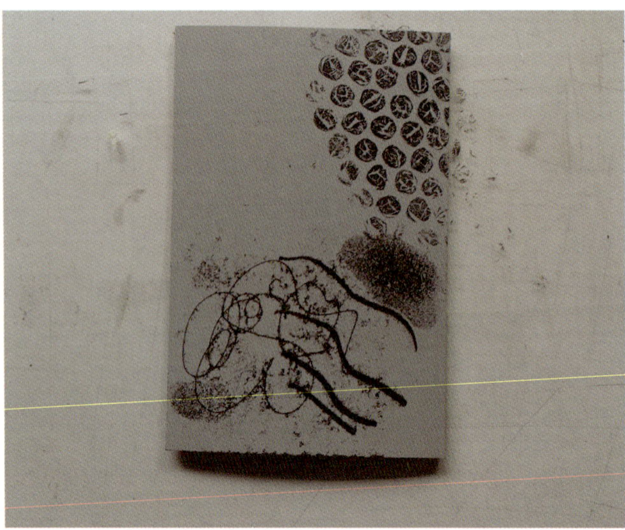

The resultant hand stamping print on the lino.

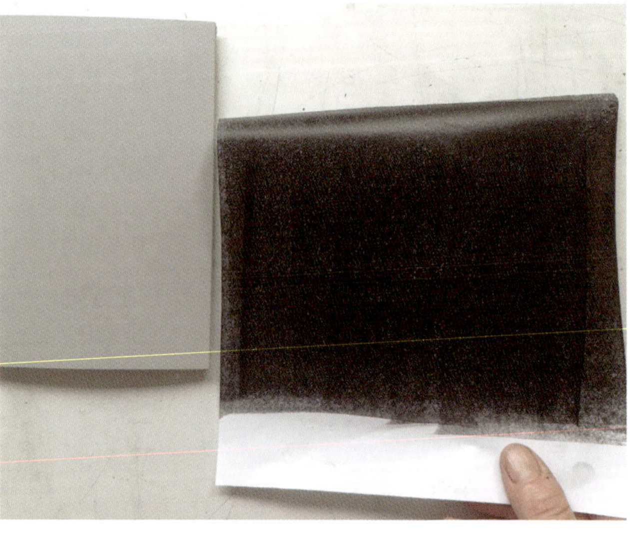

Copy paper rolled up with a thin layer of oil-based ink.

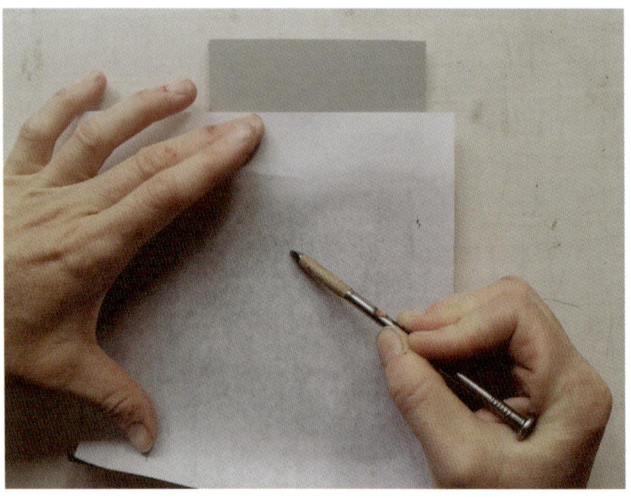

Place paper ink side in contact with lino and draw on the back with tools.

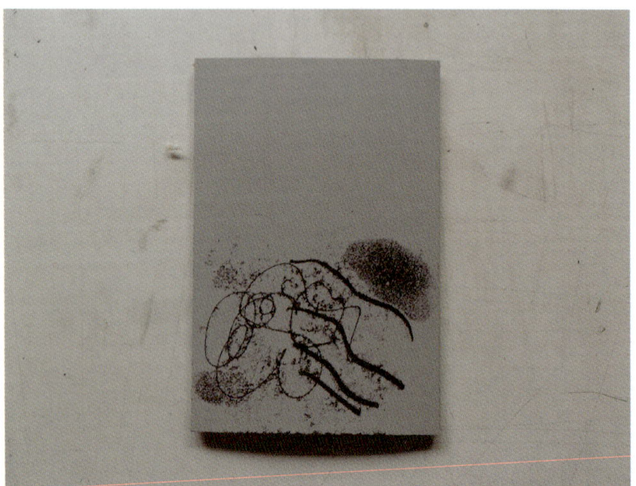

The resultant ink transfer drawing on lino will print as is.

MONOCHROME LITHINO

This example will introduce you to the basic process of processing a black lithino drawing. It is designed to allow you to test the materials used to draw and understand how they translate to print. Try not to think about creating an image here; this is a test sheet of material use. This example takes place over a period of a week. The drawing stage occurs first and then the lino is stabilised under gum Arabic. This needs to sit for a week before printing. Here we have printed using a press with one compressed felt blanket, but you can also hand print your lithino by using a baren. We will talk further on this later.

Materials

Sheet of traditional lino, approximately A5, with drawing complete and dry
Traditional oil-based ink
Roller and roll-out area
Press set up for lino, with runners. If hand printing, a metal teaspoon is a great baren
Gum Arabic
Printing paper. Smooth surface, anywhere between 120gsm and 220gsm works well.
Wide, flat paint brush
Clean sponge and container for water

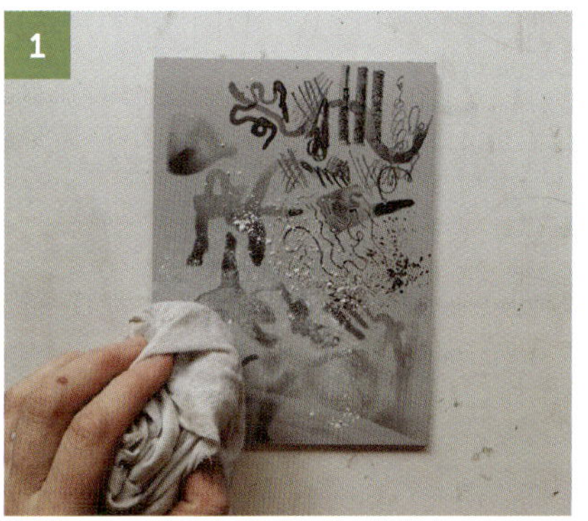

Apply a dusting of whiting and puff out evenly over the dry litho drawing.

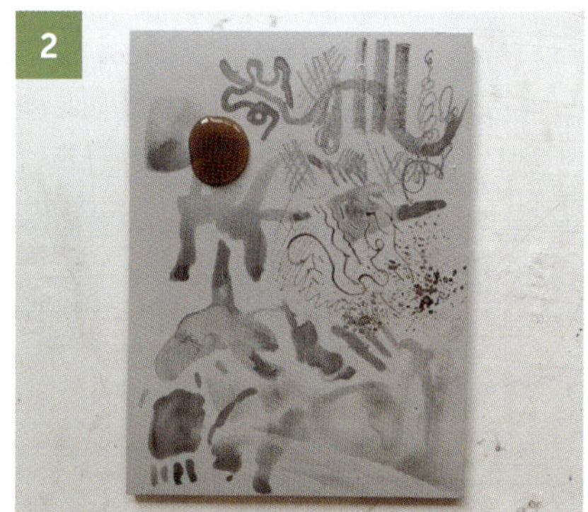

Place a 50p-sized amount of gum Arabic onto the lino.

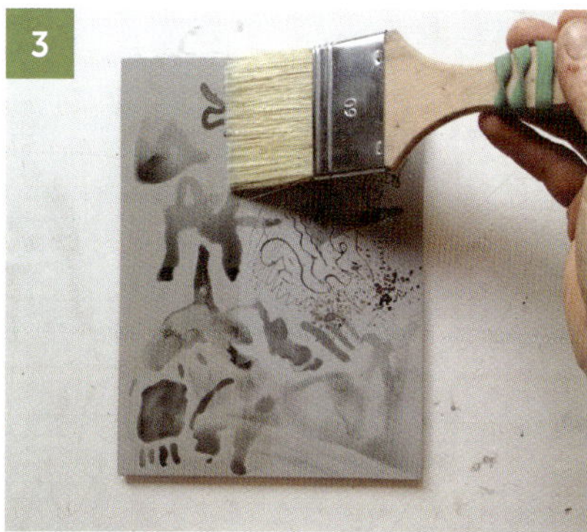

Spread out the gum evenly using a wide, flat brush.

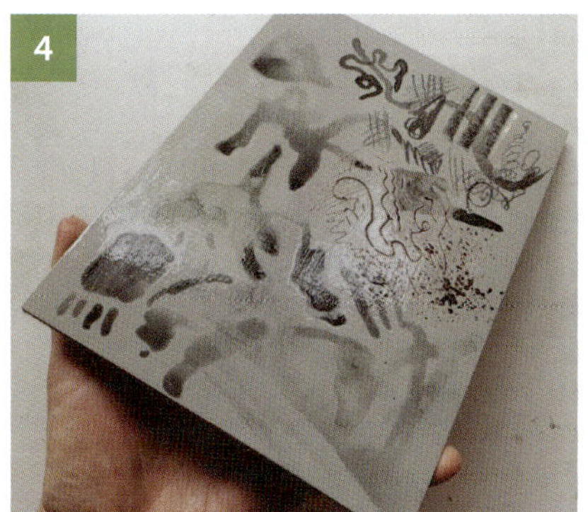

Check in the light for an even, thin layer. Leave for a week.

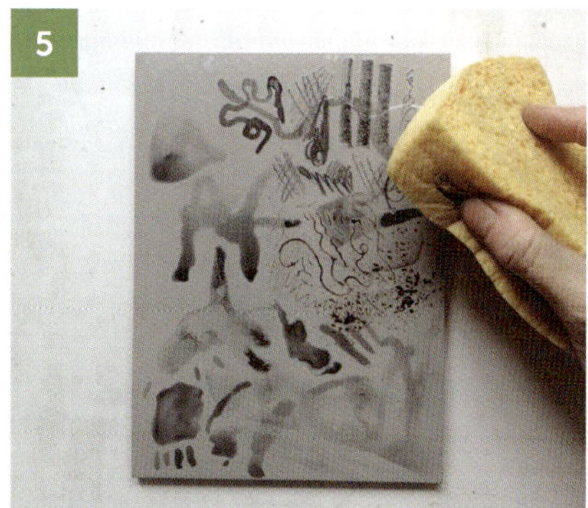

Before inking up, remove the gum with a wet sponge.

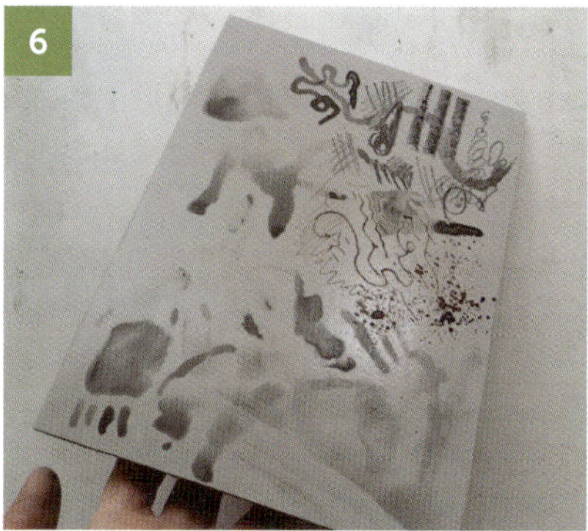

Using a damp (not wet) sponge, wipe over lino creating a thin film of moisture.

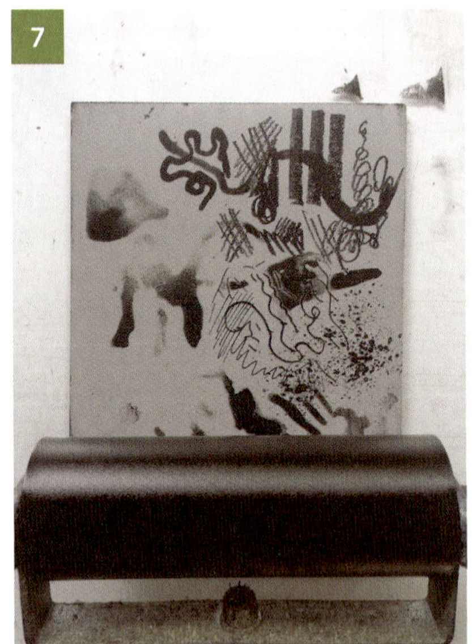

Roll the lino up with a thin layer of ink. Keep lino damp if needed.

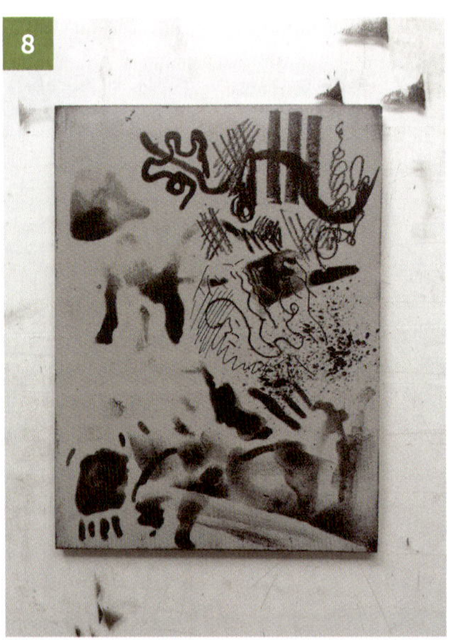

When all marks are building nicely and filled in, you can print.

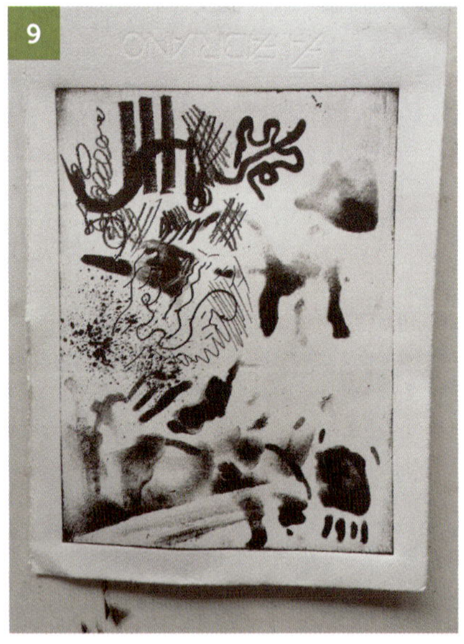

Print with damp paper under an etching press set up for lino.

Why do we 'etch' the drawing?

In lithographic terms, the word 'etch' is being used to describe the stage when gum Arabic is being applied to the drawing to stabilise the image areas and the non-image areas. This means that your lithino is more likely to produce a stable edition. In an ideal world, the gum Arabic should be left on the lino for a week – in fact, the longer the better. However, because of the nature of life, this is not always possible and if you leave the gum on your plate overnight (approximately eight hours) then you can still get a fantastic first impression and a few impressions to follow before the plate wants to fill in with ink in non-image areas. As an artist who works on unique prints, I have no problem with only getting the first impression beautifully true to the marks. The interest for me is in the quality of the lithino mark marking rather than the edition.

Editioning

Lithino is not stone litho. It will not print 500 copies. To be honest, I am not entirely sure what one is meant to do with 500 copies of anything anymore, so quite frankly, that

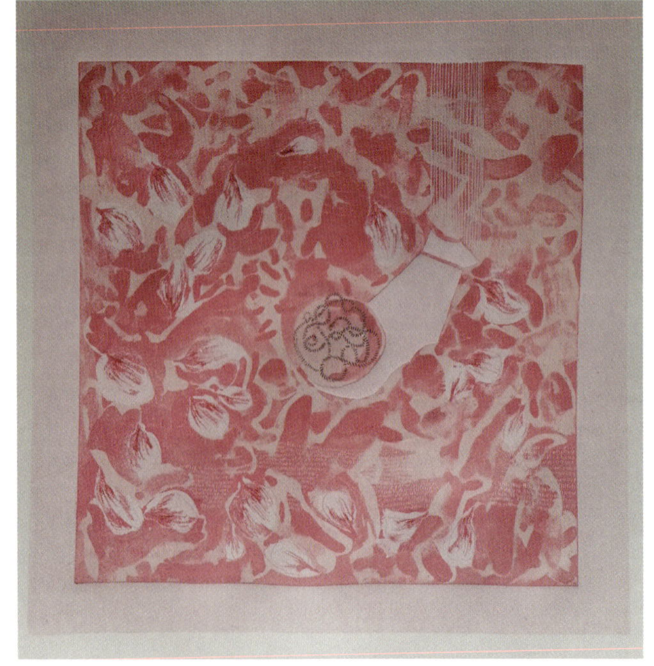

The first impression of a pink tusche lithino, showing the wash depth.

works out well. Lithino is about a unique approach to mark making on a completely biodegradable product. Its strength lies in the beautiful quality of mark and its ability to be flexible and accessible. Unlike stone or plate litho, lino can be cut up into jigsaw elements, it can be transported easily, it can be carved into easily and it can be re-used for other methods of printmaking after lithography. It is amazingly versatile. However, if one is interested in creating an edition, lithino can do this. The key is in the plate graining, the sanding process. The better the sanding you give the lino surface, the less likely the ink will fill in the non-image areas (known as 'scumming up' in lithography). I have happily printed 15 prints of a monochrome lithino, with barely any scumming up and a reasonably stable image. You cannot really over sand with the wire wool, but you can under sand.

Printing in colour

If you wish to print your lithino in colour rather than black, it is as simple as rolling on the chosen colour instead of the black ink. The lithographic drawing materials should not transfer any black to your print and the impression will simply be a coloured version of the lithino.

Working with colour in lithography requires practice because of the nature of the thin layer of ink applied – it can be very transparent. This works in your favour when building up colour layers with multiple plates because you can get to play with colour overlay to generate further colours in the impression. However, if for instance you have a lovely tusche wash drawing, inking it up in primrose yellow will mean that many of those lovely subtleties will be lost because the yellow on the white paper struggles to showcase the contrasts. If you inked it up in a green or a blue, you may find you have

A beautiful example of a two-plate colour lithino drawn in crayon. *After Edvard Munch I* (2024), Nina Gross.

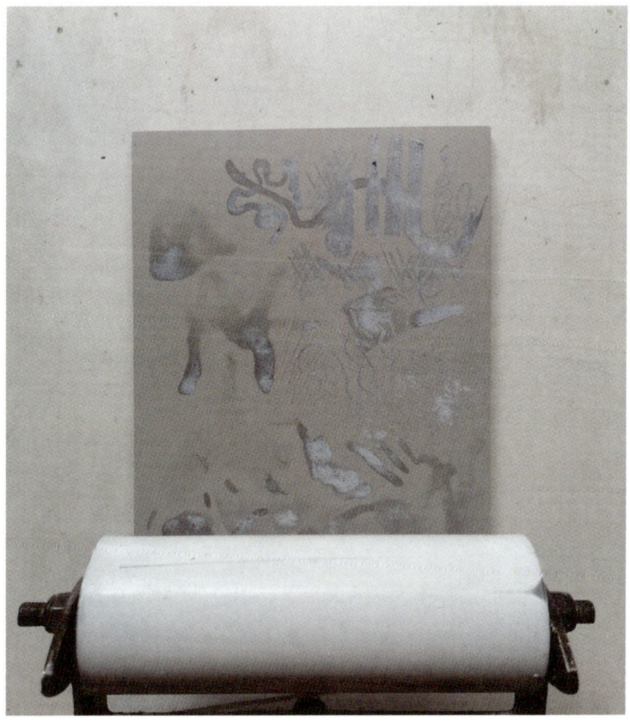

Inking up the lithino in opaque white, loosened with a little oil.

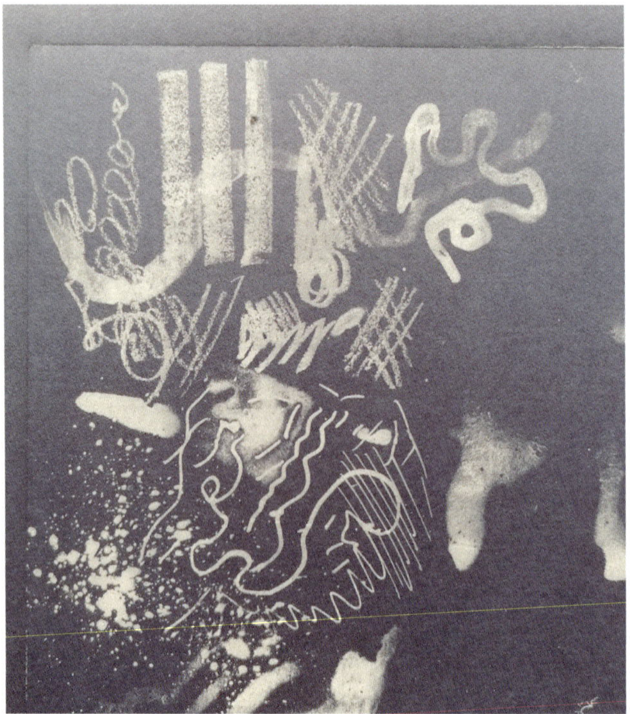

Detail of the white lithino printed on dark blue paper.

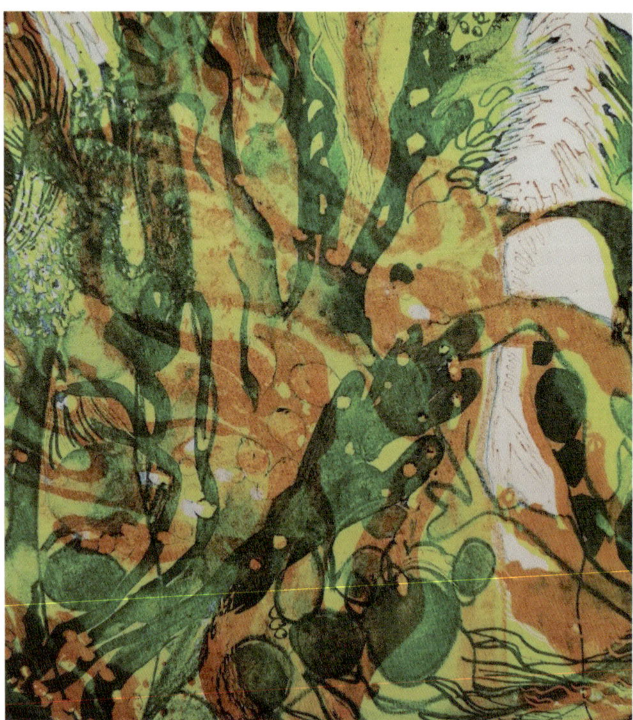

A tester piece by a student of four different colour lithino plates.

kept more of the beautiful wash contrasts. On saying that, if you inked up your lithino in white and printed it on black paper, then you will be amazed at the quality of the results. It really is worth having a play.

Press printing or by hand

Lithino prints beautifully under an etching press with the rollers supported by lino runners. Lino runners are strips of lino set either side of the press bed edges to support the weight of the top roller. This prevents the roller hitting the lino matrix and bumping up or off the lino and causing a shift in the impression or damage to your press. Lino runners need to be inserted in the press by loosening pressure evenly, inserting the runners and then tightening the pressure evenly on both sides to finger tight. Once finger tight,

the suitable pressure for lithino is tighter than if you are printing a straight-up relief lino cut, and so I turn another half turn after finger tight pressure. Next you will need to check that the lino is not being stretched under the pressure of the etching press. If your lino gets stretched, it makes it impossible to register any subsequent layers.

To test the stretch, run a piece of scrap lino under the set pressure press with a piece of your printing paper and once run through, check the sides of the lino against the emboss created. The sides of the lino should be matching in size to the emboss created. If the pressure is too tight and a stretch has been created, then you will notice that the emboss is longer than the actual lino matrix. In which case you will need to loosen the pressure and re-test.

Printing by hand is as simple as getting a printing baren and applying pressure. A smooth, hard printing baren works the best, such as a metal spoon. You will need to apply a decent amount of pressure in small circles and hold your paper with your non-printing hand. Because the lithino has a very thin ink layer, the paper does not naturally stick to the lino matrix, so it can shift if it is not held tight. Switching to a lightweight washi paper will also help and mean that you need not apply so much force. Try something in the range of 25gsm to 75gsm, such as a Tosa washi paper sitting around 28gsm. You still want as smooth a surface as possible for the best representation of your marks.

INTRODUCING LINO CUT MARKS

Lino is known more commonly for its relief work, created with lino cut carving tools. The advantage of lithino is that you can combine the lithographic expressive mark making with more graphic lino cut marks. The combination is beautiful and unique. What is more appealing is a unique aesthetic thing that the lino cut marks create when printing using the lithographic technique. When printed up, around the edge of each carved mark is a little black outline. This is because the edge of the carved lino mark catches a bit of the ink when inked up lithographically. It is quite exquisite and beautiful, and unique to lithino.

This mark is only visible when the lino carved areas are on a non-image area. This means you can visually see the black outline against a white background. The best way to showcase this is through a demonstration of integrating lino carved marks within the lithographic imagery. We will be able to see this happen more clearly with a step-by-step project.

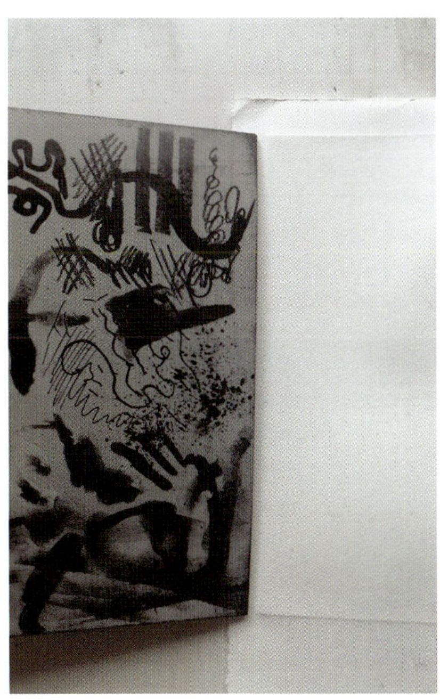

Check the pressure emboss with actual lino to check for stretch.

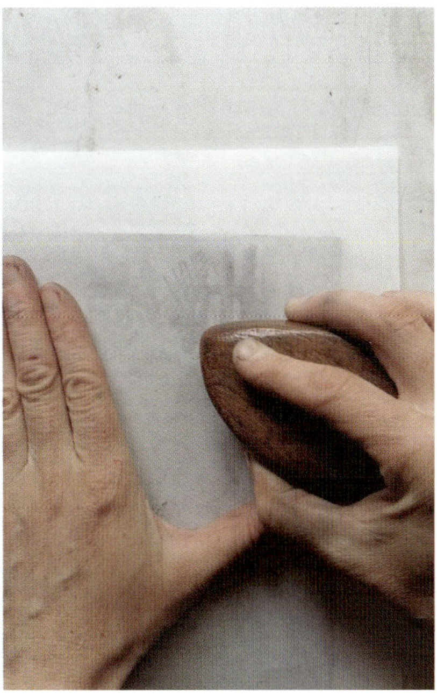

Hand printing an inked lithino onto 39gsm paper.

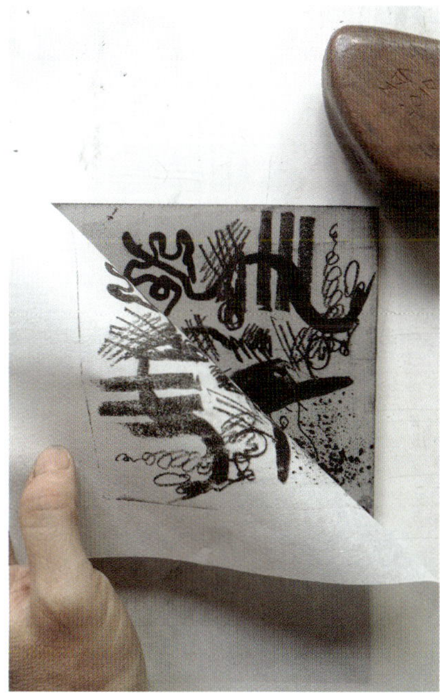

The resultant impression is still strong.

INTRODUCING CARVING

For this demonstration, you will need a pre-drawn and gummed up lithino plate. Focus on a range of mark making on the lino, and again see this as a test plate. Make sure to give it a good sand prior to mark making. The materials listed below are for the process of carving and printing after the gum has been applied and allowed to dry.

Materials
Lino carving tools
Traditional oil-based ink
Roller and roll-out area
Sponge and water
Smooth paper between 120gsm and 220gsm
Press set up with lino runners

Working with the carving
The results from the carved marks are really beautiful and you can easily just work with those even without any lithographic mark making. It is quite unique to lithino. Sand your lino as if you were to draw lithographically, then apply a layer of gum Arabic, let it dry and then carve into it with lino tools. Ink and print it like a lithographic layer, removing gum, keeping plate damp, rolling up and so on. The resultant print will be a white background and lots of black outlines to carved marks. Very unusual and has a great potential to play with.

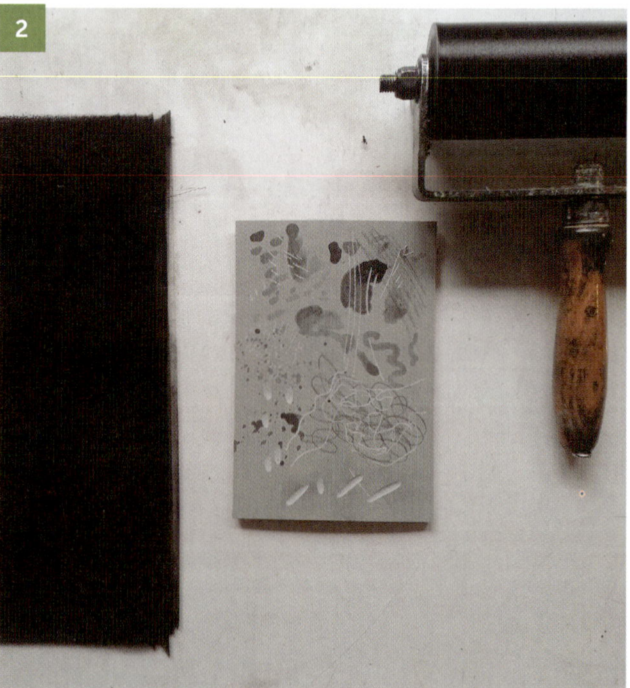

Carve into a prepared, gummed-up lithino plate using lino tools.

Remove gum and get prepared to roll up lithographically.

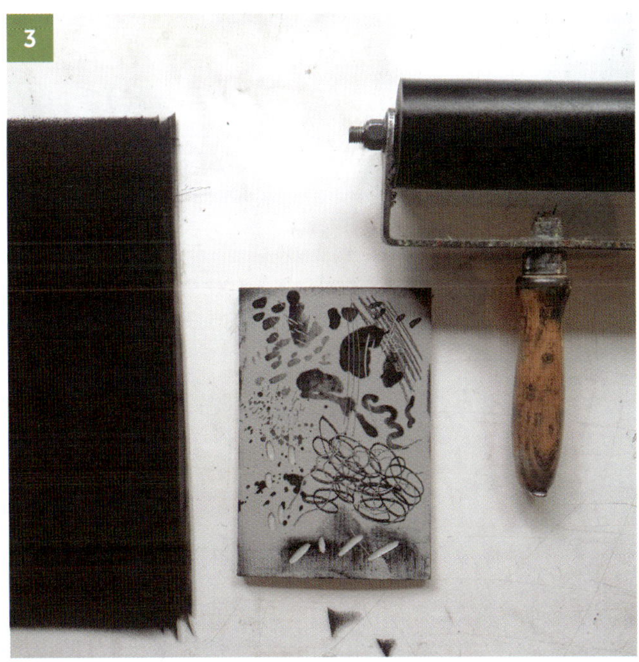

Once the lithino marks have taken, you are ready to print.

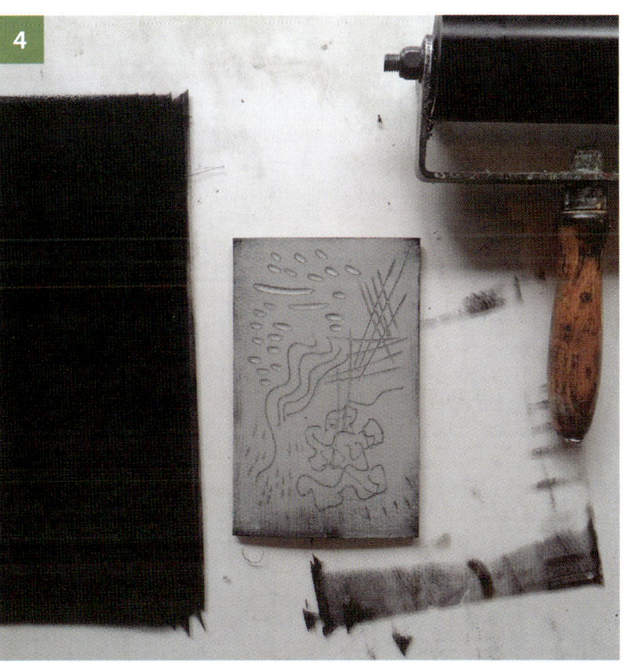

A lino with carved marks inked lithographically. Note the white outlines.

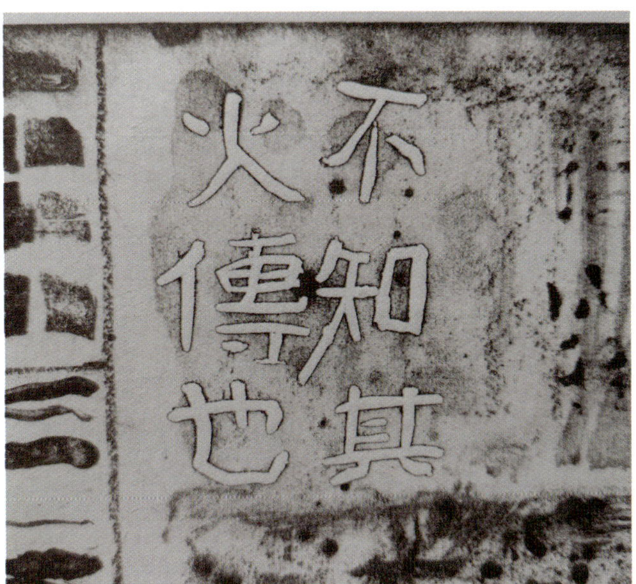

A detail of the white outline on a student's lithino print.

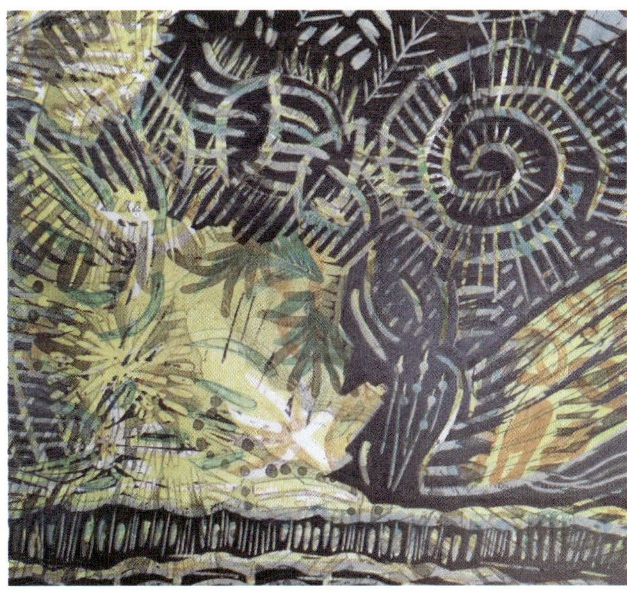

A complex layered lithino sample with carving at each stage. The outlines of carved marks add complex details at each layer.

DRAWING WITH GUM ARABIC

Gum Arabic is an amazing thing. It is essential in lithography, but can also be used as a drawing material in its own right. Wherever gum Arabic is applied, the lithographic marks under the gum will print true to their form. Where gum is not, the matrix will roll up with ink. This can be clearly demonstrated with a test piece example. Instead of applying gum all over to etch the lino, it is applied in spots as a partial gum etch. The results are beautiful.

The use of gum as a drawing material is a method used across all forms of lithography. It is not common, but I believe it really is very versatile and wondrous. To develop it further, you could add some carved marks in your lino combining the bold gum resist with the little white outline effect of carved marks. This would be unique to lithino and thus very exciting.

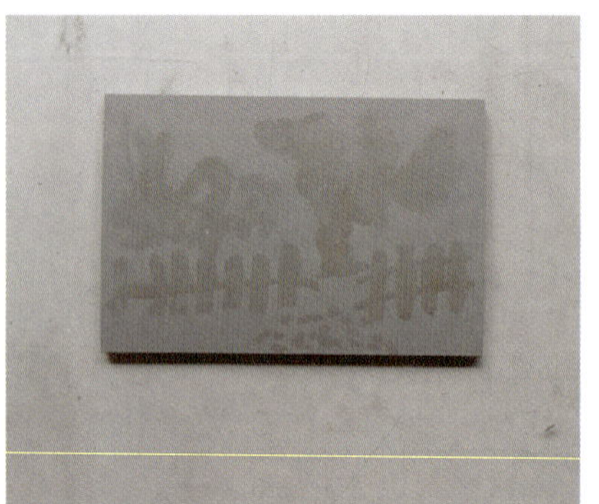

A drawing painted with gum onto a sanded lino plate.

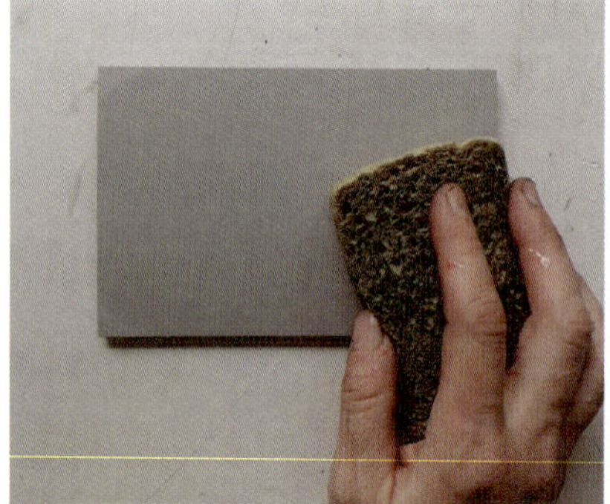

After the gum has etched, it is removed with water.

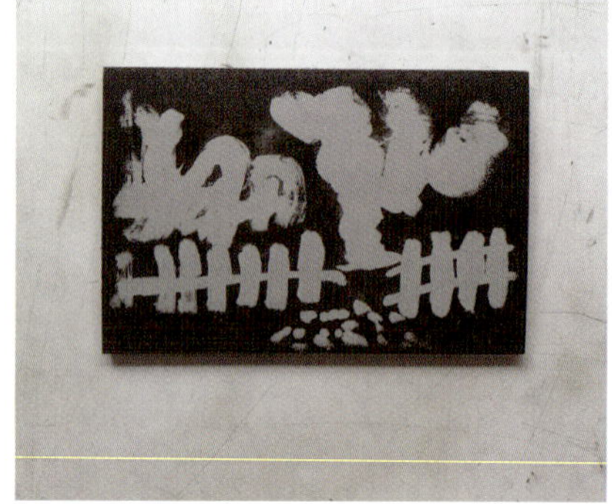

The plate is kept damp and inked up in black.

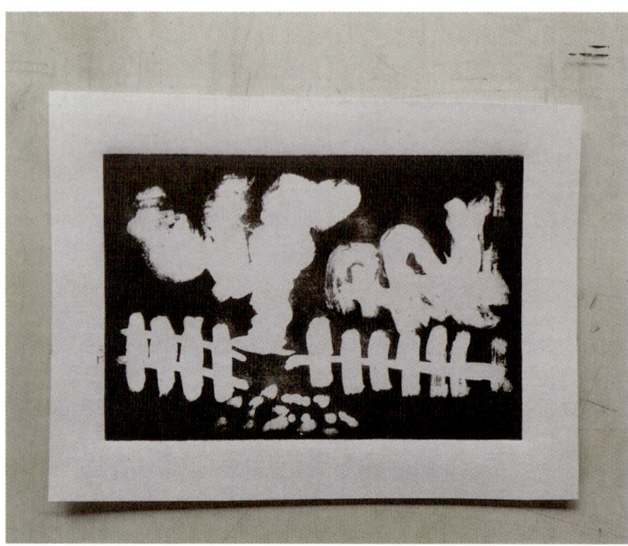

The resultant bold gum-resist lithino.

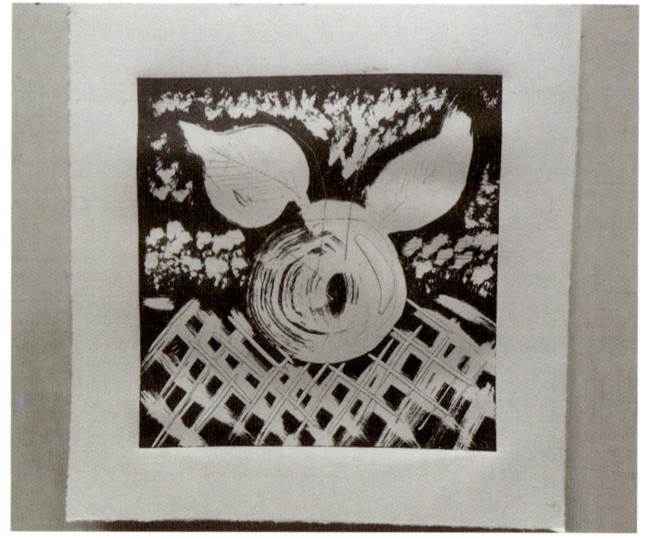

A gum-resist drawing combined with carved lino marks.

Painting with gum and a viscosity roll

This method really works best under an etching press. It can be hand printed, but if you are wishing for the rich black, then a press is the way to go. We will integrate a quick viscosity roll over to turn the white areas into a coloured section. After inking up standard in black, you will need to let residual moisture on the lino plate evaporate before the red viscosity roll. This takes around five minutes. If it is not dry, your oil-based viscosity roll will not adhere to non-image areas.

Materials

A piece of lino pre-sanded with wire wool
Gum Arabic
Paintbrush and tools to 'paint' with (such as feathers or sticks)
Traditional oil-based inks, black and one other colour
Roller and roll-out area
Copperplate oil weak
Press set up with runners
Smooth surface paper between 120gsm and 220gsm

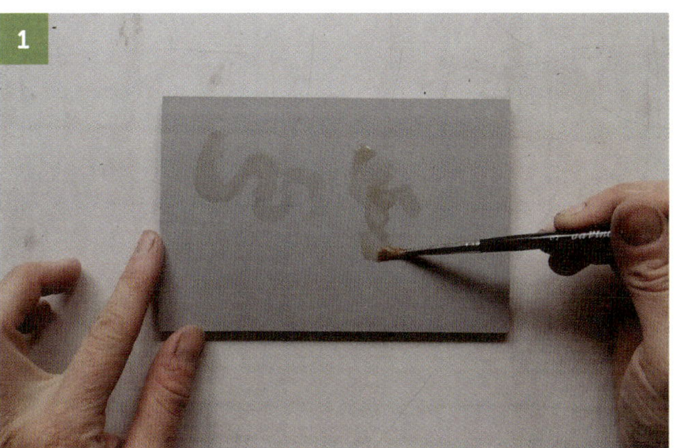
Draw your gum-resist drawing onto sanded lino. Leave to etch.

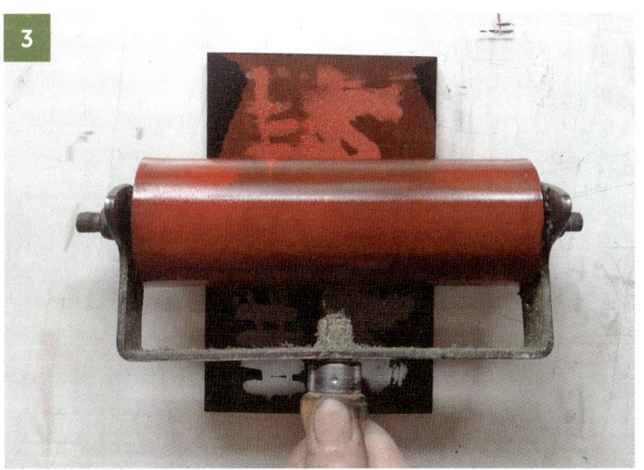
When ready, remove with water and sponge and roll up black.

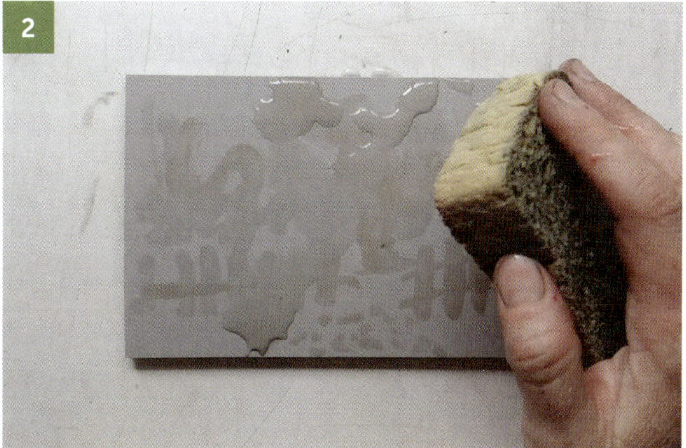
Using the viscosity roll method, roll over a red roll on top of black.

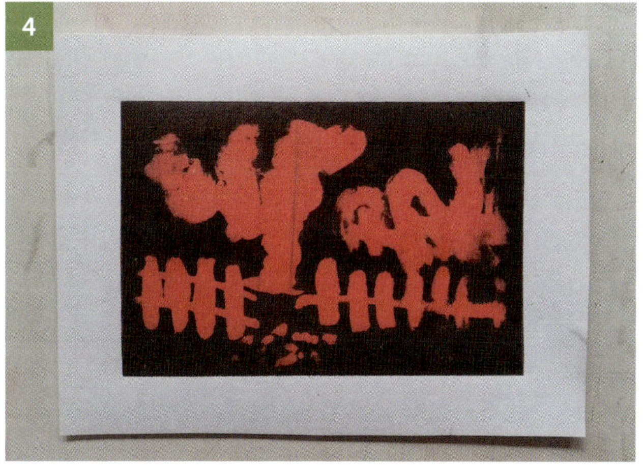
Print on damp paper revealing a bold and clean lithino print.

CRAZY GUM

Gum Arabic, if applied thickly and evenly, will do a beautiful etching job. If you apply it a little more thickly, then it has a tendency to crackle and craze. Where the gum crackles, it does not etch the lino surface and so on your impression you will get the most lovely crackly marks. This is definitely something to work with in areas of your print, and applying the gum more thickly in certain parts allows an element of control as to where this crackling is taking place.

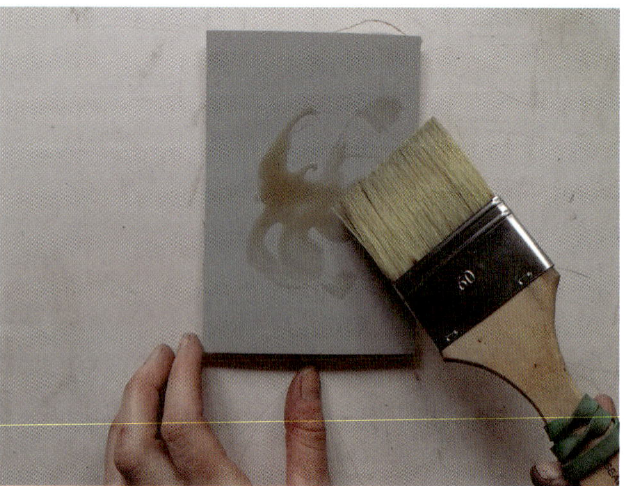

Add pools of gum Arabic onto sanded lino and leave to etch.

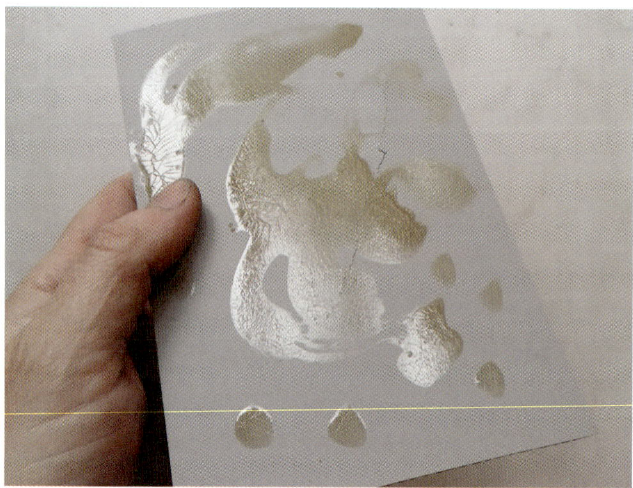

Remove dried gum with plentiful water and gentle rubbing.

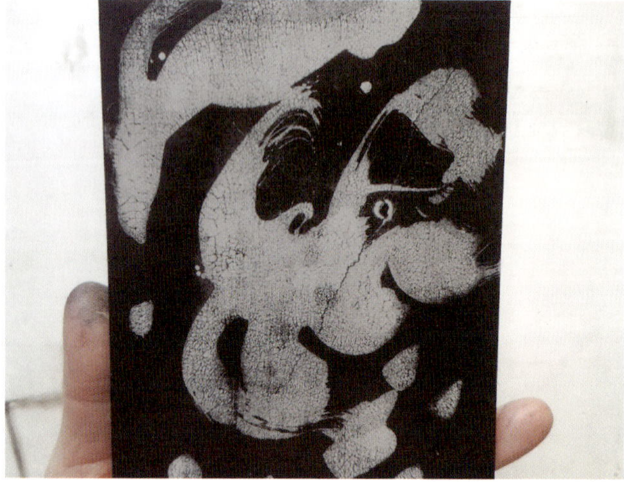

Roll up as standard with damp plate and black ink.

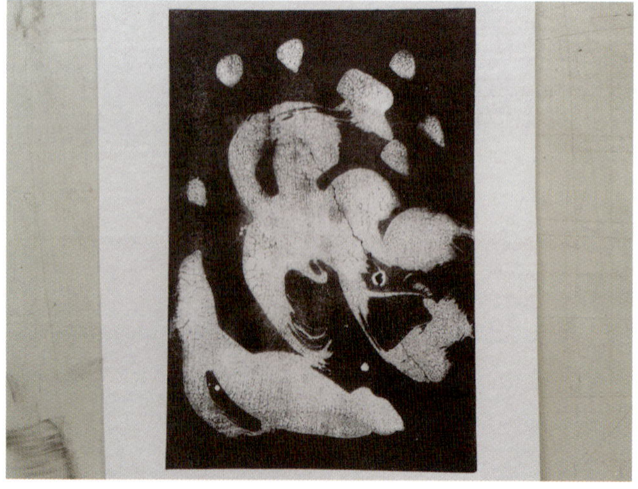

The printed impression clearly showing the crackling.

REPLACING GUM ARABIC

Gum Arabic is a natural product that derives from the sap of an Acacia tree. The Acacia tree is not an indigenous tree to the area I live, which is northern Europe. I use a lot of gum Arabic, and although it is a completely natural and biodegradable product, I was still interested in whether I could potentially find another tree sap that sits around a similar pH value (3–4) and derives from a tree that is more indigenous to the land I live in. It is always a balance. And gum Arabic is an amazing ecological product. I had the landowner's permission to collect and test samples from certain trees which were exuding excess sap one spring. The collection of this sap did not damage the trees, so it seemed an opportunity not to miss. Sometimes you can spot crystallised sap on poorly trees and if you have the landowner's permission and you are not causing any damage to the tree or the lands, then it is worth investigating to see if it works as a gum replacement. When it comes to approaching ecological printmaking, an inquisitive mind and sensitive approach is a must. If you are lucky enough to find a resin that works well, and are able to collect a good amount, then it can be dried out and stored as a resin and dissolved in warm water for use. I have found the resin from a standard cherry tree works superbly. It can be stored dry in lump form It does not store for long when in solution, but popping it in the fridge will extend shelf life. It is amazing how little you need to create a lot of lithino works.

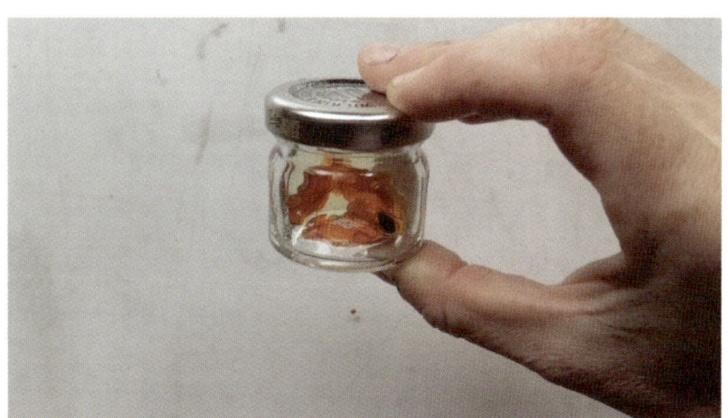

Dried cherry resin collected with the landowner's permission.

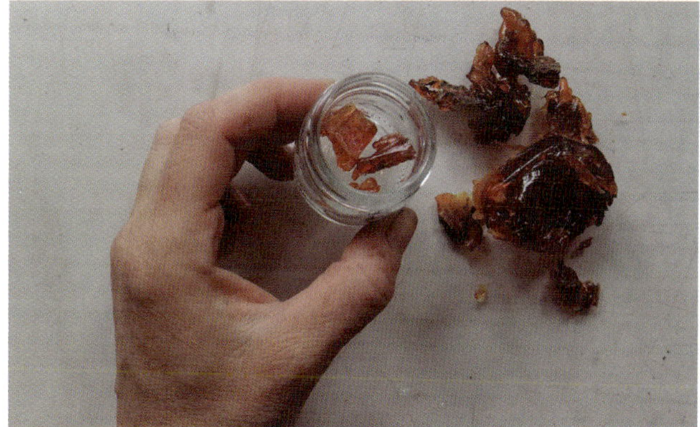

Add a small amount of resin to a jam jar and add double the weight of hot water.

Shake vigorously and leave for an hour or so until dissolved.

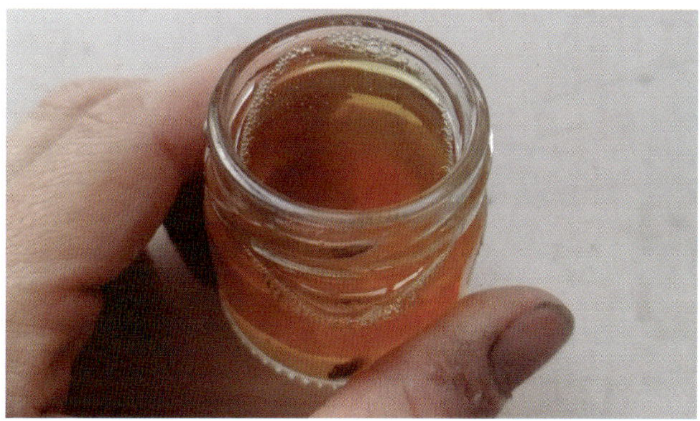

The finished resin solution is ready to go. Store in the fridge.

RE-USING LINO

Lino for the use of lithino can be re-sanded and used again. And again. And again. It really is quite amazing. All lithography requires that the printing matrix be grained prior to use and lithino is no different. In some methods of litho this is done with chemicals, in other methods this is a physical graining process, as with lithino. I have learnt to love the sanding, particularly with the wire wool because it does not make the horrible sanding sounds that send zig-zag shivers down my arms. If you have printed a lithino and you have finished with the lino matrix, clean off the oil-based ink with a tiny amount of vegetable oil and then a good water and soap scrub. The lithographic materials will stay on the surface, because they require spirits or turpentine to remove them, neither of which I am interested in promoting. Instead, once the lino is dry from the water and soap clean, just re-sand. It does require some effort and it is not instant, but it works beautifully and you can then work on the piece of lino again.

If you have carved into the lino, you will retain your carved marks. This is really useful if you are working on a reduction lino cut because it means that you can drop in a lithino layer at any point of the print in amongst the classic relief areas. So long as the matrix has been sanded between each layer, you can switch between lithino, lino, lino, lithinio in any order you so wish.

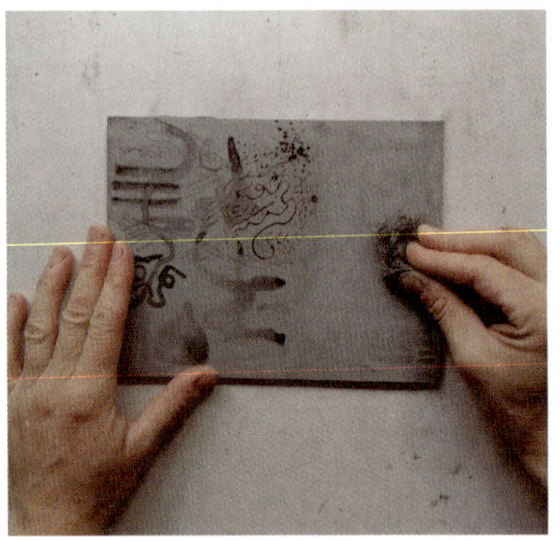

Sanding old lithino plates after the ink has dried on the surface.

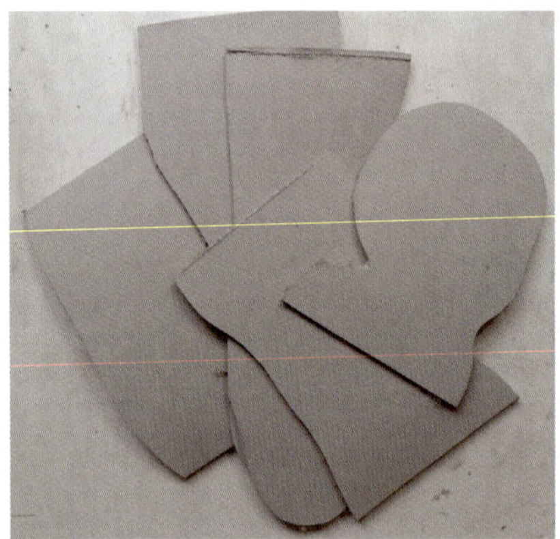

A batch of re-sanded lithino plates ready to rock and roll.

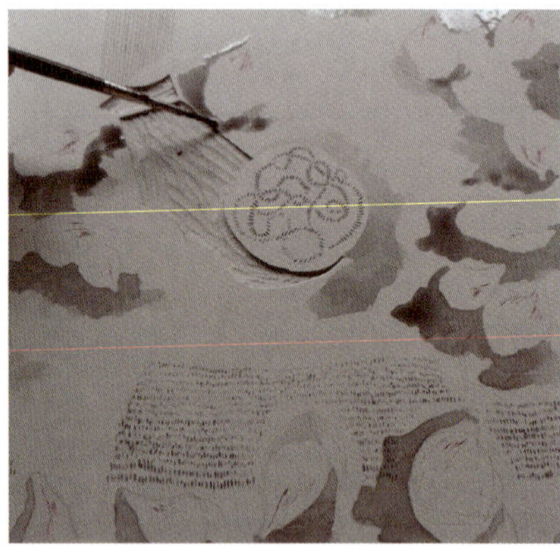

Working with tusche on a lithino layer on re-sanded lino.

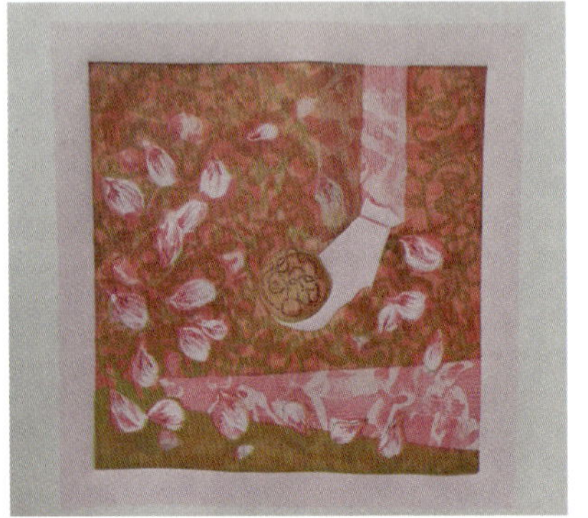

The work in progress of the resultant lithino, all worked on the same lino sheet.

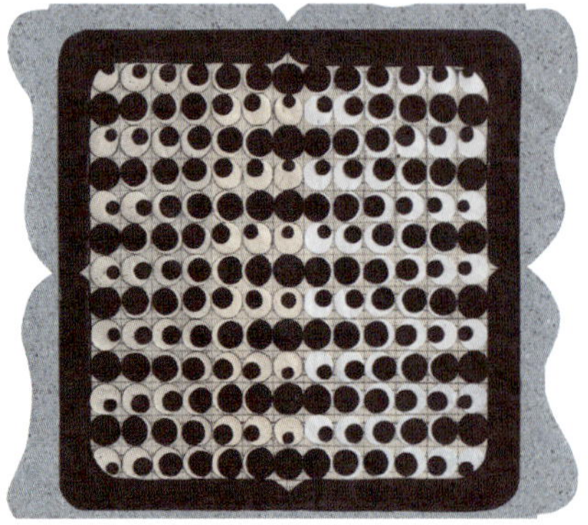

A stunning lithino on handmade linen paper working with the bold effects the medium can offer. *When In Doubt, Blame the Moon*, Alice Zakharenko.

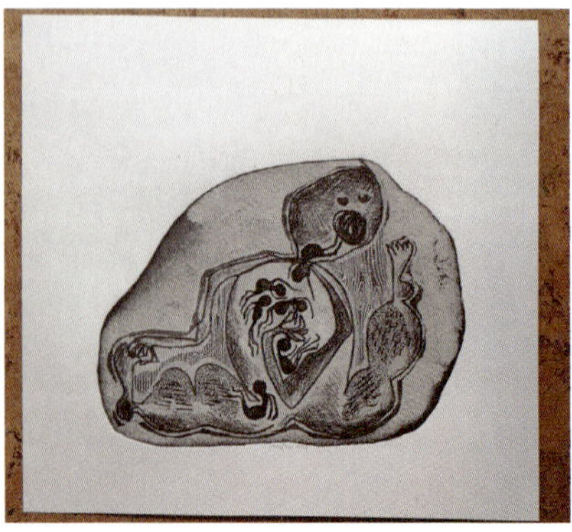

This lithino was made by reclaiming and resanding an offcut from a jigsaw relief lino. *Greed*, Mary Dalton.

Some artists with whom I have shared this re-sanding technique have loved it so much from an ecological perspective and got three or four completely different lithino prints out of their one lino matrix. One even commented that she found the lino was more responsive and printed better on the surfaces that had been re-sanded.

Emergencies!

Don't panic. If your lino plate scums up when printing, this means it fills in all over with ink, then most likely it means that you have not dampened your lino plate. It can be resolved to an extent, but try not to let it happen too often as the lithino is sensitive. Keep an eye on the moisture level of non-image areas, particularly if printing in hot weather.

Where to go with lithino

Lithino is truly a remarkable medium, which still has so much development and investigation time to go to reveal its full potential. It was essential it was included in a book about ecological printmaking because lino as a matrix is one of the best ecological surfaces that one can work on. In this chapter I have given you the basics of the medium, but think outside of this box. Can you combine intaglio and lithino on the one plate? What happens if you monoprint and included viscosity rolls on the lino? Are you able to do a multi-plate lithino? And jigsaw lino? So many options and so much exploration!

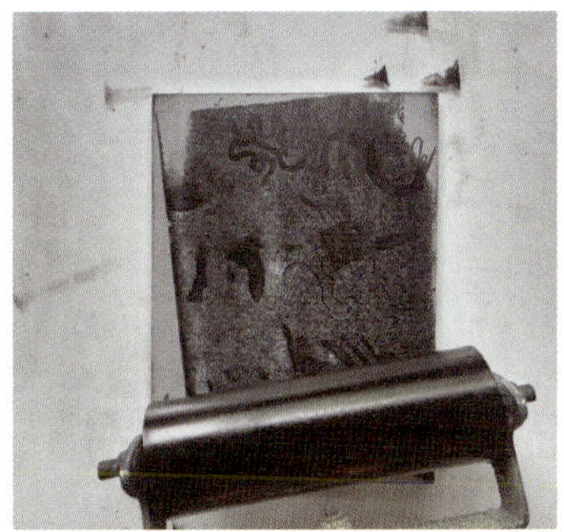

Scumming up is mostly a result of the plate being too dry.

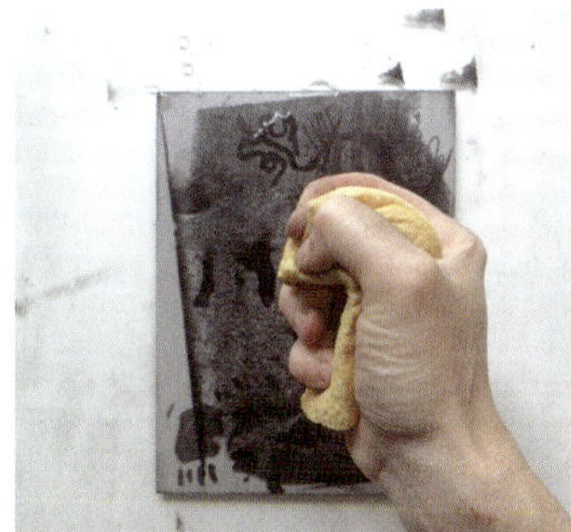

Squeeze drops of water onto the plate immediately and distribute.

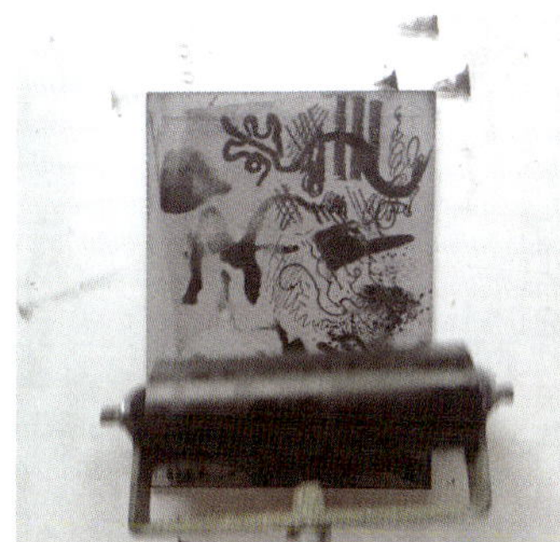

Roll with quick light rolls to snap off scum and continue to ink-up.

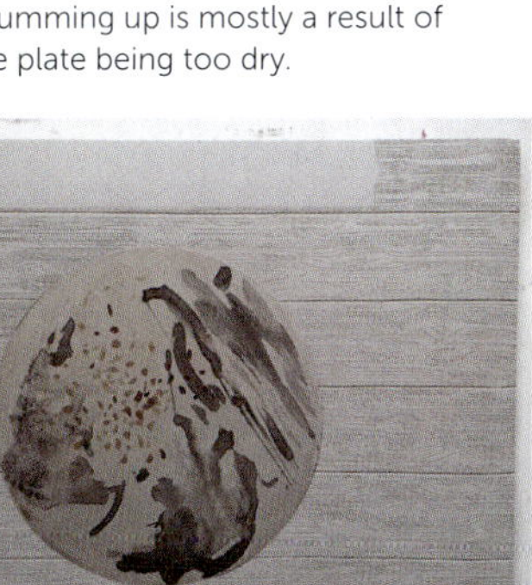

A lino carved up as a jigsaw with lithino circle and intaglio lino outside.

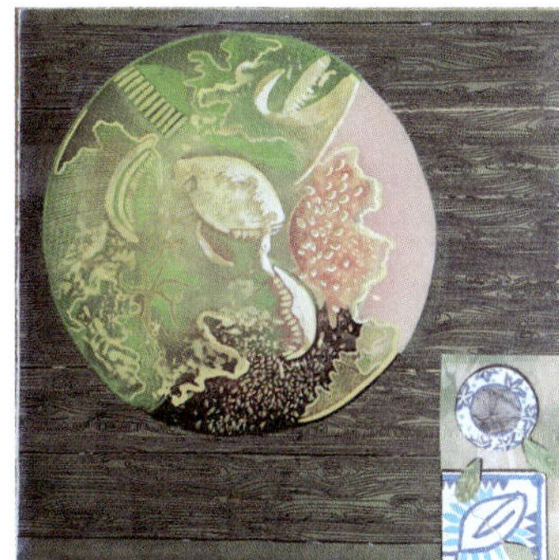

The completed print after multiple re-sanding layers, celebrating lino. *Compost Study*, Mary Dalton.

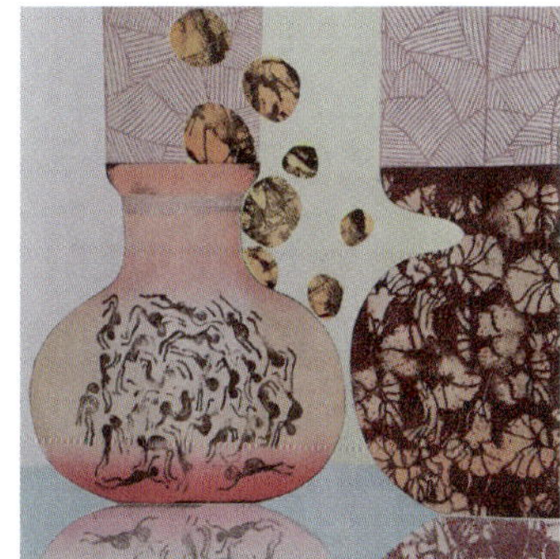

A detail of lithino in a hybrid print. The vases and orange blobs are all lithino cut to jigsaw elements with viscosity rolls and monoprint.

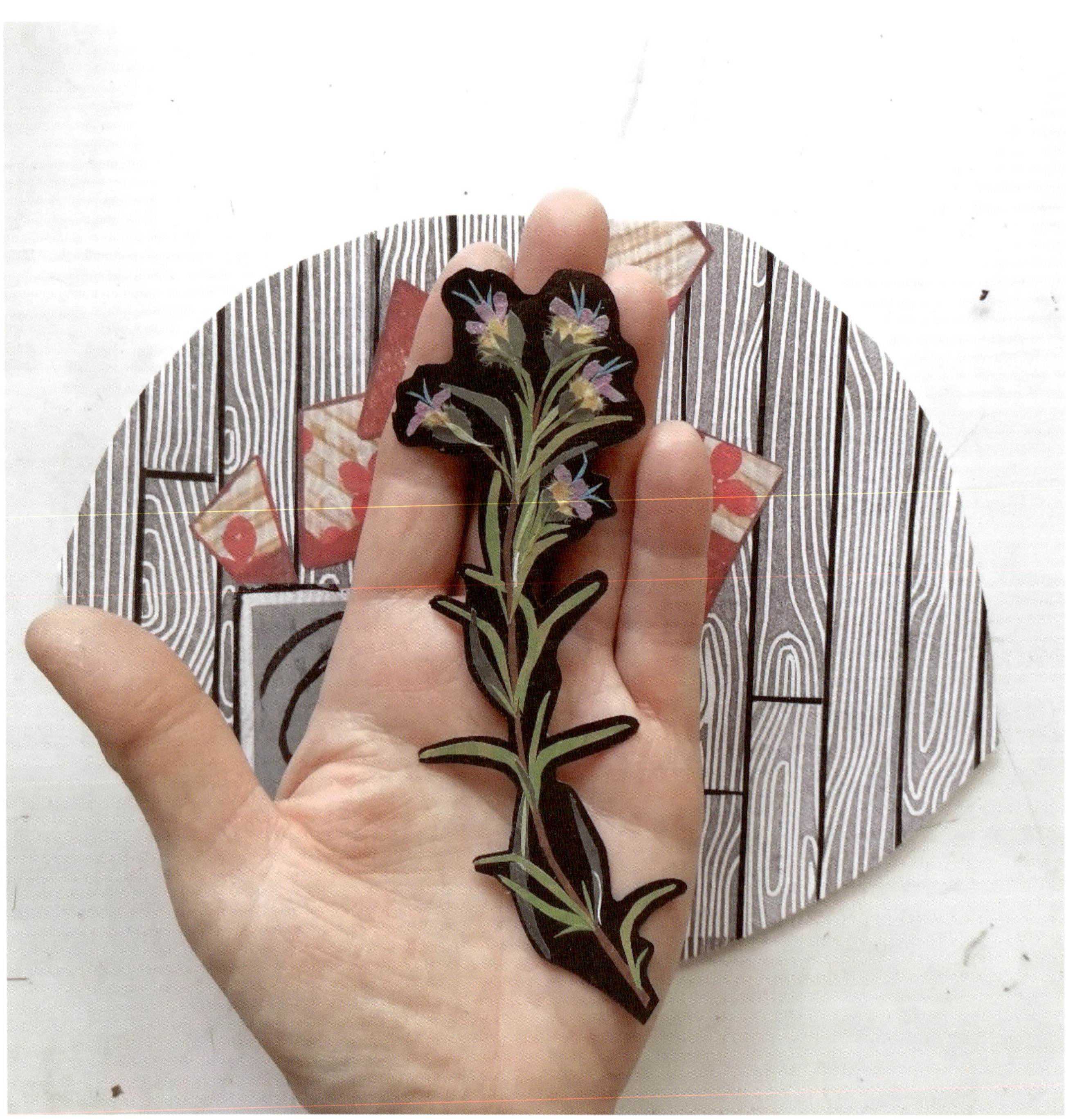

CHAPTER 7

THE MATRIX: PRINT AS OBJECT

Print does not have to exist upon a flat surface of paper or similar substrate. Print has huge potentials to be incorporated into mediums beyond the two dimensional – object, film, sculpture, performance and more. From an ecological perspective, looking at print off paper and how it is incorporated into other mediums allows one to question further the sustainability of the end product. If the print exists in a digital film rather than 100 paper editions, is this a more ecological approach? If the print is used to apply texture and pattern to fabrics that are used in a performance but then worn as clothing subsequently, this has a fascinating ecological perspective, does it not? Always enquire and always question. There are so many wondrous ecological alternative approaches out there.

This chapter will take an overview of a few approaches to print off paper. It will hopefully fuel a questioning imagination as to the many possibilities.

PRINT IN ANIMATION

Using printmaking in animation, films and so on is not a new idea. The textures and mark making lend themselves to illustrations and subsequent animated films. In recent years the use of prints in stop-frame animation has taken off, and this probably follows the advent of very user-friendly and free stop-frame animation apps available for home phone users. They are incredibly high quality and easy to use, even for those not used to the integration of technology. Approaches to the creation of the stop frame vary according to the artist. Some choose to see the printed elements as individual objects that playfully come to life on the screen. Others utilise the element of the edition within print and generate multiple individual frames that are minutely different from one another to generate movement. Sometimes print is even just used as the stationary background element to the film. It varies hugely and is wonderful to observe this element of prints being developed more.

CREATING A STOP FRAME

In order to have a go at a stop frame, you will need to download a basic stop frame animation app for your phone. They are readily available and many basic ones are free. Recommending a particular brand at this stage will be pointless because app technology changes so rapidly, my recommendations would be obsolete quickly. Once you have one, you will also need a tripod for your phone to hang overhead. And when I say tripod, mine involved two pieces of rope attached to a washing line that was screwed into our ceiling. It worked. Start by taking a simple and effective approach to a print stop frame by animating three pre-selected printed shapes moving across a printed background. Simple, fun and effective.

How can this become more print-specific?

The previous demonstration was a way to get used to using a stop frame app. It could have been done with a banana, an apple and two grapes, we just happened to include printed pieces of paper. So, how are artists making the stop frames more specific to printmaking? One fantastic approach is to utilise the natural editioning qualities of some print matrices and how this can be altered each time. This can be captured perfectly by a stop frame animation to showcase a changing printed impression. From an ecological

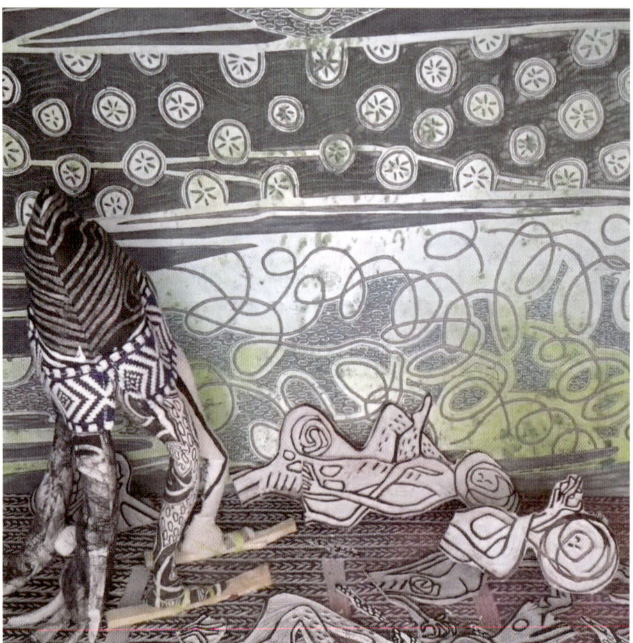

A still from a stop-frame animation using printed objects as the set. *Farmer* (2021), Mary Dalton.

perspective, this is an interesting approach. On the one hand, you are still having to use paper to create each one of the individual frames, but on the other hand, the end result, the actual artwork, exists solely in digital format and is not

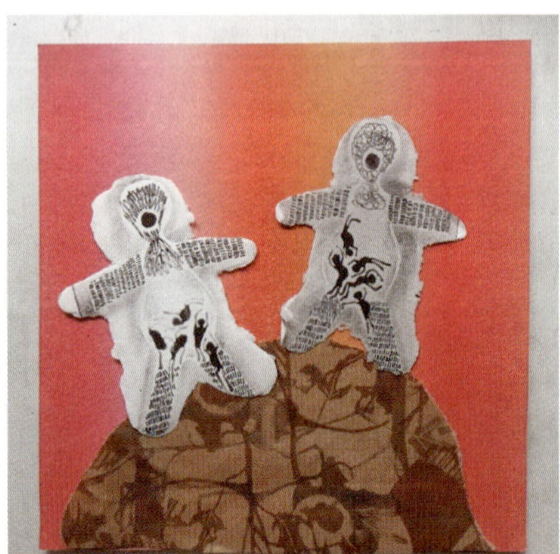

Selecting bold and moveable printed elements works well.

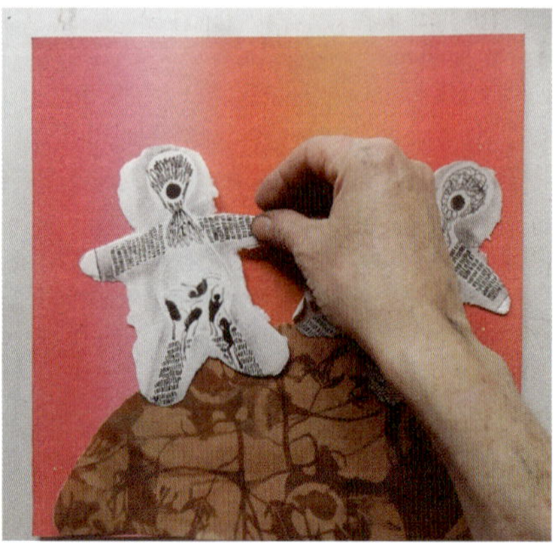

For each still, the elements need to be moved marginally.

consuming more materials over time. On the other hand, the downloading of the digital product by users creates an ecological footprint, whereas a paper print handed between two humans takes no energy in transportation. It is complex and an approach to ecological printmaking means keeping eyes and ears to the ground and to not rule out any process without full investigation. I think what is interesting about the digital approach to print is that it is very much in tune with the way the world is going, and it can really be pushed by a generation of artists who have grown up with technology as a common language. This is exciting and this keeps print alive. If print stays alive, the very same generation of artists will also question print's ecological footprint. If print has killed itself through holding onto old traditions that are not relevant, then a new generation of artists see no purpose in using it, let alone pushing its ecological credentials.

Print for all

Printmaking in animation is a fantastically exciting avenue to explore. It really is very interesting to pursue and can open up whole new languages in print and expression. Play, have fun and watch this space as the medium builds in interest. A digital download copy of an artwork is also a very engaging and accessible approach to artwork. Printmaking has always been a means to communicate to the mass audience, but now the way to communicate these stories may be shifting. Digital works are talking to a young generation and reaching out to more through social media. Sometimes it is worth trying these things out to see where it goes and what doors it opens. Is it more ecological than an object-based print? I am still weighing that one up as discussed previously. But it is so vital to include digital-based artworks in this book as a way that does question our approaches to object-based sustainability and how the future is looking for alternatives.

An app will collate all the stills and generate an animation.

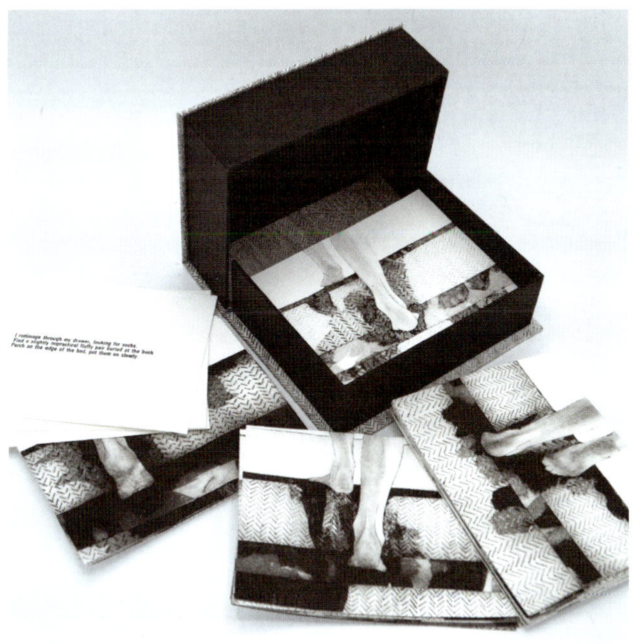

A selection of varied dry points used for stop-frame animation. *Imperceptibly Different* (2022), Nina Gross.

PRINT INSTALLATION AND ENGAGEMENT

In this chapter we are looking at printmaking being applied as a medium in other art genres. We know that print can be used to apply texture, pattern and surface to a variety of medium and this can therefore be used to enhance props that may be used in installation or immersive works. Printed textiles are a fantastic way to incorporate print in installation, be it through clothing worn or props used. It is an undercurrent branch of printmaking, but one I think is fascinating, and certainly a great use of the medium. From an ecological perspective, if the print is being used to create a one-off installation or performance, then in many ways material resources are less and also it become a community piece, rather than a commodity. Secondly, the printed items may have a secondary use beyond the installation, again increasing ecological awareness.

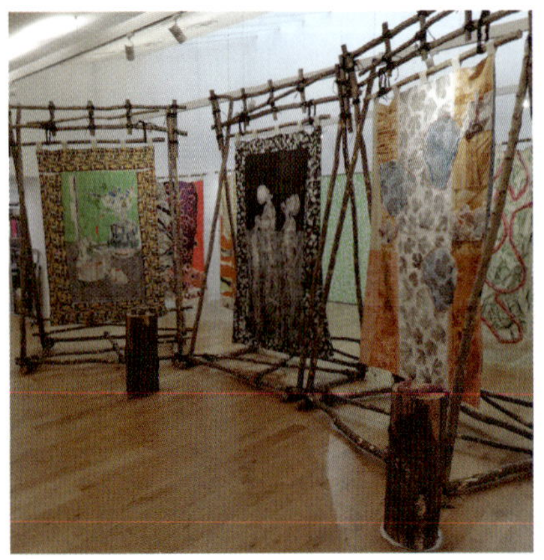

An installation shot of hand-printed textile banners, lino wallpaper and printed objects. From 'The Worlds In Between' exhibition (2023), Mary Dalton.

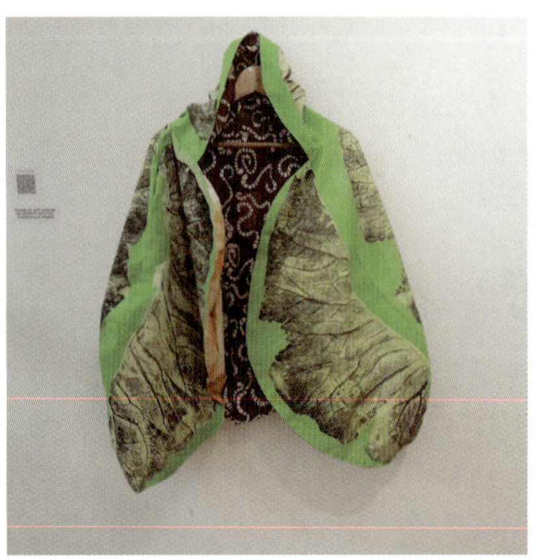

Printed textiles used in performance such as the cabbage leaf and lino-cut printed cape take print out of frames. *Cabbage Leaf Cape* (2023), Mary Dalton.

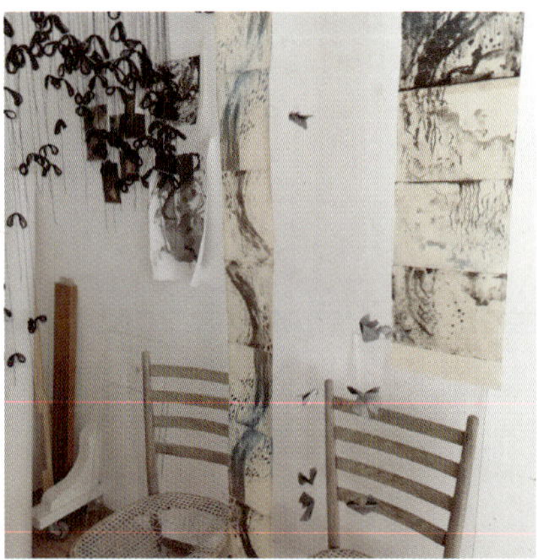

Planning printed elements of installations takes consideration and thought. Mock-ups are useful to understand logistics. Work in progress (2024), Peon Boyle.

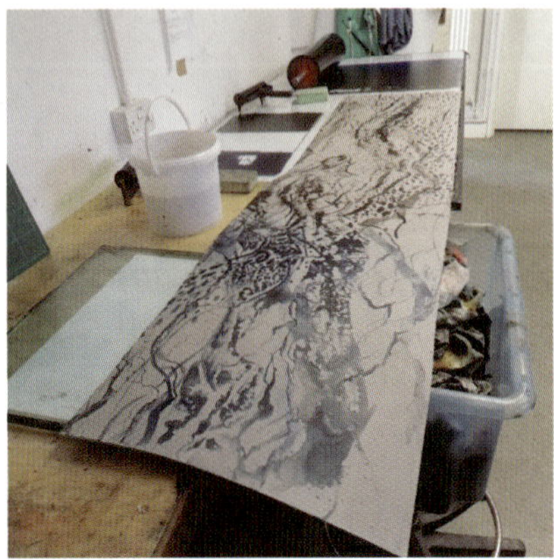

Printing large-scale works for installation is a technical, fun and challenging feat.

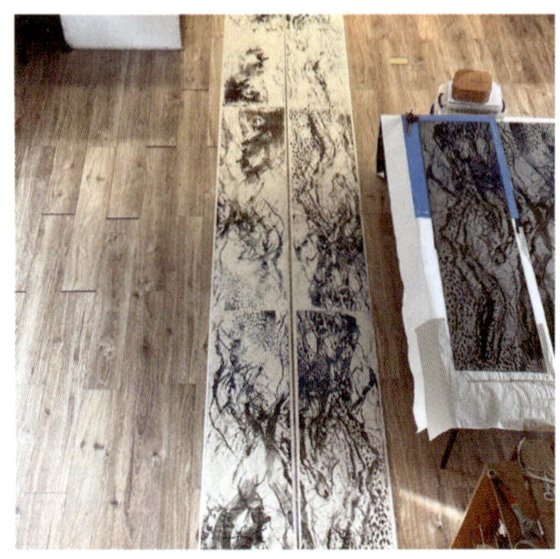

The resultant prints will form part of a bigger mixed media installation by Peon Boyle.

Print as object

Printmaking has a long history in works and editions on paper, for use in books, artworks, illustrations or posters, predominately two-dimensional artworks. Now print does not have to be restricted to that. Paper in itself is hugely versatile as a means to add decoration and expression to three-dimensional surfaces. In Japan, printed papers were often used for decorative purposes including making three-dimensional items. The strength of the washi paper allowed for it to be turned into screens, lampshades, paper dolls and even clothing. Chiyogami papers were traditionally screen printed with beautiful repeat patterns. Although we do not approach silk screen in this book, the principles of using patterned papers as a means to apply pattern to a three-dimensional surface is a fantastic and clean way of introducing print into objects.

Creating the papers

The first step is to make some hand-printed papers. This could be a random approach to create a textural field, or a planned approach to create a repeat pattern. The first allows for a freedom of creation that can be spontaneous, the second will produce a block that tessellates across a larger area and can be used multiple times over. Both have their use and different ways of expressing the pattern. I often set aside time to make a batch of the random patterns because this method of working often goes a bit more with the flow, and the more sheets you create, the stronger the textural field becomes. I end up generating several sheets in this method and they get stored for the times I need to rummage and find a suitable paper for a project. The repeat tile approach requires a design to be made and a more considered approach to printing, so I often design the repeat block with a specific project in mind.

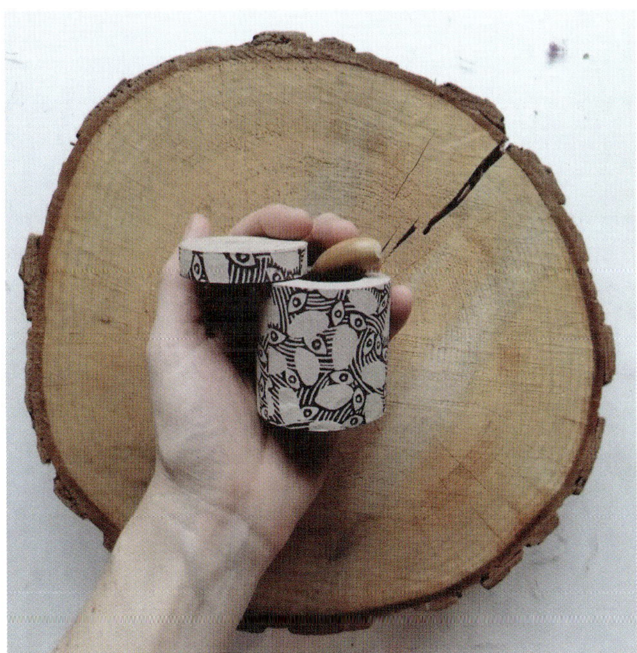

A small handmade seed pot from holly timber, covered with lino-cut paper.

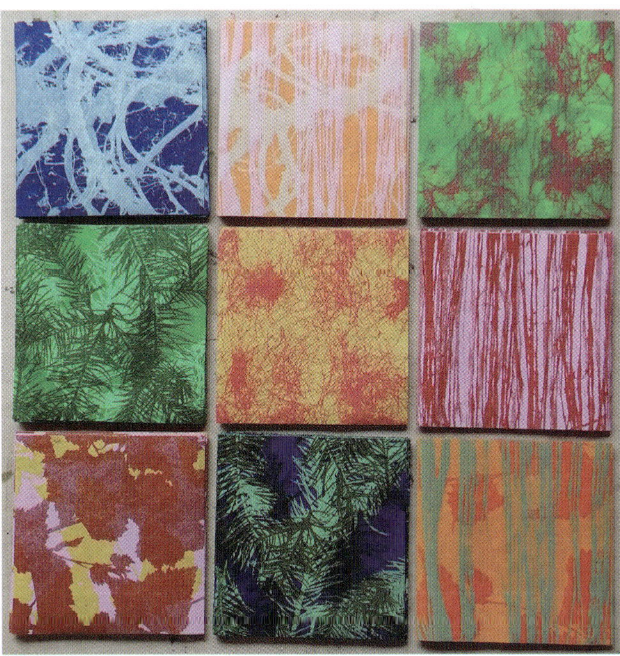

A selection of hand-printed papers in a range of patterns.

Printing the textural field approach really is as simple as getting ink out and printing onto a backing paper using whatever method takes your fancy. Try overlaying old carved lino block in different patterns. Ink up a sheet of aluminium, make a monoprint and repeat with different monoprint layers. Hand stamp vegetables, screws, threads. The approach is fun and freeform, resulting in some brilliant papers. We will take a deeper look at the repeat block approach.

The paper choice plays an important role before you print. If the paper is being used for a specific project, then just ask yourself a few questions. Firstly, is the printed paper going to be used on a flat surface (collage or covering the sides of a box for example) or a three-dimensional surface (such as covering a wooden toy). If it is for a more three-dimensional or undulating surface, then a lighter weight paper choice would be best as this allows it to be manipulated more easily. You would be looking at anywhere from 9gsm up to 20gsm as ideal. This means a bit of clever and delicate printing, but all works very well. If working on a flat surface, a paper sitting from 25gsm up to 40gsm is good. For my flat paper work I use a 32gsm paper that does a great job. Washi papers are your best friend in this process. They are strong yet lightweight. You can get a range of papers and they increase in cost the more natural fibres are included. For instance, a 100 per cent kozo paper (paper made from the fibres of the paper mulberry tree) will be significantly more expensive than one made with 10 per cent kozo, some gampi and some cellulose pulp. All the washi papers are strong, so find one that suits your budget and your means. For the demonstration on repeat block printing, I am using a 32gsm mixed-fibre washi – some kozo for strength, but also cellulose pulp for budget reasons. From an ecological perspective, the natural fibre paper is amazingly sustainable because the fibres used traditionally come from managed kozo trees, coppiced rather than cut and killed. As with many ecological questions, transportation of the papers from another country always has an impact on the footprint of the planet, so when I use the papers, I try to order in bulk to at least save one more journey.

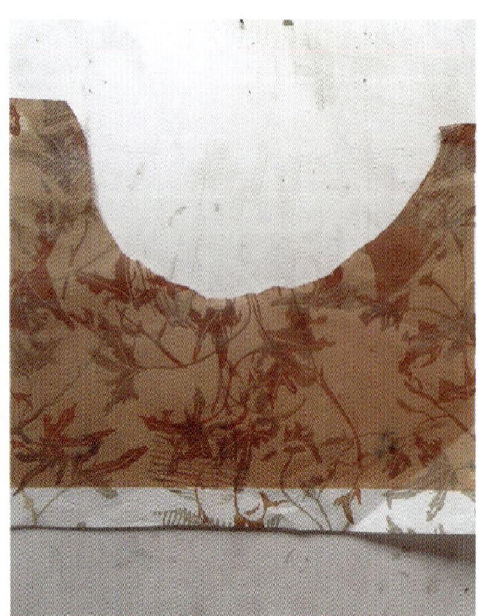

An example of a random lino-printed paper, with pattern overlays.

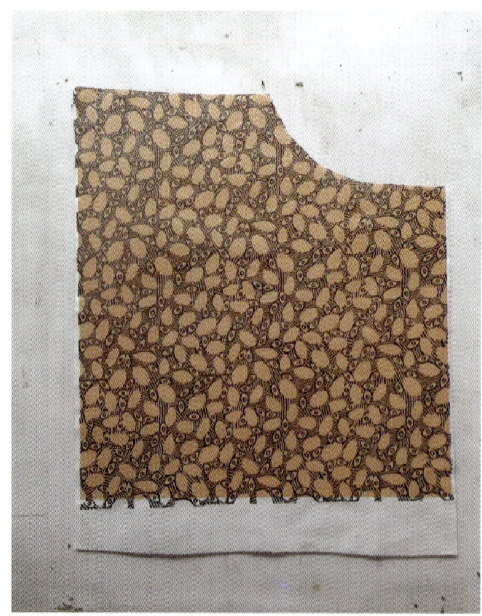

A more formal repeat pattern lino-cut paper.

A multi-plate monoprint paper.

CREATING A REPEAT BLOCK PRINT

This demonstration will allow you to create a single colour repeat block carved out of lino. We will be matching the pattern on all four sides of the lino block, so that the tile may be repeated across a larger sheet of paper or fabric. Here I am printing on old serviettes that I found in a rag bin. I am using a set square to give me a straight edge to work from because the repeat block in this instance has few printed corners or straight sides to register with. I have also chosen to start the repeat design from the top left corner, but you may also start, for instance, in the middle of your paper and work out so the pattern is evenly distributed at the edges. The folding method used here to generate the repeat is simple and effective. The more you get into repeat designs, the more detailed you can go and you may wish to measure edge-matching with a ruler. Many now use a repeat pattern-making app on their digital devices. Forgive me, I'm old school.

Materials

Square of lino 10cm × 10cm
Lino carving tools
Paper and pencil for drawing out work
Paper or fabric
Ink colour of choice, roller and printing set-up
I am using a press set to lino pressure with runners. Can be hand stamped

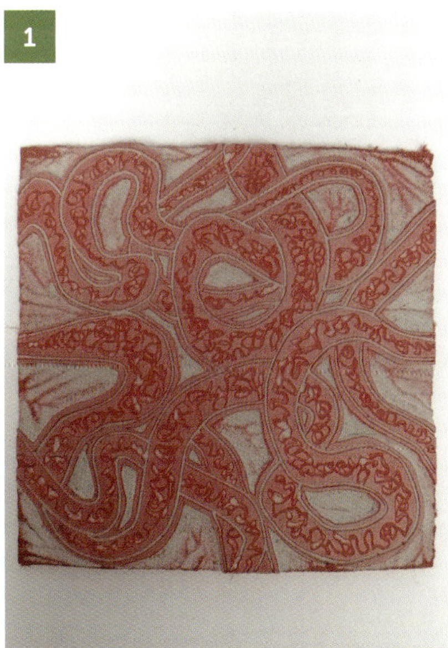

The repeat block we are working towards; 10cm × 10cm.

Cut a piece of copy paper or similar to the same size as the block.

Fold paper in half, then into quarters on each side.

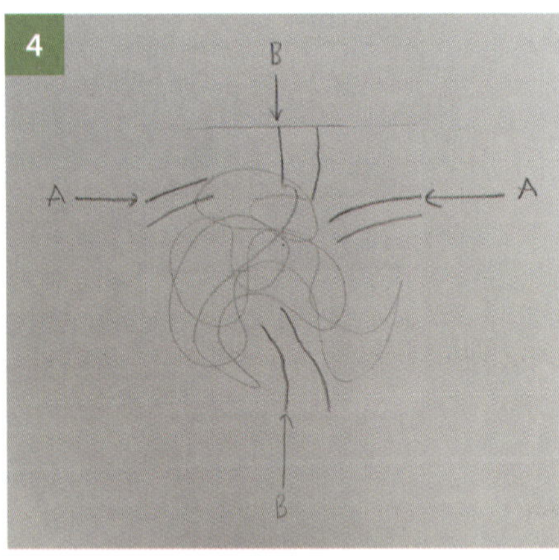

Draw the design in pencil, using the fold lines to align lines at the edges.

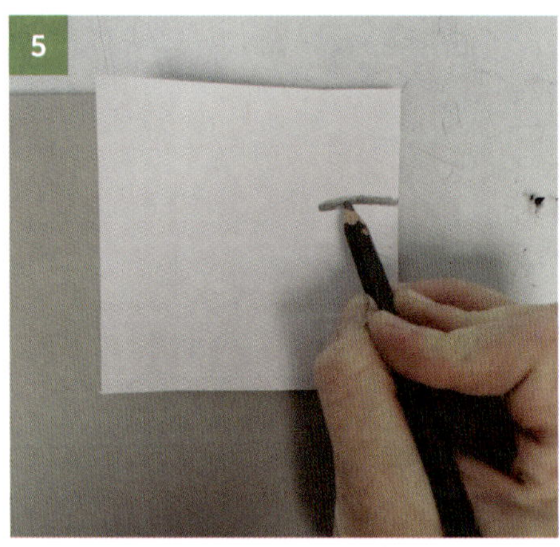

Turn completed drawing over and place onto lino surface.

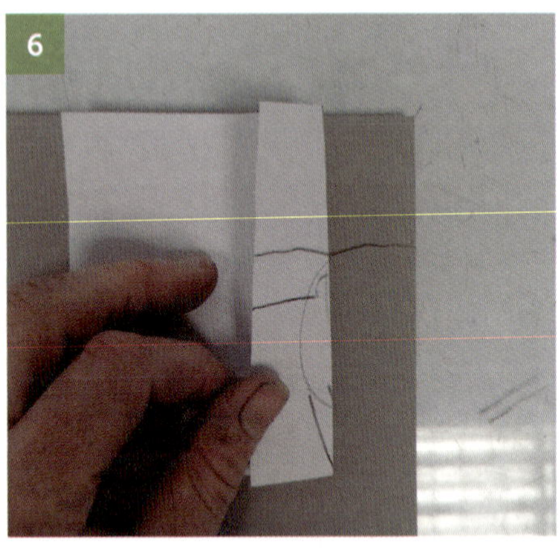

Rub on the back with pencil to transfer drawing to lino. Carve.

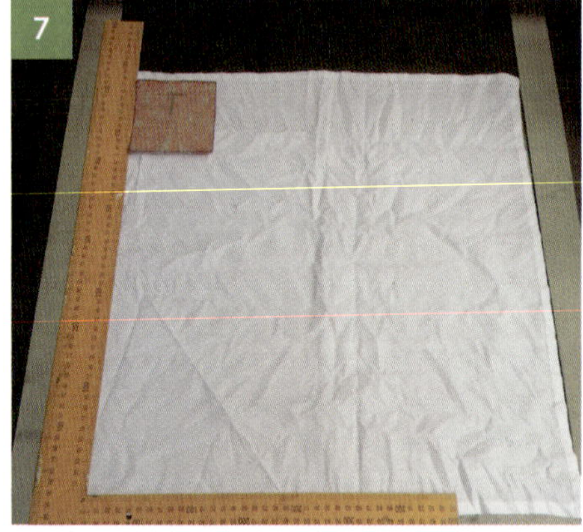

Ink up the lino and place the first block lined up with a straight edge in position.

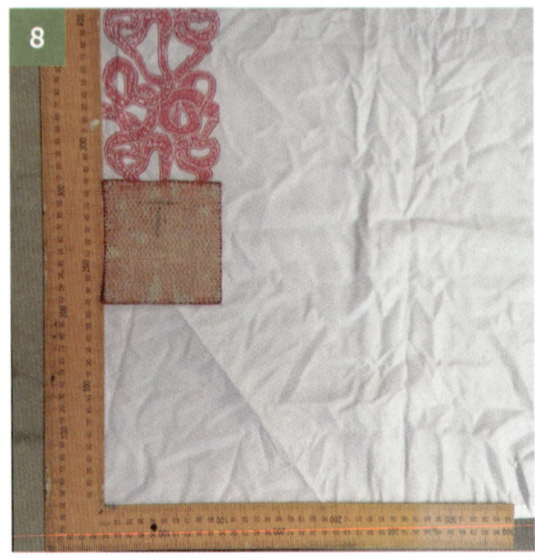

Continue to use a straight edge or your eye to register the next block. Always remember the top.

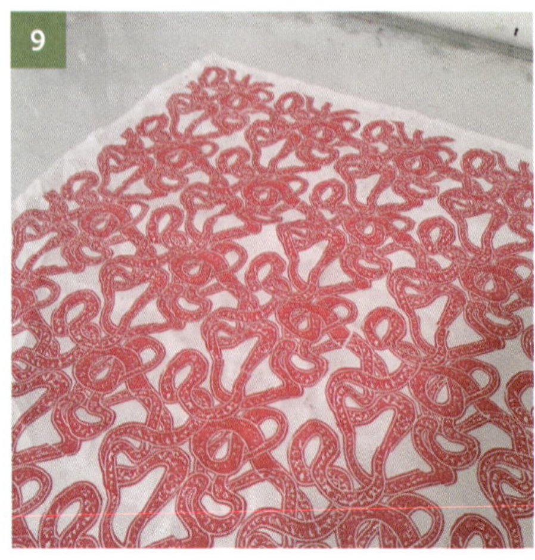

The completed repeat pattern over a 45cm x 45cm serviette.

USING YOUR PAPERS FOR OBJECTS; A NOTE ON GLUE

As we highlighted earlier, the heavier weight washi papers are fantastic for flat surfaces including chine collé and collage. Let us take a look at the repeat pattern paper we carved and the various applications it could be used for. Because of the 32gsm weight, there are three main processes I wish to bring attention to. Collage, chine collé and object pasting (I'm trying to avoid the word decoupage, but in essence this is what it is!). All the methods of paper use require glue. The paper has to be stuck with something. Now many will revert to PVA or other plastic-based glues at this stage because of the ease of use and quick drying time. However, from an ecological perspective they are appalling, and even from a conservation perspective they are highly questionable. Instead, it is worth trying and looking into rice paste and wheat paste glues. They may require a slight shift in a habit of working, but they are cheap, biodegradable, immensely strong and paper-to-paper, nothing beats them. You can buy pre-made rice paste glues which can be diluted or used neat and are brilliant to have around. They do come in their own plastic tube, so this then raises a material waste question. In which case, you can also make your own rice paste or wheat paste glue, which can be made in bulk and frozen in ice-cube trays that can be brought out when required. Making paste glue is a whole art form, and the following method truly is the most basic. Once you have a glue, you can start pasting paper.

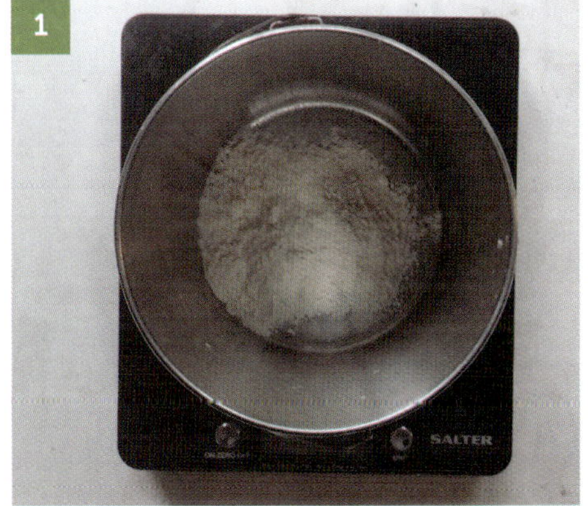

Add 20g white rice flour to a pan.

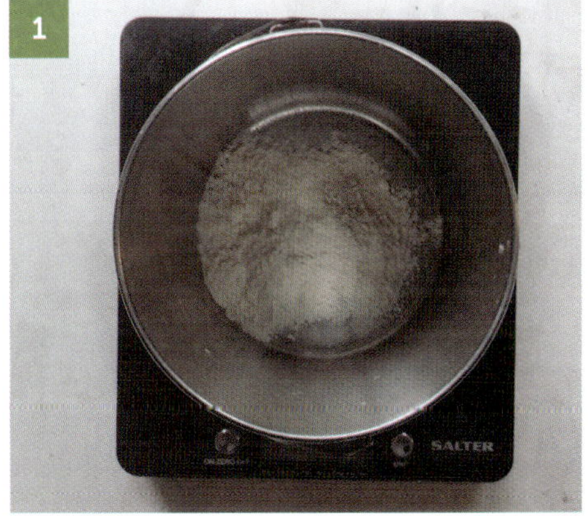

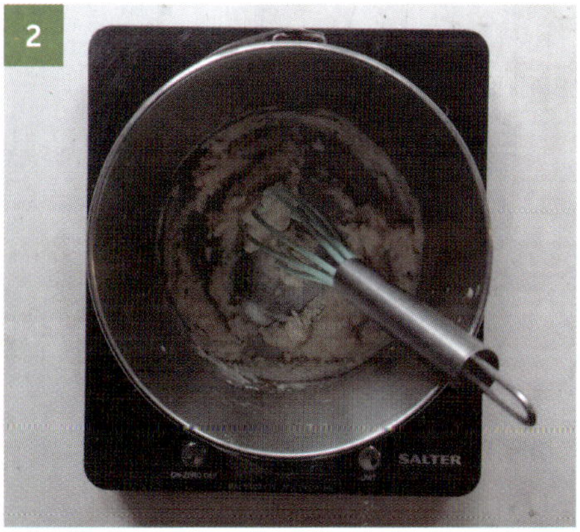

Add 100ml warm water and mix to a paste.

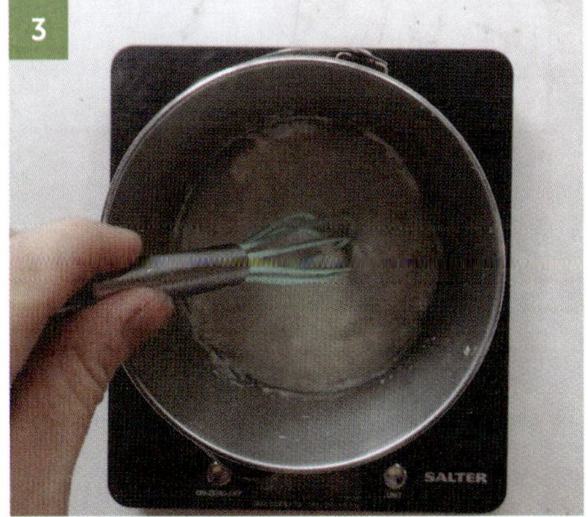

Add 150ml boiling water and gradually mix in.

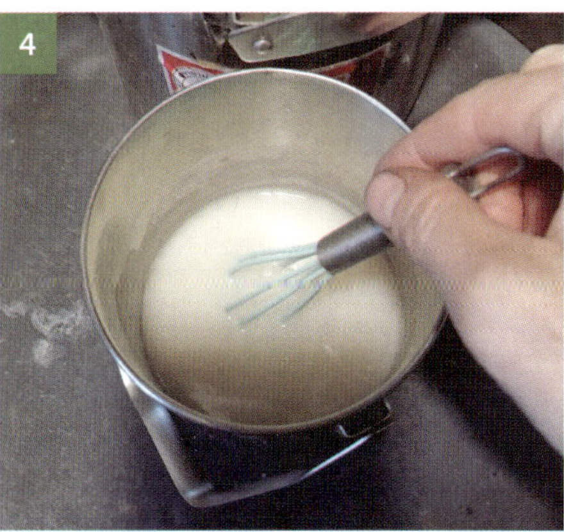

Heat glue mixture, stirring, until clear.

CHINE COLLÉ

This method of pasting decorative lightweight papers onto a heavyweight backing impression paper literally is and has been commonplace in print for many a year. It is a great way to introduce pattern and colour into a print. The beauty of chine collé is the seamless bond between the decorative paper and the impression paper. Chine collé works best under an etching press, as the high pressure bonds your lightweight decorative paper with the impression paper. I have seen artists use powdered glue granules, spray glues, stick glues and all manner of sticky and frustrating methods that will put you off for life. The method we are exploring involves pre-coating your paper with a layer of paste glue, letting this dry, cutting out your required shape and then fusing it to damp impression paper through a press. It is simple, clean and effective. And highly addictive. In the step-by-step project we are applying chine collé paper on top of the surface of a pre-made and dry monoprint, to add a bold collage section. We will also briefly look at adding chine collé at the same time as printing your inked matrix, so that the inked lines sit on top of the chine collé paper.

Materials

Pre-made and dry monoprint, approximately A5
Tissue or hand-printed collage paper
Rice paste glue
Ramekin for mixing
Clean brush
Etching press
Paper for printing and facilities to dampen

If working with drypoint or similar intaglio methods that are printed onto damp paper, then you can run a chine collé paper through at the same time as printing your impression. After you have put your inked impression on the press bed, you place your pre-coated chine collé paper glue side up, so it will be in contact with the impression paper, on the printing plate. Then print as usual with damp paper and high pressure. It means that your printed lines from your matrix will be on top of your chine collé paper, so a great way to introduce colour or pattern into works.

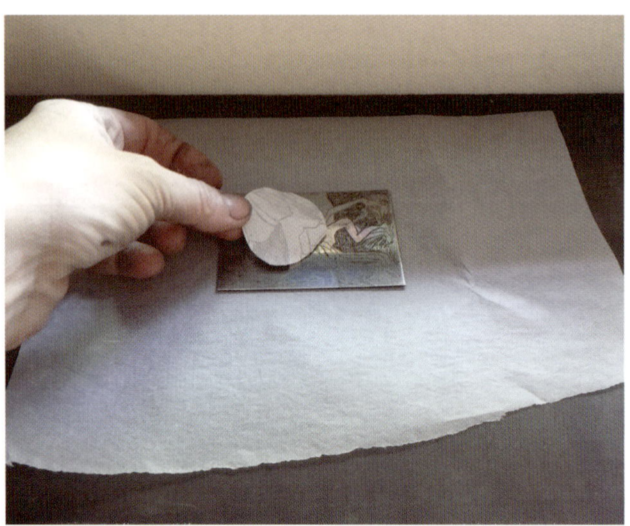

Adding a prepared chine collé paper glue side up onto an inked metal plate.

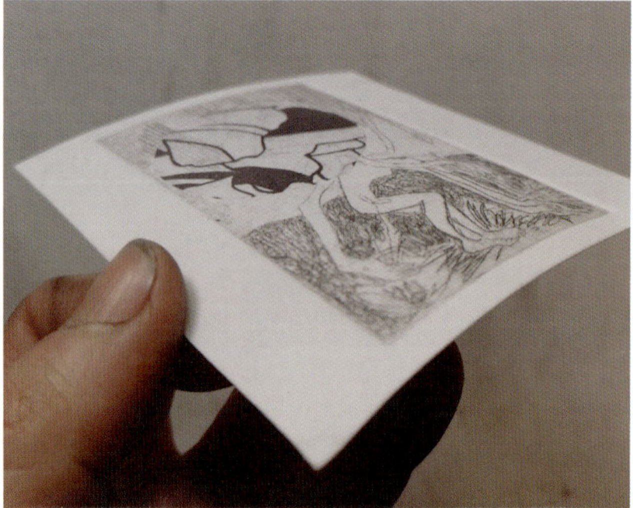

After printing, the chine collé is fused seamlessly with the impression paper and the print is also printed.

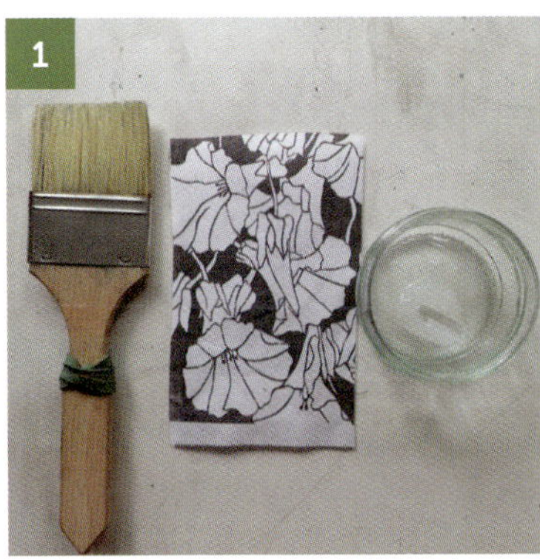

Materials needed to prepare a chine collé paper.

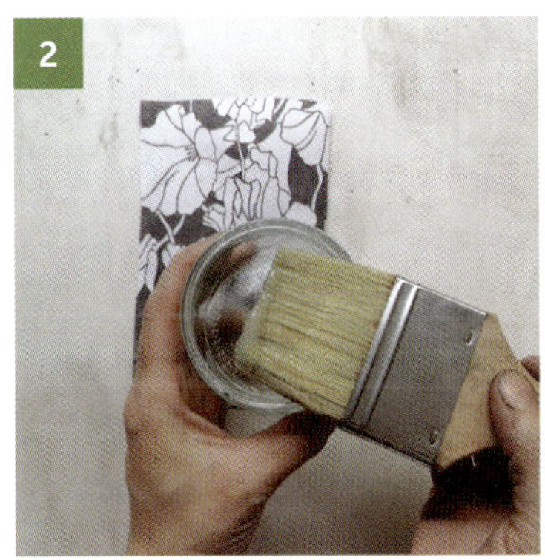

Dilute the rice paste glue until it reaches a thick custard consistency.

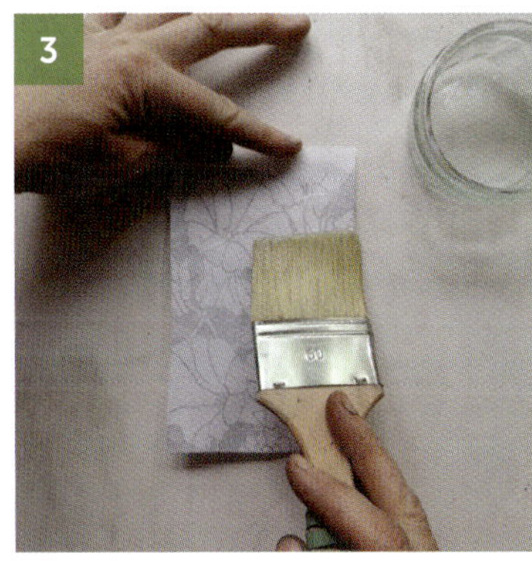

Coat the back of your paper with glue and leave to dry.

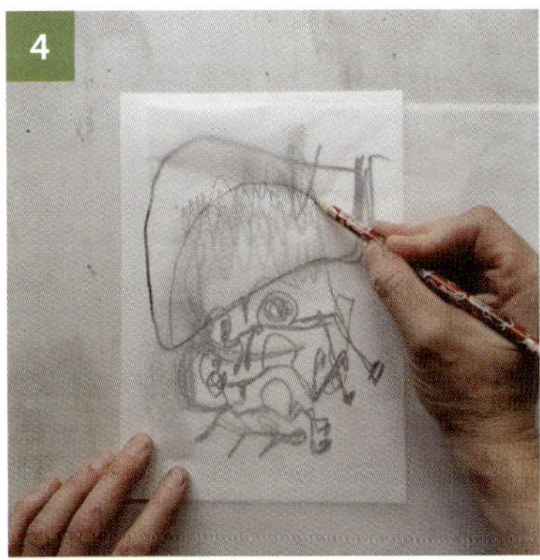

Trace the area of the prepared impression you want to collage.

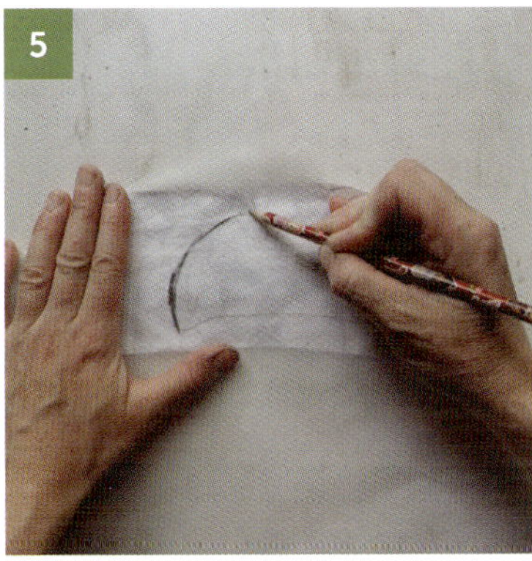

Flip over the tracing paper, transfer the outline onto the back of chine collé paper.

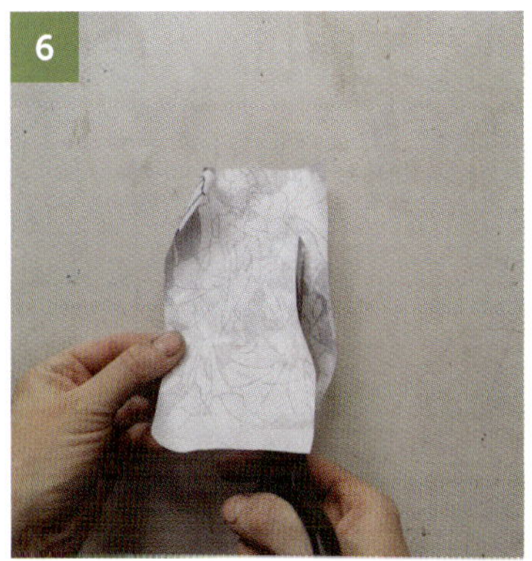

Cut out your shape.

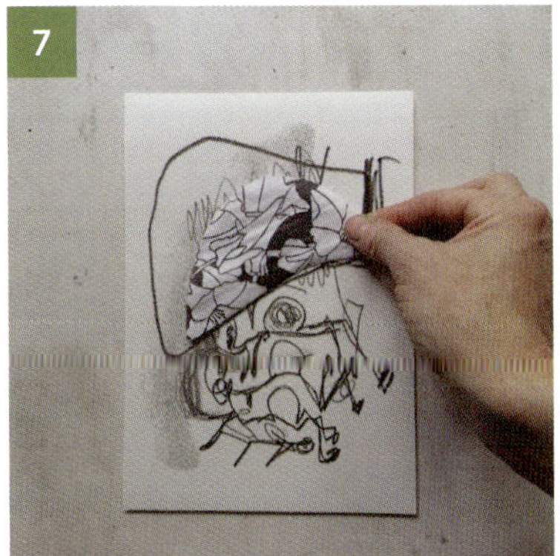

Test the size and fit of the shape over the impression. Dampen impression.

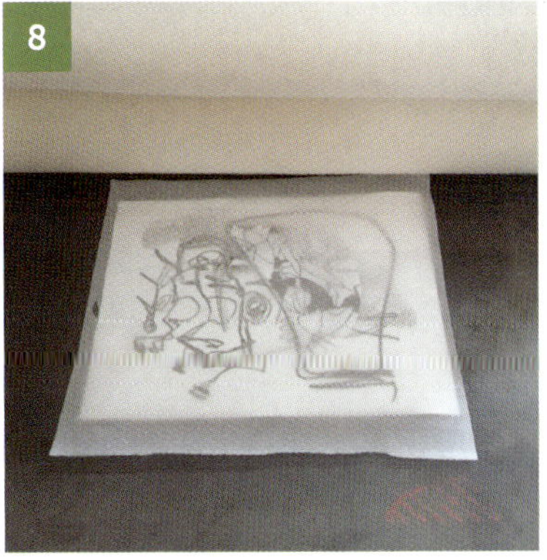

Place impression on press, chine collé glue side down and tissue on top.

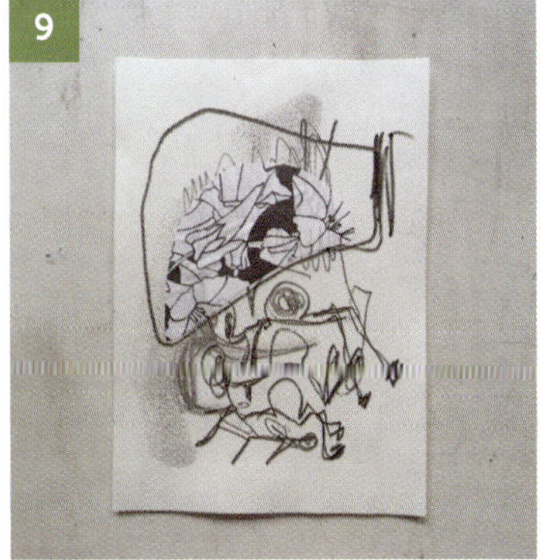

Print under high pressure and the chine collé will fuse.

HAND COLLAGE

Collage is such fun and so liberating to just cut from paper without any pencils controlling the free shape-making. The chine collé method can be used to create collages on impression paper, you just don't add a print matrix. However, if you do not have access to a press and wish to make a beautiful collage, then the following method works very well. It takes the principles from chine collé in as much as we have pre-coated paper. If you stretch your paper according to the instructions in Chapter 5, your paper will dry flat as you work with the rice paste. This method allows you to work without stick glues, wet PVA or other very sticky methods. You will need to have a few sheets of pre-coated papers when following the chine collé method.

Collage is a beautiful way to work with printed paper and can be achieved on any scale.

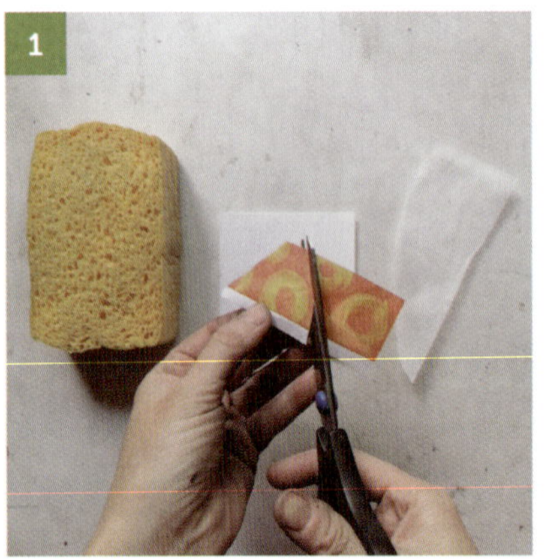

Cut out shapes from a pre-coated and dry chine collé paper.

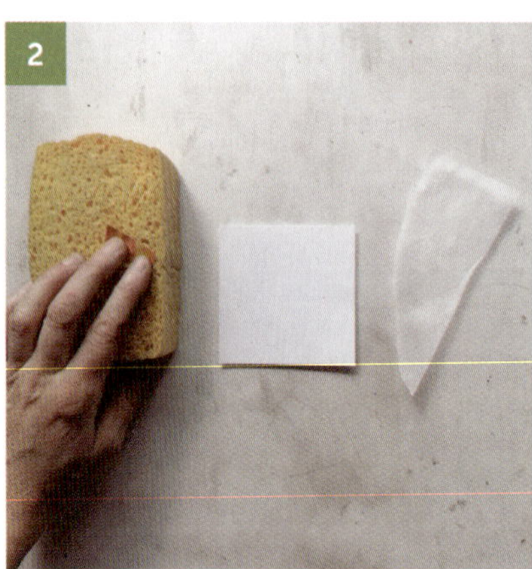

Press the back into a wet sponge to re-ignite the glue. Or sponge the back.

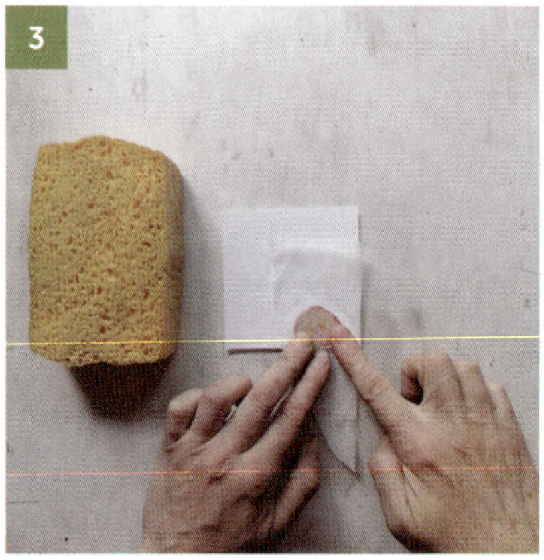

Apply the paper onto your impression paper and rub firmly in place.

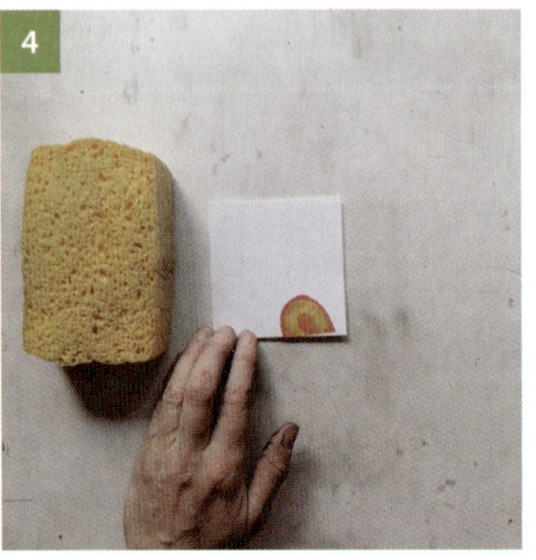

The completed hand collage shape sitting flush.

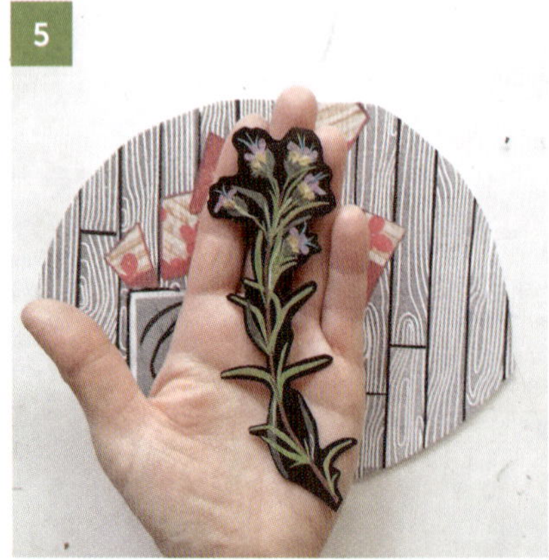

A miniature collage made with handprinted papers.

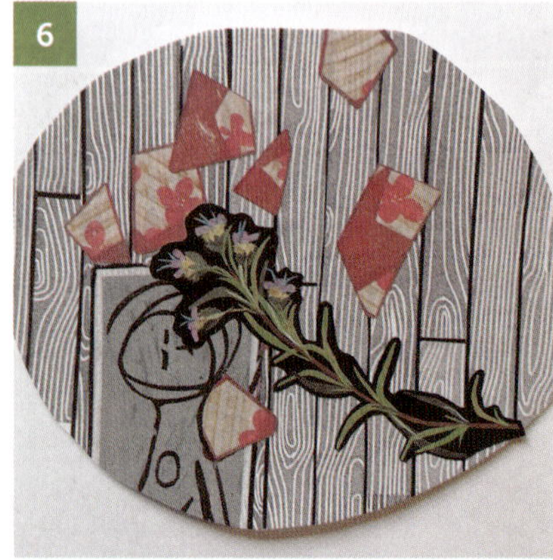

Still Life with Rosemary, Mary Dalton (2023).

DECOUPAGE

This is the method of gluing papers onto a backing object. A beautiful method of working and very satisfying if done well. We will work this as a step-by-step project, with the item of your choosing. We are working with an object with a flat surface for this example. The glue I use is a thicker rice paste glue than the one used for the chine collé, to allow for a strong bond. I am working here on an object I have made from plywood that I reclaimed from a scrap bin. I rarely purchase plywood anymore because of the use of the less ecological glues, but reclaiming from a skip at least gives the material a second use before landfill.

Materials

One object with flat surface (a box for example)
Collage papers *without* rice paste glue backing
Rice paste glue, brush and pot
Scissors and craft knife

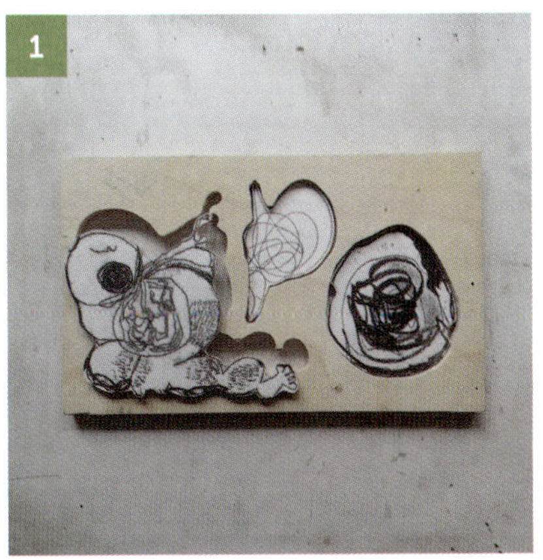

The object of my choice already has some monoprint applied in sections.

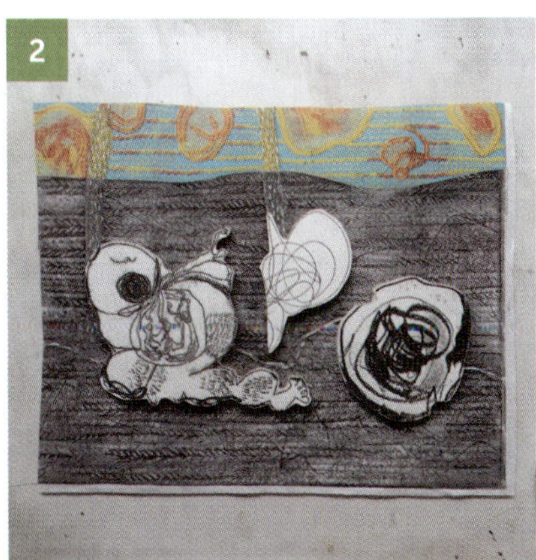

Make a selection of paper and make sure you have enough.

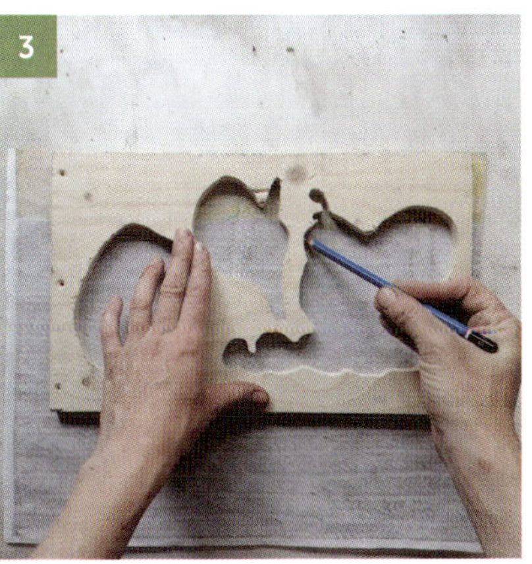

Draw around the object you wish to cover on the back of the paper.

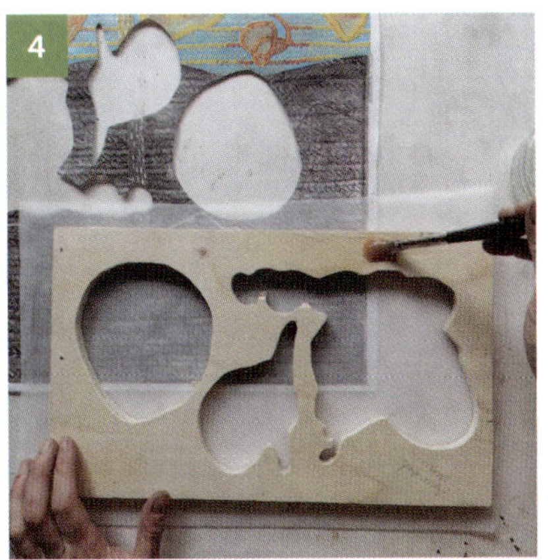

Apply an even layer of rice paste glue directly to the object.

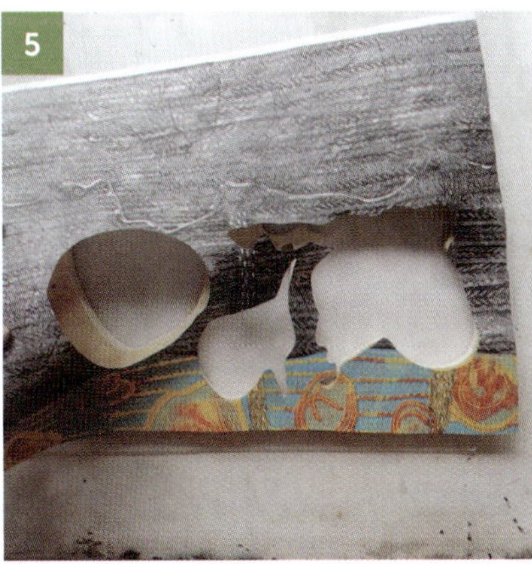

Gently place paper in place. You can move it in place.

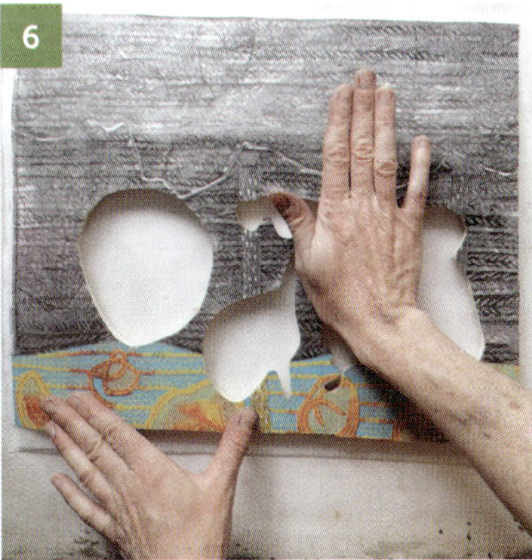

Apply pressure with your hand to flatten paper out.

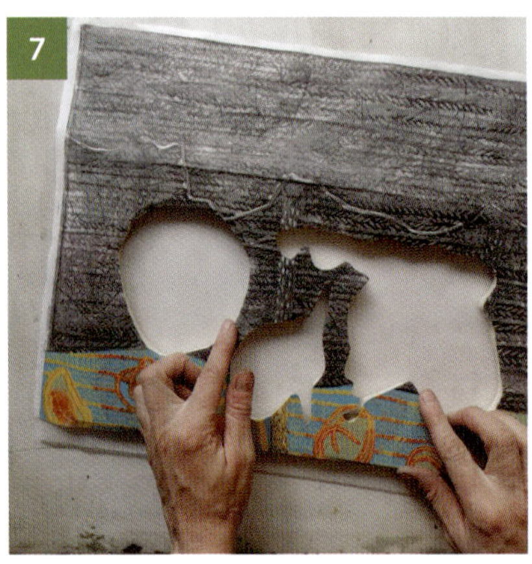

Use fingers to make sure paper is right up to the edges.

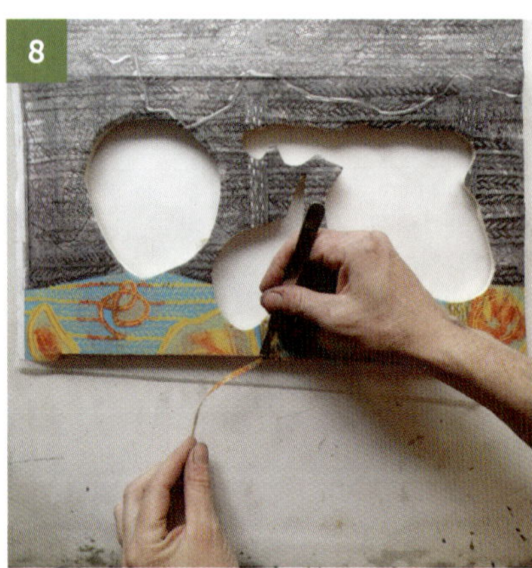

Use a fresh blade to trim off excess once glue is dry.

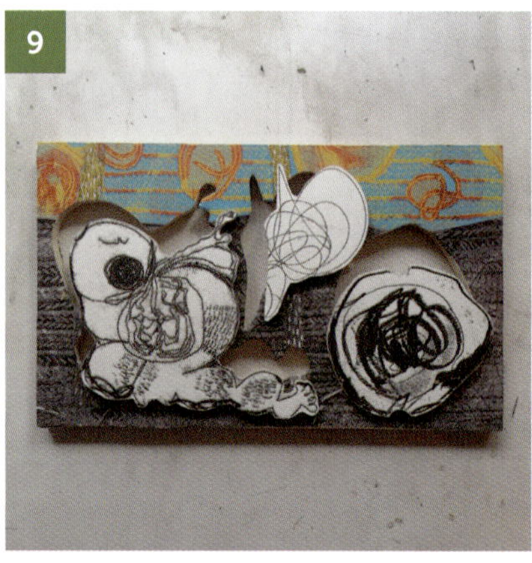

The completed object is seamless and inviting.

If you are wishing to cover a non-flat surface, it is entirely possible if you print onto or use very lightweight paper. Think tissue paper weight and then you can apply this using rice paste glue and smooth as you go with your hands. If you are printing with any method that would ordinarily require damp impression paper, then there is a little trick to avoid dampening the lightweight washi. Lay your impression washi onto your inked matrix on the press bed, then place a dampened piece of cartridge paper on, and then your blankets. Run through the press as usual. The moisture from the damp cartridge will seep through into the washi but it means you do not have to spray or handle very wet washi paper.

GOING BEYOND THE PRESS BED

As printmakers, we often are restricted by the press bed size when using techniques that require a press. However, as we have already looked at, printing on fabric alleviates this. You can also print continual sheets of paper the width of your press bed, if you can loosen the pressure after each pass and move the paper through, reapply pressure and repeat. It works really well.

And never be afraid to go maximum press bed size and then tesselate the prints afterwards. Stretching your wings a bit often opens up possibilities of print beyond paper.

And then there is momigami, and toys and fun

And so we have seen how ecological print is not all greyness and soggy oatmeal biscuits. It is vibrant, challenging and full of expressive storytelling life. And there is so much more that you can explore. How about momigami, manipulating kozo paper with starch paste to turn it into a fabric-like material? Give it a go. Or what about making toys with printed elements? Go raid a carpenter's scrap bin, wonders are found in there! And fancy a new pair of funky trousers? Why not print them? And as you can see, print is alive. And so is this planet. We can work together, in harmony, to tell the stories of our world without hurting it.

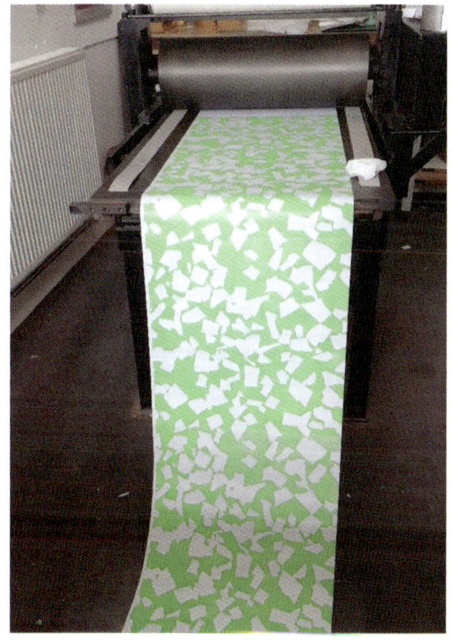

Printing 50m rolls of continual lino repeat wallpaper under a press.

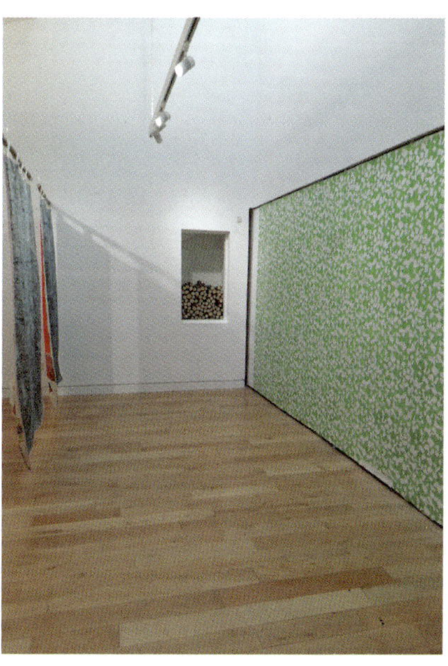

The completed wallpaper in situ has matched beautifully.

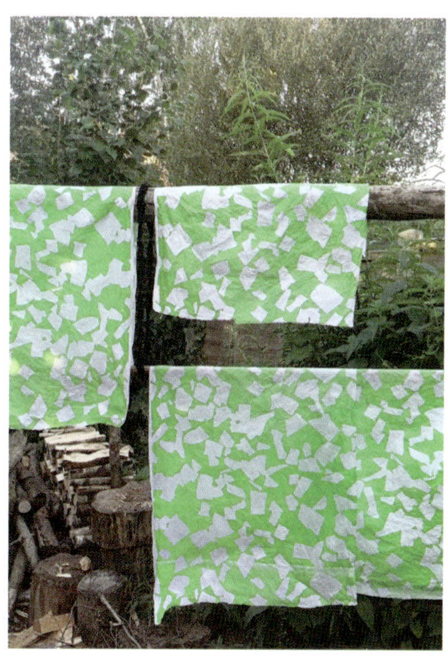

Momigami prepared lino cut papers drying in the garden.

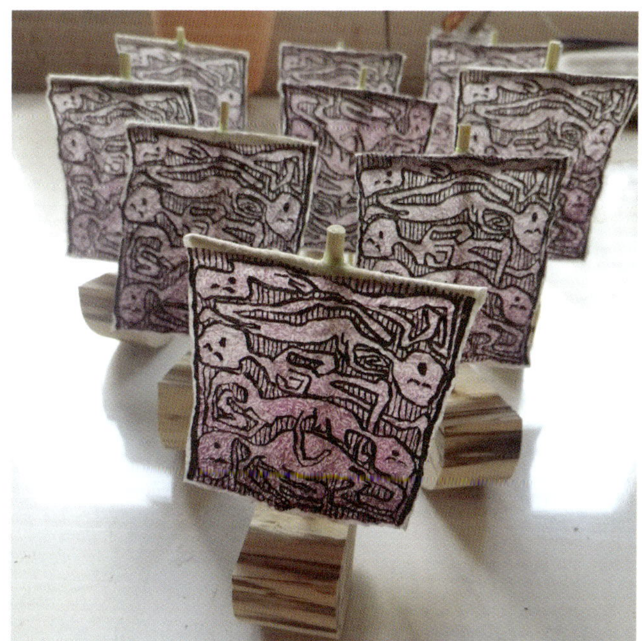

Handmade toy boats with hand-printed momigami sails.

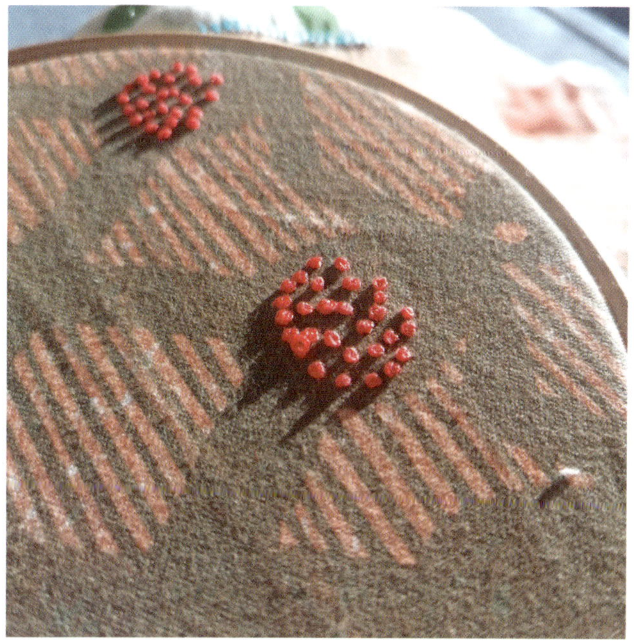

Embroidery on a hand-printed napkin. Well, why not.

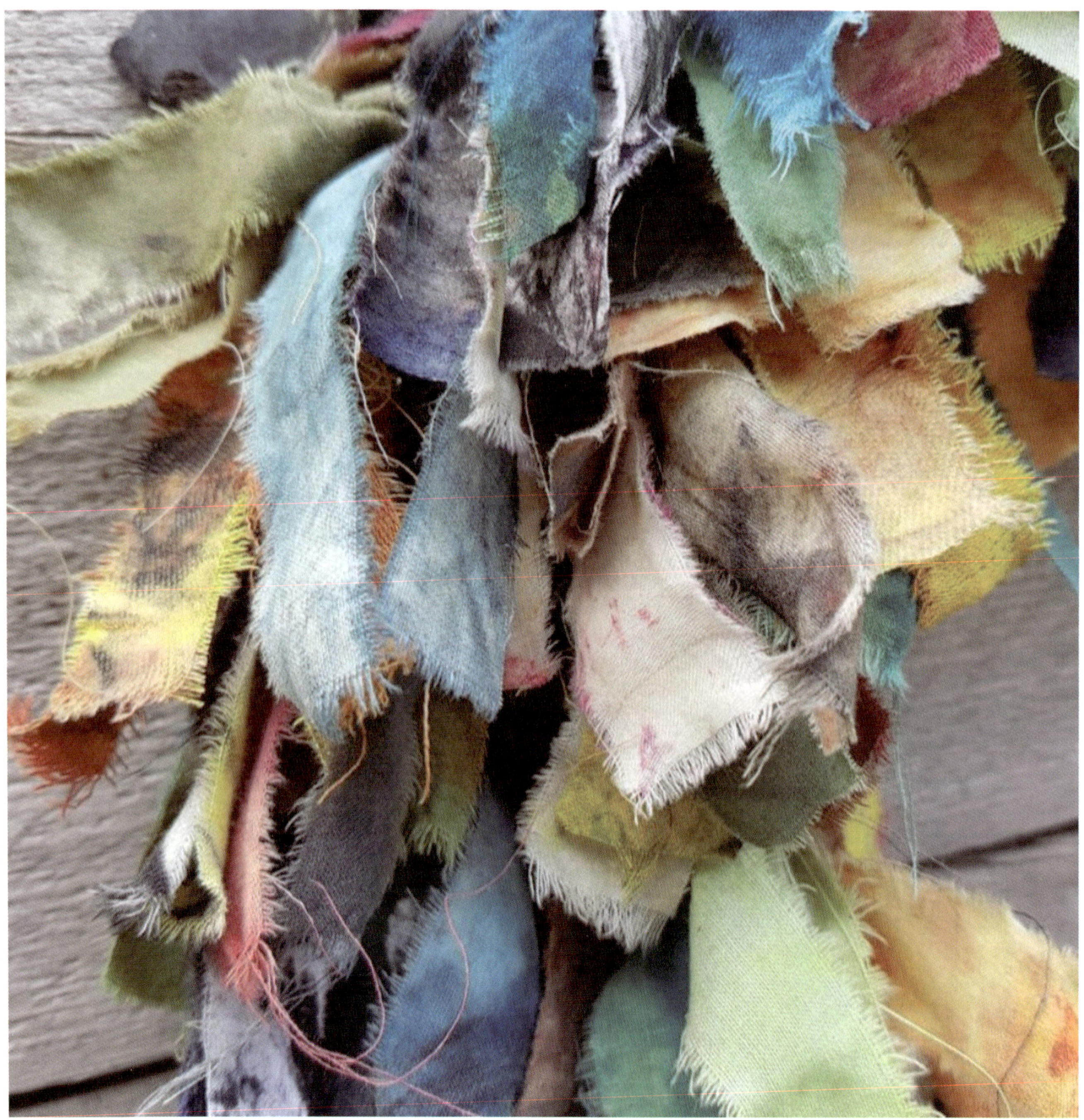

CHAPTER 8

THE ECOLOGICAL WORKSHOP

In this final chapter we will take a look at how you can set up your space to take measures to be more ecological in approach, material resources and water management. And this includes all types of spaces from professional set-up, educational ventures and kitchen tables! We can all take responsibility for our work area with small incremental changes. Some of the workshop basics such as raising rollers for lino have been addressed in the previous chapters; this is more about ecological tips and tricks for your practice. It is almost impossible, and very daunting, to make all the changes at once, so why not pick one, and see if you can integrate it into your practice so it becomes the norm? Then pick another and so on. There are inevitably more than mentioned in this chapter and the process of improving ecological awareness in one's practice and space is ongoing.

INK

We know we have been using oil-based ink throughout this book, which we also know stays open for a long work time. But depending on your practice and how much you use, choosing the correct ink storage container can avoid waste and prevent oil-based ink hardening up in its container. If you only need small amounts, then ink comes in metal tubes of around 150ml, just like oil paint. This is a great way to store the ink because you can screw the lid on securely, make sure it's air-tight and you waste little. Roll up from the end as you use the ink.

Next in volume is a 150ml cartridge. Not all companies stock this, and some will then provide tins at this weight. A cartridge has to be inserted into a silicone sealant gun to allow you to squeeze ink out. They are really useful if you do a lot of teaching or run open access workshops/spaces. No air can get into the cartridge, so it cannot dry up and you do not waste any because it is also being pushed down tight to the ink level.

Finally, we have tins of ink, which can be anywhere from 300g up to 2kg. If you use a vast amount of ink, then tins make sense. I have a lot of tins because I like the way they all stack in a small space. The oil-based ink does take time to dry, but air exposure in the tin will eventually harden the top layer after many years. You can usually scrape this off to reveal the fresh ink below. However, if you are constantly using the ink in the tin, then this never really becomes an issue. Some artists add a layer of water on top of the oil-based ink after use to prevent air penetration, or a greaseproof seal. When taking ink from a tin, never dig a palette knife in and scoop out because you make a big hole in the ink which increases surface area for a skin to dry. This then means it becomes difficult to remove the skin and you get bits in your ink. Always use a push knife (that is the flat, wide knife) to scrape a layer off the top, leaving a flat surface.

If you have made some handmade ink and wish to store it, then you have a few options. Depending on the size, if you have made a small batch, you can simply place it in a folded foil envelope with an ink sample on top to help remember what it is! If you have made a larger batch, you can purchase empty aluminium tubes which you fill from the bottom and roll up, allowing you to store your own inks.

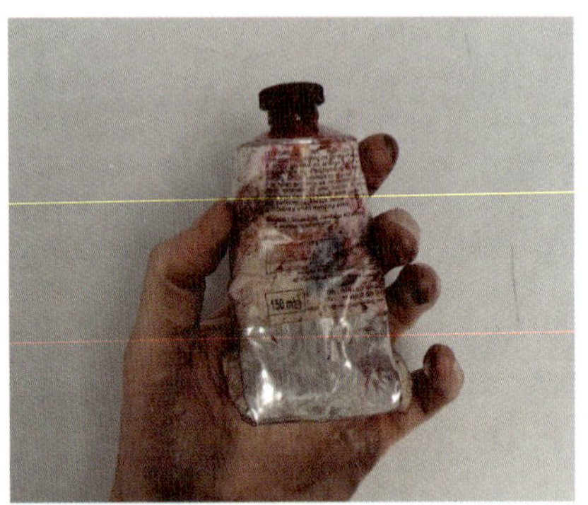

Tubes of ink are great solutions for small amounts.

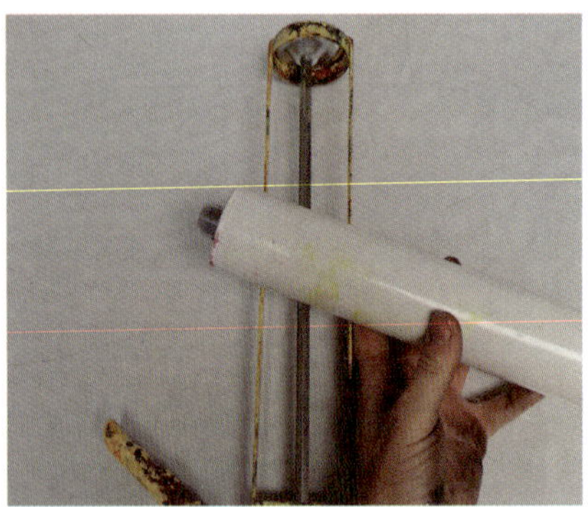

A 300ml cartridge stops the ink from drying up.

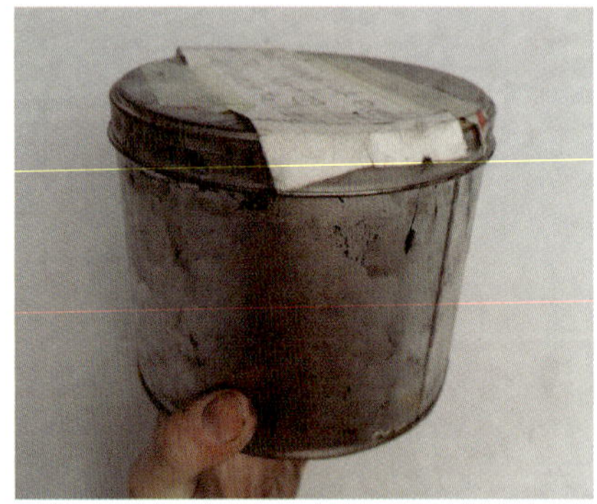

A large 500g tin of ink has a shelf life.

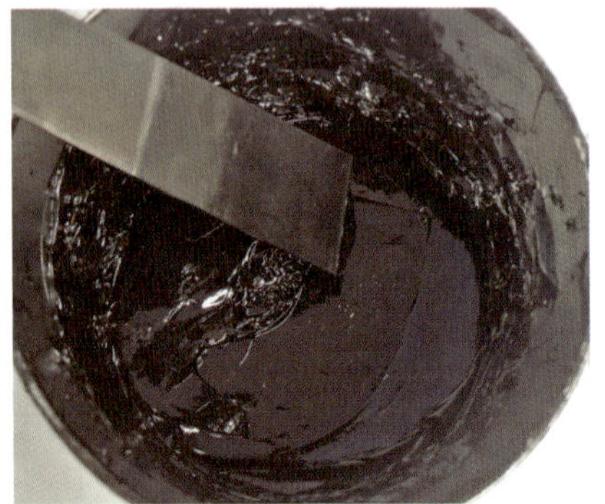

Always scrape ink level from the top of the ink.

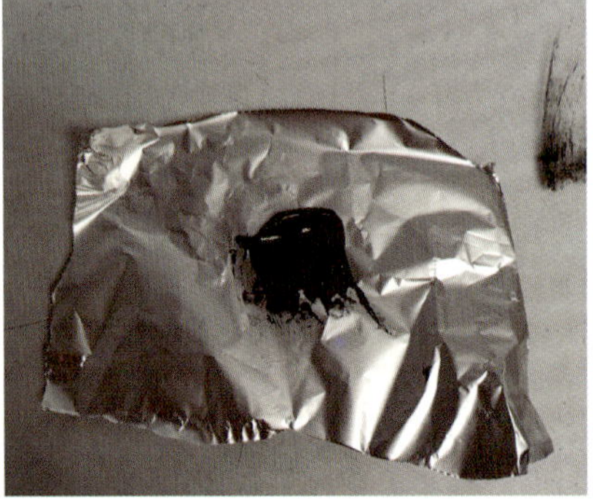

Storing ink in little foil envelopes works well for small batches.

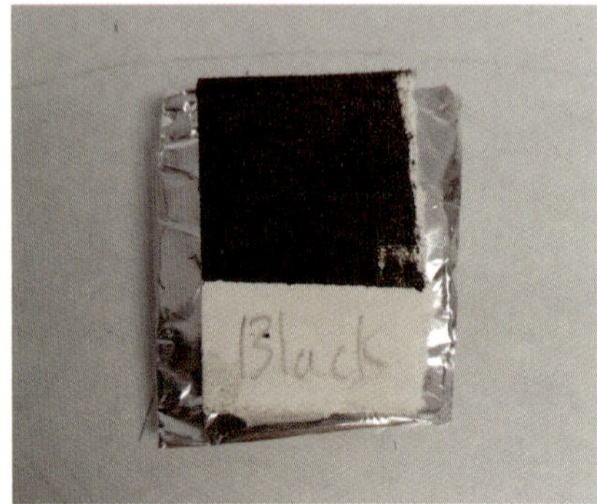

Do not forget to label the ink that is inside!

WORKING WITH OIL-BASED INK

Oil-based ink is a sticky, wonderful thing as we have discovered. But it does have a habit of getting everywhere. Here we look at a few tips to control its spread and to help clean up.

Cleaning up oil-based ink requires no solvents whatsoever, so it's fantastic from an ecological perspective. Furthermore it is neat and quick with no splashing or water use. I use whatever oil I can get in my top-up shop at the best value, which is usually a vegetable oil. This is the only time in printing I wear gloves; a pair of washing-up gloves that I replace once every few years. The soap solution used for the last wipe down is simply diluted bar soap in water. You can also use a degreaser such as ecological washing-up liquid and water or similar.

If you choose not to wear gloves when printing, hands can get inky, particularly with the intaglio processes. Cleaning the worst off your hands can also be done with a small amount of oil rubbed in to loosen the ink. Once it's all loose, just wash with soap and water to break up the oil and the worst should be off. You can also use a substance called barrier cream before you start getting inky. It is rubbed into hands like a moisturiser before you work and then when you go to wash hands, the ink all just washes off. I choose not to use it as it is just another material to purchase and store and I am careful what we add down our watercourse. But, as with all these things, the choice from an ecological perspective is entirely up to the individual and if barrier cream negates the use of disposable gloves, then that balances out.

If you are working on many prints, then washing your hands each time you go to handle paper is excessive for water use and also for your skin's health. Instead, you can use paper fingers to allow you to handle paper without getting inky fingerprints. Paper fingers are made from the offcuts of paper in studios, or if you wish to make a permanent pair, you can use a thin sheet of aluminium (for instance a flat pack drinks can) and then these can be wiped down if you ever need to clean them.

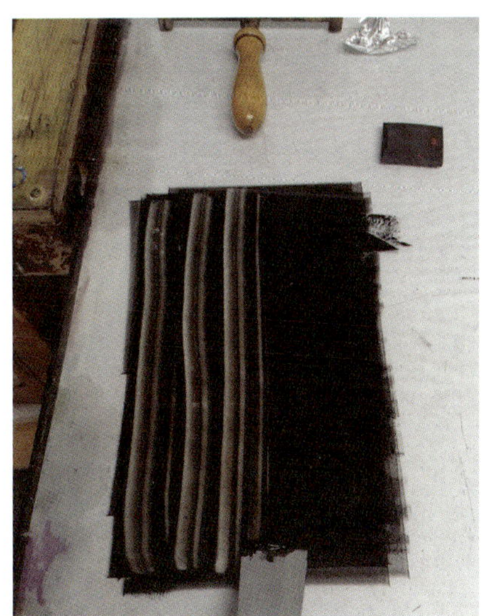

Scrape up any spent ink and put it in a scrap of paper. Bin.

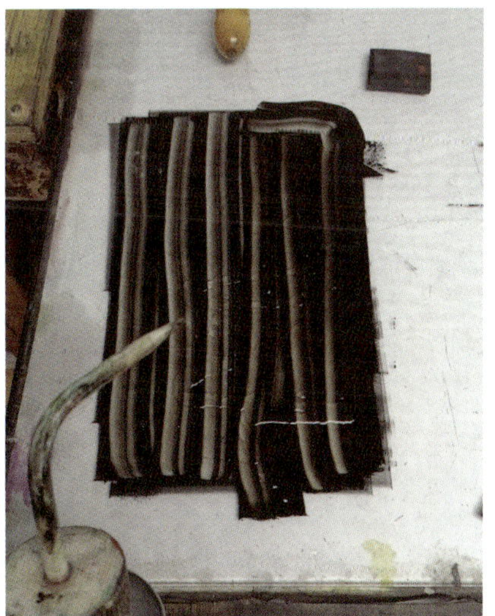

Cover the inky surface with some oil.

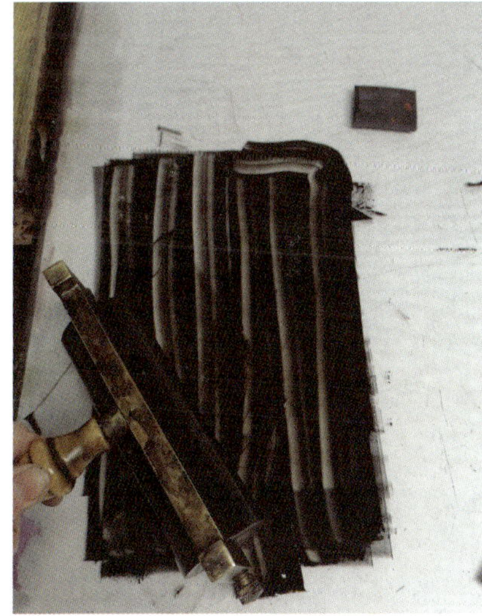

Use a palette knife or your roller to spread oil out.

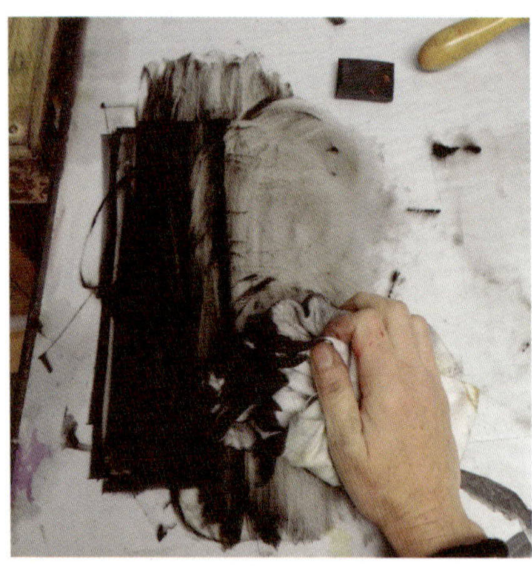

Using your dirtiest rag, remove the first layer of ink.

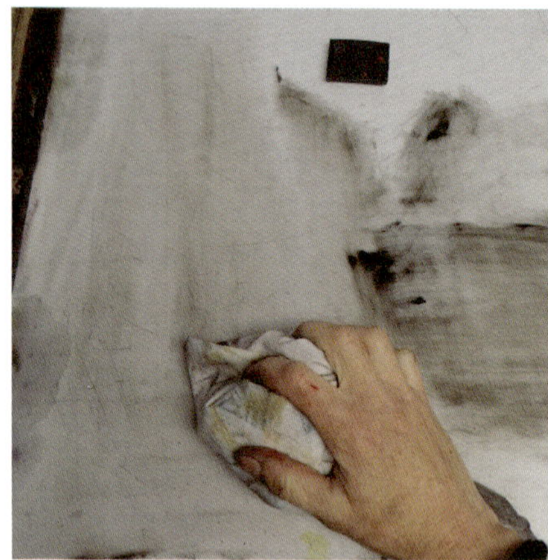

Move onto a cleaner rag for the next pass of cleaning off ink.

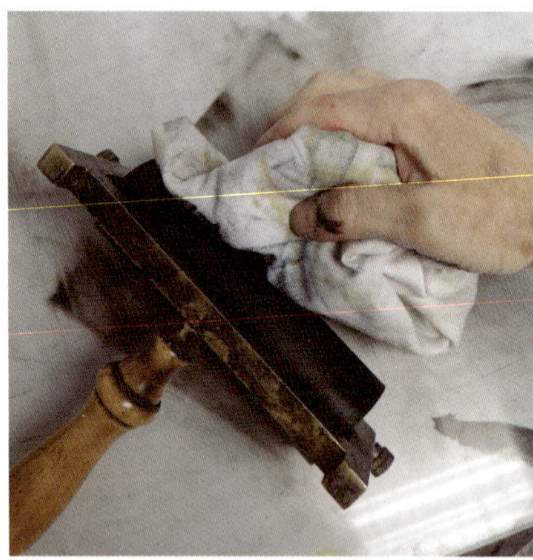

Wipe off ink and oil from roller.

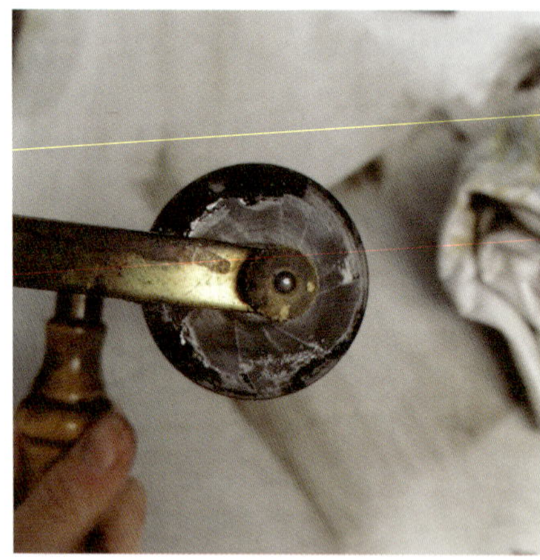

Make sure to get roller edges.

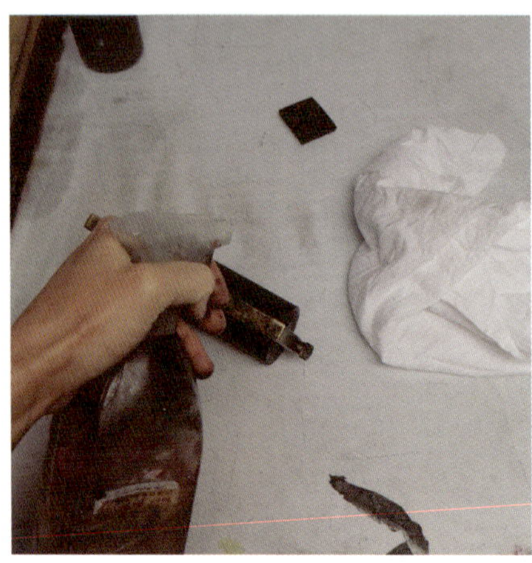

Spray everything with soap solution, including equipment.

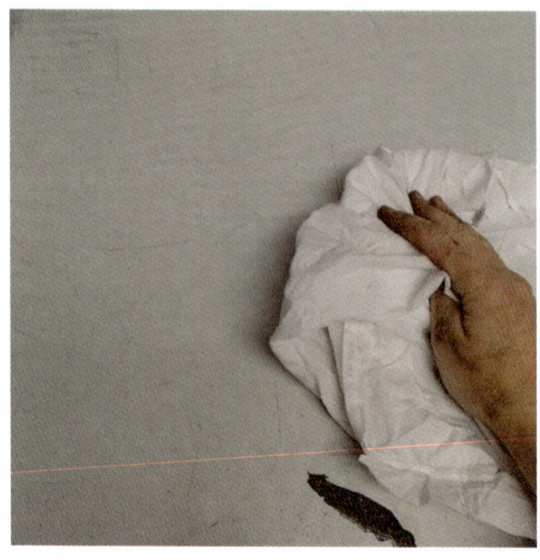

Final wipe down with the cleanest rag.

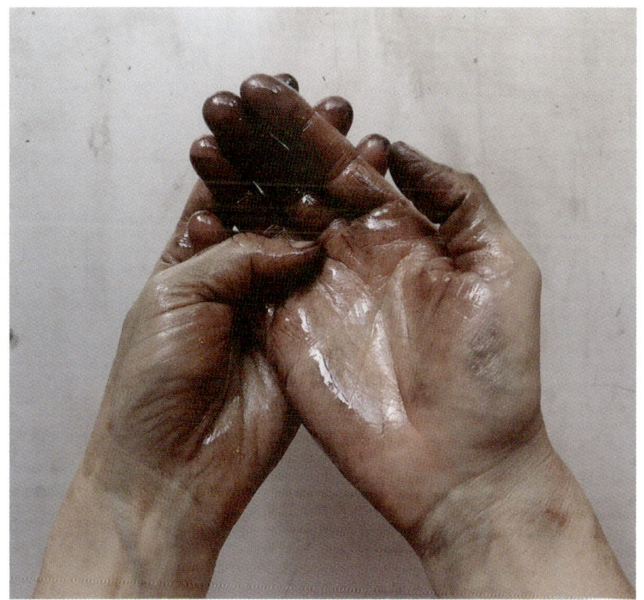

Oil does a great job removing ink on hands. Finish with soap.

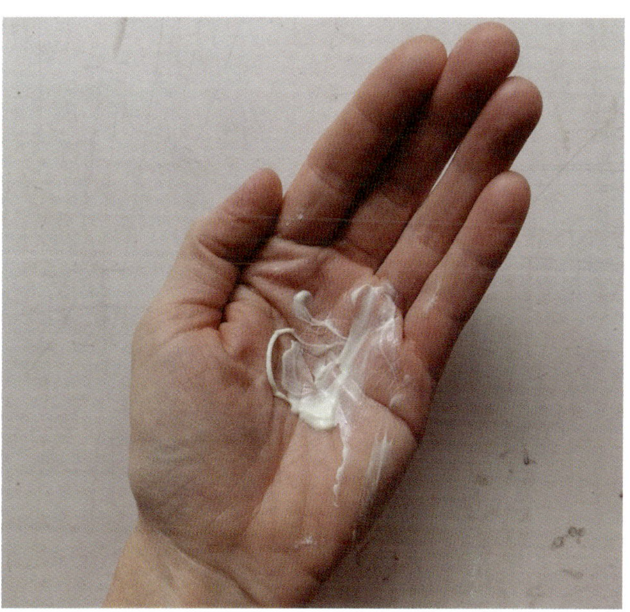

Barrier cream can help clean ink off hands more easily.

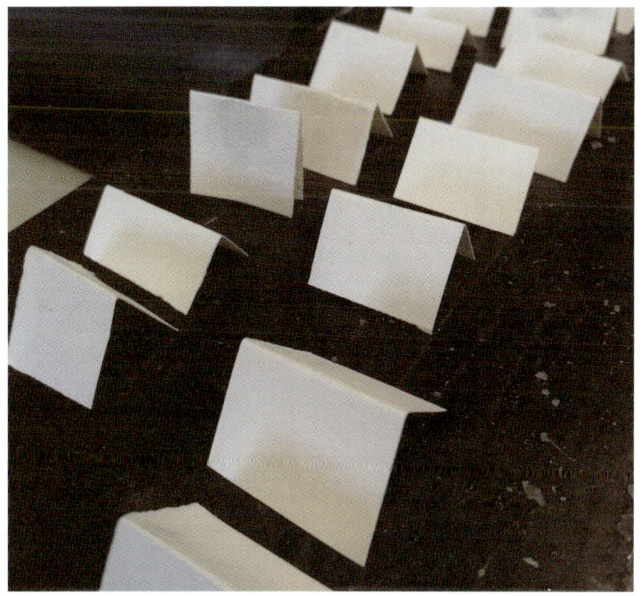

Having a stack of pre-cut paper fingers ready to use is invaluable.

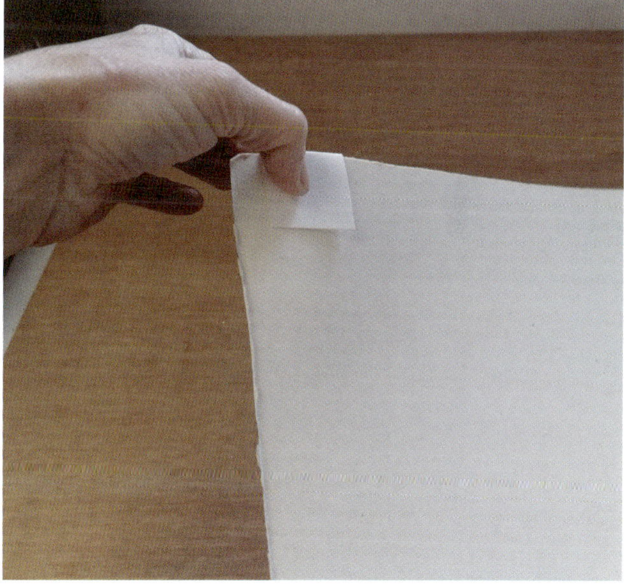

Paper fingers allow you to handle paper no matter how inky your hands.

MATERIAL RESOURCE AND PROCESSING

Humanity seems to use a lot of stuff and generate a lot of stuff these days. If we can look at our individual practice and be more responsible for both materials coming in and processing of materials going out, then that is a hugely positive approach to sustainability. In print, we use a lot of paper. We have already looked at making paper, reducing edition size and understanding that paper is a valuable resource. However, we do use it in print, so what steps can we take to reduce consumption and process our waste? Firstly, re-use. Tissue paper that has been used on press beds and only has a few inky blemishes can be re-used. Simply stack in a pile that you know is secondary paper and once the ink is dry, you can use again. The same goes for newsprint.

Paper scraps that are not covered in huge amounts of ink can obviously be recycled. Although we know recycling does take a vast amount of energy, and in that way is not perfect, it is better than just wasting it.

Rags used for clean-up can be sourced from old clothing or old bed sheets. Just ask around politely and you will often find people are happy to give you things for rags. I always ask for 100 per cent cotton only, which is very easy because it corresponds to most people's old bedding. Bed sheets make a huge amount of rags. Rags can be used multiple times before they are finally spent. I have a cycle of using really dirty ones first, then moving into cleaner ones. The extremely inky ones I leave for a week or so to dry a little and then re-use again for my first dirty clean up. I am looking into shredding and composting rags after use, but that is where one needs to be careful of the pigment used in the inks that you printed with. This makes it tricky, but at least if you can re-use them that is brilliant.

I know an artist who goes that bit further and dries inky rags and then uses them to make stunning, evocative artworks and textile items. A beautiful re-use of an item otherwise destined for the bin.

Commodities in the print room, such as blankets, can have multiple lives before binning. Once a set of blankets is spent, the facing and middle blanket can be set aside and destined as embossing blankets or ones for lithino where the pressure is high, but three intaglio blankets are not required. Blankets that are just stained can be washed on a cold washing cycle with low spin or hand washed in a bath. Oil-based ink will not come out, but it does remove grease, dust

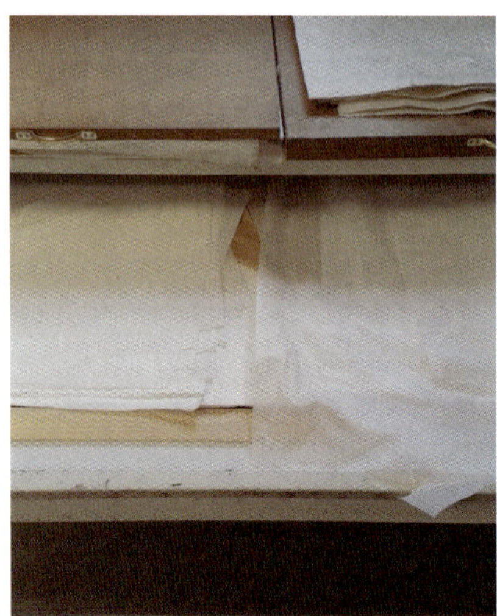

Tissue paper drawer separated into new paper (left) and re-used paper.

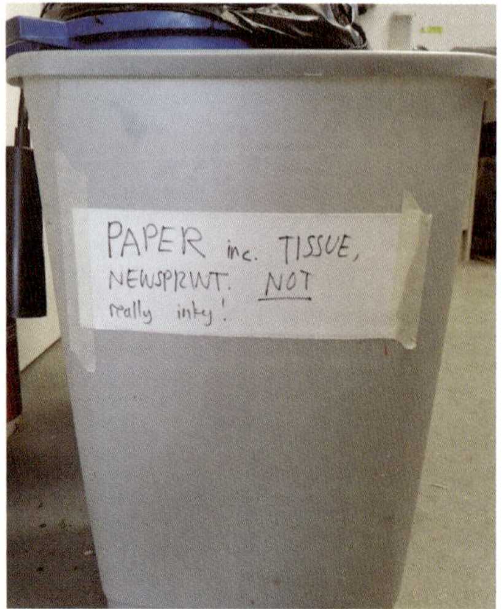

Recycling and sorting studio waste helps minimise landfill.

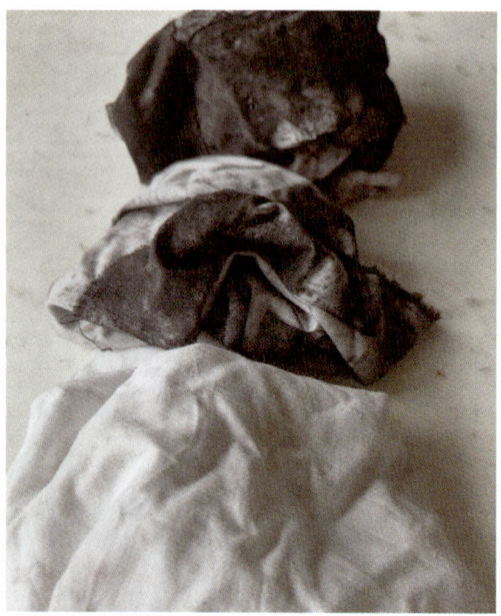

Rags can be re-used multiple times, even inky ones.

and general dirt. They will shrink a little, but will re-stretch again after use.

Compostables are abundant in the print workshop. Lino cuttings can be composted without any nasty leaching into the soil. They can take their time, and the choice is entirely individual and dependent upon the composting system you employ. It is worth trying and monitoring the results as it is a great material processing resource. Likewise, scraps of paper without ink can be composted. Again, experiment with your own system to understand the degradation process.

General workshop basics

When making changes to a more ecological approach, there are a few simple switches in the workshop that can make a difference. An important one is switching from masking tape to gum tape. We have used traditional gum tape to stretch our paper in Chapter 5, but you can also buy pre-gummed paper tape which you can use in a similar way to masking tape. It is non-plastic based, completely recyclable and many are also biodegradable. Some makes are stronger than others, so have a little explore.

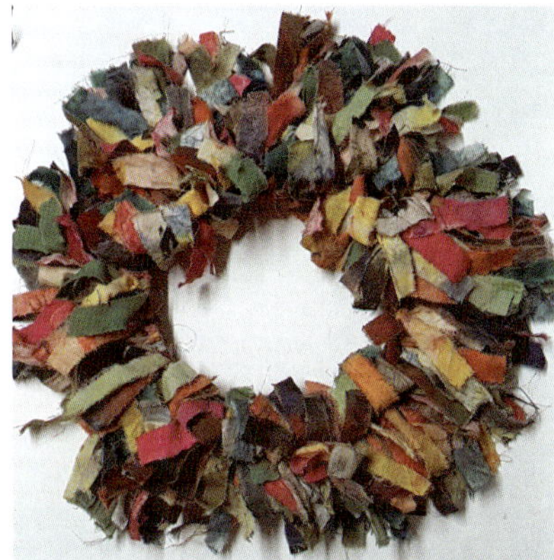

One person's rags are another's riches. Re-using is a beautiful ecological approach, as displayed here in a glorious wreath made from old printing rags. It brings such joy. *Circle of Life*, Jule Mallett.

Old blankets are perfect for deep embossing blankets or lithino.

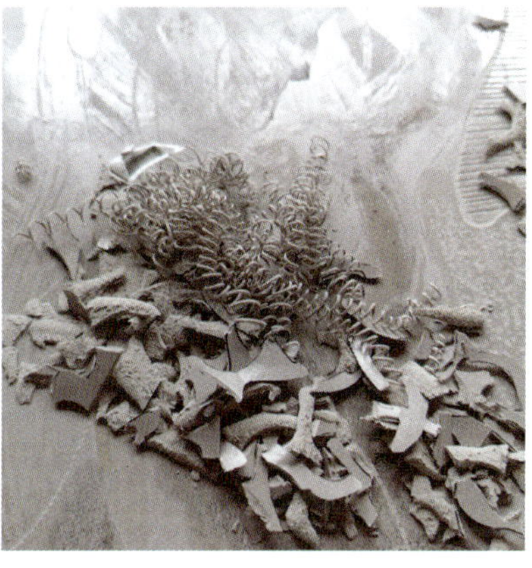

Composting items is worth experimenting with at home.

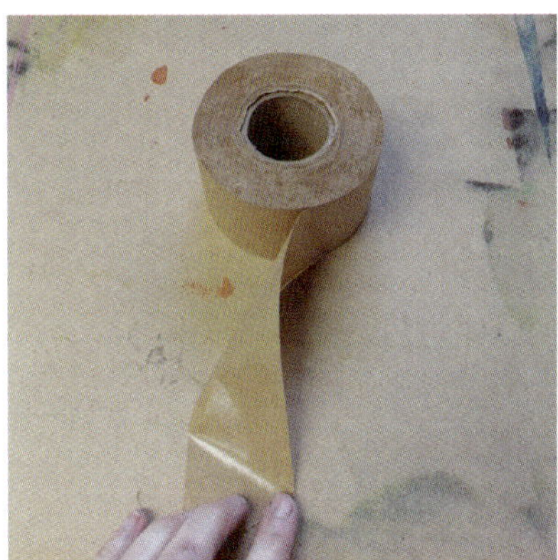

Recyclable and biodegradable gum paper tapes can replace masking tape.

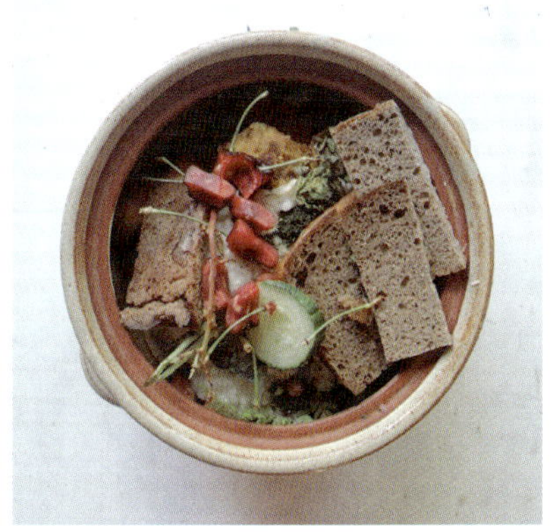

Keeping a small compost selection on site encourages waste management.

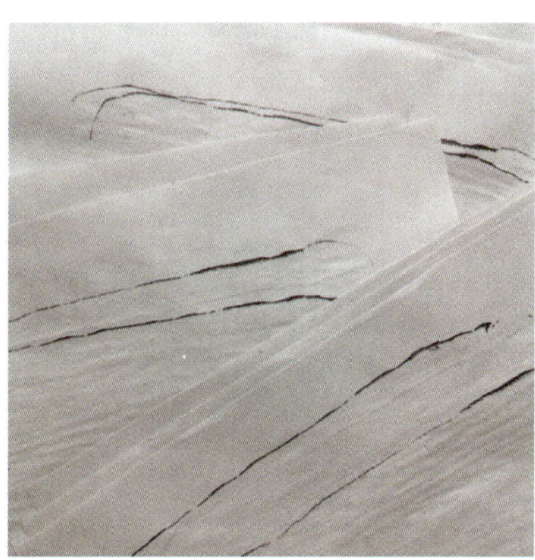

Old newspapers provide a useful inking station in smalls spaces.

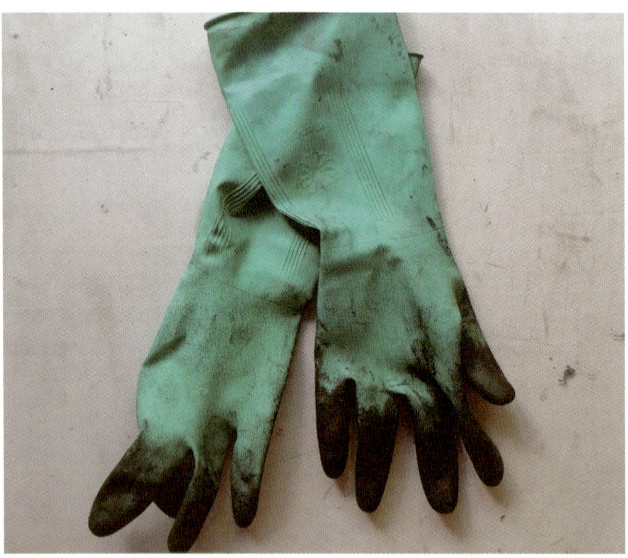
Alternatives to single-use disposable gloves are easily found.

I am fortunate to have access to a garden and a great composting system, so I do make sure I always have to hand a small reclaimed bag or tub to put all my compostable waste in whilst at work. If it is there, you are less likely to throw it away in a bin and more likely to sort your waste.

Picking up waste newspapers from public transport or other places can provide really useful intaglio inking stations. It is a product that will get thrown away daily, and yet if working in a small space it can be invaluable for inking up dry point pieces without worrying about getting your surface underneath dirty. The little amount of ink on the newspaper sheet after inking up still enables it to get recycled. It really helps if you are small-space working.

Try switching to re-usable gloves as opposed to single-use disposable ones for any inky clean up or activities. They at least last that bit longer than the single-use plastic variety. We looked at options also for cleaning hands with oil if you wish not to use any gloves at all.

Paper dampening and water use

We work a lot with both damp and dry paper throughout the book. I often employ a surface dampening method because I rarely need damp paper throughout a print, I often switch from damp to dry to damp for example. If one were to use properly soaked paper, then you would have to rely upon your paper being stretched and then dry before employing a further print method on the dry paper. This could take a long time and stop a creative flow. By employing a surface dampening method, you can print onto the paper for dry methods pretty much straight away. Filling up a water bath to soak paper takes a lot of water use and sometimes it is only used for the one or two sheets, then emptied. If you are planning an edition or you know you are just printing paper dry point intaglio, then having a tub of water to soak your paper in makes sense. Other than that, my suggestion is always to just give the paper a surface dampen.

A surface dampen literally means giving the printing side of the paper a spray with a fine water mister or a gentle wipe with a sponge. Then a little blot off with acid-free blotters and you're good to print. You must print straight away after dampening the surface because otherwise the water will evaporate whilst you're standing around and your paper will be dry. So make sure everything is prepped on the press bed and ready to go.

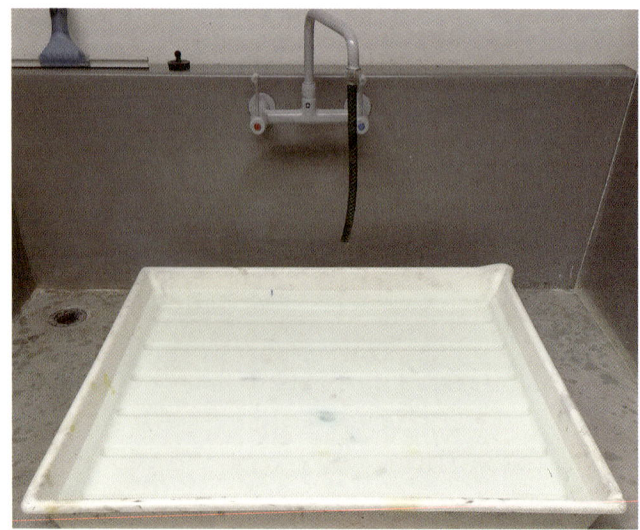
Paper soaking baths take a lot of water, use them wisely.

The quick method for pre-soaking paper requires that you fill a tub or water bath big enough to take your paper. The paper sits in the water for five to ten minutes before you are ready to print and then it is pulled out, left to drip from the corner and blotted off. This is ready to print. If you are printing an edition or working on a batch that requires damp paper, you can employ a proper overnight soak. Feed all your sheets into clean water one at a time. Leave for 20 minutes. Gather the bundle together in the water, pull out, and let drip. Then place the whole wet bundle between two sheets of clean glass or Perspex, and add a weight on top, like a stack of books. Leave overnight. The following morning, take the top sheet of glass off and individually peel and blot off each damp sheet. As you blot off each sheet, restack them on the top glass. Once all are blotted off, put the second sheet of glass back on top of the stack to prevent evaporation. They are now all perfectly, evenly dampened and ready to go. The water that is left in any of the paper soaking baths can be re-used for plant feeding!

We do a lot of washing of hands as printmakers, so remember to not leave the tap running if you are not using the water. In the oil washing method or even a sugar soap solution wash, you only need the water for the rinsing or soaping up. Every little helps.

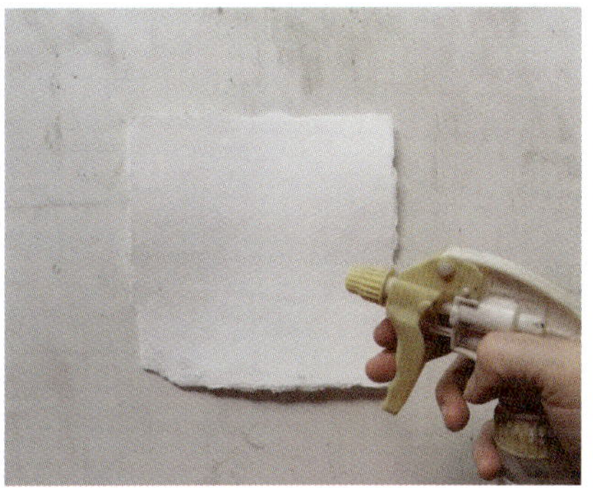

Spritz the paper with a fine mister or wipe gently with a sponge.

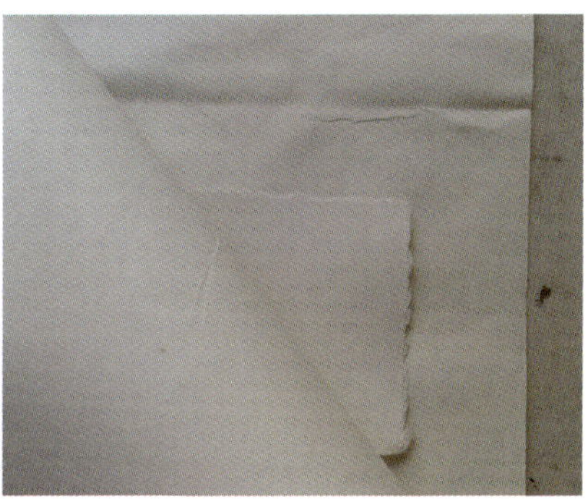

Blot off any excess or water rivulets with acid-free blotters.

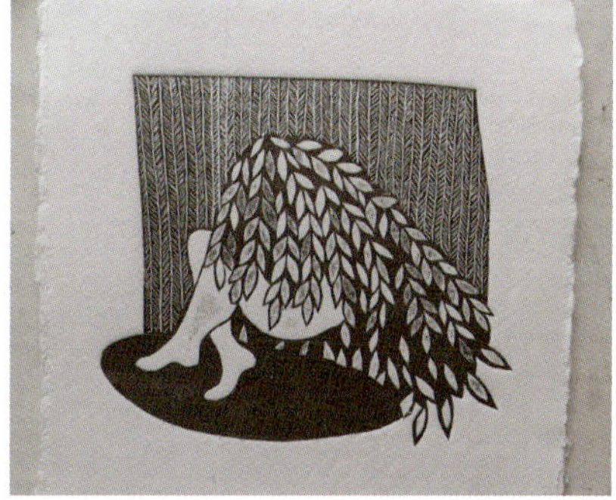

Print straight after dampening the surface.

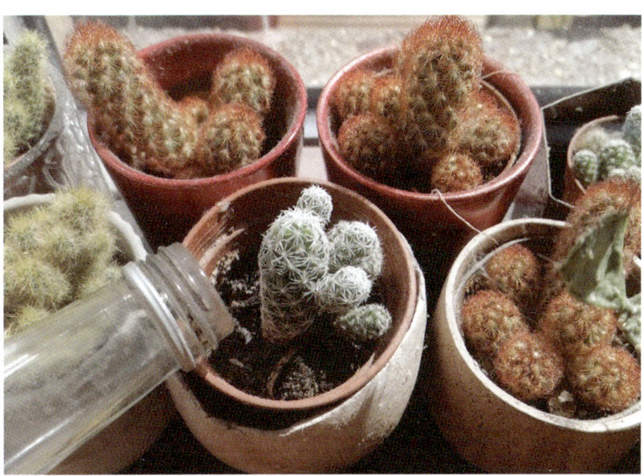

Paper soaking water can be re-used for plant feeding.

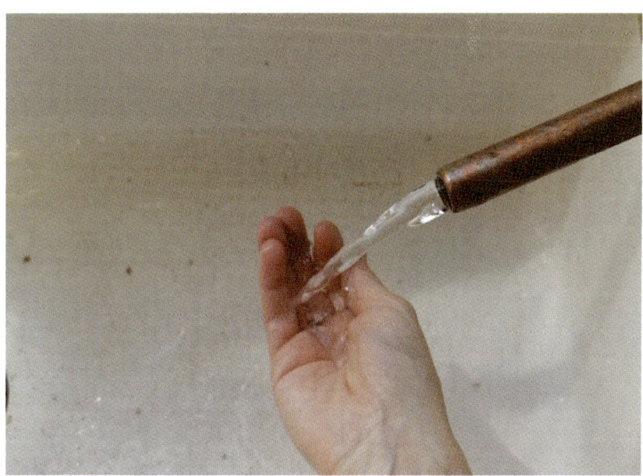

Don't forget to turn off the tap when not rinsing hands.

INDEX

First published in 2025 by
The Crowood Press Ltd
Ramsbury, Marlborough
Wiltshire SN8 2HR

enquiries@crowood.com
www.crowood.com

British Library Cataloguing-in-Publication Data
A catalogue record for this book is available from the British Library.

ISBN 978 0 7198 4479 9

Cover design by Sergey Tsvetkov

Typeset by Envisage IT
Printed and bound in India by Parksons Graphics